MW01002988

A History of Neglect

A History of Neglect

Health Care for Blacks and Mill Workers

in the Twentieth-Century South

Edward H. Beardsley

THE UNIVERSITY OF TENNESSEE PRESS / KNOXVILLE

Copyright ©1987 by The University of Tennessee Press / Knoxville. All
Rights Reserved. Manufactured in the United States of America. First
Edition.

Frontispiece: Black midwife carrying her bag out on call in rural Georgia,
c. 1935. Courtesy of the Georgia Department of Archives and History.

The paper in this book meets the minimum requirements of the American
National Standard for Permanence of Paper for Printed Library
Materials. ∞ The binding materials have been chosen for strength and
durability.

Library of Congress Cataloging-in-Publication Data

Beardsley, Edward H.
     A history of neglect.

     Bibliography: p.
     Includes index.
     1. Afro-Americans—Health and hygiene—Southern States—
History—20th century. 2. Afro-Americans—Medical care—Southern
States—History—20th century. 3. Cotton textile industry—Employees—
Diseases and hygiene—Southern States—History—20th century. 4. Cotton
textile industry—Employees—Medical care—Southern States—
History—20th century. 5. Textile workers—Diseases and hygiene—Southern
States—History—20th century. 6. Textile workers—Medical care—Southern
States—History—20th century. 7. Southern States—Social conditions. 8.
Southern States—Economic conditions. I. Title. II. Title: Mill workers in
the twentieth-century South.
     [DNLM: 1. Blacks—history—United States. 2. Health Services—history—
United States. 3. History of Medicine, 20th Century—United States. 4.
Socioeconomic Factors. WZ 80.5B5 B368h]
     RA448.5.N4B33 1987   362.1'0425   86-24949
     ISBN 0-87049-523-2 (alk. paper)

To my children,
Eleanor, Lewis, and Tyler

Preface

"It is bad enough," said G.H.T. Kimball of the Twentieth Century Fund, "that a man should be ignorant, for this cuts him off from the commerce of men's minds. It is perhaps worse that a man should be poor, for this condemns him to a life of stint and scheming, and there is no time for dreams and no respite for weariness. But what surely is worse is that a man should be unwell, for this prevents his doing anything much about either his poverty or his ignorance."[1]

A History of Neglect is the history of the health of two groups of people living in the American Southeast who have been largely unwell — and poor and ignorant — through a substantial part of the twentieth century. In fact, for these two groups — Southern blacks and cotton mill workers (nearly all white) — ignorance and poverty were both cause and effect of ill health. But their high illness and death rates resulted from other things, as well, sometimes from what Progressive Era reformers would have called "social sins." For blacks, of course, ill health was often closely linked to the effects of racism and segregation. Yet white cotton hands also suffered social isolation and disdain, and those attitudes, in turn, encouraged and seemed to justify a policy of economic authoritarianism among mill owners. Partly because of the near-feudal life-style that resulted from such a policy, mill workers confronted health problems equal in magnitude to those borne by blacks.

A History of Neglect thus attempts to do more than simply describe *what* the health status of blacks and mill workers was as the century unfolded. It also tries to tell *why* it was what it was, and why changes occurred — generally, but not always, in the direction of improvement. Like other works in the social history of medicine since about 1960, such as *The Cholera Years, The Butterfly Caste, Medicine and Slavery in Virginia, Bad Blood,* and *The Germ of Laziness,* the present study tries to move beyond a concept of health as the product of biological events and to see it as the product of culture as well.[2] Malaria and pellagra, for example, were on one level simply the result of the presence of *Anopheles quadrimaculatus* and the absence of sufficient nicotinic acid in the diet. But they were just as much the product of social facts such as poverty, racism and classism, unconcerned white (and black) doctors, penurious politicians, domineering landowners and mill owners, and New South boosterism. Likewise, when health improved, the change was caused not only by the draining of streams and (for pellagra) the distribution of brewers' yeast, but also by the expansion of federal authority and an awakening of textile owners (as a result of global war) to the interconnectedness of worker productivity and health.

A broadly conceived health history, however, has potential for more than just examining and confirming the cultural basis of physical well-being. It can also hold up a mirror to the larger society. It can, for instance, allow us to measure how well that society fulfilled or even tried to act out its basic ideals. Surely the acid test of a good society is the ability of all its people not merely to survive but to enjoy a fair measure of well-being. *A History of Neglect,* then, permits a measurement of such Southern ideals as democracy, individualism, and Christian charity. It concludes that for blacks and mill workers, at least, those ideals were more a matter of rhetoric than reality.

Finally, a caveat or two. This book makes no claim to be a survey of all Southern poor, just some of them. White tenant farmers, the Appalachian poor, and migrant workers are all excluded, not because their stories were less important, but because to have included them would have enlarged the scope beyond that of a single book. The broad subject (Southern health history) is one in which there is, thus far, little secondary work, and the health of blacks and mill hands, by themselves, proved task enough. Moreover, focusing on the cotton hand allowed an exploration of one area of Southern health history that was possible with no other group: industrial health. An adequate telling of the health history of blacks and mill workers, though, required the inclusion of several other groups who played key roles in the health stories of the primary parties. Among them were the white medical profession, black physicians, mill owners, and state and federal health establishments.

In like manner, *A History of Neglect* also does not attempt to cover the entire South, just three states in its southeast region: Georgia, North Carolina, and South Carolina. For the present study, however, they offered an ample and suitable target. Each had a sizeable and roughly equal black population through the period under review (1900 to 1970). For most of the era textiles was the dominant industry in all three states (and by 1930 those states were also the nation's textile center). While each was primarily rural and agricultural, all three had sizeable and growing urban centers. Moreover, the same social and political ideas were dominant in all of them — ie., individualism, white supremacy, and the belief in states' rights and a limited federal government. Those ideas, furthermore, were linked to a common, almost obsessive desire to move from farm-based to industrial-based economies (the New South idea). Thus while there were important differences among the target states, as the book tries to make clear, it is possible to generalize about the three as if they were a single entity, with a common heart. The reader is therefore put on alert that when the terms "South" and "Southern" are used, the region usually being referred to is the book's limited, three-state area.

Just as no attempt was made to be inclusive as to geography or population, there was also no effort to cover all health problems or all facets of each group's health history. The book gives no attention to mental illness in the South, for example. Such would be an important study (a supplement to Gerald Grob's fine work), but it was one that lay well outside the scope of the present work.[3] Nor has any attention been given to investigating the health of aged blacks and mill workers, partly because, until later in the century when life expectancy improved, there were not that many over sixty-five-year-olds for the historian to be concerned about. If anything, though, life for elderly members of these populations was even worse than that for their younger relations; and that story, too, merits a book of its own.

Even if its scope is not comprehensive, a project that has been in the making as long as this one has accumulated many, many debts, which can never be repaid but must be gratefully acknowledged. Creditors of this book fall roughly into two categories, those who aided the large task of gathering mostly scattered and hidden source material and those who helped in interpreting and organizing it. The first group have largely been recognized in the notes and bibliography, but a second thank-you is in order here, especially to Dr. Paul Cornely of Howard Medical School, Mrs. Modjeska Simkins of Columbia, Dr. Charles Watts of Durham, Dr. Lee Heaphy of Winston-Salem, Dr. Hubert Eaton of Wilmington, and Mr. Francis Bell, retired vice-president of the Springs Corporation. There were also colleagues and archivists who helped identify valuable material and whose aid has not been noted elsewhere. They include my colleague Dr. Tom Terrill, Mrs. Ann K. Donato of the Waring Medical History Library in Charleston, Dr. Tom Johnson of the South Caroliniana Library in Columbia, and Mrs. Ann Bishop of the Duke Endowment in Charlotte.

The second group of benefactors not only assisted the author to make sense of his welter of material but also saved him from making many silly errors. Thanks on these scores are due to Dr. John Ettling of the University of Houston, Dr. Sol Benison of the University of Cincinnati, Dr. Martin

Pernick of the University of Michigan, and the staff and associates of the Wellcome Unit for the History of Medicine at the University of Oxford, who in 1980 not only accorded the author working space and congenial company but the opportunity to test his early work on an audience of skillful critics. Two other colleagues need special acknowledgment. Dr. James H. Cassedy of the National Library of Medicine is probably not aware of it, but at the beginning period of research he made valuable suggestions which helped define the project's scope. To Dr. Todd Savitt of the East Carolina University Medical School at Greenville goes the author's largest thanks. He gave a careful reading to the whole manuscript, and his detailed and constructive criticism led the author to take many needed second looks. Finally, gratitude is also due to many of my colleagues at the University of South Carolina. As a kind of captive scholarly audience, they had little way to escape my appeals for aid. But even so, they remained, throughout, generous with their time, interest, and help. Drs. John Sproat and George Rogers, successive department chairmen, provided financial and other assistance at critical times, while the University of South Carolina, through the Carolina Venture fund, gave generous aid to the preparation of a finished manuscript. In addition, Professors John Scott Wilson, Grace J. McFadden, Ronald Atkinson, and Lacy Ford read portions of the manuscript in its final stages and gave shrewd guidance as to its improvement.

Finally, I have debts to acknowledge among those who are neither historians, businessmen, or physicians. To Ms. Cynthia Maude-Gembler and Ms. Lee Campbell Sioles of the University of Tennessee Press, my appreciation for both their support and their hard work in making this a better book than I could have produced alone. To Mrs. Polly Brown and Mr. Homer Steedley go my thanks for teaching me to be computer literate. And to Mrs. Majken Blackwell, an equal measure of gratitude for producing the graphs and figures.

To all of these colleagues I would say that if the book has areas of merit they can largely take credit. Errors of fact and interpretation remain the author's alone.

Much of the material in Chapter 4 was previously published in E.H. Beardsley, "Dedicated Servant or Errant Professional: The Southern Negro Doctor before WWII," in Walter Fraser, Jr., and Winfred B. Moore, Jr., *The Southern Enigma: Essays on Race, Class, and Folk Culture* (Greenwood Press, Westport, CT, 1983). Copyright © 1983 by Walter Fraser, Jr., and Winfred B. Moore, Jr. It is reprinted by permission.

The author also gratefully acknowledges the permission of the Johns Hopkins University Press to republish material originally appearing as articles in the *Bulletin of the History of Medicine*. E.H. Beardsley, "Making Separate, Equal: Black Physicians and the Problems of Medical Segregation in the Pre–World War II South," *Bull. of the Hist. of Med.* 57 (Fall 1983): 382–96, forms part of Chapter 4; and Beardsley "Goodbye to Jim Crow: The Desegregation of Southern Hospitals, 1945–70," *Bull. of the Hist. of Med.* 60 (Fall 1986): 367–86, makes up part of Chapter ɪɪ of the present volume.

Contents

Illustrations and Figures

Illustrations

Figures

Introduction

In the decades prior to World War II, most observers of the American South perceived it as a biracial society. There was indeed that dualism, and yet to focus on the black-white division alone was to obscure another important dimension of the region's social structure. In the major textile manufacturing states of North Carolina, South Carolina, and Georgia, for example, only some whites were actually supreme. There the social order was better described as a three-tiered edifice, with "respectable" whites (a group including even most of the region's farm tenants) on top, blacks on the bottom, and textile mill hands (almost exclusively white) occupying an intermediate level, but one far closer to bottom than top.

If disparaged and often reviled, textile hands were not, of course, as badly off as the region's blacks. Mill workers, after all, did escape the confinements of Jim Crow legislation; they exerted some political influence, probably had more occupational mobility than blacks, and enjoyed a measure of psychological satisfaction from the mere fact of being white. At the same time similarities between the two groups were at least as striking as their differences. It was the fact of those similarities — in status, living condition, and image — that shaped the author's decision to join the health histories of the two populations in a single narrative.

Health, in fact, was one of the points of closest comparison between the two groups. Not only was each burdened with pain and sickness, but for both, poor health emanated from the same basic source: that collection of attitudes governing the South's response to those it regarded as being among its lower orders. At the center of these attitudes was a habit of exploitative paternalism acquired during earlier centuries of dealing with black slaves. By the time the mill village population had begun to reach sizeable proportions at the end of the nineteenth century, the South's economic and social leaderships and their middle-class allies were well practiced in identifying inferiors and keeping them in their place.

It was then that attitudes and practices learned in dealing with blacks — personal disdain, social control, economic exploitation, and even political disfranchisement — began to be applied with almost equal force to the expanding body of mill workers as well. The impulse was largely economic. If textile manufacturing was to fulfill the large dreams of New South boosters, a cheap and abundant supply of white labor was every bit as necessary as a "mud sill" of slaves had been to the ante-bellum plantation economy. Yet marshalling that white industrial force created a panoply of fears for the entrepreneurial class, reminiscent of those that had haunted earlier slave masters. Mill owners were especially concerned over the next decades that outside agitators, in the guise of union organizers, would turn the industrial population against the system — in the manner of abolitionists (and later the NAACP) working among blacks. Thus, if textile labor was to be used to greatest advantage in fulfilling the dream of Southern economic revitalization, it must be managed, restrained, and isolated — by methods already proven successful with blacks.

But the regimentation of the rural Southerner-turned-cotton hand was not the work of factory owners alone. The rising Southern middle class also played a part, and class impulses were involved as well as economic ones. As historian David Carlton has shown in his recent study of the piedmont South, around 1900 the region's new urban middle class — its cotton merchants, bankers, and shopkeepers, as well as ministers, journalists, physicians, and other professionals — became much alarmed by the growing presence of the mill hand. Although low, mean whites — "crackers" and "sandlappers" — had been objects of fear and contempt long before they transformed themselves into factory workers, mill laborers seemed a particular menace because they were concentrated in such large numbers and were so close at hand.[1]

To the new urban middle class, still insecure in its status, the expanding mill population, planted mostly on the borders of established towns, represented a lawless, ignorant, almost barbaric element — in sum, a grave threat to the urban social order. One cultivated Southerner put it thusly: mill hands were the kinds of people "who carry pistols in their hip pockets, . . . expectorate upon the floor, . . . have no toothbrushes, and comb their hair with their fingers."[2] As long as such people had been dispersed on Southern farms and in mountain hollows, they could be safely ignored and were welcome to claim the special privileges of the white race. By 1900, however, those one-time sharecroppers and mountaineers were close at hand, and Southern respectables began to wonder if white supremacy need "entail white equality."[3] At the very least cotton hands had to be kept under firm control and inculcated with middle-class respect for law, decency, and property. Thus the Southern middle class fully approved giving the mill owner a free hand to discipline his people as he saw fit.

The most visible feature of that discipline was the company-owned mill village. Its chief advantages were that it provided owners an assured and ample labor supply, as well as a means of controlling these hands, on the job and off. In 1946 Robert Stevens, chairman of the mammoth J.P. Stevens organization, recoiled at a fellow mill executive's suggestion that he consider selling his village houses to workers. "Never," Stevens exclaimed. "I'll never do that. We'd lose control of our workers."[4] Though in 1946 Stevens's outlook was no longer representative of the industry, in the pre-war era it had been without question the consensus view.

Control was chiefly aimed at quarantining village and mill against alien elements who sought to plant disruptive notions of the possibility of higher pay and better conditions. Union organizers were feared the most, though their insensitivity to mill workers' values was legend and allowed owners easily to take their measure and defend against them. But *anyone* who questioned the wisdom and reach of management was suspect. In one South Carolina mill village a visiting seminary student grumbled openly that owners paid preachers' salaries so that they could control what was said from pulpits. The mill president hotly denied the charge and then fired the "young fool" for being a damned liar.[5]

The basic disdain of the ruling class for white industrial workers, together with its fear of losing control of them, interacted with the fantastic hopes for mill development in that era and helped shape a status and life style for the average Southern mill hand that was barely distinguishable from those of black Southerners. Carlton found that middle-class progressives in the South were so appalled by the mill populace that they came to reject traditional ideas of white supremacy in favor of a social order in which *some* whites would rule over lower orders of both races. In a study of a later period, John Kenneth Morland discovered that cotton operatives in upcountry South Carolina regarded townspeople with more than just fear and resentment: they also seemed to accept the townsman's claim of superiority. For their part, townspeople were as insistent on segregating the mill worker as they were the black. Sinclair Lewis, who had a keen eye for such things, visited the piedmont South in the 1920s and found the class gulf there to be wider than anywhere else in the country.[6]

If the South's "better" classes did not actually read the mill population out of the white race, much of the imagery associated with cotton hands was indistinguishable from that traditionally used to describe blacks. To the middle class, mill people were shiftless and undisciplined. They had a bent toward homicide, differentiated from that of blacks only in that they used pistols, while Negroes killed with knives and razors. Male heads of mill families were often drawn as lazy no-accounts who preferred to live off the wages of wives and children rather than hold jobs themselves.[7]

On the other hand, mill owners (who could not openly disparage their work force) played down their workers' defects, preferring to see them as children who needed continued guidance from more mature heads in making life's basic decisions. Like the slave owner before him or the sweater of black labor in his own day, the mill president also talked much about the loyalty of his hands and the strong and mutual affection between management and labor which he proclaimed to be a prime feature of industrial relations in Southern mills.[8]

If similar imagery was used for mill hands and blacks, the reality and quality of life for both populations offered an even stronger parallel. Wilbur J. Cash was only the earliest of many to observe that the plantation system served as a model for mill village organization. Although Cash and other contemporary critics might have exaggerated the extent to which the mill village was a closed society, twentieth-century owners were almost as thoroughgoing in their will to control as slave masters had been, providing not only housing for their hands but commissaries, schools, churches, and policing. White sharecroppers and tenants were enmeshed in dependency, too, but only mill hands, Cash insisted, approached the abject state of blacks, and only mill masters asserted the "old paternalistic prerogative" with such force.[9]

The mill owner did not of course exert any kind of property right over his employees. Cotton hands could and frequently did register their displeasure with an owner by deserting his employ and seeking work in another mill. But such shifting about usually brought little gain. Though their economic prospects were not as dismal as blacks', upward mobility for most cotton operatives, whether social or occupational, was pretty much closed off—largely because owners were determined to preserve cheap labor as a bargaining chip in playing for Northern capital. Economist Broadus Mitchell might have had an axe to grind, but his sentiments found frequent confirmation in industry-wooing statements of Southern business leaders. Mill workers, said Mitchell, "are being offered on the auction block pretty much as their black predecessors were, and their qualities are enlarged upon with the same salesman's gusto."[10] Far better, said mill observer and Columbia University historian Frank Tannenbaum, that those benighted Anglo-Saxons "had remained on the farm and scratched the soil with their hands." Many might have gone mad, starved, or died in family feuds, but at least a few poets, preachers, and legislators would have risen to the surface.[11]

If cotton hands protested their situation and sought to alter it, they quickly found that, like blacks, they had to contend with opposition from the organized forces of the community who were determined to uphold the independent power of employers. Middle-class opinion was one bulwark of owner power. Organized religion was another, for its spokesmen nearly always stood with Property in contests between Labor and Capital. In 1917 one piedmont South Carolina preacher went so far as to call mill development "the largest single opportunity the world has ever seen to build a democracy upon the ethics of Christianity."[12] And, when needed, management could also call on the police power of the state to enforce its will — as happened during the Gastonia strike of 1929 and the region-wide general strike of 1934.[13]

Congruence between the lives of mill hands and blacks even extended to the political sphere. It was true that disfranchisement (in the 1890s) did not touch the mill population in any way comparable to its impact on blacks. Nonetheless, a large proportion of poor whites (many of them mill hands) lost their place in the political process, either because they failed to take advantage of loopholes in literacy tests or fell prey to poll-tax requirements.[14] And in South Carolina's piedmont, townspeople were so convinced of the corruptibility of the mill vote that around 1900 some were demanding its elimination (just as they had done with the black vote a few years before). Reflecting the fears and desires of fellow citizens in Columbia, South Carolina, newspaper editor N.Z. Gonzales tried (unsuccessfully) to get local mill villages struck from the city's voting rolls. Although urban disgruntlement never had any impact on the operation of state Democratic primaries, where operatives voted freely, it did result in a reduction of the mill vote in some city elections, through stiffer enforcement of tax and residency requirements.[15]

But political disability took other forms than simple loss of the ballot. Not until the New Deal thirties, and the appearance of leaders like Olin Johnson of South Carolina, would mill hands find spokesmen willing to pursue their interests against those of mill corporations. Before then, politicians of the stamp of Eugene Talmadge of Georgia and Cole Blease in South Carolina might speak in the vernacular of the "mill boys" and court them vigorously at election time; but once in office (thanks partly to mill votes) they turned their backs on their followers to support conservative policies of the economic *status quo*. Too often such candidates, when on the hustings, did little more than play to mill prejudice against blacks. Such rhetoric may have provided textile hands some psychological satisfaction, but it was gained at the cost of obscuring pressing economic problems. As Southern writer Lillian Smith saw it, the region's economic and political elites duped poor whites (from both farm and mill) into making a very one-sided bargain. By its terms "Mr. Rich White" got the right to "boss the money," but "Mr. Poor White" got only the right to "boss the nigger."[16] Considering what the political process actually delivered to textile operatives in the pre–World War II South, white industrial workers were victimized by a politics of neglect only a little less than their black adversaries.[17]

As noted earlier, nowhere does the victimization of both groups show up more clearly than in the realm of health care. There, the needs of mill hands and blacks were enormous. Yet mill corporations, who asserted the right to deal with the former, and state and local governments, which had a mandate to assist the latter, both defaulted on their responsibilities. Not even a realization that ill health among the lower orders threatened the rest of the South was enough to frighten its leaders into action. On occasion boards of health were stirred to move into mill villages to contain some deadly epidemic. But action was spasmodic, often because both owner and hands were reluctant to comply. Moreover, health departments soon learned that the prerogatives of private property set limits on public action, however necessary. As for black health needs, racism posed an equally potent check on effective response. Funds for public health were sharply limited, to begin with, by the South's historic aversion to social spending. Then, when those scarce resources and programs came to be allotted, racially biased calculation always insured that blacks got less.

Unable or unwilling to meet the needs of the poor, health officials resigned themselves to expending funds and energy in those places where results would attract most favorable attention from, and do least to alienate, influential whites. For their part, political leaders saw no advantage in making strenuous efforts in behalf of black populations who had little political clout and, hence, nothing to offer in return. As for meeting the health needs of mill hands, both political and health leaders were reluctant to take initiatives, reasoning that government intervention in the affairs of the textile industry would only encumber the latter's ability to develop, bringing on at the same time the enmity of a powerful economic class.

For blacks and white cotton hands alike, the Southern solution was to assign responsibility for health and welfare to supposedly better and wiser hands — to spokesmen for a racist white majority in the first case and to a small, but powerful economic interest, in the second. Such consignment was not only an affront to the ideal of democracy, it even offended the notion of *white* democracy that the South had long claimed as its standard. But the South preferred to embrace paternalist fantasies rather than uncomfortable realities. Black militant W.E.B. DuBois understood that tendency and deplored it. "No man," he insisted, "is so good, intelligent, or wealthy as to be entrusted wholly with the welfare of his neighbor."[18] The South's political, racial, and economic leaderships, however, believed otherwise, so far as blacks and mill hands were concerned, and decades of preventable ill health and disability were one result.

Yet for all the congruence between blacks and mill workers, their health histories are best presented as two distinct, if parallel, stories. For although there were similarities between Southern mill hands and blacks, there were differences as well, differences that set the two groups and their histories—whether of health or other matters—apart in important ways.

For one thing, until the 1960s (when mill work was desegregated) these two Southern populations lived almost as far apart as citizens of separate states. According to Cash, and as confirmed by industry leaders themselves, mills were created in part as a sanctuary for falling whites to afford them an escape from deadly economic competition with blacks. Accordingly, mill work became quickly and essentially white-only employment, with (the relatively few) blacks working only at menial and mostly outdoor tasks.[19] By World War I the custom was being bolstered by law. In South Carolina, for example, the Segregation Act of 1915 wrote the exclusionist practice into law, banning blacks from most categories of mill jobs. A similarly rigid segregation marked the mill village. Unlike the rural South and the rising Southern towns, where whites and blacks lived often in close proximity, in mill communities blacks were restricted to the village fringe. Only the entry of an occasional black domestic broke the racial sameness of milltown.[20]

Like distinctions marked the provision of health care—and the health record itself. Whereas state, city, and county health agencies had a responsibility for securing the health of blacks (a responsibility most did not meet), Southern health departments had almost nothing to do with illness in village and mill, agreeing to leave those matters to textile owners. Rural health improvement, for example, was almost an obsession of early twentieth century public health leaders, but no Southern state health officer (nor most Northern ones, for that matter) ever made more than passing reference to problems of industrial hygiene. Even after occupational health programs were instituted in the New Deal thirties, their administrators proved to be little more than advocates of the old policies of laissez-faire.

Cared for (or, rather, neglected) by different parties, blacks and mill operatives also had their own characteristic health profiles. Mill hands received more private professional care than blacks, though normally from physicians whose primary allegiance was to owner rather than patient. Mill operatives naturally had a higher incidence of industrial illness, although blacks employed in tobacco and lumber industries (a far smaller number) suffered in equal measure from hot and dusty environments. As for specific diseases, cotton operatives had far more hookworm and substantially more pellagra than blacks, while the latter had a greater incidence of venereal disease, tuberculosis, and illnesses (and deaths) associated with maternity and infancy.[21]

For such reasons, the twentieth century health histories of Southern blacks and textile mill hands are best told as parallel stories. In turning to them, however, the reader should bear in mind that they related to groups who were linked together in fundamental ways as victims of a society built on economic exploitation and on class and racial hierarchies and who because of those links bore for far too long a disproportionately heavy burden of illness, physical pain, and emotional despair.

PART I

Problems Defined

CHAPTER I

The Health of Southern Blacks, 1900–1930

In 1914 a perceptive white physician from Selma, Alabama, told a Southern Medical Association meeting in Jacksonville, Florida, that blacks were backward and inefficient, not because they were an inferior people but because they "are a sick people, outrageously sick, pathetically sick. . . . "[1] Had that Alabama doctor been inclined to historical observation, he could have added that serious and general ill health had been the lot of Southern blacks for a very long time.

In fact, the most arresting feature of the health status of blacks was the scant change it had undergone in the long period from the late slavery era to the start of the Great Depression. With the major exceptions of the elimination of cholera and yellow fever and the possible moderation of tuberculosis, the morbidity and mortality pictures for blacks during slavery remained substantially unaltered during the first two generations of freedom. What changes there were tended to be additions of illness as often as deletions. By the 1920s cardio-vascular disease, already a serious threat to whites, became a major problem for blacks as well. Moreover, it was only after emancipation, apparently, that blacks began to fight a major (and losing) battle with syphilis and gonorrhea. By causing significant increases in sterility and stillbirths, these diseases also helped account for the sharp decline in black fertility between the Civil War and the Depression. Malaria, although a problem in the ante-bellum era (with blacks having greater resistance than whites), became by the early twentieth century a relatively greater threat to blacks, as their lower economic status denied them the environmental and nutritional improvements that whites by then were increasingly enjoying.[2]

Lying behind this picture of continuing ill health was the fact that blacks endured much the same harsh living and working environments that they had faced in slavery. In the rural South, which as late as 1930 contained some 55 percent of all Afro-Americans, housing remained squalid and often overcrowded, with sanitary facilities and clean water in short supply. Work, too, remained as physically demanding as before, with black freedmen continuing to be subjected to the multiple hazards of labor in the out-of-doors. Starting in the early 1900s a rising number of blacks, hoping for economic and social improvement, left the rural South for the cities of that region and of the North. But until the 1920s, due to intense urban crowding, losses in health outweighed gains.

    Whether or not they migrated to cities another problem blacks faced was the inability to earn sufficient income to pull themselves above the bare subsistence level. In the rural South blacks fell increasingly into the penury of farm tenancy and sharecropping, while in cities — North or South — they were limited primarily to the most minimally rewarding service jobs (shoeshining, janitorial work) and to low-paid domestic employment.[3]

    If material deprivation was a major health factor, so too was the racism which held blacks to the very bottom rungs of the national economic ladder. By the 1890s, with the codification of segregation in the South, white racism was once again as virulent as it had been during slavery. Even physicians were captives of such thinking. Until the early twentieth century most white doctors believed, as had their ante-bellum counterparts, that blacks were biologically inferior and subject to a different pathology from that governing whites. Further, they regarded blacks as psychologically unfit for freedom and for the most part uneducable in the ways of better hygiene. Among many white doctors, the thinking was that it was futile even to try to rescue black health.[4]

    Fortunately, the sick Negro of the late nineteenth century was not completely dependent on the racially biased white physician. In the post–Civil War era a black medical profession made its appearance with the creation (by 1900) of nearly a dozen medical schools, such as Howard Medical School (Washington, 1868), Meharry Medical School (Nashville, 1876), and Leonard Medical School (Raleigh, 1882). By the late 1800s, having failed to gain acceptance into mainstream medical institutions, black physicians were also creating medical societies and hospitals at an impressive rate. The first important facility (1868) was Freedmen's Hospital in Washington, a government-endowed institution which soon became the clinical arm of Howard Medical School.[5]

    A rising black medical profession was no panacea, however, for black doctors remained in short supply. More to the point, they could provide only symptomatic treatment of medical problems that were primarily the result of deep-seated social pathologies. As black activist and educator

W.E.B. DuBois observed in 1933, the excessive rate of black deaths was due to nothing but poverty and discrimination. As for early black hospitals, their services — often inadequate and inferior — touched only the minority of blacks who had shifted to cities and, among them, served only a still smaller group with sufficient income to afford an expensive hospital visit, though Freedmen's, Meharry, and Leonard Hospitals generally treated indigents for free.[6]

Because of the persistence of such conditions, the mortality rate among Southern blacks declined at a glacial pace in the late nineteenth century. In fact, there was some evidence that death rates actually increased in the first decade after the Civil War. But even long-term mortality improvement, especially for mothers and infants, was so meager, and declining Negro fertility so apparent, that demographic experts prophesied the extinction of the Negro race. That prediction (based to a large degree on flawed census returns of 1870–90) proved groundless, but mortality progress in the 1900–30 era was fragile enough to make black ill health a serious and persistent dilemma.[7]

Thus the Alabama physician of 1914, in marking blacks as pathetically and outrageously sick, but not inferior, took a far more progressive view of the health condition of Afro-Americans than most of his colleagues. He also gave recognition to a situation which had existed for at least the preceeding half-century.

In exploring the validity of that doctor's observation for the early twentieth century — the aim of the present chapter — the historian first becomes aware of the problem of tuberculosis (TB). For blacks and whites, alike, that disease was far and away the most frightening and deadly health problem of all. In South Carolina in 1900 it took the lives of 219 blacks out of every 100,000, a rate nearly three times that for whites. Although the toll of TB deaths fell to 174 by 1920, the black rate remained 2.7 times the white. In North Carolina the situation was similar: a Negro rate in 1920 of 144, about 2.3 times the Caucasian. The middle 1930s saw a further decline in black deaths, but the South Carolina rate of 92 then stood at more than three times the white, and the differential in North Carolina was about the same.[8]

The greater virulence of TB among blacks, especially those of younger age, had several causes. Malnutrition was one. The diet of a great proportion of blacks was generally deficient, and the absence of key vitamins is now regarded as a factor in the inability to resist infection from tuberculosis bacteria. In addition, twentieth-century blacks still suffered from the fact that, unlike whites, they lacked historic experience with TB. Having encountered the disease only with the coming of whites to Africa (or with blacks' transplantation to the New World), blacks had yet to build up an effective immune response to the disease. It was such immunologic deficiencies that made blacks far more susceptible than whites to miliary TB (galloping consumption), an especially deadly form of the disease, in which the body's defenses are overpowered by a rapid and simultaneous invasion of many organs.[9]

Finally, the absence of effective medical care also contributed somewhat to the mortality differential. Blacks ill with TB either did not seek care in time, or if they did, found no help available. Most Southern states did not establish sanatoria for Negroes until the 1920s, several years after they provided them for whites. South Carolina's facility, State Park (near Columbia), began operation in 1916, but blacks did not have a place in it until 1921, and they got it then only because they paid for a substantial part of it, themselves. Only slowly did the problem of bed space improve. Even with black death rates three to four times higher than white, black hospital admissions in South Carolina did not reach parity with white until the 1950s, just about the time that new drug therapy was making such care unnecessary. In 1934, 833 blacks succumbed to TB. Although the recommended national standard that year was one hospital bed for every TB death, South Carolina provided its blacks only 148 places. For whites, the standard was met.[10]

Fortunately TB underwent a steady decline among blacks, even without much help from the state. The situation was different for heart disease, which increased at an alarming rate among blacks during the early twentieth century. The census bureau in 1920 grouped a large number of diseases under the label "diseases of the heart," but the more significant contributors to death included endocarditis, myocarditis, angina pectoris, and diseases of the coronary arteries.[11] By 1925 in South Carolina and 1930 in North Carolina and Georgia, heart disease had not only surpassed TB as the leading killer of blacks, it was also claiming their lives at a far greater rate than whites'.[12] One of the first to recognize the problem was South Carolina physician Robert Wilson, president of the state board of health, who in 1915 noted the extremely high death rate among blacks in Charleston and Augusta, Georgia (where the rate was 190, more than double the white). The unevenness of mortality was so great that it raised in Wilson's mind the likelihood that "we are in error when we assume that the negro is the physiological counterpart of the white man."[13] Other Southern doctors came to share Wilson's concern, but not until the late 1930s, when federal money was available, did Southern states bestir themselves to take action against heart disease among either race.

The third major category of killers of Southern blacks was that of diseases and conditions associated with maternity and infancy. According

Black tuberculins at Camp Alice in Sumter, South Carolina, c. 1930. One-half of the sanatorium's costs were paid by the Duke Endowment. Courtesy of the Duke Endowment.

to the census bureau (in 1928) the leading causes of maternal death were puerperal albuminuria (a kidney disease), puerperal septicemia, accidents of labor, and hemorrhage, while infants succumbed most frequently from premature birth, birth injury, congenital malformations of the heart, and hydrocephalus.[14] Most tragic because they were mostly preventable, deaths of black mothers and babies were a measure not only of the despair that marked the lives of most black families but also of the ineffectiveness of Southern public health work in the early decades of the century. Maternal mortality among Negroes was not high by comparison with mortality from TB or heart disease, and like TB it was in steady decline, falling in North Carolina, for example, from 41.3 deaths per 100,000 in 1920 to 23 in 1935. Yet by comparison with the white maternal death rate in the Tarheel State (27 and 12, for the two years), the black rate was far higher and falling more slowly.[15]

More serious were infant deaths. Out of every 1000 black babies under one year of age in South Carolina in 1920, 159 died. In 1940, 10 percent still perished. White mothers suffered as well, but their losses were fewer, standing at 86 and 54 per 1000 for those two years. Infant mortality was closely associated with economic status. Black babies born into affluence were at little risk. The problem was that most Southern blacks were among the poorest of the poor. Maulsey Stoney's experience, if not typical, was illustrative. Mrs. Stoney, a servant on Edisto Island, South Carolina, had given birth as best as she could recall to eleven babies. None survived. Some were stillborn. Others died in infancy, one baby, she believed, smothering in his own covers.[16]

The mortality picture for most other ills during the decades before World War II was equally discouraging for Southern blacks, if not as devastating. The only important diseases which killed whites at greater rates were scarlet fever, diphtheria, and cancer. In the latter case, however, black deaths were not only rising but also slowly approaching the frequency for whites. For typhoid fever, whooping cough, pellagra, malaria, and syphilis the black rate, though in decline, remained well ahead of the white. Malaria and syphilis were comparatively unimportant as killers of Negroes (though syphilis rates were on the rise at least from 1920), but they caused a great deal of sickness and disability.

Finally, a word about pneumonia: in the pre-penicillin era, pneumonia carried off great numbers of whites and blacks, operating as a kind of executioner after victims had been substantially weakened by other illness. And from that disease, too, blacks suffered greater losses. Historically, blacks have always shown a higher susceptibility to respiratory disease than whites. As was true for TB, the explanation apparently lay in the fact that Negroes had no experience with the bacterial pneumonias until the sixteenth century when they began to encounter Caucasians. Although the differential in mortality declined over time (as blacks acquired defenses similar to whites), the black death rate remained higher.[17] In 1920 in South Carolina, for example, 298 Negroes of each 100,000 died of pneumonia, while the white rate stood at 197. Both rates were uncommonly high, a result of the 1918–19 influenza pandemic. But in 1935 the Negro rate still hung at 172, while the white level had dropped more sharply to 109.[18]

To make matters worse, when blacks died from their various ills, they often died without medical attention. One estimate of the national situation in the 1930s put the figure at 25 percent. In the South it was even higher. About 28 percent of blacks who died in South Carolina in 1935 had no doctor in attendance, while only a fifth as many whites faced such neglect. Besides the emotional agony and stress that those figures all too poorly convey, they also suggest that true mortality rates for specific diseases were considerably higher than reported for both blacks and whites. Certainly, the large number of Southern Negro deaths falling into the "ill-defined" or "unknown" category confirms that assumption. In the two Carolinas and Georgia, deaths from unknown causes rivaled even those for TB until about 1935.[19]

The human meaning of such cold statistical analysis was that life for American blacks was far more cruel and much shorter than it need have been. In 1910 black males in the United States could expect to die four years earlier than white, and black females lost over nine years. The end of the next decade saw little relative change for Negro women and a worsening for men. Looking back over the first four decades of the twentieth century, one black epidemiologist concluded that since 1900 Negroes had made little gain in life expectancy, except in the first years of life. And between 1920 and 1940 black males aged twenty to fifty fell three years further behind whites.[20]

But mortality was only a rough index of the health of a people and the conditions under which it lived. Given the fact that about 98 percent of Southern blacks survived each year, it would be more to the point to describe the health of the living. Regrettably, the historian can sketch only the roughest dimensions of Negro morbidity before the 1920s, because neither the national government nor the Southern states had much insight into the health or ill health of black citizens. In fact not until the 1950s did the subject of morbidity (for either race) begin to receive on-going, detailed attention. Yet if one were willing to forego precision, an estimate of Negro morbidity in the earlier twentieth century South is possible. That estimate suggests that Southern blacks were, as the Alabama doctor claimed, "outrageously sick."

Morbidity data are most plentiful for black children, largely due to fairly frequent medical inspections of schools, undertaken primarily out of a desire to contain the spread of epidemic disease among whites. Begun in many Southern cities and towns between 1910 and 1920, inspections seldom gave as much attention to black youth as white, but as an index of child health in the region, they were fairly reliable. In 1912 Spartanburg, South Carolina, became one of the first Southern cities to make a medical inspection of its Negro school children. Ironically, the study was made just about the time Governor Cole L. Blease was vetoing a bill establishing statewide school inspections on the ground that they would require young girls to disrobe in the presence of possibly lecherous male physicians. The Spartanburg study found that 56 percent of black children had at least one significant "defect," such as enlarged tonsils (41 percent), swollen glands, or defective teeth (30 percent). By contrast, only 42 percent of white youngsters had serious problems. A Columbia, South Carolina, study of about the same time found problems to be far more abundant, affecting 88 percent of black children and 95 percent of white.[21] Although the better black showing was surprising (and exceptional) it pointed less to the relative healthfulness of Columbia's black youth than to the poor living standards of both races.

Approximately a decade later Charleston health officer Leon Banov, a dedicated physician and a Russian immigrant, surveyed pre-school children of rural Charleston county, a largely black area. Banov discovered 28 percent of them to be malnourished, and 6 percent anemic. The most widespread problem underlying nutritional deficiencies was intestinal parasites: over 45 percent of black children showed the presence of hookworm, ascaris, or some other infestation. Scabies, impetigo, and severe dermatitis were also common, particularly among the very young. Some of these ailments were due to parents' ignorance of basic hygiene. One Negro baby remained in Banov's memory, and he wrote that, in order to examine the infant: "we had to remove about seven thicknesses of woolen clothing, including a very heavy red flannel petticoat. The weather was rather warm and needless to say, the child was cross and fretful, and the skin was extremely irritated from the excessive perspiration."[22]

The racial differential in morbidity among children was pointed up by a 1924 Baltimore study of those under fifteen years which showed that black children contracted TB, syphilis, and pneumonia at far higher rates than white. Morbidity from broncho-pneumonia (902 per 100,000), for example, was twice as great, while that for syphilis (235) was nearly ten times larger. A survey of rural Maryland children about that time showed that 70 percent of black youngsters under two had signs of rickets, while only 30 percent of white babies were so afflicted.[23] A South Carolina black woman who was active all over the South in the Negro health field in the 1930s believed that anyone who had not lived through that time would find it impossible to imagine how different the black children's appearance was from that of latter-day blacks, with all the malaria, impetigo, scabies, rickets, typhoid fever and pellagra that was present.[24]

Most black children survived to adulthood, but if they left the child-hood diseases behind, they did not cast off the burden of ill-health. One of the most serious problems of black adults was syphilis. In the white im-agination Negroes were a "syphilis-soaked race," but not until the late 1920s did Southern states, thanks to aid from Northern foundations and the federal government, attempt to measure just how severe the problem was.[25] What they found was bad enough: a syphilis rate among blacks varying from 10 to nearly 30 percent of the population. And the problem stubbornly resisted efforts at reduction, though before the 1940s those efforts were underfunded, spasmodic, and often conducted in ways that were insulting to the blacks they were purporting to serve. In 1930 a foundation study of syphilis in Glynn County (Brunswick), Georgia, found 26 percent of blacks with the disease. Seven years later a retest of that same population discovered a 27 percent infection rate. The awful touch of syphilis meant more than just debility and death. In a pregnancy, syphilis, whether carried by mother or father, could mean spontaneous abortion, stillbirth, or serious defects in the newborn infant.[26]

A disease whose clinical effects were registered more immediately was malaria. According to time-honored belief, Afro-Americans enjoyed sig-nificant immunity to the disease. And, indeed, for the ante-bellum period that appeared to be the case. Not only did contemporary observers remark on it, but modern science has discovered among twentieth century Africans a genetic basis for malaria immunity. The primary protections were two: the absence of a specific antigen in the blood (the Duffy antigen) among most blacks, which gave them a resistance to *vivax malaria,* and the presence of the sickle cell trait (which occurred when an individual inherited the sickling gene from only one parent), which conferred some immunity in perhaps 30 percent of blacks to the more deadly form of the disease, *falciparum malaria.*[27]

But if blacks enjoyed a measure of natural protection in the nineteenth century, whatever advantages it gave them over whites seemingly disappeared by the early twentieth. By 1920 mortality statistics for the Southern states revealed a black death rate from malaria which was two to four times that of the white. The reasons were not clear; but most probably blacks (despite genetic immunities) had a harsher experience with malaria because of a combination of social and economic factors that increased their exposure to mosquito bites over that of whites. According to modern epidemiologists, by the early twentieth century relatively more blacks than whites lived near mosquito breeding sites and slept in houses without screens. In addition,

A group of black men receiving intravenous treatment in a Georgia venereal disease clinic, c. 1937. Individual chemotherapy sessions lasted about four hours, and the whole course of treatment could stretch to eighteen months. Courtesy of the Library of Congress.

work and social activities of black people occurred more often out-of-doors, which put them in special jeopardy during periods of peak mosquito activity. Finally, blacks on average had a lower nutritional status, which weakened natural immunities and increased susceptibility to malarial infection.[28]

Deaths, though, were not the most important measure of malaria's impact. In most Southern states (by 1930) TB, heart disease, pneumonia, cancer, diseases of maternity and infancy, even syphilis, claimed more black lives than malaria. What made malaria a significant health problem was its ability to weaken, even incapacitate, an individual for years on end.[29]

And it was blacks, not whites, who bore a greater proportion of those burdens. By the 1930s malariologists were concluding that for every malaria death there were at least 200 cases of the disease, and in 1932 assistant surgeon general Thomas Parran estimated that the South as a whole had 2 million cases of malaria every year. Given their greater incidence of infection, Southern blacks had to contend perhaps with 1 million of them.[30]

Among them, the ones who suffered most were rural blacks, who as late as 1930 made up about 80 percent of the South's black population. They suffered because until the late 1930s they were largely ignored. When the (Rockefeller) International Health Board and the Public Health Service (PHS), along with state boards of health, launched the first demonstration projects in malaria control just after World War I, sponsoring agencies decided to concentrate on urban areas. The primary aim of the projects, after all, was to impress the public with the effectiveness of lowland drainage, stream oiling, and other modes of malaria control in order to win backing for large efforts. Given limited funds, it was thought that working in urban areas would garner a greater payoff in popular support. Rural regions were too poor to aid such trials, and the extensive drainage required made malaria control there virtually impossible.[31] The strategy made sense (though not even towns responded as hoped), but the consequence was a continuance of malaria infestation among rural blacks.

As for TB, the presumption of Southern physicians and health officers was that morbidity among blacks showed the same excessive rates as did their mortality. Fortunately, that turned out to be incorrect. When Southern states inaugurated their first case-finding efforts in the early 1940s, they found that Negro morbidity rates (about six cases per TB death) were no higher than white. Those results were confirmed by World War II induction physicals, which showed black morbidity rates to be, if anything, a bit lower.[32]

Obviously, no one can say precisely how sick the Southern black populace was in the early decades of the twentieth century. Only a handful of people hazarded even the most general estimate. In 1922 Monroe C. Work, sociology chairman at Tuskegee and long-time editor of the *Negro Yearbook*, pronounced that 6 percent of Southern blacks were "seriously sick all of the time."[33] But as he found the same percentage of gravely ill in every Southern state and major city, his findings were somewhat suspect. Two decades later Roscoe Brown, head of the Division of Negro Work in the PHS, made another kind of projection. In 1941 Brown suggested that blacks showed the same excessive rates of morbidity (compared to whites) that they did of mortality.[34] But to translate that into actual numbers of Negro sick, one had to know the white morbidity, which was also unknown. So the scholar was back again at square one.

Selective service examinations during World War II offer a rough approximation of Southern Negro morbidity in the late 1930s, although these figures have to be used with caution, for they pertained only to younger males and did not distinguish Southern blacks from those living elsewhere. But if one examines draft data in conjunction with occasional local morbidity studies, certain tentative conclusions are possible. By the mid-to-late 1930s it is likely that as many as 20 percent of adult blacks in the South had syphilis and another 3 to 4 percent, gonorrhea. Upwards of 13 percent may have harbored malaria, with South Carolina and Georgia blacks showing an even higher proportion. Seven to 8 percent showed signs of heart disease, and fewer than 1 percent had TB. Approximately 1 percent suffered from kidney ailments, and about 5 percent had hernias. If one allows for a fair amount of multiple illness, it is entirely possible that 35 to 40 percent of adult male blacks in the South were fairly sick, or just about to be, in any given year. Although it took its measurement a decade earlier, the Committee on the Cost of Medical Care, the blue-ribbon panel named by President Hoover to survey the nation's medical needs, implied a black morbidity rate of similar magnitude. In its final report (1932) the Committee noted that blacks "have health problems which are, on the whole, considerably more serious than those of whites. The Negro is America's principal marginal worker, and he suffers in the North as well as the South from . . . poorer housing, less adequate diet, less sanitary surroundings, more employment of married women and great economic insecurity."[35]

As for black children, there is no reason to think that they were any more healthy. They shared a substantial amount of the malaria present in the Southern black population and some of its venereal disease. They were the main victims of the so-called childhood diseases, though probably no more than white children. They showed an excess of worm infestation and nutritional disease, though how much was uncertain. Moreover, school surveys revealed that at least 50 percent of black children struggled with debilitating disorders, such as inflamed tonsils and decayed teeth. Like their fathers and mothers, Negro children, too, were nearly as often sick as well.

Such widespread ill health was the product, however, of problems more deep seated than the mere prevalence of acute illness and infection. Chief among them were racial discrimination (and accompanying persecution) and an economic situation that black sociologist C.S. Johnson character- ized as "an almost hopeless struggle against feudalism."[36] Rather than en- dure that sort of grinding existence, after about 1900 an increasing number of rural blacks began to flee their growing imprisonment on deep-South tenant farms for what they hoped would be greater economic opportunity (and better social conditions) in America's cities.[37]

Before the war those black belt migrants had gone mostly to Southern cities, to such places as Atlanta, Birmingham, New Orleans, and Mem- phis. Accordingly, between 1900 and 1910 the South's urban black popula- tion had swelled by nearly 1,490,000, while that of cities in the North and Midwest had increased by only 194,000 — the latter population consisting mostly of blacks from the border South who had had some previous urban exprience.[38]

But after 1915, drawn by the high labor demand of wartime, the stream of black migration changed course and began to flow to cities like Detroit, Chicago, Philadelphia, and New York. Between 1910 and 1920 the urban South still counted 396,000 additional blacks, but their numbers in the urban North grew faster, by some 474,000. In 1920 the United States Census reported that of 1,487,000 Negroes living in the North and West (the vast majority in urban areas), 781,000 of them had been born in Southern states. The number of black South Carolinians who migrated to Pennsylvania, alone, rose from 2100 in 1910 to 11,600 in 1920.[39]

In several ways this migrating black peasantry fulfilled its expecta- tions. Higher wages, greater freedom, and education for its children were often the rewards of moving to the city. But health presented a different story. Whether in Northern or Southern cities, through the 1920s at least, the health of newly urbanized blacks deteriorated significantly. Like the early nineteenth-century British industrial cities, which attracted millions of that country's rural poor, American cities made no provisions for its black (or poor white) newcomers, leaving reception to those who stood to profit most from unregulated immigration, such as realtors and property owners. As one black physician noted, "just as soon as Negroes move into a neighbor- hood, even in our liberal Northern cities, rents rise, promoting overcrowding, the sanitary standards are lowered, [and] garbage collections and street clean- ings become fewer."[40] Chicago, noted one of its historians, "expected the Negroes to stay in the [urban] 'Black Belt' and the 'Black Belt' was already overcrowded."[41]

Although statistics of mortality for urban blacks were scanty (and those for rural Negroes virtually nonexistent), by the early twentieth century the urban Negro's dilemma was clear. In Northern cities like Newark, Chicago, and New York, their general mortality rate ran from 50 to 60 percent higher than the white rate, and black babies perished two to three times more often than white.[42] Southern towns offered worse chances for survival. In 1914 Jacksonville health officer C.E. Terry compared mortality rates for fifteen Northern cities with nineteen in the South and found that, while the Southern white rate exceeded the Northern by 212 deaths per 100,000, the Southern black rate was 657 higher. Of all major and preventable infectious diseases, only the rate for TB suggested that blacks were better off staying in the South. But whether they ventured northward or to their own capitals, blacks were without question putting health at risk when they left their farms.[43]

Yet if it did nothing else the black trek to the cities brought the question of Negro health to national attention. While blacks remained on the land they could be (and were) ignored. But once in the cities, where public health agencies were fast maturing, they had to be noticed, if for no other reason than that they seemed to menace whites. The "Negro Question" that pressed so insistently upon the national consciousness after 1900 was largely a product of this urban migration, and while it had many dimensions — crime, unemployment, political participation — one major concern was health.[44]

The first to give attention to rising urban mortality were blacks themselves. Even before 1900, faculty and students at Atlanta University were becoming increasingly alarmed about the problem. After discussing the need for a more systematic investigation of general urban conditions with his trustees, university president Howard Bumstead convened in 1896 the first of a series of Atlanta University Conferences on the Negro. As the most pressing problem of all, Negro mortality was made the focus of the initial gathering, which sought to define its extent and discover its causes and possible solutions.[45]

Although uncertain about the extent of mortality because of sketchy data, participants had no doubt about why blacks died. Ignorance and intemperance were to some degree responsible, as whites often charged, but blacks perished chiefly because they were impoverished and neglected. A Savannah social worker noted in 1903 some of the health risks he saw in urban migration. To save money a black family usually took a one-room apartment. "The landlord will not agree to have this cleaned before they move in, although it has not been cleaned or repaired in a score of years, and during that time as many different families with each a different disease have lived in it."[46] Although modern medicine has rejected notions about the viability of old diseases, housing of this sort still posed threats from exposure, flaking lead paint, rats, and other vermin.

Yet behind the painful awareness of the handicaps that plagued them lay a confidence among blacks that as environmental conditions improved, mortality would surely decline. Some even understood that the immediate cause of higher rates lay in the Afro-Americans' sudden shift to a new disease climate to which they had not had time to adjust. As one Negro educator saw in 1909: races "which have for centuries lived in cities acquire a greater immunity to some diseases, especially TB, than those who have more recently given up rural for urban life."[47] There was no reason why blacks, too, would not adjust to the new conditions of urban living. Meantime blacks and whites, together, could speed the process by extending to Negro city dwellers the kinds of programs that were proving successful among whites. Meharry Medical College dean George Hubbard (a white) told the 1913 Atlanta Conference that what was needed were health education in schools and churches, more and better services, and ampler opportunities for blacks in state TB hospitals. Techniques for disease prevention were well known, said Fisk sociologist Charles S. Johnson, and whites could not sit idly by and let the Negro "stumble blindly through new problems . . . "[48]

Many whites were concerned about the collapsing health of black migrants. But if black leaders had been guardedly optimistic, white physicians and health officers were less sure that the future would bring improvement. When white medical and health organizations finally began (about 1910–15) to discuss the implications of the Negro's high urban mortality, many doctors — echoing a belief which had appeared with emancipation — argued that the new statistics merely confirmed the black's inability to survive in an urban-industrial society. As for the future such a belief extended only the prospect of racial extinction. White medical experts who took that view, a position that won greatest adherence among the South's private, rather than public, physicians, saw no purpose in mounting costly public health campaigns among a people who were merely undergoing the inevitable.[49]

Although most white professionals stopped short of embracing the race extinction thesis, that did not make them optimistic about Negroes' chances for healthful urban living. They agreed that the Negro was ill-prepared, by virtue of historic conditioning and racial temperament, to master successfully the epidemiological and economic challenges of urban life, but they recognized, too, that survival was conditioned by environment. If that could be improved, urban blacks had as good prospects as whites.

Therein lay the problem. Not only were environmental changes impeded by political and economic realities but by racial ones as well. Even enlightened whites saw the Negro temperament — their presumed laziness and improvidence, coupled with unclean, sexually promiscuous habits — as a primary part of their environment.[50] Up to the middle 1920s urban mortality statistics seemed to bear out the gloomiest predictions. In both Southern and Northern cities Negro death rates, though dropping, still towered above those of whites and kept well ahead of those of rural blacks. In 1923 and 1924 there was actually an increase in Negro mortality, which some attributed to the rising northward migration. Even Louis Dublin, medical director of the Metropolitan Life Insurance Company and a white who welcomed blacks' escape from the South, was concerned by the unexpected mortality setback. The best that he could make of it was that it was "somewhat confusing," for while the Negro rate had increased in Chicago and Detroit and risen significantly in the South, it had decreased on the Pacific Coast and held steady in New York. Yet even if the overall situation was unfavorable, Dublin was sure that the setback was temporary and that the downward course in urban black mortality would soon resume.[51]

Possessed of a hindsight that Dublin and contemporaries did not enjoy, the historian can see not only that urban mortality resumed its fall but that in the long run Southern blacks who migrated to Northern cities made a wise choice from many standpoints, including that of health. Even by 1910 adult Negroes in major Northern cities like New York and Newark enjoyed markedly better chances for life than those whose transplantation took them only as far as places like Raleigh, Charleston, and Atlanta. For Negro infants, whose mortality was a surer measure of overall health and the community's will to maintain it, Northern cities became safer places by the early 1920s. Mortality fell so rapidly in Northern metropolises, in fact, that by around 1930 Northern blacks had about as good a prospect for avoiding deadly diseases (with the exception of TB) as Negroes who remained on Southern farms. Black infants in the North achieved that sort of parity about 1935.[52] That is not saying a great deal, of course, because Southern rural blacks had abundant health problems in the 1930s, but it does indicate the speed at which black health in the North improved and suggests that Southern rural blacks who fled northward after around 1930 found increased freedom and opportunity without giving up anything to ill health.

As to why Northern blacks were doing relatively better by that time, several reasons suggest themselves. Some credit was due to the work of urban health departments. In places like New York, Providence, Buffalo, and Newark there already existed, by the time the flow of black migrants began, a vigorous tradition of public responsiveness to the health needs of the poor. In 1916 the New York City Health Department, working with the Urban League, began an effort to reduce the high infant mortality rates among blacks. Like an earlier venture (1908) among white immigrant families, the later campaign was also a notable success. After one year deaths from diarrheal and respiratory diseases, which by 1915 claimed the lives, respectively, of 71 and 80 of every 1000 Negro infants, were reduced to a rate of 48 and 50. Of course not every Northern city was so vigorous. Hospitals and health agencies in Terre Haute, Indiana, about that time were virtually ignoring the needs of Negro citizens.[53]

Northern blacks also found more medical services at their disposal.

Public hospitals made fairly ample provision for them (which was unheard of in the South), and, while care was always segregated, hospitals were in easier reach of the Negro populace. There were also more and better black-owned hospitals, at least in major Northern cities. Doctors in general and black doctors in particular were also more numerous, many black physicians having migrated from the South for the same reasons that their patients did. Between 1910 and 1930 the black doctor-to-patient ratio in New York state and New Jersey held at about 1:1900, while the proportion in the Carolinas and Georgia averaged around 1:7600.[54] In the early twentieth century, of course, medical intervention could produce only limited results, but the value of what doctors and hospitals could do was steadily increasing, so that a people with a relative abundance of those services was better off than one without.

Equally important factors in improvement of their health status were changes in the way urban blacks ordered their lives. Some were apparently inherent in urban living; others were tied to the wider economic opportunities in the North. For one thing, urban black women (North and South) had significantly fewer babies than their rural counterparts. In South Carolina farm communities in 1930 there were 566 children under five years for every 1000 women of child-bearing age. In North Carolina and Georgia the numbers were substantially the same. Urban blacks, by contrast, had only about half as many children. Whether urban births fell because children were no longer an economic asset or for some other reason, the result was that the average urban black family was smaller by about two children.[55] Given the fact that higher earnings were available to blacks in the North, those families obviously had more resources for such things as food and medical care.

Housing, too, had obvious consequences for health. In the North much of it was of better quality than that in the South—both rental dwellings and owned homes. In Columbia in 1930 the median value of homes owned by Negroes was $1464, while the average renter paid $10.81 per month. In Philadelphia the corresponding amounts were $4662 and $30.43 and in Akron, Ohio, $4076 and $25.50. Even after adjusting for higher Northern prices and conceding the existence of much slum property, one could conclude that Northern blacks, on average, lived in more commodious and sanitary structures than their brothers and sisters in the South.[56]

Certainly improved education was another reason why Northern blacks enjoyed better health. That widespread illiteracy existed among adult Southern blacks was well known. While it had declined by 1930 to about 27 percent in South Carolina and 20 percent in Georgia and North Carolina, there were some predominantly rural counties in those states where over 30 percent of blacks could not read or write. In the North things were different. Black illiteracy in New Jersey in 1930 was only 5 percent; and that was on the high side, for in New York it was 2.5 percent.[57] Commenting at about that time on the improving life prospects for black infants in Northern cities, Grace Abbott of the United States Children's Bureau said that fewer babies were dying because it was easier to educate the mother.[58] That task was simpler, she might have added, because most Northern black adults were able to read and write, put a higher premium on education, and were thus responsive to efforts to guard their lives and those of their children.

The great majority of blacks, however, the ones trapped in the rural South, experienced few of those health gains. In fact, in the first decades of the twentieth century rural blacks sank increasingly into the nether world of sharecropping and tenant farming, until by the end of the 1920s some 80 percent of South Carolina blacks, like those elsewhere in the region, were barely surviving as they endured a slavelike existence of chopping and picking cotton. And for those who moved to Southern cities, life was even more perilous — at least until after World War II.[59] In Charleston and Columbia, two of America's most unhealthy places, the general death rate for blacks in 1930 (per 100,000) was 3330 and 3040, respectively, which compared unfavorably to an average of 1649 for all the state's blacks.[60]

Although poverty was surely the primary factor explaining ill health and excess death in the South, it was not the only one. Good health or its absence was the result of many variables, all interconnected and most related to economic status. Not only sanitary environment, but also nutrition, level of education, stress, the way one viewed and responded to illness, the availability and acceptability of medical care — all helped determine whether one was sick or well, lived or died. And for blacks, especially those in the South, racism and institutionalized segregation heightened the effect of every other variable. America's health and medical professions and its political leadership groped very slowly toward an understanding of the economic, social, and cultural parameters of health. They moved even more haltingly in developing the will to change the system of life that bound blacks to their fate of ill health and early death.

The effects of poor housing and lack of sanitation in urban black neighborhoods have already been alluded to. For rural blacks environmental conditions were almost as bad. What black tenant farmers gained by the dispersal of housing, they lost to greater congestion within each dwelling. In the Carolinas and Georgia, black farm families were 60 and 70 percent larger than city families. As late as the 1920s most of those families, besides being isolated from medical services by a lack of telephones, autos, and useable roads, were normally squeezed into one- or two-room shacks, which were unscreened and without running water. Water came instead from surface wells, which were often contaminated by human feces, as 90 percent of black tenant families either made do with a foul, open-backed privy or simply relieved themselves in surrounding woods.[61]

The same sort of sanitary arrangements prevailed in Southern Negro schools, although scool officials took some care to protect black children from unsafe water, by having them either bring bottles from home or borrow water from a school neighbor. In some ways it was fortunate that those drafty, ill-heated, unsanitary facilities were open only three to five months of the year.[62]

Another aspect of Negro life affecting health was diet and nutrition. One problem was ethnic food preference. Until federal food supplement and school-lunch programs began in the 1930s many blacks, like day laborer George Brown of Etiwan (Daniel) Island, South Carolina, considered corn and other vegetables as "buckra" (white) food and resisted suggestions that they add them to family diets.[63] Partly because of such tastes and also because there was pressure to devote every square foot of ground to the money crop, few blacks planted gardens. Moreover, as pellagra surveys showed, poor blacks and to a lesser degree poor whites, relied far too heavily on fat pork, grits, and molasses as standard fair.[64]

In the 1920s nutritional research still lacked precision, and diets tended to be graded according to the consumption of key foods rather than on the basis of minimum daily requirements of important vitamins. Nonetheless, nutritionists were convinced that the dietary habits of Southern rural black families (and to a lesser degree, white families) posed serious risks to health, especially in children. In 1929 the Agricultural College of South Carolina (Clemson) surveyed the nutritional condition of young children and reported that Negro parents generally had little understanding of the relation between diet and health. For the most part, food preferences of adults (usually, males) determined those of children. One-half of Negro youngsters got inadequate quantities of all the foundation foods, which then included milk, eggs, vegetables, potatoes, fruit, and cereals. Insufficient milk consumption was a special concern, as experts regarded it as the perfect food. One quart per day was long considered the standard, and black children fell far short of attaining it (the intolerance of many blacks to milk was not yet suspected). Overall, the 1929 study showed that 95 percent of black children were getting "questionable," "inadequate," or "grossly inadequate" diets. It found further that 50 percent of black pre-schoolers (and 40 percent of white) were underweight and that few got sufficient rest, their parents generally letting them keep adult hours.[65]

Ten years later a re-survey of the coastal area, which had the greatest concentration of blacks, showed that little had changed nutritionally. Though a farming people, more than half of all inhabitants had no cow, with the result that white children averaged just a quart of milk a week, while black youngsters got little more than a cupful. Sixty percent of black diets were low in other protective foods as well — such as potatoes, leafy vegetables, tomatoes, and citrus fruits; and for the great majority of black families, pellagra remained a constant threat. In every category blacks fell dangerously behind the whites, whether in vitamin C intake (half the blacks got too little), overconsumption of fatty foods, or the amount of iron in the diets of pregnant women and children (where, again, half were deficient).[66]

What investigators found in South Carolina was true elsewhere. A 1935 sampling of black children in Tuskegee, Alabama, discovered an alarming rate of anemia. Though that might not necessarily result from under-nutrition, researchers reported that children's diets also lacked milk, eggs, and fruits, which their parents considered luxuries and which had to be replaced with other, cheaper foods to satisfy their youngsters' hunger.[67] A little later, in eastern North Carolina, nutritionists examined a small mill and farming community and found that, while white textile workers and farmers did poorly in terms of vitamin intake, blacks were more at risk. They got only one-third of the needed amount of vitamin B_1, one-third of the riboflavin, and about one-half of the iron. Those conditions, the report added, described rural black families across the state.[68]

Nutritional problems were in part the result of blacks not knowing what to eat. Yet even had they known, most did not earn enough to buy what they needed. As one elderly Charleston black told a health nurse who chided her for not feeding her children the recommended diet, "I sho' wish I could give 'em the sorta food you tell me they ought to have. . . . But best I can do is give 'em 'nough to keep 'em from starving."[69] Not even federal cash and food supplements of the 1930s made up the difference in many areas where blacks were at the mercy of white landlords. In eastern North Carolina, plantation owners reportedly had an understanding with county relief directors to hold back loans to blacks and to overlook landlords' practice of charging for supplies that they were supposed to receive free. Their rationale was that they had to do those things to "prevent the 'demoralization' of their Negro labor."[70] Of course not all Southern blacks were in the tenant class, but even the minority who could affort a suitable diet sometimes had problems with nutrition. One thing commonly observed by home nutritionists of the 1930s was the bland diet of black clients. In addition, most blacks with money had to live with the ever-present possibility of falling suddenly back into poverty. Such fears acted as a brake on any food expenditures the family felt were not absolutely necessary.[71]

Besides the obvious links between poverty and health, there also existed two more subtle and complex ties. The first was the dependence of poor people — black and white — on nontraditional medicine, a reliance shaped not only by poverty but also by cultural heritage and geographical isolation. Although some folk remedies and customs had value — and certainly many did little harm — many also had negative results. The other connection has only recently been clarified. In the post–World War II period a new group of scholars calling themselves medical sociologists found that poor people of all races responded to illness differently from members of more privileged classes. When a class-connected system of illness response deferred needed treatment, ill health was often the result.

Part of the folk medical tradition among Southern blacks was a heavy reliance on "hoodoo" or root doctors, a common practice until the 1920s. Maude Callan, a South Carolina black nurse-midwife who began serving blacks of low country Berkeley county in 1923, faced serious competition from lay healers when she started up work. "The believed in root," Callan recalled, "and I told them that if I believed in root, I'd be dead." But she found it no easy task to wean people from these healers. Her approach was to challenge blacks to explain why, if the root doctor's medicine was so good, he did not work among whites. One black was quick with an answer: "hoodoo" medicine was ineffective against the white man "cause he hair too slick."[72]

Resorted to mostly by those with emotional problems or those seeking to repair a case of alienated affections, "hoodoo" doctors also offered treatment for a wide variety of major and minor ills. Their stock in trade was a concoction or potion which the patient buried or wore on his or her person to banish the evil spirit causing the trouble. Often the supposed source of illness was an enemy who had engaged a rival "hoodoo" to put a curse on the afflicted individual. The second root doctor prepared a prescription to counter the hex. In the arena of the mysterious a "hoodoo" doctor found it easy to retain credibility. If patients recovered, and the odds were that they would, then the "hoodoo" won increased esteem. If no recovery ensued, or death occurred, the root doctor could claim that the patient had not followed directions.[73]

By the 1930s, though, credulity was waning, and while a large percentage of blacks continued a reliance on patent medicine and the flamboyant, mass-audience kind of faith healer like Bishop Daddy Grace, root doctors' practices shrank to embrace only older blacks or those in particularly isolated areas, such as the Sea Islands of Georgia and South Carolina. Others might occasionally resort to their services, but they were apt to seek the help of regular physicians, as well. Reverend I. Dequincey Newman, civil rights leader and itinerant Methodist minister in South Carolina in the 1930s, believed that by then root doctors existed only "in the twilight. They were sort of referred to in whispers. If you patronized a root doctor it was not publicized."[74]

Side by side with "hoodoo" doctors was a self-help tradition of magical

medicine. Passed down orally through the generations, these ancient superstitions and rituals (which are extant in some measure today) were widely
known among Southern blacks and whites in the early decades of the twentieth century and covered virtually every known illness. To prevent blood
poisoning from a nail puncture one held the wounded area in the path of
smoke from burning woolen rags. A reputed cure for appendicitis was to
walk slowly up and down stairs and then take a laxative. Poplar bark was
supposedly a specific for pellagra, while diphtheria was cured by blowing
sulfur down the patient's throat. Typhoid fever did not require medication:
there, the remedy was to tie wreaths of cabbage leaves about the victim's
wrists, ankles, and head.[75]

How much and how long blacks relied on such practices are unclear.
Some evidence suggests a fair degree of dependence existed down to the
1930s. For one thing, the existence of "cures" for recently publicized diseases
like pellagra and diabetes suggests that the tradition of magical healing remained viable.[76] Moreover, several early students of Southern folklore witnessed such rituals about that time. Fisk sociologist Charles S. Johnson noted
in 1926 that the practices were still in wide use. That "is rather bad," he added,
because where those practices do not bring their own infection, they retard
nature."[77] Indeed, where the patient was seriously ill—with something like
pellagra or diphtheria—the resort to ritual cures would delay or deny more
effective treatment (assuming of course that it was available), with possibly
fatal results.

In addition to superstitious beliefs about treatment of illness, blacks
also harbored a number of notions about health maintenance that were often
equally dysgenic. Meharry's DeanHubbard noted that they kept "every door,
window, and other opening of sleeping rooms . . . tightly closed," and while
asleep they buried their heads under thick blankets. Sunlight was as
unwelcome as night air. Houses whose windows were covered with curtains
or shutters in daylight hours were a common sight in black communities.[78]

But folk medical practices of Southern blacks were not without value.
Many of the teas and other natural remedies of the herbal medical tradition
of both white and black America had curative or at least restorative value,
as modern medicine is continually discovering. One remedy for upset
stomach, common in Southern Negro homes into the 1930s, was a tea made
from boiled chicken gizzards. It worked, though no one knew why until
a recent investigation showed that gizzard lining contains pepsin, a known
specific for digestive disorders. Modjeska Simkins, a black teacher and health
worker in South Carolina, recalled from her girlhood that rural blacks commonly had herb gardens in which they grew sage, mullein, hoarhound,
boneset, and sassafras, which they made into teas to be administered for
a variety of ills. Children grew up knowing the different uses of white and

black snake root and red and white sassafras. Most black homes contained a bucket of water in which fat pine roots lay soaking; as needed, a cupful of the turpentine-water mix would be taken for colds or congestion.[79] Although modern science has discovered some medicinal value in nearly all these plant remedies, the heavy reliance on them by poor blacks and whites alike was also a function of the tendency among uneducated people to think of the body in mechanistic terms, as a kind of elaborate plumbing system which occasionally got clogged or rusty and needed to be cleaned, unclogged, or flushed out.[80]

It was usual, then, with the first appearance of symptoms of an illness for blacks to resort to self-medication, whether with home preparations or patent medicine. If sickness persisted or symptoms worsened, some might then resort to a root doctor or experiment with other medicines or remedies. Seldom did the individual seek what the modern world called qualified professional help, at least not until illness had reached the stage at which it was interfering with the person's ability to earn a living or manage the home.

To account for such behavior merely in terms of the unavailability of professional help or the lack of money for doctors is too simple an explanation, in the view of medical sociologists. One also has to consider average blacks' outlook on illness and death, as well as their habit of resorting to a rather unusual procedure for coping with serious illness, a procedure which put the doctor's office and the public health clinic at the end of a lengthy process of help-seeking behavior.

Poverty, among black or white, produced its own attitude toward health. Inducing both fatalism and pessimism, poverty also acted as a brake on the kind of response to illness natural to middle-class Americans. Early in the century Meharry's Hubbard observed this negativist thinking at work. Blacks, he said, too often took the view that no man could die before his time. Accordingly — and foolishly — they put off calling for the physician or surgeon until it was too late.[81] Such fatalism was stubbornly persistent. As late as the 1930s many blacks continued to regard TB as a form of divine retribution for sin, against which there could be no defense. Others saw it as an inherited condition, not to be escaped — nor passed along to anyone else, for that matter. Whereas the better-educated and more affluent might perceive the body as a fine piece of equipment which needed continual maintenance for tip-top operation, the poor thought in terms of a machine whose lifespan was limited and unalterable, which could be used until worn out but not repaired. As head of preventive medicine at Howard Medical School, Paul Cornely had a close acquaintance with black health behavior. His view was that Negroes tended "not to give a damn about preventive services because to them this is something for the future which they don't think they will see."[82]

Medical sociologists have frequently noted the feelings of futility and powerlessness existing among the poor, who tend to see doctors and hospitals as a system run by and for the middle class, but not for them. The poor seek only to hold on, to survive. And survival, especially in the period before federal welfare, meant economic survival — holding onto the job at all costs, keeping up rent payments and, if possible, burial insurance. While fighting that battle the poor faced more than their share of family disputes, crop problems, and — for blacks — the added stress of racial intolerance and the ever-present threat of white retribution if racial norms were transgressed. In the face of such immediate and insistent crises, concerns over health simply did not rate a high priority. One might, after all, get well, given time and a change of medicine. The possibility that one might get worse, maybe die, was not something that easily prompted the habitually fatalistic Southern black to action. Besides, possibilities were things that belonged to the future, and the exigencies of the present gave them more than enough to think about. In effect, the poor could be ill, but they could not afford to be patients.[83]

Denial of illness was reinforced and extended by the existence of what medical sociologists call the lay referral system, an integral part of the structure of low income communities. Often when illness struck, the sick person appealed to friends or relatives to supply some other explanation for the symptoms. When finally the fact of serious illness had to be faced, the patient sought their advice about a course of action. In the early decades of the twentieth century, recommended action was normally something other than a visit to a doctor or clinic, which was ruled out for any or all of a number of reasons. The friend or relation appealed to might be ignorant about outside avenues of help or might put greater reliance on home remedies or on the skills of a local healer. More important, other family or community problems might be too pressing to assign the impending illness a high priority. If the verdict was that the individual's problem had to wait, the sick person was under pressure to accept it, for the patient was usually under many obligations to those friends or relatives and often shared certain responsibilities with them. To assume what sociologists term a "sick role" (ie., to become a patient) would mean abdicating those duties. Besides the societal pressures for delaying a visit to the doctor, many blacks had an inclination to avoid the profession, as past experience with the outside medical or health system had often been frustrating and demeaning.

Not only did the poor resort to the lay referral system on the way *to* the doctor but on the way back as well, a practice that often had the effect of slowing recovery. Public health physicians and nurses frequently had to battle patient reluctance to follow medical advice, usually because friends or relations had dissuaded the patient from complying. Mattie Ingraham was a health nurse in the 1930s who served a largely black population in the South Carolina low country. One of her mothers had an infant with a serious case of rickets. Ingraham had given the mother cod liver oil for the condition. But the next visit revealed that the young black woman had stopped administering it. The nurse, incredulous, asked why. "Somebody tell me," the mother admitted, "I've been give him too much already."[84]

If poor blacks' fatalism and their habits of self-treatment and of resorting to a lay referral system delayed their getting medical attention when needed, the general unavailability of health and medical services lengthened that delay further, often shutting patients off from treatment altogether. Not until federal assistance became available in the late New Deal period would state boards of health make an earnest effort to extend services to their whole population (see chapter 7). And before the launching of a national hospital construction program in 1946 (chapter 7), hospital care was simply unavailable for a large fraction of the Southern black population, although the hospital program of the Duke Endowment (chapter 5) filled some of that gap after 1927.

Insofar as private physician care was concerned, the situation was more complex. It is not correct to say simply that there were not enough doctors to serve Southern blacks. Given the high patient-to-doctor ratio in the pre–World War II era, if most blacks had been in the habit of seeking regular physician care, certainly there would not have been enough doctors to go around. But most blacks were not in that habit, and the low demand for physicians in most of the rural South was one explanation for the short supply (which, in turn, helped keep down demand).

One thing that can be said with assurance is that there were not enough *black* doctors to meet the need. Most Afro-Americans preferred to be treated by members of their own race, but black doctors were virtually nonexistent in many parts of the South. In South Carolina, along with Mississippi the state with the fewest black physicians, there were only sixty-six black professionals in 1910, and that number remained fairly constant for twenty years. Also about 40 percent of them were concentrated in five or six of the state's largest cities. Even had there been geographical balance, each black physician would have had around 12,000 patients, compared to a white ratio that varied between 560 to 800 in the period up to 1930. Thus most Southern blacks had recourse only to white doctors — who tended to be in cities, too, far from the bulk of the black populace.[85]

Some blacks, of course, did not want to be treated by a black physician. According to North Carolina (black) doctor Hubert Eaton, a family's preference for a white physician seemed to be passed down through the generations, like the family Bible or tastes in food. Sometimes whole communities tended along that line, said Eaton, as if they felt that the "white man's ice is colder."[86]

Whatever the physician's race, he or she expected to be paid, and the inability of the average black family to make even the barest provision for physician care made that service less accessible. Etiwan Island sharecropper George Brown never took any of his children to a doctor unless one of them became "desperately ill." The nearest one was eighteen miles away and across a bridgeless waterway. In the 1930s his charge was five dollars a visit and Brown lamented that his budget just "will not take care of this."[87] In rural acreas black tenants could rely on white landlords to get them to a doctor if an illness became serious enough to impede work. However, landlords often deducted physician charges from Negroes' pay at the end of the season, a policy which must have forced their employees to endure illness as long as possible before appealing for help.[88] In rural Georgia that was certainly the case: in the mid-1930s over 60 percent of blacks who were disabled by illness for a week or longer never saw a doctor.[89]

Added to all the other factors inhibiting blacks from seeking medical help were barriers of race and class. Charleston black leader Septima Clark recalled the anguish her family faced around 1910 when her brother had to be taken far downtown to a white physician. Although the child had suffered a bad burn, the mother had to wait until the doctor had finished with every white patient before he would see the boy.[90] Even when black doctors were available, class differences could sometimes pose problems, too. As illiteracy fell among Southern blacks (by 1930 it had dropped below 25 percent), those who could not read prescriptions were increasingly ashamed to expose that problem to a black doctor and would sometimes avoid treatment because of it.[91] In the final analysis, racial, cultural, economic, and geographic factors combined in the pre-1940 era to isolate most blacks — even those greatly needing help — from physician care.

The same assortment of problems surrounded Negroes' use of hospitals. First, in many parts of the rural South there were no hospitals for anyone, black or white, until passage of the 1946 Hospital Construction Act. In South Carolina, as late as 1930, none existed in twenty of the states' forty-six counties. As was the case with physicians, most of the South's better facilities were located in cities. Not until about 1930 did they begin to open their doors to black patients, with some continuing to exclude blacks until the 1960s (see chapter 11). Columbia's major public hospital refused to accept black patients until 1934 and did so then only because a foundation considering aid to the hospital made it a condition of funding.[92] Many facilities that denied blacks admission made exceptions for surgical emergencies, but such hospitals normally refused post-operative care. L.W. Long of Union, South Carolina, a leader in both state and national Negro medical circles, recalled that as late as the 1930s the white hospital in his town sent black patients home in the back of a wagon while still under anesthesia.[93]

Where blacks were admitted, the segregated Negro ward of the 1930s was often a wretched place. Typically, the black ward was overcrowded, ill-equipped, and often located in a basement room. Blacks were naturally reluctant to go to such places, and their fears were compounded by a wide belief that white physicians would use them for experiments, a conviction that persisted until well after World War II. Even so respected a figure as Negro sociologist E. Franklin Frazier maintained in 1924 that white physicians regarded his people "simply as experimental material."[94]

The alternative to the white facility was the small hospital and nurses' training school run by black physicians. Before the 1930s it was often the only place where blacks could go for medical attention, and so it filled an important community need. Even though such facilities never reached more than a small fraction of Southern blacks, mostly in urban areas, they multiplied at a fairly rapid rate between about 1910 and the late 1930s. And despite abundant problems of funding and staff, most managed to survive beyond World War II. The nine black hospitals in Georgia in 1913 increased to sixteen by the late 1930s, with only four collapsing along the way. The six in North Carolina also increased to sixteen in that period, with but one casualty.[95]

If most Southern black institutions managed to stay in business, few gave what the major accrediting agency regarded as adequate care. In 1928 there were about a hundred black hospitals in the South. Of that total, only nine had earned passing marks from the American College of Surgeons.[96] One of the unaccredited was Charleston's Cannon Street Hospital and Nurses Training School. It began in 1897 on a shoestring, and although it was long-lived there was no evidence that the passing years brought anything but continued deterioration in structure and equipment.[97] Lawrence Lee, white city physician of Savannah, was not surprised that most blacks feared hospitals. The ones he had seen, he reported in 1914, "are warranted to repel and even terrify people less superstitious than the Negro." Black institutions were also seriously overcrowded. Savannah's facility regularly admitted ten to fifteen more patients than there were beds. The overflow ended up sleeping on chairs, the floor, and often with another patient.[98]

Apart from Meharry's Hubbard hospital, blacks in the deep-South could claim only four first-rate facilities in the pre-1940 era, according to black physician and editor Montague Cobb. They were the John A. Andrew Memorial Hospital at Tuskegee Institute, Flint-Goodrich in New Orleans, Lincoln in Durham, and Community in Norfolk. The rest were mostly cramped, converted houses or cast-off hospital structures no longer good enough for whites but considered amply sufficient for blacks—the medical equivalent, as Cobb put it, of "old clothes for Sam."[99]

Adequate hospital care was not only inaccessible to most of the black

Graduates of a midwife training course conducted by the Georgia Board of Health, 1926. Instructor stands at the far left. Courtesy of the Georgia Department of Archives and History.

community, it was also unsought. Because of cost and the popularity of folk medicine, hospital care was not an expectation of Southern blacks — not even in those situations where for Southern whites it had become customary. Maternity care provides a good illustration. In the pre–World War II era, the only help which most Southern black women received during pregnancy and childbirth came from untrained, mostly illiterate midwives, whose numbers were then legion. In North Carolina in 1910 officials counted 1400 midwives. But that tally was surely low, as the state board of health five years later found some 9000 at work, delivering every year about 80 percent of black infants (and 20 percent of white). In South Carolina their numbers were fewer and in Georgia, greater, but both states' midwives delived the same high percentage of Negro babies.[100]

Almost to a man, doctors and health officers were convinced that reliance on midwives was largely responsible for the high maternal and infant mortality among the black population, citing the fact (as one North Carolina health officer did in 1917) that twice as many black babies as white died in the first six weeks of life. Although part of their alarm was surely due to professional conceit, it was true that until about 1920 midwifery was entirely unsupervised in the South.[101]

As a group these women had no training and little notion of sanitary technique, and their ritualistic approach to birth beggared description. Lavinia McKee started practicing midwifery in South Carolina's low country about World War I, and she recalled that when labor pains were especially hard it was common practice to give the mother a tea made with dirt-dauber's nest. If that was unavailable, pains could be "cut" by placing a sharp tool like a knife or hoe under the patient's bed or by rubbing her body with sulphur and lard. For severe birth pains, the midwife placed under the bed an old pair of shoes turned upside down. Rituals included practices with newborns, as well. Immediately after delivery the midwife usually placed the baby underneath the mother's bed to insure that it would always be a good child. If the infant was born with a caul (a membranous covering from the womb) over its head, the substance was dried and later fed to the baby to insure happiness. On the Sea Islands of coastal Georgia, midwives considered it a major error to wash the baby until the ninth day. In sanitary surroundings such practices might not have done much harm, but in the grime of a tenant house, ritual was closely associated with infection, and one Florida health officer noted that tentanus, convulsions, teething, hives, and colds appeared with disturbing frequency on death certificates returned by midwives.[102]

About the early 1920s Southern state boards of health, under pressure from medical associations, began trying to train midwives in more modern procedures and to eliminate the worst of the lot through licensing. Though

Black midwife carrying her bag out on call in rural Georgia, c. 1935.
Courtesy of the Georgia Department of Archives and History.

many were banned from practice during the decade (nearly 1500 of 3900 known midwives in Georgia), reform was slow. There was really nothing and no one to prevent a rural black woman from consulting an unlicensed midwife until local health departments became more widely established, which did not happen until the New Deal era.[103]

Before that occurred, though, the health status of Southern blacks would take a downturn, if such were imaginable. With the start of the Depression in 1929, the basic public health services (immunizations, some support for mothers and infants) that had been delivered to Southern blacks since the end of World War I were sharply curtailed. With services and family income reaching an all-time low, already high maternal and infant mortality rates began to climb. But the major force affecting health in the Depression was the elimination of income. In the rural South increased numbers of blacks and whites were forced into tenancy or off the land entirely. For urban blacks, who were slowly forming a habit of using doctors and hospitals, loss of jobs had more striking impact on health. In 1933 Atlanta's Neighborhood Union, a black organization involved in Negro welfare since the early 1900s, surveyed 277 black families to gauge the Depression's effect. The overall conclusion was that life for Atlanta Negroes was in collapse—in regard to health and everything else. Every family had sustained at least one serious illness within the previous three years. As for care, 103 had to seek treatment in the free clinic at Grady Hospital; 71 had consulted a private doctor; 43 had used home remedies, and 28 had gotten no treatment. Outcomes were equally bad: 107 had recovered, 123 still lay ill, and 18 had died.[104]

Blacks, however, were not the only group confronting serious health problems in the early twentieth-century South. Although statistics do not exist to prove it conclusively, in the pre–World War II decades the general health of Southern cotton mill workers was probably every bit as troubled. While economic deprivation was a primary cause of poor health in Southern mill villages, it was not the total explanation. The mill hand was also the victim of certain prevailing economic and social ideas, which not only bound him to a sort of feudal status but caused him to be scorned and ignored— almost as if his skin were black.

CHAPTER 2

Health of Mill Hands

The Village Environment, 1900–1930

Dazzled by the possibility of economic revitalization through the manufacture of textiles, the South's commercial, political, and medical leaders proved more than willing to consign the welfare of mill employees to the keeping of their mill-owning employers, who for their part offered elaborate assurances about what they were doing to secure the health and well-being of the people put in their charge. The only problem was that there was little substance to owners' claims. Rather than health, what their underpaid workers found in crowded, unsanitary mill villages and in hot and dusty factories was a cycle of disease, exhaustion, and more disease that emptied too many lives of any meaning other than bare survival.

But workers' problems could not be laid at the feet of mill owners, alone. Those same commercial, political, and medical supporters of mill development also bore responsibility, for as mill hands became a visible feature of Southern society, its "better" elements came to disdain them almost as completely as they did the region's blacks. To the rising urban middle class, even to most rural Southerners (from whose midst most cotton operatives came), the cotton hand was a white who had fallen from grace. Shiftless, primitive in habits, resistant to improvement, mill operatives were not only viewed as socially irredeemable but seen as having only themselves to blame for whatever health problems they faced.

A few Southerners, working in government, the press, and the health professions, recognized the plight of the mill hand. But by the time owners' welfare promises were found to be false, they enjoyed so much authority in legislative halls and in the Southern economic imagination that none dared call them to account.

Had the size of the South's mill-working population been small and static, public indifference and employer exploitation, though regrettable, would have been of only limited social and historical significance. But the fact was that that population underwent an enormous growth in the late nineteenth and early twentieth centuries. While some features of textile development, such as expanding profits, multiplication of factories, and increasing job opportunities, were rightly matters of regional pride, the health conditions inside those mill villages—the subject of the present chapter—were an occasion for Southern, even national, shame.

Like Topsy in *Uncle Tom's Cabin,* the Southern cotton textile industry grew at a breathtaking rate in the two decades bracketing the start of the twentieth century. Particularly rapid was the growth in the eastern cotton-belt states of North Carolina, South Carolina, and Georgia. North Carolina, which quickly became the region's textile leader, already counted 177 mills by 1899, a number that increased to 281 by 1909. In second position, but with a greater proportion of large-sized mills, was South Carolina, whose factories increased in that same ten years from 80 to 147. Georgia, which would never fall as completely under the sway of textiles as its two neighbors, was still a major mill state with 116 establishments by 1909.

To measure the economic impact of these mills—and the political and social power of their owners—one had only to recite the mounting worth of the goods they produced. Their value in North Carolina rose at a rate that surely fulfilled the expectations of the most eager New South prophet: from $28.4 million in 1899 to $72.7 million by the end of the next decade. In the lower state the money-making magic of textiles was equally potent, the value of South Carolina's product actually leading that of North Carolina until 1909, when it reached a total of $66 million (compared with $48 million in Georgia). If one recalls that only thirty years before nearly all the profits of cotton manufacture were being harvested by New England industrialists, the changes in the South's economy are doubly dramatic.[1]

Equally impressive was the employment which the industry provided a wage-hungry region. By 1900 textile jobs in North Carolina had already surpassed 30,000. Over the next ten years an additional 17,000 would be added. In South Carolina some 45,000 rural folk had taken up mill work by 1910, and in Georgia 18,000 had done so. Reserved almost exclusively for whites, these jobs were held mostly by former tenant farmers, their wives, and children, although mountain families and a few land-owning farmers, working part time, also joined the flow to the mills. Not only were mills the largest employers in the Carolinas and Georgia by the century's turn, but mill people made up significant (and growing) portions of each state's population. This was especially true in South Carolina, where around 1905 better than one of every six white persons lived in a mill village.[2]

To listen to the Southern mill owner, though, revitalization of stagnant economies was of secondary importance. The greatest contribution of the textile mill was the blessings bestowed on the poor white families whom it was rescuing from social and economic devastation. Caught in the tightening grip of farm tenancy, facing a future that offered equality only with the black, the Southern poor white, according to New South lore, found in the cotton mill not only work and cash wages but education for his children, a decent home for his family, and a chance for a healthy, happy life. In short, the early mill owners saw themselves primarily as philanthropists, whose chief work was saving lives and assuring the future of a whole class of Southern people. Possibly owners would get rich in the process, but that was no more than their due. As one friendly chronicler of such good works put it, if there was great prosperity for the few, there was also "much well-being for the many."[3]

Had the average mill hands been privy to the claims of mill owners, however, they would hardly have recognized them as applying to their situation. In fact, anyone inquiring closely into matters of mill village health in the century's early decades would have been struck by the disparity between publicists' claims and actual conditions. Although paucity of records prevents a detailed accounting of mill morbidity and mortality, as was more nearly possible for blacks, enough studies and observations were made to warrant the conclusion that all the way up to World War II life was lived on the margin by most families in most Southern mill towns.

That that was so was sometimes hinted at by Southern leaders, themselves. In 1913 North Carolina's respected state health officer, Watson Smith Rankin, advised his younger brother, also a physician, that the mill town of Kannapolis was a promising place to begin a practice. Conditions would not be very good, said Rankin, who had once had a rural practice in the textile region, himself. But a young doctor would really learn his trade there, for the "amount of sickness in a place of that kind exceeds the amount . . . in other places."[4]

Rankin's view was amply confirmed by a United States Bureau of Labor study of that period (published in 1911), which examined living standards in three typical mill settings. These included a large industrial city (Atlanta), a small town with several mills (Greensboro, North Carolina), and an isolated rural area (Burlington, North Carolina). Focusing on twenty-one families, the study also made a rough comparison between Southern conditions and those in the North, by examining fourteen mill families in Fall River, Massachusetts.[5]

Among Southern mill workers larger families were the rule. On average they numbered eight to nine members (20 percent larger than in Fall River), including usually a boarder or lodger taken in to help defray expenses. The normal American family, one with a single wage earner, was almost unknown in Southern mill towns. Of the twenty-one families in the Labor study, sixteen had three or more members at work. The normal family was underrepresented, said the report, simply because "it is almost impossible [economically] for it to exist."[6]

More striking was the amount of serious illness among the Southern families. Only four of twenty-one enjoyed what could be called general good health. Although exact comparisons with Fall River were impossible, it was at least suggestive that seven of fourteen New England families had had an illness-free year. To be sure, health records, compiled from interviews and observations, lacked precision and reliability. Even so, Southerners displayed a virtual catalogue of the ills to which humans were prey. There were cases of "female trouble," poor digestion, typhoid fever, malaria, tuberculosis, and bronchitis. Congenital defects appeared with distressing frequency. Crossed eyes, crippled limbs, and lumps on faces were common, as was the boy or girl typed simply as too delicate to work. Women seemed to bear the heaviest burdens. Besides those who had died young or lost infants to miscarriages, others struck government interviewers as "old and worn out" before their time.[7]

Not untypical was the Atlanta family of five whose male head had been injured in the mill, with a subsequent loss of six weeks' wages. The mother had lung trouble. One daughter was frail and a heavy consumer of patent medicines, and a working daughter had just recovered from a serious illness that cost the family twenty-four weeks' pay and a large medical bill. Families in the other settings had their share of illness, too. The mother in a Burlington family of eight was only thirty but looked fifty. The father had had malaria and lost two weeks of work, and two children had suffered bouts of measles. Having no cushion of savings, the family had to borrow money from the mill superintendent to get by during the father's illness. Wages had gone up some since the couple married, but "rations," said the wife, "had gone up more."[8]

Villages seemed as decrepit as their occupants. A Winnsboro (South Carolina) man, reflecting on the early twentieth century village of his boyhood, recalled it as a "dreary lot of unkempt, unpainted houses on a hilly spot south of the town. . . . Thin gray lines of smoke issued from kitchen chimneys in the daytime, and yellow kerosene lamp lights shone out of small windows at night. . . . The persons making their way through its unkempt streets sometimes would have to hold their noses to keep out the stench of pig pens or cow stalls."[9] Boston writer Marie Van Vorst visited Columbia in 1903 to gather material for a book on women workers. Her recollection of the villages where she stayed, posing as a mill hand, was one of muddy lanes, treeless lots, and drab houses. Cramped, ill-furnished interiors were depressing enough, but what drove Van Vorst nearly to distraction, besides the necessity of sharing a bed with another lodger, were the bed-bugs and mosquitoes that swarmed at night.[10]

Keeping such homes warm in winter was another burden. The fireplace was an ample source of heat, but thin walls and floors made it impossible to retain much of its warmth. It was common on entering a mill house in winter to find mother and children huddled there. Although owners provided fuel at what they said were wholesale rates, the average Southern family actually spent more on heat than workers in Fall River.[11]

Out of such conditions came the inevitable: major problems with infectious, insect-borne, and parasitic diseases. Especially in the first decade of the twentieth century, infectious illness was probably a more serious menace in mill villages than elsewhere. To add to the problem, most owners did not view epidemic control as their responsibility. Yet state health boards had neither funds nor requisite legal power to keep watch over mill villages. Thus in South Carolina in 1903 smallpox broke out in mills around Anderson and Spartanburg, and diphtheria in and about Darlington. Four years later scarlet fever appeared, with epidemics reported in Greenville County. (The board of health responded in all those cases, but only after a crisis had appeared.)[12]

Smallpox was easily the most serious problem early in the century. Its root causes lay both in the migratory habits of mill hands and in owners' unwillingness to cooperate, either by having families vaccinated or by controlling movement of disease victims. Toward the end of the decade health officials in South Carolina felt that owners were giving more cooperation but that workers remained intractable. As one frustrated public physician said, the lower class would not do what you told them to prevent disease.[13] A Winnsboro minister accounted for workers' resistance as a result more of individualism than ignorance: "it was regarded [by them] as an invasion of personal rights to even require vaccination of the children in a home."[14]

Another contagious illness that bore heavily on mill village families was tuberculosis. Regarded at the time as the result of long and constant exposure to cotton dust and mill germs, TB was actually (says modern opinion) the product of home crowding, poor nutrition, fatigue, and of course the presence in the household—or mill—of an infected individual. But whatever its origin, the incidence of (and mortality from) TB was thought to be extremely high. Although Southern health officers made few efforts to determine the extent of the problem among textile operatives or any other population group until World War I, such was not the case in New England. There, detailed investigations were made, a few of them attempting comparisons with the South.[15]

One such study, by the Massachusetts labor bureau in 1912, analyzed

A Tifton, Georgia, mill family in front of their mill village house, 1909. The widowed mother and the five oldest children worked in the mill. Courtesy of the National Archives.

TB mortality among mill-working and non-mill-working females in Fall River, Manchester, and Pawtucket. Its finding was that the female operative was two and a half to five times more likely to die from TB than the woman outside industry. But bureau investigators also examined available TB statistics on mill populations in Atlanta, Augusta, and Raleigh. Though sketchy, the Southern data suggested that Southern mill women died at a rate that was about one-third higher than their New England sisters.[16]

A third common illness, as debilitating as TB if not as deadly, was malaria. Concentrated primarily in rural regions of the lowland South, the disease was endemic in parts of the textile piedmont as well. Exactly how serious it was before World War I is unfortunately beyond the historian's knowing. Not even Southern health officials knew. Yet every Southerner knew that malaria was a problem, even though few did anything about it. Its victims, mostly the poor, tended to accept it as just another of life's burdens to be borne in silence. Rather than seek professional help, the great majority preferred to rely on patent medicines. Those who might have responded, such as health boards and business leaders, preferred saying as little as possible about it for fear of discouraging outside investors and settlers.[17]

The vulnerability of cotton operatives cannot be doubted, even though hard statistical evidence is scanty. Most pre-war mill villages offered all the necessary pre-conditions: a highly transient population, ill-constructed and unscreened houses, and ample breeding places for *Anopheles quadrimaculatus*. There was also some direct evidence of malaria's substantial presence in Carolina and Georgia mill villages. The 1911 Bureau of Labor study of twenty-one mill families found active cases of malaria in five. Heavy infestation was also reported about 1912 in mill communities in Rockingham, Lumberton, and Roanoke Rapids, North Carolina.[18]

The Roanoke Rapids situation pointed up the seriousness of the problem. In 1913 the company physician reported that for the previous three years some 75 percent of the town's population had had a bout with malaria.[19] Besides the suffering and lost wages visited on individual families, the disease was costly to the mills. Management had to provide housing for far more families than normally needed, in order to have enough workers to keep spindles turning. As one mill president said, "You knew you would not have John Jones tomorrow because that was his chill day, and so you had to have somebody who did not have one on that day to take his place."[20]

Mills with this serious a problem were the first to see a need for preventatives. In 1914 Roanoke Rapids owners launched an ambitious anti-malarial campaign in cooperation with Public Health Service officers who had just returned from a successful mission against yellow fever in Panama.

Swampy areas were drained, ditches cleaned, and devices installed to spray oil on slow-moving streams. Results the first year were dramatic: doctors' calls fell off nearly to zero, and mill employees enjoyed their first summer without major disease problems. Owners were equally elated, one manager reporting that the money his mill spent "was more than regained in one month's operation."[21]

A few other mills, such as the ones at Rockingham and Lumberton, took similar steps in the pre-war years, but where the problem was less serious and less obvious, little was done. A fairly high rate of absenteeism was taken for granted by mills, and where it did not interfere with business operation, management did not unduly concern itself with its cause. Nor was much attention given to the problem by county health departments, even though those agencies were beginning to proliferate in the South after about 1912, with several starting up in North Carolina's textile region. As a result malaria continued to be a troublesome presence in Southern textile villages, as it was in rural black communities all the way down to the 1930s, when major eradication projects were undertaken by the federal government.

Perhaps those early state and local health departments should have done more against malaria, but there was fair reason why they did not. Their attention and energy just then were focused on a more prevalent and pressing illness. Scientists knew it as *uncinariasis,* but its popular name was hookworm disease.

The emphasis was rightly placed, because among Southern poor whites—whether in factory or on farm—hookworm was the most widespread medical problem of the pre–World War I era. Although the disease had probably been common in the South at least as far back as the Civil War, it was only in 1901 that it was identified with certainty and its cause attributed to a parasite thought (wrongly) to be uniquely American. But it was not until the end of the decade that its seriousness was generally conceded by the South's health and medical communities and a campaign organized (by outside leadership) for its elimination.[22]

Well before then hookworm victims, though as yet unidentified as such, were a common feature of the Southern landscape. Pale and listless, with vacant stares and winged shoulder blades, those "lazy" Southerners were so visible in cotton mill villages that their condition was assumed to be a result of working amid cotton dust and was even called "cotton mill anemia." Young people were most often its victims—one survey estimated that 60 percent of cases were under sixteen—and the boy of fourteen with a seven-year-old physique and a thirty-year-old face appeared with such regularity that he came to be thought of as the "typical cotton mill child."[23]

Victims not only looked bad; they functioned poorly as well. There was of course a range of disability, depending mostly on the number of

A South Carolina hookworm victim, 1912. The boy on the left is a healthy 14-year-old. The smaller lad has hookworm. He is 16 and has a mental age of 6. Courtesy of the National Archives.

worms a person carried hooked onto the intestines. Fifty would make a light case, whose only symptoms would be a little blood loss. But infestation could exceed five hundred, in which event the victim's very life was threatened from exhaustion and cardiac arrest. In moderate infestation, which described the great majority of cases, the red blood count fell off sharply, and the victim became anemic, undernourished, and listless; eventually there was physical and occasionally mental retardation. Pregnant women were at special risk as they could not retain the higher level of minerals and nutrients they needed. As a result, they had problems in labor, and a higher proportion of their infants were stillborn.[24]

The disease was originally most prevalent among white tenant farmers, whose primitive sanitary habits caused continual reinfection. One early twentieth century survey of rural waste disposal facilities in the textile South found that about 35 percent of that class of farmers had no privy at all. Most of the remainder had crude, foul set-ups that "are rarely or never cleaned."[25] In drawing workers mostly from that population, textiles inherited a hookworm problem of nearly equal proportions. Federal government zoologist Charles Wardell Stiles estimated in 1910 that of every hundred farmers coming to Southern mills, about thirty brought worms with them. Operatives from other mills, a far smaller group, had less disease, but even among them one in ten was infected. In many villages, however, far more than this 25 to 30 percent had hookworm.[26]

Unlike the case of malaria, effective preventive and curative measures were taken against hookworm early on, among both mill families and rural whites. The story of the Rockefeller Sanitary Commission for the Elimination of Hookworm Disease (1909–15) is too familiar and too recently addressed to be detailed here, but the relation of the Commission's work with Southern mill families and their employers merits some attention.[27]

Zoologist Stiles was a major catalyst of the Commission's formation, and Southern mill owners were among his earliest converts, a few even backing up their interest with money. Columbia's Olympia Mills shifted the emphasis of its clinic from malaria to hookworm after Stiles persuaded company physician William Weston that uncinariasis was more serious. Another mill later offered Stiles $50,000 to undertake an anti-hookworm campaign, a gift he ultimately declined, owing to Public Health Service fears that acceptance would implicate it with "exploiters" of child labor.[28]

That kind of generosity, though, was not typical. Most mills were only willing to give Stiles moral support. They looked to someone else to undertake the expense of hookworm treatment. Indeed, in 1907 Olympia Mills physician Weston was trying to convince South Carolina owners of the obvious economic advantages of hookworm prevention. The disease was "so easily cured and with so small expense" that he believed it would "pay the

A free, traveling dispensary for the treatment of hookworm in Jacksonville, North Carolina, 1911. Dr. C.W. Stiles of the Rockefeller Hookworm Commission is standing furthest inside the tent, to right of the physician with stethoscope. Courtesy of the Rockefeller Archive Center.

managers of manufacturing establishments . . . to have them [i.e., work-ers] treated at the expense of the establishment."[29]

Once Rockefeller work began there was much less need for mill fund-ing. Backed by a start-up gift of $1 million the Commission initiated a wide-ranging program of education and treatment in nine Southern states, in-cluding the two Carolinas and Georgia. Working through the existing pub-lic health structure in the states the Commission relied at first on educating doctors and teachers about hookworm in hopes that they could prevail on parents to get their children treated if tests showed presence of worms.

Then in 1911 the Commission shifted emphasis from education to treat-ment, adopting an approach that had recently proven successful in Missis-sippi: the traveling dispensary. Taking the doctor to the people (rather than trying to push them to him) proved hugely successful. As historian John Ettling has shown, this was partly because treatment (thymol) was free — if potentially dangerous — but mostly because the dispensary embodied all the characteristics and flavor of the religious camp meeting with which Southerners were already familiar. Going to the dispensary for thymol was like going to the revival to get religion. Even the picnic on the grounds was included.[30]

By 1915, when the program rather abruptly ended, some 750,000 South-erners had received chemotherapy from dispensary physicians. If not elimi-nated, hookworm was on the run in the South. Between 1910 and 1914 the rate of infection was reduced by over 60 percent in Georgia, halved in North Carolina, and cut nearly two-thirds in South Carolina. After the Rocke-feller campaign hookworm still existed, largely because many Southerners resisted taking sanitary precautions. But if they did not eliminate it, South-erners at least knew how to recognize and treat it. As a result, its cruel physical manifestations largely disappeared from the Southern scene.[31]

As for the role that textile mills played in the Commission's work and the benefits that their operatives received from it, the picture was not clear. Certain general points can be made, however. While mills had an interest in eliminating the disease, few took an active, direct part in treating vic-tims. Contact between mill management and Commission officials, for ex-ample, was virtually nonexistent, which indicated that mills did not as a rule establish their own treatment clinics or dispensaries — or encourage Commission doctors to hold theirs on company grounds. Quite possibly mill management were among those who supported the creation of county health departments to put hookworm treatment and other measures on a permanent basis. But if they did, they were not very successful in getting such units in their counties, at least not in the pre-war era. Of the eight county departments created in North Carolina prior to 1917, only three were set up in the nineteen counties where textiles were dominant. South Carolina organized five county units during that period, two of them within the state's seven textile counties.[32]

More important than hookworm *treatment* was prevention of the disease, which necessitated an interruption of the hookworm cycle and was most effectively accomplished by the sanitary privy or sewage disposal system. Although not assisted by Rockefeller — it would have been prohibitively expensive — the idea of sanitary waste disposal was promoted by the Commission as a proper object of private (and public) attention. But until World War I there were only few signs of mill owner interest. In 1910 Stiles, a firm friend of the mill movement, admitted that sanitary conditions in "so many" Southern mill villages were "miserable" and argued that owners had a duty to improve them.[33] Over the next decade progress was made, but it was slow and scattered and tied to the whim of individual owners who happened to take an interest in clean toilets. That such men were in a minority was shown by a 1916 PHS study of seven mill villages in and around Spartanburg. Only two had sanitary waste systems. The others provided families the kind of foul privy that was an encouragement to hookworm and other infection. There was little way that the state could improve things either: South Carolina had no law requiring villages to install sewage systems, and there were too few sanitary inspectors to encourage much in the way of voluntary change.[34]

But if owners took little part, hookworm was at least brought under control by about 1915 (though by no means eliminated). The same, however, could not be said for another disease stalking Southern mill hands in that day, a far harsher, more mysterious and fearful malady known as pellagra. A diet-deficiency disease closely associated with poverty, pellagra is now known to be caused by a prolonged insufficiency of nicotinic acid (niacin). Before about 1910 hardly anyone in the South except a few physicians even knew the disease existed, much less its cause. They knew only its symptoms, which were both widespread and grim.[35]

Called the sickness of the four "D's" — diarrhea, dermatitis, dementia, and death — the first sign of pellagra was a reddening of the skin on hands, arms, feet, and face. Often confused with sunburn or poison oak, pellagra's symptoms became unmistakable when reddened skin crusted over and peeled away, leaving tell-tale butterfly-like lesions on the face. Accompanying the skin condition was a serious digestive disturbance and a general feeling of malaise. In severe cases depression became dementia, and victims frequently were committed as insane. The death rate of asylum patients was extremely high and was at first thought to reflect pellagra mortality in the general population. Later work showed, however, that mortality was only about 3 percent, meaning some thirty-three cases existed for every death.[36]

Although pellagra was perhaps a greater threat to rural poor whites,

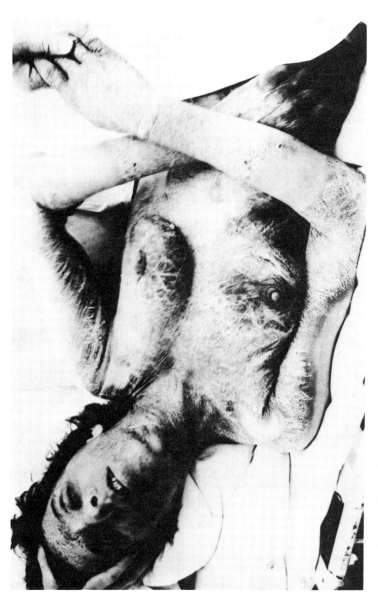

A white female pellagra victim, 1917. The darkening and crusting of the skin was a common pellagra symptom, though this is clearly a severe case. Courtesy of the National Archives.

its most visible victims were the region's institutional population and its cotton mill hands, who were in a way institutionalized too. For that reason prisons, orphanages, insane asylums, and mills attracted most of the attention that health officials began to pay pellagra after 1910.

But as awareness grew that mill workers were especially prone to the malady (a 1912 study in South Carolina showed that about ten of every thousand villagers had it), owners, town boosters, and local doctors dependent on mills became chary of having the problem scrutinized for fear of hurting a mill town's "good business climate." One group of executives and physicians, however, refused to shut their eyes to the problem. They were the residents of South Carolina's Spartanburg, Oconee, and Chester Counties, who willingly cooperated with private and public studies which ultimately proved crucial to tracing pellagra's etiology.[37]

Closely associated with the brilliant PHS epidemiologist Joseph Goldberger, the South Carolina studies not only confirmed the seriousness of mill pellagra but also revealed that its primary cause was not biological but economic. It lay not in spoiled corn (as first thought), disease-causing germs, or insects, but rather in the mill family diet — a poor people's diet, heavy on salt pork, molasses, and corn meal but woefully deficient in eggs, milk and butter, fresh meat, and green vegetables.

One of the Atlanta mill families from the earlier Bureau of Labor study had several children with pellagra symptoms. The contents of that family's larder could also have been found in virtually every mill home. In December the mother bought meal seven times, oil six, lard three times, and salt pork and sausage twice. Except for the Christmas turkey, one order of steak, and one head of cabbage, there was no other purchase of fresh meat, greens, or eggs. On New Year's Day the thirteen-member family ate a breakfast of sausage, butter, biscuit, and coffee; a lunch of salt pork and white peas, greens, corn bread, biscuit, and cake; and a supper of leftovers, minus the greens, but with a serving of milk. The only thing different that day was the presence of butter and milk, for unlike most mill families they owned a cow. But divided thirteen ways, those valuable foods surely did not give much nutritional protection.[38]

The frequent result of such a restricted wintertime diet was pellagra in the spring. Most hard-hit were children and non-working women. Among the villages studied by Goldberger, such women (in the twenty to forty-five age range) contracted pellagra ten times more often than their working men. The large differential was mainly due to the inability of child-bearing females (presumably the majority of the non-workers) to maintain a margin of nutritional safety. During pregnancy and especially lactation, nutritional needs of the fetus or infant are met from the mother's reserves. Among the population Goldberger studied, such reserves were virtually nonexistent, and a high rate of female pellagra was an inevitable result. In addition, excessive pellagra may also have stemmed from a willingness of non-working wives and mothers to defer to those who did work, in allotting food.[39]

If poverty was the root cause of the mill family's deficient diet and subsequent suffering, it was not the whole story. Custom and convenience were surely additional factors. Meat, meal, and molasses were traditional Southern fare. It was tasty enough and well-suited to a people lacking luxuries like refrigerators and having little spare time for food preparation. Availability of food was also a factor. One curious feature of pellagra's distribution that critics of Goldberger's nutrition thesis played up was the immunity of some villages to disease. One such community (called "Ny" in his study) lay in Oconee County. Its relative freedom from pellagra baffled Goldberger until he noted some curious differences in regional marketing practice. The nearby mill town of Inman, a place with much pellagra, had several stores, but none sold fresh vegetables, meats, or dairy products. "Ny," on the other hand, had a store which offered an abundance of fresh food. The explanation involved neither uncaring mill owners nor inefficient shop keepers, simply different agricultural practices. Around Inman were mostly cotton growers who in typical "King Cotton" fashion raised little else. What produce and meat were produced were drained off to the major market of Spartanburg, with little of it reaching Inman. By contrast, farmers about "Ny" had diversified. And having no nearby urban market, they sold their goods instead to villages like "Ny."[40]

Still, poverty remained the ruling link between pellagra and diet. In Goldberger's villages, two-thirds of the working population earned less than $10 a week (per adult male unit) which was the break point between a substandard and a minimally decent living style. As income dropped through the lower range, pellagra rose. Those families with less than $6 had forty-three cases per thousand of population, while those earning more than $14 suffered only three and a half. As income fell pellagra-preventive foods disappeared from family larders. Compared to their more affluent neighbors the poorest mill workers bought less fresh meat, green vegetables, fresh fruits, eggs, butter, and milk—and more salt pork and corn meal.[41]

By 1916 Goldberger and associates had gathered abundant evidence of the dietary basis of pellagra. The most convincing and dramatic proof had come in 1915 when he succeeded in inducing the disease in a group of healthy Mississippi prisoners who had volunteered for a controlled feeding experiment that restricted them to an unrelieved diet of cornbread, molasses, and fatback. Within weeks, the group had developed characteristic signs of disease and were begging to be released from the test. The test received wide publicity among Southern physicians and health officers, but not all were convinced. Vitamin research was then in its infancy, and the notion that healthy people could be made sick by a deficiency of something seemed fantastic to doctors who had cut their teeth on the germ theory and the concept of insect-vectored disease. Perhaps the loudest scoffer was South Carolina's health officer, James A. Hayne, who held rigidly to the idea that pellagra was due to some yet-unfound germ.[42]

But those who accepted or were at least willing to give a hearing to Goldberger's theory were equally numerous. Nineteen fifteen had been the worst pellagra year on record in the South, with some 100,000 estimated cases, and the dietary theory, although not absolutely established, at least offered a point of attack. So in 1916, with Goldberger in the vanguard, Southern boards of health began their first campaign to educate people to the need for a better diet. Some went further. A Wilmington, North Carolina, physician opened a clinic in the local court house to educate and treat pellagra victims. A lumber company in central Louisiana started a hospital for afflicted employees.[43]

Laudable as they were, such efforts were doomed to failure. Barring a massive nutritional aid program, until the economic status of mill and farm hands changed, pellagra would continue to stalk the South each spring. Even home gardens were no answer as long as mill families were unable to get off work before dark to tend them during crucial planting months of March and April. The only truly effective solution was a fatter pay envelope, but in the several years before 1916 the very opposite occurred: rises in mill wages fell behind food price increases.[44]

Then came World War I, and with it the first flush times, ever, for textile hands. Higher wages that mill owners would not pay on their own, wartime labor scarcity now forced them to pay. In 1914 the average annual income of the South Carolina textile hand was $311. By 1919 it was $757. In North Carolina the rise was roughly the same, from $294 to $730.[45] Food costs vaulted too, but not as rapidly. The impact of the new prosperity on pellagra was astonishing—though only what Goldberger had predicted. From a 1915 high its incidence fell by 1920 to the lowest level since statistics-keeping began. Goldberger still saw cases in Spartanburg villages, but the disease had lost its terror. From all appearances, pellagra was on the run. Certainly that was the view of the Spartanburg County Medical Society, which gathered to fête Goldberger and co-workers in 1920. But festivities were not just to honor Goldberger, doctors said; they were also to "bury pellagra."[46]

If that were so the funeral was premature. A malady so tightly tied to economic conditions, Goldberger warned, could be revived by bad times as easily as it could be subdued by good. In 1920, as the war boom collapsed, the nation's agricultural sector suffered a severe depression. The cotton South, hit by the boll weevil at the same time, suffered more intensely

Dr. Joseph Goldberger, the Public Health Service officer and hero of the anti-pellagra campaign, who established conclusively the dietary basis of the disease. Courtesy of the National Library of Medicine.

and longer. Textile profits plummeted, and that brought sharp cuts in mill wages. The fall in earnings at Georgia's mammoth Pepperill Mills showed what was happening. There, average pay, which in 1921 had reached a record high of nearly $24 a week, fell by 1923 to about $15.50. As wages fell pellagra began its frightening comeback. Deaths in South Carolina rose 20 percent between 1920 and 1921, and at the single village of Inman, Goldberger saw the number of cases increase from fourteen to thirty-one over the same period. But that was just the beginning. Like a freight train gathering momentum, pellagra continued to increase through the 1920s, as farm and textile families made inevitable dietary adjustments to shrinking income. By 1927–30 pellagra was striking 200,000 Southerners every year, and deaths reached an all-time peak.[47]

Merely to note the rising menace of pellagra, the continuance of malaria, and the persistence of hookworm, however, gave little clue as to the total amount of sickness in 1920s mill villages. Although a precise morbidity picture was impossible to draw, there were a number of studies of absenteeism in the industry, which allowed at least a rough appraisal. In 1923 agents of the Woman's Bureau (United States Department of Labor) visited eighteen cotton mills—nine in the South and nine in the North—in an effort to determine the amount of time lost by female workers and why. Two conclusions emerged: women had a higher absentee rate than men, and Southern women (and men), a higher one than their Northern counterparts. Southern female operatives on average missed over 27 percent of possible work days (the male figure was 20.7), while Northern women lost 16.4 percent (10.7 for men). Absenteeism in both regions was also proportional to length of working day and week. As for causes of lost time, interviews further revealed that personal illness was the primary factor, accounting for nearly one-quarter of all absences and affecting the working time of about 61 percent of all women. Other reasons were illness of another family member, a need to rest, pressure of home duties, and recreation. For Southern female hands, especially (who made up 40 percent of the 1920s textile force), health problems and fatigue constituted a weighty, day-to-day concern.[48]

A 1926 investigation of one Southern mill gave an insight into the causes of illness. It found that leading ills for men and women were respiratory complaints (accounting on average for 22 percent of days lost to illness), digestive disorders (14 percent), and boils (8.5). Compared to Northern mill hands, Southern operatives had considerably less trouble with respiratory ills and far more with digestive problems.[49]

Management had long been familiar with the problem of absenteeism but had traditionally explained it in terms of a lack of industrial discipline. As farmers—so the argument ran—these families had gotten used to an alternating cycle of hard work followed by inactivity, and when they became mill hands the habit of missing work when it suited them was too strong to break. Accordingly, management tended to dismiss suggestions that health problems lay behind workers' frequent absence.[50]

Lack of stick-to-itiveness might have marked the Southern factory class at century's turn, but it hardly fit mill hands of the 1920s. As second generation operatives, most were fully resigned to factory routine. Moreover, in a period of textile recession, as parts of the 1920s were, few workers were apt to miss work (and wages) frivolously. It could thus be assumed that when Southern hands stayed home sick, they were very sick.

The full measure of the effects of illness and disease, however, went beyond the counting of immediate victims. There were secondary casualties, too, such as a spouse or older child who was forced to take up the slack when a major bread-winner went down. Children surely bore the greatest burden, for more than well-being was lost: hope and future often vanished, as well.

A case of this sort, exceptional only in the weight and duration of the burden, was that of Evelyn Barnett, a child of Greenville mill parents. In 1913, before Evelyn was a year old, her mother died. After four years of wandering from mill to mill with his baby in tow, Barnett remarried and eventually settled the family in Rock Hill, where both parents worked in a mill, and Evelyn attended school. Then in 1927, after another move and another school, Evelyn's stepmother developed pellagra and had to abandon work. That forced Evelyn at fourteen to leave school and enter the spinning room of the Lockhart Mill to help support the younger children. Later, Evelyn admitted that leaving school was the hardest blow of her life, for she wanted desperately to become a nurse. Yet although she cried and begged her father to let her continue, he told her that he had no choice but to put her to work.[51]

Four years later her prospects brightened. The family's financial situation had stabilized to the extent that Evelyn, now eighteen, was able to take a mill job in Greenville and start a life on her own. But suddenly hope was dashed again. Her father had a stroke and was totally disabled. With an invalid wife, he was now fully dependent on his eldest child. Evelyn had no alternative but to move her parents, four brothers, and a sister to Greenville. As she related stoically, "her parents took care of her when she could not take care of herself. And its her duty now to take care of them through their troubles and triles." She hungered for more in her life, but God "had not intended [it] to be. . . . " Though her burden was great, "She will Bear it Gladly."[52]

CHAPTER 3

Health of Mill Hands

The Mill Environment, 1900–1930

In one respect the Evelyn Barnetts of the South and their families were worse off than Southern blacks. Where health was concerned, cotton operatives faced a sort of double jeopardy. They were at risk not only from having to live in near poverty in unsanitary mill villages, but from their work environment as well — the hot, humid, noisy, and dusty setting of cotton textile mills.

Virtual captives of a tightly paternalistic system, mill hands had no one to turn to other than mill owners in seeking relief from debilitating work conditions. Yet until World War II, most owners either ignored occupational health problems or denied their existence. Such deliberate neglect was possible in part because Southern labor and health departments, in awe of the industrialists, did not do their own job of identifying work hazards and communicating that information to employers and legislative leaders. Yet owners and politicians could not claim ignorance as an excuse, for if local public agencies were long silent on matters of industrial hygiene, the same was not true of health and labor agencies in Northern states and Washington. From those quarters, from the early twentieth century on, studies appeared with some regularity on the ill-effects of textile dust, heat, humidity, noise, and fatigue. To understand the origin of such conditions and the problems they created, one must begin with an understanding of the cotton textile milling process itself.

Except for minor modifications the cotton mill presented an unvarying environment during the first four decades of the twentieth century. Hence the industrial hygiene problems of 1940 were essentially those of 1900. To be sure, 1940 did not see the child laborers who had been much in evidence in early mills. And by the later date the pace of work was greatly increased over that of the early 1900s, owing to the introduction of the stretch-out system, which required fewer operatives to tend more machines. In addition, there was no longer the volcanolike eruption of dust four to five times a shift, when carding machines were cleaned. However, owing to the introduction of higher-speed equipment, overall dustiness was hardly reduced, and, a few changes aside, cotton textile manufacture—and the threats it posed to workers' health—altered very little in the four decades before World War II.

Although milling involved twenty to twenty-five operations and many complex machines, the basic procedure for converting baled cotton into finished yarn or cloth was relatively simple. The first step was the preparation of the raw cotton. Utilizing machines termed openers, pickers, and cards, first-stage processes cleaned the baled cotton of dirt and trash and then raked fibers into parallel alignment (carding). The product, a long, untwisted rope called a sliver was coiled mechanically into tall, wide-mouthed containers ready for spinning.[1]

In spinning, the sliver was first combed; then several strands of sliver were combined, stretched, and given a slight twist on machines called drawing frames and slubbers. Their product, a loosely twisted rope of uniform weight called slub roving, was wound on large bobbins and delivered to machines called ring spinners. They further stretched the roving and gave it additional twist, producing the final yarn, which was rewound on another set of bobbins, ready for weaving.

The final stage in the production of cotton cloth—weaving—involved taking yarn from many bobbins and winding it in parallel coils onto a long beam (which formed what was called the warp). Individual strands of the warp were then attached to the harness of a loom. Actual weaving commenced as the loom began rapidly raising and lowering alternate warp strands while simultaneously firing thread-bearing shuttles back and forth across the loom and through the raised and lowered warp threads.

The peculiarities of cotton fiber and the side-effects of running machines were also part of the milling process—and of the health environment of workers. One characteristic of cotton was that it could not be worked under low humidity. Without sufficient moisture, fibers tended to snap under tension, making drawing and spinning difficult. In addition, dry air produced an unmanageable amount of static electricity, causing fibers to stand out from the central axis, further lowering tensile strength. Accordingly, moisture had to be added to mill rooms by means of steam jets, evaporation pans, cold water vaporizers, or similar equipment. Since the amount of moisture necessary to sustain a certain humidity level varied directly with room temperature, Southern mills tended to be particularly damp, for there was not only the naturally hot climate but heat from fast-moving machines as well. Compounding the problem, and the discomfort, of high tempera-ture and humidity was the tendency of superintendents to add an extra measure of moisture for safety's sake. After all, yarn breakages and shut-downs were costly both to mills and operatives.[2]

Another peculiarity of textile milling was that material had to be con-stantly watched and tended to. Besides breakages, sliver cans, roving spools, spinning bobbins, and shuttles were forever filling up or being emptied. Failure to respond in time meant work stoppages, lost pay, and rebukes. So except for warp loaders and children, no one got to sit and rest. And following the introduction of the stretch-out in the 1920s, the pace of work and level of fatigue mounted higher.

Then there was dust. Every part of the mill was dusty, but it was worst in preparation rooms, for that was where dirt and short-fibered lint (or fly) was beaten or clawed out of raw cotton as it made its way through openers, pickers, and cards. Workers reported that those areas were sometimes so dusty that fellow hands at the end of a long aisle simply disappeared in the haze.

The major dust producers were carding machines, large whirling cyl-inders with millions of tiny steel "teeth," whose function was to tear the raw cotton fibers into parallel alignment. Besides dust from normal runs, every two to three hours drum teeth became so badly clogged with fiber that they had to be cleaned. Until about World War I this procedure involved two op-eratives positioning a stationary brush against a rotating card. Called strip-ping, the process took forty to fifty minutes, and the cloud of dust it created not only engulfed the strippers but was pulled through the whole room by ex-haust fans. About 1912 enclosed, vacuum strippers came into use and reduced substantially the dust eruption during cleaning.[3]

Finally, there was noise, especially in weave rooms. The effect of thou-sands of shuttles striking with blinding speed against the sides of metal looms created a crash of sound that left unaccustomed visitors stupefied, if not in actual pain. Although the technology of noise measurement was not de-veloped until the 1920s — and not utilized to regulate mill environments un-til the late 1960s — recent studies of mill noise suggested that levels of 90 to 110 decibels were common in Southern mills, with some weave rooms top-ping that mark. What that meant was that weavers worked day-in and day-out amid noise levels ranging from that of a pneumatic drill pounding ten feet away (90 decibels) to that of a closely passing, high speed express train (105 decibels).[4]

In addition to milling process and associated atmospheric conditions, one other health-related environmental factor was mill sanitation. Until the 1920s when factory hygiene became the object of some state regulation, conditions were grim. A particular problem in Southern mills were toilets. A 1910 national survey of working conditions of female and child workers reported that water closets were plentiful enough. The trouble was that they were so foul. In one typical mill, the floor of the men's toilet was covered with "quids of tobacco and murky pools of tobacco juice together with pieces of paper. . . . " The floors were "wet and slimy, and the odor decidedly offensive."[5]

The report was nothing new to managers, but they put the blame on workers, who they said were still uncivilized. The 1910 report demurred: although some fault lay with operatives, many conditions were due to owner neglect and disinterest. Little attention was given to privacy: male and female toilets were often only a thin partition apart and sometimes partitions did not even extend to the floor. Some toilets were built within the workroom, making already stale air worse. Almost nowhere were soap and washing facilities provided, and the common drinking cup was in wide use, at least until the 1920s.

One unsanitary feature for which workers were to blame was spitting, common in North and South. If there was any regional difference it was the Southerner's combination of spitting with the use of tobacco and snuff. Whenever one entered a Southern mill, said a visitor, one was "welcomed with a great spray of tobacco juice" from women and men. The average mill worker, lamented a South Carolina sanitarian, thought he had a "right to spit where he pleases, and he usually pleases to spit upon the floor."[6]

A final health risk was the weaver's practice of threading shuttles by sucking yarn through by mouth. Shift workers and substitute weavers got thereby a good opportunity to exchange germs. But the risks surrounding the suck-shuttle were not localized. As one North Carolina weaver recalled, when shuttles were threaded "we'd get a mouthful of lint and have to spit it on the floor." With the advent of newer automatic-loading shuttles about the time of World War I, those kinds of dangers were eliminated.[7]

Evaluating the impact of such conditions on the health of Southern workers in the pre–World War II era necessarily involves considerable speculation because evidence is scanty and indirect. The explanation for such a void is simply that no one there was much interested in health evaluation, neither medical leaders, unions, nor mill corporations. The region's physicians and health boards were preoccupied with infectious disease, and its fledgling unions, with survival. Corporations (and state legislators) mostly looked the other way. Consequently, little hard data on work-related mortality or morbidity were ever generated for Southern mill hands as a distinct population group, compared to that for blacks, infants, and rural and urban Southerners.

Yet the relationship between job and health did not go unexplored.

Doffer boys at work in 1911 in a cotton mill owned by the Cherryville Manufacturing Company of North Carolina. Lewis Hine who made the picture noted of the two youths that there were "plenty of others." Courtesy of the National Archives.

By 1910 a broad-based occupational health movement was slowly emerging within the federal government and in a few Northern industrial states, such as Illinois and Massachusetts. Some of the early studies focused on the health implications of mill work and occasionally even examined Southern mills.[8]

The most common assumption of early investigators was that there was a close connection between mill work and pulmonary TB, particularly among women. As noted previously (chapter 2), a 1912 Bureau of Labor study found among New England girls a close correlation between TB and mill work. The connection appeared even tighter in the South, leading investigators to conclude that "operatives' work is prejudicial to the health of females, that the combination of operative work with matrimony is especially harmful, and that . . . the female operative is . . . in most danger from tuberculosis."[9]

When investigators inquired into the specific mill conditions responsible for such high TB rates, little agreement could be found. One group argued for direct transmission within the mill, and another held that mill conditions merely predisposed a worker to disease. For both groups, however, cotton dust was the offending agent. According to the direct transmission school, germs were carried from individual to individual astride particles of lint, which acted as so many tiny vectors of disease. As for the source of germs, a Massachusetts sanitarian had no doubt that they came from "the habit of spitting." Other hygienists saw dust as merely a secondary infective agent, which weakened lungs and readied them for later attack by TB organisms. One industrial hygienist, writing in 1912 in *Scientific American,* suggested the mechanism: sharp fragments of particles within dust lacerated delicate tissues and started local irritations and wounds, providing "favorite points of attack for the tubercle bacillus."[10]

Epidemiological theory also regarded high humidity as a predisposing cause. In the pre–World War I years some medical scientists were convinced that a damp atmosphere favored the development of consumption, but none offered evidence of the relationship. Others suggested that it was not humidity itself that was the danger but the change from humid to dry environment at the end of work. According to the Bureau of Labor the result of such sudden climatic shifts was a lowered resistance and an increased susceptibility to pulmonary, bronchial, and catarrhal infections.[11]

The direct transmission school was closest to the modern understanding. But instead of identifying dust as the disease-carrying agent, today's epidemiologists point to the dried remains of mycobacteria droplets, called *droplet nuclei,* as the culprits. Sprayed into the air as a fine mist by coughing or sneezing, *droplet nuclei* have the capacity to hang suspended for a long period and are small enough to be inhaled into the terminal air passages, where bacterial multiplication and disease can begin.[12]

Although humid air itself is no longer seen as a predisposing cause of disease, the mill humidifying process was a legitimate health concern. In the first decade of the century, textile mills began to switch from live steam to use of humidifiers, which sprayed a fine, cold-water mist into the work room. Offering the advantage of more precise humidity control, the apparatus was also a bacteria breeder. Southern states had no standards for humidifier water purity, and water was usually recycled with scant attention to filter maintenance. The result was a buildup of bacteria, which were continually sprayed into the work room. A 1912 Massachusetts study found that where spray humidifiers were used the bacteria count was far higher than in rooms without such devices, with peak concentration directly underneath the sprayers. Investigators used harmless bacteria, but the clear implication was that such systems, if contaminated by pathogenic organisms, posed a high risk of dangerous infection.[13]

Another bona fide worry of those early industrial hygienists concerned the unusual combination of high humidity and high temperature, which was characteristic of the mill working environment, especially in more torrid Southern states. Although mill hands seldom confronted the kinds of conditions and muscular demands which brought on heat prostration and heat stroke, they did face temperatures and humidity high enough to produce intense fatigue, which itself had implications for health and well-being.

An early warning about the interconnections between mill work and fatigue (and about health risks from the latter) was sounded in 1908. If Bureau of Labor claims were exaggerated and cloudy, they did identify a problem that would attract sizeable and continuing interest. According to the report, the physiological effect of continuous heat exposure was a drawing of blood to the body's surface to facilitate heat dissipation. As blood was diverted from internal organs, the "tone and nutrition of stomach, lungs, heart, and other organs are lowered." Accompanying clinical damage supposedly included a loss of appetite, languor, and increased susceptibility to disease. High humidity intensified all these ill effects.[14]

Interest in fatigue was international. A 1911 British study reported that over time the natural "tendency is for . . . muscular work to be diminished. Yet in a weaving shed the machine sets the pace, and the worker must neglect the dictates of his sensations. . . . " By day's end, "many of the weavers complain that they have no energy left, have no great desire for food, and need only drink and rest."[15] Back in America two 1916 investigations confirmed the British findings and went on to claim that the ill effects of fatigue were cumulative. Over a period of days, efficiency dropped, accidents rose, and there was a build-up of psychological problems, as well as a lowered resistance to infectious bacteria.[16]

Later researchers would find that such early reports vastly overstated the destructive effects of fatigue. While disease susceptibility may rise with severe fatigue, the claim of cumulative deterioration has no basis in clinical measurement. In fact, modern investigators' primary finding is that humans have a remarkable ability to adapt to hot environments, so long as working conditions are not so torrid as to bring on heat cramps and stroke. Yet that is not the whole of it. Where there is a combination of humidity *and* high temperature, the body does have serious difficulty throwing off its own heat output, with the result that the cardiac system is put under considerable stress, often accompanied by elevated temperature. And if over the long term fatigue is not a serious health risk, on a day-to-day basis it is enormously costly in terms of vitality and simple well-being. As a late 1930s U.S. Bureau of Mines study put it, high heat and humidity took a "tremendous toll" on factory workers, especially in the South in summertime.[17]

While Northern industrial hygienists were raising alarms about dust and germs, heat-humidity, and fatigue, one other objectionable feature of mill work went unnoticed—by everyone but workers. That was the intense noise in weave rooms. While hearing impairment was its most obvious and certain result, later investigators would discover a number of more insidious effects, such as fatigue, increased blood pressure, and decreased working and mental efficiencies.[18]

Obviously, scattered reports and claims of Northern industrial hygienists, though suggestive, are of limited value in estimating the impact of mill work on the health of Southern textile hands in the pre–World War II period. By the time occupational health had earned high visibility and favor (in the 1960s), most of the problems which had plagued an earlier generation of operatives no longer existed, owing largely to changes in the production process.

Fortunately, the historian does not have to rely solely on the claims of pioneer hygienists, who were strong on concern but short on evidence. A useful supplementary source is the testimony of Southern mill hands, themselves, who told interviewers working for the Federal Writers Project (a division of the New Deal's WPA) about the toll that work had taken of their physical and emotional well-being. Considered together, these provide the kind of direct evidence of industrial ill health in the South that contemporary studies lacked.

A common, perennial complaint concerned the deafening uproar in spinning and weave rooms, which new workers, particularly, found almost unbearable. Modern research has set the threshold of painful sound at 130 decibels, with 120 decibels being the point at which noise can actually be felt. Weaving areas were never that punishing, but noise levels did sometimes climb substantially above 100 decibels. To be put into such an environment was, as one hand expressed it, awfully "scareful."[19] An Asheville hand recalling her first day at work said that "when I got there and went in it seemed like the racket would pick me up and carry me right bang against some of the machinery."[20] While many workers adjusted to the loom's roar rather quickly, some found accommodation hard. One man, after spending some months in a Seneca, South Carolina, mill complained to his wife: "I don't know as I'll be able to stand the racket much longer. Work I'm used to and don't mind, but such a racket is liable to put a body crazy."[21]

Like most, the man made an adjustment; but getting used to noise brought its own problems. One seasoned weave operator noted that when you begin work each morning "your head just roars."[22] And it was the same at day's end, when it would usually be a half-hour before a worker could hear anything. For many hands, perhaps half, the cost of accommodation was a loss of hearing. It was common to find retired workers who were only able to converse by reading lips.[23]

As workers aged, years of adjustment took another kind of toll, one measured in increased nervous stress. A female weaver in North Carolina's Brandon Mill, who started work about 1900 at the age of seven, was not bothered one whit by the din of the loom when she was a child: "Lots of folks said the noise nearly drove 'em crazy, but I wove it into a song of my own, and you know I loved the noise 'til three year ago when I had my operation, and my nerves went to pieces on me. Now the wheels don't sing no time; they worry me and make me wish sometimes I didn't have to work."[24]

Just as mill work rooms were intolerably noisy, they were also at times oppressively hot and humid. It was true that most workers had little complaint on that score, perhaps because heat and dampness did not strike the senses or the memory with the impact of crashing looms. Also in the South work was always hot and therefore meant to be hot — and to some, the heat appeared even beneficial. Retired South Carolina mill worker Coley Lynch took the view that heavy sweating was healthful, for it eliminated poison from the system.[25]

Yet there were a few recollections drawing a quite different picture. A Mr. Edmonds, a weaver in Caesar Cone's Proximity Mill in Greensboro recalled (and perhaps exaggerated) the lack of atmospheric controls and the tendency of superintendents to set conditions solely according to presumed production needs. Consequently rooms at times were unbearably hot. About 1925, said Edmonds, "they'd got hold of a idea somewhere that the looms run faster and made better cloth if the weaveroom was kept at an awful high temperature."[26] It was allowed to climb over 100°, and the effect was shattering. Women went "all day in that unbearable heat with their clothes stuck to their bodies like they had been dipped in a pool of water. Going up and down their alley weeping, working all day long. . . . "[27]

One January day when inside temperatures reached 104°, Edmonds threw open weave room windows and threatened to go to the state capital if the superintendent did not reduce the quantity of steam. Although he nearly lost his job, Edmonds ultimately got management to agree to drop the temperature to 90°. Unfortunately there was not an Edmonds in every plant, and there generally was a floor superintendent who believed that the way to insure a successful production run was to elevate temperature and humidity levels.[28]

More than noise, heat, humidity, and even dust, what mill operatives most remembered and resented about their jobs was numbing fatigue, not just at the end of the day but all through it. The product of long hours, heat, humidity, and noise, fatigue was intensified by the demands of the milling process and the personnel policies of management.

There was, for example, the matter of sitting. Despite claims of recruitment literature, which pointed up the number of seats for female operatives (required by law in most places by about 1910) and the ample opportunity to use them, textile work was not sitting work.[29] Except for warpers in the weave room, all jobs required standing, for tasks were widely dispersed. In addition, operatives had to give constant attention to possible breaks in material. During the Progressive Era much was made of females' need to sit at work, but in the cotton textile industry, production did not allow it. The upshot was that many workers wore out. That did not mean that they quit work: they could not afford to do that. They simply endured pain and discomfort. Mary Abbott had gone into the Virginia mills as a child. By the late 1930s, when she was in her forties, she was used up. "When I was young, I'd never mind standin' up, . . . but now I'm getting old, my laigs an' back aches so bad at times an' my eyes get to waterin' so bad I can't hardly see."[30]

Management might have checked the build-up of physical and emotional strain had they allowed rest periods. But before the thirties, at least, textile owners, managers, and foremen regarded such an innovation as a coddling of workers. At the end of the 1920s there was a brief discussion of the issue in the textile literature. The consensus was summed up by one mill foreman who argued that to allow regular rest breaks "would cause disorganization, bad work, and loss of production." Of course an overseer must try to make allowances for girls and women, but men did not need rest periods.[31]

Often there was not even time for eating — for women or men. In the First War nutritionists began arguing the need for industrial lunch rooms offering balanced meals and time to digest them, but textile employers chose to follow the policy of catch-as-catch-can. If operatives could get a few minutes ahead of their machines, they could break out lunch pails and bolt a quick meal. Most managed that, and Burlington, North Carolina, weaver Almeda Brady told how it went, even as late as the 1930s: "We don't have no time off so I work to get my looms to runnin' good and then I set right down flat on the floor and eat. That restes me a little. It's a rare thing for me to set down any more durin' the day."[32]

In the middle 1920s the stretch-out came to the American textile mill. While its effects were also felt in the North, Southern workers experienced it in its rawest form, for owners there were less inhibited by union or governmental checks. Although Southern operatives resisted the new routines, to the extent of initiating union contacts in the late 1920s and striking a number of mills, owners imposed their will relentlessly. By the 1930s textile work, which had long been exhausting, was now so demanding that many hands were physically and emotionally undone.

As the name implied, the stretch-out was a system of extending an operative's labor and supervision over a greater number of machines. Weavers who might before have run eight looms, by the late 1920s had responsibility for thirty. Spinners went from 800 spindles to 1600. A product of textiles' belated discovery of "Taylorism" (the industrial efficiency movement), the stretch-out was an attractive proposition to owners. They were able to boost production with fewer hands, and, while remaining operatives enjoyed a share of the savings, owners kept more. Charlotte spinner Mrs. M.C. Campbell had earned $9 a week for tending 800 spindles. After the stretch-out doubled her load, her new wage was 40 percent higher. Employers argued that the system was a boon to operatives, who got higher pay for expending about the same amount of energy. If they ran more machines, said management, they no longer had to do subsidiary tasks as before. Those were performed by lower-paid help, freeing the principal worker to specialize.[33]

Whatever the wage increase, to workers it bore little relation to new work demands. The system came to Cone's Proximity Mill in 1925. Weaver Edmonds recalled that after one-third of weave-room hands were let go, remaining workers were pushed almost beyond endurance. "Day after day weeping women had come to me and said . . . , 'Surely there's something somebody can do for us. We cannot stand the load they've put on us.' It wasn't a pleasant sight," he added, "to see my own daughter come home worn to a frazzle." Two men had nervous collapses and had to be hospitalized, Edmonds claimed. There was little but "awful misery ahead for working people."[34]

The increasing number of strikes was a measure of the strain. Twice between 1927 and 1930 normally passive mill hands at Proximity walked off their jobs in protest. In the first instance workers came back when management promised adjustments. But these were not what the hands had expected. An efficiency expert, Edmonds recalled, came up with a new wrinkle: he let the fastest worker set the loom-tending requirement and then made others try to keep pace. A 1930 strike was the result, led this time by the United Textile Workers of America. But the company broke the strike and fired all known unionists, including Edmonds.[35]

Work stresses at Cone were typical. A spinner in a Durham mill said that she "had never dreamed that eight hours of work could be so hard." Once, she had been able to get ahead and enjoy several ten to fifteen minute breaks. But the introduction of new machinery in the late 1920s had doubled her spindles, leaving her forever fifteen to twenty minutes behind.[36] In Charlotte, J.H. Reynolds was a card tender, and when his company suddenly doubled his responsibility his life changed radically. "I didn't know nothing about work 'til this thing come about. . . . I am so tired when I get home I don't feel like doing nothing but laying down and resting."[37]

Looking back on those years Wake Forest (North Carolina) textile worker Mary Branch summed up in a few poignant lines of verse her feelings about life and work in the mills. What she wrote voiced the despair of thousands. The life of a textile hand, she said,

> is trouble and worry and fears,
> We can never get through what we are expected to do
> if we work at it ninety-nine years.[38]

Hyperbole no doubt. But the facts remain that well before the Depression 1930s, workers saw mill labor as a torturous experience, and a growing number of outsiders were suggesting that it entailed serious medical consequences as well. Owners had repeatedly pictured themselves as being close to workers, sensitive to their needs, and attentive to their welfare. Their relation to their hands, they insisted, was that of a father to his children. But to most mill hands this "father" proved unresponsive and negligent — sometimes even a tyrant. Not only did owners keep their hands in a state of dependency, they also failed to meet workers' needs in the areas of wages, housing, sanitation, recreation, and health.

Mill workers were subjected to the same sort of ethic of iron-willed paternalism with which Southern blacks were long familiar; and, as in the case of blacks, mill hands, too, found that promises of paternalism were not kept. Instead, both groups were held in contempt and at the best ignored. One result, for each, was a harvest of ill health which remained a dominant fact in the lives of most blacks and mill hands until about the time of the Second World War.

Yet, discouraging as it was, the situation was not hopeless. Long before the war the health problems of one of the two populations, Southern blacks, had become a matter of serious concern to a number of groups in American society, who had begun to seek ways to alter the dominant pattern of illness. In the early twentieth century, especially, the group most closely involved with black welfare—because of their origins and training —were black physicians, who, if they did not do all they might have, did keep fellow blacks from slipping backwards in that bitterly racist period. Mostly they were Southern doctors, but they also included a number of Northern black physicians. Although free of the South, themselves, they still felt responsible for their brothers and sisters left behind. To be a part of such health reform efforts, however, required uncommon zeal, for whether their base was North or South, black doctors first had to fight for their own survival.

PART II

Problems Addressed

Blacks in the Era of Segregation

CHAPTER 4

Black Physicians and the Health
of Their People, 1900–1940

Until well after World War II black physicians in the South and, to a lesser extent, in the North as well were virtual prisoners of American racism and the segregationist structures it spawned. Denied the training and income of white doctors and unable to keep abreast of new developments once in practice, many Southern black physicians could not deliver to their patients the quality of medical care that they needed. Though many doctors tried, neither could they do much to raise (or cause to be raised) the overall level of health of the Southern black populace. The "Southern way of life" not only stunted the growth of an entire professional group but, in shackling black doctors, added yet another chain to hold down the people they served.

One problem facing the young black who aspired to a career in medicine in the early twentieth century was the availability and quality of professional education. For all practical purposes the only places open to blacks were Negro medical colleges. Between 1869 and 1900 eleven such schools had been established, with nine surviving into the twentieth century. All of them, however, faced an uncertain future due to rising medical standards and the need for ever-larger endowments. By the early 1920s seven of the nine had ceased to exist, five of them victims of Abraham Flexner's shattering medical school survey of 1910, which concluded that only Howard University Medical School and Meharry Medical College showed sufficient viability to merit foundation support and to continue in operation.[1]

Most white schools in the North and West, it was true, admitted black students. But they did so on a quota basis, and the quotas were small. The University of Michigan's class of 1932, with its four black medical graduates, 77 had an uncommonly large number. Before 1940 the fifty-five or so white schools that took black applicants produced altogether no more than twenty black physicians each year. By contrast Howard and Meharry annually graduated somewhere between 100 and 125.[2]

So Howard and Meharry offered the only real opportunities for the aspiring black student. But until the 1930s, when substantial foundation support (begun in the mid-1920s) finally produced a general upgrading, the quality of the average Howard and Meharry graduate left something to be desired. Between 1902 and 1946 an average of 54 percent of Meharry's graduates and 26 percent of Howard's failed their medical boards. That fraction compared poorly with the average 6 to 7 percent from Harvard and Washington universities — or the 13 percent from Southern white colleges — who had to re-sit their exams.[3]

One reason for the poor performance of black graduates was inadequate undergraduate preparation, which not even four years of medical school could correct. As one Negro medical educator said, "the Jim Crow preliminary educational system is a shameful example of national neglect and inadequacy."[4] But there was also no escaping the fact that after the Flexner Report and up to the 1930s Howard and Meharry did not stand on a par with the average white institution. Neither had been able to attract sufficient private or public support (which was generated by Flexner's report) to enable them to overcome earlier deficiencies. As a result, both had to make do with facilities and faculties that fell ever further behind.

Unquestionably, the two black institutions had turned out a number of very able graduates, and to them the low standing of their colleges was painful. In 1928 Peter Marshall Murray, a Howard man then building an enviable New York City practice, complained bitterly about the dismal showing of Howard graduates on a recent national examination. All six had failed, and Murray felt "utter astonishment because these men . . . were according to our standards brilliant men. . . . "[5] Obviously, Murray concluded, something was "radically wrong" with the way the Howard faculty taught their subjects. Unless every department was modernized, "one morning we shall awaken and find our rating gone and our one-time leadership taken by Meharry." Meantime, he lamented, "we are daily made to feel that our diploma . . . represent[s] less and less in terms of solid scientific medical training."[6] Fortunately, neither Howard nor Meharry lost their accreditation, thanks to timely assistance from the General Education Board and the Rosenwald Fund. Beginning in the mid-1920s those two foundations generously supported a number of programs, including faculty improvement at Meharry and new facilities and equipment at both schools.[7]

But a more obdurate problem remained: the inability of many black graduates to find acceptable internships. In the 1920s the number of accredited positions available at Negro hospitals averaged about 70 per year, which was only 60 percent of the number needed; and nearly all those places were in institutions outside the South. By the 1930s the total had increased to about 90, but that still left blacks 30 to 40 short. Negro doctors could apply to Northern white hospitals, but they were more rigidly segregated than white medical schools and preferred to let hundreds of internships go unclaimed rather than accept black applicants. Roscoe Giles, a black who would later demonstrate his ability by winning a fellowship at the University of Vienna, could find no openings in leading Northern hospitals when he applied in 1930. "I suppose I can truthfully say," he wrote Peter Murray, "that I have had the doors of more hospitals closed in my face than probably any other Negro and *mirabile dictu* at least five of them in New York City."[8] Black physicians who failed to get an accredited post had no recourse but to give up the internship year or accept positions in small, backward facilities. Either way their professional development suffered.

If internships were hard to find, residencies, which would open the way to medical specialization, were virtually nonexistent. In fact, aspiring black specialists were often discouraged from pursuing that course. Future editor and activist Montague Cobb enrolled in the graduate program at Western Reserve and was promptly told by one of his professors that there was no need for Negro specialists.[9]

It was in medical practice, though, that the black physician felt the warping and dulling effect of segregation most. While Northern doctors were by no means beyond its reach, Southern physicians and patients were its major victims. In some places the white medical establishment contested (or abridged) the Negro's very right to practice. In South Carolina's heavily black Marlboro County the first black doctor, a Meharry graduate who set up a practice in the county seat in 1908, was able to work only under supervision of a white physician. In Mississippi not until 1921 were black doctors automatically licensed upon passage of the state boards.[10]

The Southern black physician's greatest handicap was his inability to practice in white hospitals. Every institution, public and private, followed the custom of restricting facilities to physicians who were members of local AMA affiliates. Since no county organization in the South admitted black members — and would not do so until after 1950 (see chapter 11) — doors of established hospitals were firmly closed to black practitioners. Even after white hospitals begin admitting black patients into segregated wards in about 1930, Negro physicians were still turned away. Clearly, the much prized doctor-patient relationship was less important than maintaining professional segregation.

Exclusion from county medical societies had other drawbacks as well,

for both black doctors and patients. Since local and state health departments were nearly always under control or influence of white medical associations, black doctors had no regular relationship with official health agencies. Accordingly, Negro physicians were excluded from post-graduate courses
and fellowships which health departments offered to spur continuing education. In the 1920s when free refresher courses became a common practice,
only about 1 percent of Southern county health departments opened them
to blacks.[11] Medical societies also promoted such training, at their conven-
tions and seminars, but black professionals were excluded from these, too,
largely out of fear that attendance at scientific sessions might encourage
blacks to push themselves into social gatherings as well.[12] This sort of public and private discrimination subjected black doctors to a kind of double
jeopardy, for it gave their own patients added (if unfair) cause to question
their abilities. As earlier blacks had done, some of these patients came to
associate good medicine with white doctors and to shift their patronage
accordingly.[13]

Because of racism and professional exclusion many able black physicians fled the South. The career of Louis T. Wright illustrates the outflow
of talent. In 1917, after finishing training at Howard, Wright returned home
to Atlanta because he felt he was needed. He did not stay long. His first
professional encounter with Georgia officialdom convinced him that his future lay elsewhere. Sitting in the Fulton County courthouse one day waiting for a clerk to register his license, he heard a voice calling: "Louis! Louis!"
Realizing it was he who was wanted Wright upbraided the clerk, telling
him that his name was *Doctor* Louis T. Wright. The clerk wandered off but
soon returned, calling "Wright! Wright!" The doctor refused to reply,
whereupon the clerk kicked his foot, challenging: "you aren't going to sell
any dope, are you, or do any abortions?" Shocked, Wright exploded: "Let
me tell you something. I'll choke you right here if you open your god damn
mouth again." Once he cooled off he realized that if he stayed in Atlanta
he would end up in prison, or worse. So at first opportunity he left the
South for good and ultimately became a successful and influential physician in New York City.[14]

Not many black doctors had so dramatic a reminder of how regional
prejudice worked, but many shared Wright's view of medical prospects in
the South and, like him, got out. In 1930 the editor of a South Carolina
black newspaper noted with questionable pride the number of homegrown
blacks who were succeeding north of Dixie. One had recently won appointment to the staff of Harlem Hospital. Another, a bacteriologist, had joined
the faculty of MIT. And a third was building a successful surgical career
in Cleveland.[15]

That outflow of talent was also mirrored in the *Journal of the National*

Medical Association (NMA)—the black counterpart of the AMA, but without its racial exclusiveness. From 1946 to 1962, the *Journal* highlighted careers of ninety-six black physicians who had entered practice between 1900 and 1935. Of them, fifty-six could be labeled Northerners, and among them were twenty-four doctors who had migrated from the South, either after medical school or following a brief Southern practice.[16]

Even choice black academic posts in the South had drawbacks. Early in his career Montague Cobb entertained the possibility of leaving Howard to become head of anatomy at Meharry. What decided him against the offer was Meharry's relationship to its more prestigious neighbor, Vanderbilt Medical School. Maintenance of links to Vanderbilt would be crucial to Cobb's success, yet the links were so tarnished by subservience on one hand and disdain on the other that Cobb knew he would not be able to abide the job. In procuring cadavers for anatomical teaching, for example, Vanderbilt got the pick of the lot, and Meharry got what was left. While Cobb could borrow books from Vanderbilt's library, he would not be welcome there himself.[17]

Despite the tendency of younger black doctors to escape or avoid the South, a considerable number chose to remain. In the years between the wars, the two Carolinas and Georgia counted some 425–40 Negro physicians, with near 70 in South Carolina, and the remainder about equally divided between the other two states. Motivations for staying varied, but a good many probably did so simply because they felt more at home there, although some perhaps stayed because they doubted their ability to compete in the North. Still others were like Peter Kelly of Conway, South Carolina, who went to school in Chicago in the 1930s intending to become a foreign medical missionary. But on graduating he changed his mind and decided "to let down my bucket right close to home" because of missionary work needed in the South.[18]

There was no doubt about the magnitude of the tasks facing the black doctor in the South as he sought to build a professional spirit and extend medical care to a largely neglected populace. Nor was there any question but that a number of black physicians made superhuman efforts to address those tasks.

One primary need was professional organization. Having failed in the late nineteenth century to open the AMA and its local affiliates to Negro membership, black doctors saw no recourse but to form organizations of their own if they were to enjoy the obvious benefits of association. One of the first groups to concede the reality of segregation and to make the best of a bad bargain was a handful of black physicians and dentists in North Carolina who in 1888 established the Old North State Medical Society. In the next decade black physicians and dentists in Georgia and South Carolina would take similar steps. By 1912 such groups had come into being in nine of the thirteen Southern states. By this time black professionals also had in the National Medical Association (founded in 1895) an organization that could give and get national attention for black health and professional needs. Its *Journal,* begun in 1909, provided leaders a means of building unity, as well as a channel to reach those members who failed to attend annual meetings.[19]

In addition to forming professional associations, a number of black doctors sought to create post-graduate programs to help fellow physicians sharpen skills and learn new techniques. The earliest teaching clinic in the South operating on a continuous basis was the one begun at Meharry in 1901 by renowned Chicago surgeon Daniel Hale Williams. His sessions began a tradition of post-graduate education at the Nashville campus that attracted a regional contingent of black physicians. A clinic of equal standing, the first initiated by a Southern black, was the John A. Andrew Clinic at Tuskegee. Founded in 1912 by school physician John Kenney, who became its sustaining force, the Tuskegee Clinics soon became an annual event in the lives of the more progressive black doctors in the South.[20]

Professional-minded black physicians worked at the local level as well on a wide assortment of projects. In Atlanta there was Meharry graduate Henry Butler. Though beginning his career in the intensely racist 1890s, when able, ambitious blacks faced particular risks, Butler succeeded in establishing the city's first black pharmacy, infirmary, and nurses' training school, and in combination with other physicians helped set up not only the NMA but the Georgia state association as well.[21]

Post-graduate clinics were the first contribution of Harvard-trained Clyde Donnell of Durham, who in 1916 created a black academy of medicine in that city. The same year he began a long association with the North Carolina Mutual Life Insurance Company. Taking over as medical director in 1920, Donnell added a full-fledged clinic for Mutual's local policyholders, as well as a venturesome health education program for the company's six hundred examining doctors and its thousands of national customers.

An equally productive career was that of Pierce Moton of Birmingham, another Meharry graduate. By 1920, thanks largely to Moton's perseverance, black Birmingham had its first general hospital. An equally grave need was an emergency maternity clinic. In the early 1930s, after witnessing a black mother give birth on a city sidewalk (because the county hospital would not admit her), Moton went to work, and by 1937 the Southside Clinics were offering a wide range of services to mothers and infants and enjoying financial backing from a Northern foundation.[22]

To illustrate the achievement of black physician-reformers in more detail, the careers of two South Carolina doctors, Matilda A. Evans and L.W.

Long, are particularly apt. They reveal not just the degree of dedication required of many Southern blacks but also the problems with which they had to contend, whether from a segregated society or an indifferent Negro profession.

Evans originally had intended to become a medical missionary, but on getting her degree in 1898 from the Woman's College of Philadelphia, she decided that her hometown of Columbia needed her more. Only the second female physician to practice in the state, she soon saw that the most pressing medical need was for black hospitals, and over the next eighteen years she established and operated three such facilities. Although she enjoyed moral and some tangible support from area whites and sank much of her own income into the ventures, none survived more than a few years. Not only was money a problem, but black male physicians, apparently unwilling to accept a female colleague, resisted and even obstructed her work. One of them went so far as to bring a charge of malpractice against her. But Evans endured, as did her hospitals, in one location or another until 1916, and in the process she provided care to black patients from as far away as North Carolina and Georgia. For many, including blacks of Columbia, Evans's hospitals were the only ones available.[23]

In 1916 she embarked on a venture in the field of preventive medicine. Although her Negro Health Association, which aimed to put a black nurse in every South Carolina county, was an utter failure, Evans revealed a clear grasp of the primary health needs of her people. Taking services and education directly into black homes, she felt, was the only route to black health progress. That such a program had to be initiated privately and received no encouragement from the state's white health establishment was a telling comment on the outlook and performance of the South Carolina Board of Health at that time.

Not that Evans did not try to involve the white community in her venture. In fact, in appealing for broad community support she showed a keen understanding of white attitudes and how to play them. In the *Negro Health Journal,* the short-lived organ of her association, she emphasized repeatedly that the sick Negro not only endangered his or her white employer but the broader community as well. Every year, she told readers, illness and death among blacks robbed South Carolina of some $20 million that would otherwise have circulated through the white community. Supporting the Association would help reduce those losses, of course, but whites should also pay black workers higher wages, so that they could afford the food and medical care their health required. The cost would be fully returned to whites, Evans assured, for "no class of working people spends money as do Negroes when they have it."[24]

In 1930, after a period of private practice, Evans again turned her ener-

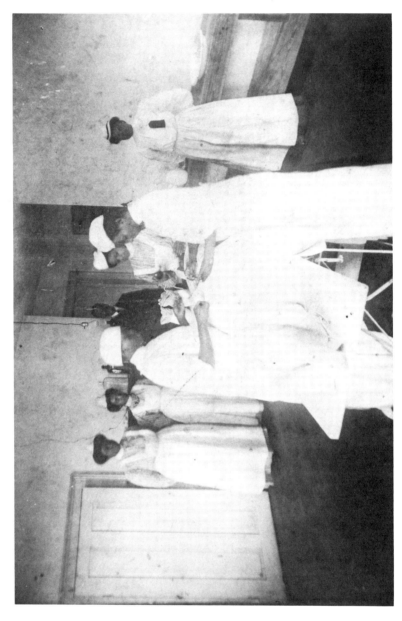

South Carolina's first black physician, Matilda A. Evans, in surgery (front, right) in her Taylor Lane Hospital in Columbia, c. 1900. Courtesy of the South Caroliniana Library.

gies to community welfare. Although the hospital situation in Columbia had improved by then, the absence of clinical facilities for black children and expectant mothers remained a problem, and when the Depression hit, Evans moved to address it. With assurances of support from black businessmen, she opened a free child and maternal clinic in the basement of a black church. Although it was begun on a trial basis, the levels of demand and medical need were so great that it became a permanent operation. By 1932 the Negro press was promoting it, and even the Richland County legislative delegation and the state board of health found places for it in their budgets. But clearly, Evans was its mainstay. In 1935 she died, and the clinic ended with her. Fortunately, the work she began soon resumed as part of the public maternal and child health program brought into existence that same year by passage of the Social Security Act.[25]

About the same time that Evans was launching her last project, an equally productive career was unfolding in the little rural town of Union, South Carolina, where in 1931 L.W. Long, fresh from studies at Meharry, set up a home-town practice. In some ways Long faced an even more barren vista than Evans had in 1900. Not only was there no hospital for blacks and no organized public health service for either race, there was only one black physician to minister to the county's 12,500 Negroes. Moreover, Union Negroes lacked the economic resources available in larger cities like Columbia, with its established black middle class.[26]

In several respects, though, Long's contributions paralleled Evans's. He established the first Negro hospital in the area and on his own undertook to provide such preventive health services as school inspections and mass immunizations, which no public agency was then offering. Ironically, that work ultimately served white children, too. Seeing that Negro pupils were receiving something that theirs were not, Union whites began to demand a health center so that they could receive similar services and reestablish their "rightful" ascendancy.[27]

In addition to those programs, Long turned his energies to problems of the black medical profession, which he found in a "state of coma" when he arrived. The Palmetto Medical, Dental, and Pharmaceutical Association, created thirty-five years before, still met annually but mainly for the purpose of "handshaking and cordialities."[28]

Long's determination to inject new purpose into professional affairs led him to initiate an annual clinic in 1932. One-day affairs that featured locally and nationally known physicians of both races, the Union Clinics offered South Carolina's black doctors a rare opportunity to keep abreast of new developments. The first attracted an audience of sixteen and featured Chicago's Charles Drew, who was already at work on his process for preserving blood. Like his hospital, Long's clinic—the only one in the state—continued without a break to the 1970s.[29]

What made L.W. Long unique among his South Carolina colleagues, however, was his stance on medical segregation. Initially he, like nearly all Southern black doctors, had gone along with professional separatism, believing that the system, undesirable as it was, was simply one of life's realities and that kicking against it would do no good and might endanger him considerably.

In 1940, however, Long rejected that posture. Confessing to colleagues that he now thought of himself as a "revolutionist," he began to argue that there were "many things that should be done immediately if we are to quicken and improve our Association."[30] In fact, by the time he assumed the presidency of the Palmetto Association in 1940, Long was convinced that the Negro profession in the South was on "the brink of destruction" and that its only hope for survival lay in its integration with the white medical establishment.[31]

A first order of business was to break down the barriers which excluded the black doctor from practice in white hospitals. As soon as he became Association president, Long began meeting with key administrators asking them to abandon the policy of forcing the black doctor to "leave his patient at the door of tax-supported hospitals." Without "workshops for our men," Long warned his colleagues, all their preparation would be nullified. Moreover, South Carolina would never succeed in attracting the black doctors it needed as long as hospital access was denied.[32] Other sorts of integration Long had in mind included employment of black physicians by the board of health and enlargement of opportunities for black medical students. Knowing that desegregation of the state's medical college was still years away, Long was prepared to settle for a system of public scholarships that would help blacks get training outside the region.[33]

In calling for a frontal attack on medical segregation, Long was moving faster and further than his colleagues cared to go. The Association's executive committee saw as premature his proposal for an immediate lobbying effort for out-of-state scholarships. Such an important matter needed more study and extended discussion by the full Association. To Long's request for a special meeting on that issue, the committee objected that such meetings were warranted "only if an emergency developed that concerned our regular profession."[34] But if the ideas Long put forward did not win colleagues' backing, they at least assaulted the prevailing complacency and helped prepare black doctors to accept such ideas when they resurfaced a decade later as part of a broad civil rights movement.

Although local physicians like Evans and Long—as well as Butler, Donnell, and Moton—labored in virtual isolation and against enormous social odds in the pre–World War II era, they did not work alone. Since the early part of the century, in fact, a commitment to improving Southern conditions had brought Northern black physicians into the region. Their stays, though brief, were beneficial. One of the earliest of those secular missionaries was George C. Hall, prominent surgeon at Chicago's Provident Hospital. In 1902 Hall began regular journeys to Alabama and Tennessee to offer surgical training to black doctors and assist them with difficult operations. He was not always welcome to white doctors. One warned Hall's sponsor: "when you need surgical assistance you had better use local talent and not send North for Northern 'niggers.'"[35] But Hall was not scared off, and thanks to his encouragement black doctors in Birmingham and Decatur, Alabama, as well as those in Memphis and Clarkeville, Tennessee, established infirmaries for the treatment of indigent blacks.[36]

It was in the late 1920s that those North-South contacts became to some degree institutionalized and assumed real significance. That was partly because Southern professional groups had matured enough by then to allow regularity of contact and because Northern visitors had attained sufficient stature to effect some change. Among the most frequent and influential of later Northern visitors were Midian Othello Bousfield of the Rosenwald Fund, Peter Marshall Murray of Harlem Hospital, and Hildrus Poindexter and Paul Cornely of the Department of Preventive Medicine at Howard.[37]

The impulse prompting these professionals to undertake their Southern missionary work was hard to pin down precisely, but it seemed to be tied to their associations with Howard. Cornely and Poindexter were part of its medical faculty; Murray had taken his degree there after World War I and in the 1920s served as surgical professor; and Bousfield, though earning his degree elsewhere, had spent his intern year in 1914 at Howard's Freedmen's Hospital. As part of the university community and, later, as an alumnus, each had heard repeatedly of his obligations as a Howard man: Not only should he develop his talents to the fullest, he should also strive to serve his brothers left behind in "captivity" in the South. Mordecai Johnson, the former Alabama Baptist minister who started his long (and to some, tyrannical) period as Howard president in 1926, continually stressed this latter duty. Every commencement found Johnson appealing to graduates to go South and improve the lives of black people.[38] While that preachment was more often honored in the breach than the observance, few Howard graduates could escape the nagging sense of a duty unfulfilled.

That is not to say that Northern doctors were impelled chiefly by guilt. Certainly their awareness of Southern problems, coupled with their high self-expectations as national leaders also turned their attentions south. In fact, three of the group — Murray, Bousfield, and Cornely — might properly be thought of as black Flexners. Not only did they try to raise the Southern black profession to a higher level; they also sought (as did Flexner) to utilize their foundation contacts to facilitate those changes.[39]

Two goals which Bousfield and Murray set for themselves (in the course of frequent discussion) were higher standards of professionalism among Southern black physicians and an upgrading of the region's black hospitals, not only for patients' sake but also for the many black medical graduates without suitable internships. Neither man had a high opinion of the general run of Southern black doctors. Murray was convinced that, like many of their Northern brethren, they were too concerned about income and not enough about giving adequate service. Bousfield was appalled by the lack of interest in professional improvement, and both despaired over the amount of wrangling that went on in most black hospitals in the South.[40] Murray believed that blacks had enjoyed so few individual rights that "it is still difficult for us to give teamwork and cooperation of the kind needed."[41]

Murray's first opportunity to address these problems came in 1931, when the NMA convened in Atlanta for its annual meeting. As president-elect, Murray not only had a chance to meet face to face with a fair proportion of his Southern colleagues but also the necessary authority to command attention to what he had to say. In special meetings with Atlanta's doctors Murray stressed the need for continuing education, the desegregation of health department staffs, and improved hospital administration and patient care.[42]

Nine months after these sessions, Murray was again in the South, in the Carolinas, meeting with black doctors in Greensboro, Durham, Winston-Salem, Columbia, and Orangeburg. His main object was to persuade them to abandon the all-too-common practice of administering their own hospitals. There was something fundamentally wrong, he told one group, when a hospital was "run out of the pocket of the doctor."[43] Some apparently paid heed, for afterward Murray wrote Bousfield: "I believe I have convinced the group in Greensboro and Columbia that the plan for lay superintendency will be their salvation."[44]

Bousfield was an equally vigorous spokesman for reform. As medical director and vice president of a major Chicago-based insurance company (until 1933) and afterwards as Director of Negro Health for the Julius Rosenwald Fund, he too could command attention. The same year Murray visited the Carolinas, Bousfield was in Jacksonville, inspecting the new all-black Brewster Hospital and seeking to encourage local doctors. "I tried to talk to them," he told Murray, about "better medicine, better preparation, the National Hospital Association, National Medical Association, Promotion of Specialization, etc.—tried to do for Jacksonville what you had done for Atlanta."[45]

But their reform strategy involved more than just prodding Southern physicians. Both also worked from their Northern bases to shape the policies of national and regional organizations that had the capability to bring about change in the South. As leaders of black medicine—Bousfield became president of the NMA the year after Murray—each enjoyed considerable influence with the Duke Endowment and the Rosenwald Fund, both of which had begun programs of black health and medical care in the 1920s.

The Duke Endowment (see chapter 5), which was launched in 1926 by North Carolina tobacco and power magnate James Buchanan Duke, set as one of its principal aims the long-term improvement of white and black hospitals in the two Carolinas. Focusing primarily on areas with inadequate (or no) service and large indigent populations, the Endowment furnished both capital and operating grants, as well as assistance in areas of administration and finance.[46]

The Chicago-based Rosenwald Fund (chapter 5), the creation of Sears-Roebuck head Julius Rosenwald, turned its attention to problems of black health in 1928. Like the Duke Endowment, the Rosenwald Fund was also interested in black hospitals, but it added a range of other concerns, such as nurse training, physician fellowships, rural health services, and reduction of black mortality from VD and TB.[47] Although Bousfield and Murray never had the influence over foundation policy that they desired, they were always able to get a hearing from Duke and Rosenwald, and of course when Bousfield joined the Rosenwald staff in 1934 his impact on that group increased significantly.

Even before 1934, as a member of Chicago's black leadership, Bousfield enjoyed a special relationship with the Rosenwald Fund, chiefly through his ties with Michael M. Davis, head of the Fund's Medical Services Division. Davis had come to the Fund in 1928 from the directorship of the prestigious Boston Dispensary, where he had devised novel approaches to the rising problem of medical costs and established himself as a national leader in the new field of medical economics. Absorbed in his first years at Rosenwald with economic issues like group hospital insurance, by the early 1930s Davis was beginning to shift attention to problems of rural black health.[48] The Fund had already supported several pilot projects in syphilis control among Southern blacks (but had steered clear of involvement in the infamous Tuskegee study), and Davis was interested as well in upgrading black hospitals, physicians, and public health work.[49]

Aware of Davis's plans Bousfield, with Murray's help, endeavored in 1932 to shape and encourage them. One thing Bousfield wanted was for Davis to get "out among the colored people." In view of "his Virginia upbringing," Bousfield thought such exposure would "do a lot of good," and in November Bousfield reported that Davis had "agreed to try to widen his contacts." Although he saw Davis as a stubborn man, Bousfield was certain that their efforts to "train him" would pay off in time: "whenever we win him completely, I'm sure he will be a wheel horse forever."[50] Davis's creation of a Division of Negro Health in 1934 and his appointment of Bousfield as head was one measure of their success.

One program for which Bousfield and Murray wanted foundation support was the improvement of Southern black hospitals, which they saw as poorly run, marred by staff bickering, and prone to scrimp on patient care. Many institutions, they knew, would resist changes. In those cases they felt that Duke and Rosenwald should be prepared to take a tough line, requiring hospitals to "measure up and continue to measure up to certain minimum requirements of hospital organization and service" as the price of support. Such firmness would insure greater progress in the long run for both patients and interns than did existing foundation policy, which gave money away without strings.[51]

In approaching the problem of the black hospital both men, but especially Murray, were motivated by a deep-seated racial conservatism. They had, for example, no immediate interest in the creation of integrated hospitals in the South or North. Their belief was that black patients and physicians would benefit most from a segregated system, at least for the time being.

Not all Northern black physicians shared that outlook, and their position highlighted the conservatism of Murray and Bousfield. A few blacks — Murray dismissed them as "demagogic" and "misguided" leaders — began demanding in the early 1930s that public and private agencies such as the Veterans Administration (VA) and the Rosenwald Fund, halt further construction of all-black facilities.[52] The center of that opposition was the all-black Manhattan General Medical Society, whose president, the former Atlantan Louis T. Wright, was Murray's chief rival for leadership of New York's black profession. The intra-racial controversy flared publicly in 1931, when Wright and New York NAACP leaders published an open letter rebuking the Rosenwald Fund for agreeing to build a new segregated hospital in the city. The next year Wright and black doctors from the Manhattan Society took on the VA, which had announced plans for a second segregated hospital in the North. Wright and colleagues argued that such a step would transplant segregation to a region where it had not yet taken firm root. Believing segregation to be a graver evil than inadequate medical facilities, the group published a strongly worded pamphlet accusing the VA of helping to perpetuate racism and demanding that hospital plans be scrapped.[53]

Murray, for personal and philosophical reasons, strongly disagreed and urged the Negro head of the VA, Oscar Depriest, not to yield to pressure, assuring him that continuance of the traditional policy had "more to recommend it than loud mouthed preachment against segregation in the abstract,"[54] But on that occasion Murray's rivals won the day. Having already created a sentiment in the black community against overtly segregated hospitals by the campaign against the Rosenwald proposal the year before, Wright and his allies were able to get the VA to reconsider and, ultimately, abandon its plan.[55]

But Murray and Bousfield's conservatism ran deeper, still. In their contacts with Duke and Rosenwald they urged not only that hospital financial management be placed in the hands of lay administrators but also that medical service, especially in Southern hopsitals, be put in charge of experienced white physicians. They had no doubt that Southern blacks would in the end become proficient enough to direct those institutions. In the meantime, Murray felt, "it is not exactly fair to these Negro doctors to throw them into a situation requiring the treatment of patients, team-work [and] cooperation, in addition to specialized modern methods" and expect them to succeed without undergoing the "slow painful trial and error method" that whites had had to face. By putting a "sympathetic and thoroughly competent white practitioner" in charge, black doctors, who like all their race "are great imitators," would have proper models from whom to learn.[56]

In their unwillingness to challenge the racial status quo and their seeming acceptance of white notions of black ability, Bousfield and Murray differed little from the great majority of black physicians of the day. What was ironic was that they were more conservative than some of the foundations they sought to influence. The Rosenwald Fund, for example, agreed with the idea of lay administration (as did Duke) but drew the line at staff supervision by whites. Rosenwald's position, as defined by president Edwin Embree, was that black physicians would learn faster if they had to run their own medical service.[57]

Although willing to accept racial separatism, Murray and Bousfield were at the same time insistent that blacks receive *equal* treatment, especially from officials concerned with the public health. Both men, as institutional leaders (and with Rosenwald backing), worked hard and with some success to get full-time health agency jobs for Southern black doctors, arguing that blacks would respond more readily to health programs if administered by their own physicians. The best illustration, though, of the use of a national forum to pressure the South to honor the full meaning of *Plessy v. Ferguson* was Bousfield's speech to the health education section at the 1933 American Public Health Association meeting. As a respected child health authority and fellow of the Association, Bousfield used that occasion to censure the white health establishment for its neglect of blacks and for the gratuitous racism that marked what contacts it did have with the black community.[58]

Though he was the first black to address the Association, Bousfield did not mince words. In the South as well as the North, most health officers did not know what health conditions were among the "less fortunate." That ignorance, he conceded, was partly due to chronic scarcity of funds, which understandably had led local boards to concentrate "efforts in white areas where the best showing could be made before influential people." But fiscal constraints were not the whole story; racism was also involved. To Bousfield, it was simply "inconceivable" that anything else could account for the fact that health officers could "so complacently review, year after year, the unfavorable vital statistical reports of one-tenth of the population and make no special effort to correct [it]."[59] Some health officers, of course, rationalized their behavior by saying that the black man was biologically different and his health problems irremediable. The result, though, was the same whether prejudice was admitted or not. "The public health worker just stands back and asks the question, 'What shall I do for the Negro,' and does nothing."[60]

White officials who did try to reach the black community usually went about it in the wrong way. Anticipating latter-day medical sociologists who would explore the obstructive role of race and class in provision of health services, Bousfield pointed out that there was a right and a wrong way to approach the black community. The first rule was that if one used the word "Negro" one must "spell it with a capital N." The second maxim governed direct address: in speeches before black audiences, it was well to "make no reference to the race question. Leave out former experiences with colored people, forego any expression of your own lack of prejudice and omit the 'darky' story in dialect." Blacks wanted to be talked to like any other group of people, with the same show of respect. Finally, there was the matter of community contacts. "The Negro community is not unorganized. There will be leaders and pseudo-leaders. There will also be the usual proportion of fools, objectors, politicians, and ambitious self-seekers and obstructionists." If health boards honestly wanted to influence conditions in black neighborhoods they had to work through true leaders. Picking contacts whose only qualification was their sycophancy toward whites, Bousfield suggested, would doom programs at birth.[61]

It is of course hard to measure the influence of this kind of attack. Most Southern delegates that year probably did not hear Bousfield, although all health officers could and the majority probably did notice his address, later, in the Association's *Journal*. Doubtless, white emotions were stirred, for Southern physicians were not used to having the prevailing racial etiquette challenged from within the profession, especially by a black. But it was equally likely that serious reflection followed in the wake of anger. After all, those in command of Southern health programs conceded the magnitude of black problems (though they did not know their precise dimensions) and wished them solved, even if that meant adjusting established racial ideas and practices. One might assume, then, that Bousfield won a wide hearing in the South and that what he had to say, things that no Southern black doctor could have said, contributed to a slowly growing realization among the white establishment that it should and could do a better job.

That realization was aided by the efforts of another group of Northern blacks, whose contribution was not the prodding and verbal goading of Murray and Bousfield but the more painstaking and less dramatic work of documenting the state of black health and sharing it with those who had the ability to bring about change. Two who were active in that enterprise were Howard's Hildrus Poindexter and Paul Cornely.

Poindexter, a native of Memphis, Tennessee, had earned his MD at Harvard in 1929 and joined the Howard faculty in 1931 as professor of bacteriology. In 1938 he was on leave, serving as temporary director of a rural health unit in Glendora, Mississippi, a tiny community in largely black Tallahatchie County. While there he made an intensive investigation of the health of black children in Mississippi and parts of neighboring Alabama. Among his findings, which appeared in the *American Journal of Public Health,* was the discovery that a significant proportion of those children were suffering from what Poindexter called "non-infectious malnutrition." Anticipating the revelations of the Southern hunger discoveries of the 1960s, he noted with dismay that while such conditions were well known to Southern health officers, they were practically never mentioned in the literature and were persistently overlooked in program planning. Sadly, the reason for neglect was that even professionals considered hunger the normal lot of the black child.[62]

The most important work of fact gathering, however, was done by Paul Cornely, a West Indian black who had come to Howard in 1934 after doing medical training and two years as a Rockefeller public health fellow at the University of Michigan.[63] Prior to Cornely's work, reliable and detailed information on Southern black health was practically nonexistent. The early twentieth century reports of the Atlanta University Conferences and the two volumes of social and economic statistics on blacks, published in 1918 and 1932 by the Census Bureau, gave considerable attention to health and mortality.[64] But none of those studies had much impact on the white medical establishment, either because they were directed primarily at a black readership or because the arid statistical format did little to seize the attention of professional leaders. Cornely's work had greater effect: his writing was lively, it presented an updated account of conditions, and he made sure that it reached a wide audience.

His initial studies were undertaken in the late 1930s largely at the urging of Bousfield, who wanted the information for the Rosenwald Fund. The investigations, which focused mostly on the South, examined such topics as changes in black mortality, health services for blacks, the role of the Afro-American press, and the status of black doctors. Cornely's basic conclusion was that while blacks had progressed, "the Negro is yearly being outdistanced [by whites] and the gap gradually widening."[65] Even though Southern states, thanks to Social Security grants, were beginning to allocate health monies in proportion to the percentage of blacks in the population, that was not enough. If the health gap was ever to be closed, spending must be raised to a level proportional to the Negro's share of disease. Yet that, alone, would not solve the problem. Like Bousfield, Cornely knew that health agencies would never convince blacks to take advantage of available services as long as insult and disdain continued to contaminate agencies' approach to Negro communities.[66]

The bulk of the work appeared in 1940 in a massive report to the Fund. Individual portions, however, were published separately in the *Southern Medical Journal* and the *American Journal of Public Health,* thus making their way directly into the offices of Southern physicians and health directors.[67] Though Cornely would continue his investigations over the next three decades, that initial work had the greatest effect because it was the most timely. It appeared just as Southern states were getting their first real opportunity to do something serious about black health problems.

Reflecting on the meaning of these careers in what might be termed the Southern medical missions field, one's first realization is that they did not fit the traditional image of members of the black middle class. Supposedly, blacks who found a measure of affluence and social status in the twentieth century were so hungry for acceptance by white America that they turned their backs on the black poor.[68] That stereotype is particularly inaccurate in the case of the Southern medical reformers, who shared in a very immediate way the suffering and pain of the blacks among whom they worked. But neither does it fit the Northern doctors. It was true that none except Poindexter worked directly with the South's sick and needy. Yet all the Northerners strove to shape — or reshape — the attitudes and practices of those who did labor among the Southern black poor. To be sure, few of their efforts brought any immediate result. But because of their involvement with foundations, the American Public Health Association, and the NMA, the Northern medical missionaries played a key role — and one which no Southern black doctor could have filled — in forcing a recognition of black health problems and initiating a discussion within both races of how best to solve them.

Individual efforts were augmented by the work of the NMA. From the early twentieth century this black association tried to get Southern health boards to give greater attention to health problems of blacks. When South-

Paul Cornely and black physician colleagues at Tuskegee Institute to attend the John A. Andrew Clinic in 1940. Cornely is in the front row, second from the right. Courtesy of Dr. Paul B. Cornely.

ern states began a major drive to eliminate hookworm and pellagra about 1910 (as discussed in chapter 2), the prevailing belief—generally correct for hookworm but wrong for pellagra—was that blacks did not suffer much from those diseases. As a result of such thinking, along with the South's habit of excluding blacks from everything, the NMA was unable to get black physicians named to Southern medical commissions concentrating on those problems. So the NMA formed commissions of its own to investigate the extent of Negro morbidity from hookworm and pellagra and to pressure white health officials to include blacks in whatever treatment programs were devised.[69]

In addition, the NMA *Journal* was frequently critical of exclusionist policies of Southern hospitals and health departments, arguing in the latter case that it was hardly fair to blame blacks for their unhealthy environment and at the same time deny them authority needed to correct it.[70] Although there was no evidence that Association appeals had any direct impact on health policy in the early twentieth-century South, criticism was valuable at least in raising the sights of black professionals and in challenging the smug contention of whites that blacks created their own problems. Had the NMA not spoken out Southern blacks would have had no one to voice their health needs, for local medical organizations were hardly free to offer that kind of sustained criticism. And if Southern officials were unwilling to listen, there were those in the North who would.

By the 1930s, under the leadership of men like Bousfield and Murray, the NMA began developing a more coherent program for improving black health in the South, as well as in Northern cities. Already the NMA, along with the Rosenwald Fund, had succeeded in convincing the National Tuberculosis Association to set up a special Negro division to foster more preventive services and fund-raising in black communities. At the NMA's Atlanta meeting in 1931 Murray revealed plans on the part of the black physicians' association to promote the training and employment of black doctors and nurses in official health departments. State boards were to be encouraged to step up health education among Negroes and to put trained black nurses in every community with a sizeable black population. Rosenwald's program of salary subsidies would help lure Southern boards in that direction. In 1935 Bousfield, by then on the Rosenwald staff, arranged a conference of black hospital administrators to put them in touch with foundation executives and to generate discussion of matters such as financing, group hospitalization insurance, interracial cooperation, and improvement of patient services.[71]

The end of the decade also saw the black physicians' association make its first move to get the AMA to integrate its Southern affiliates so that black doctors could gain access to local hospitals. Nothing came of the move: after agreeing to meet with NMA leaders at the 1939 AMA convention, AMA officials virtually ignored them. Although black doctors felt humiliated, in the long run the NMA failure taught a useful lesson. It revealed that when the test came the AMA would choose racial separatism over medical advance. As one Urban League spokesman told black doctors, the AMA attitude "is not only reactionary but indicative of an amazing indifference to one of the gravest health problems that America faces."[72] Given that outlook a black strategy of humble petition was useless in effecting change. If American medical institutions were to be opened up, they would have to be pushed by a black profession that was prepared, as one future leader put it, to "raise Hell" to get what it wanted.[73]

The reformist drive of leading black physicians did not, unfortunately, reflect a similar commitment on the part of the rank and file of Southern black doctors. It is impossible to speak with certainty about the way the average black physician defined his role and approached his tasks, but available evidence (in the records of black physicians and of foundations which aided them) suggested that at best most accepted prevailing health and medical conditions passively. At worst, far too many were (or let themselves become) less than competent, while a few consciously exploited their patients.

Even though there were Negro professional associations in most Southern states by World War I, a large proportion of black doctors did not take advantage of the one opportunity most had to exchange experiences and sharpen skills. The 1914 meeting of South Carolina's Palmetto Association attracted only 32 doctors and dentists out of about 110 in the state. Scanty records prevent one knowing if that attendance was typical, but as late as 1942 Association president W.H. Young still found it necessary to upbraid colleagues for showing so little interest in the annual meeting.[74]

The same inertia gripped the associations themselves. South Carolina's group was slow to offer members the kinds of programs they needed. When surgical and medical clinics were made a regular feature in the late 1930s, initial programs sometimes had little substance. According to a guest clinician from Howard, not only were public health issues neglected, but the "clinics were not organized. In the absence of facilities for x-ray . . . it was impractical to hold a worthwhile tuberculosis clinic."[75]

Disinterest and lack of opportunity combined to turn many doctors into back numbers who offered their patients less than adequate care. One black doctor in Baltimore in the early 1930s was dismayed by the "careless and unscientific manner in which some physicians . . . handle their patients." Frequently they failed to perform blood or Wasserman tests or advise patients to seek treatment for venereal disease.[76] South Carolina's W.H. Young agreed that many doctors were not doing their best: "In the first place, some of our offices and drug stores are too filthy for a decent person to enter. In the second place many of us aren't prepared to render the ser-vices our patients need."[77] When Bousfield visited the Jacksonville hospital in 1932 he was equally appalled: "The men in Jacksonville are away behind the time and by no means equal to the demands of such a hospital. It is pitiful." On the whole he found the city a "dreary place to contemplate from the medical point of view. . . . The brothers are squabbling over the hospital—playing five up and finding fault."[78] Wrangling and infighting among Southern physicians was widely observed by black visitors from the North and caused much concern. Murray's view that black facilities should be under white control was largely the result of his observation of such dissension.[79]

To black Southern doctors' credit, many did considerable charity and public health work. In the period before World War II half the patients of rural black doctors were charity cases. A number of physicians contrib-uted substantially to preventive medicine, vaccinating children and run-ning prenatal and adult clinics—nearly always for free. But in South Caro-lina, at least, it tended to be always the same small group who did these tasks. Apparently that was the pattern nationwide, for in the late 1920s Louis Dublin, the racially liberated medical director of the Metropolitan Life Insurance Company, took black doctors to task for doing so little in preventive medicine and for being so passive in the face of public neglect.[80] Perhaps the majority of blacks were too busy with demanding private prac-tices. Or perhaps they were like the many black physicians of Baltimore who reportedly refused to cooperate with free clinics on the ground that "they take bread from our mouths."[81]

Whether or not the bulk of Southern Negro doctors actually put dol-lars before people and whether or not blacks were more guilty of such calcu-lation than whites are questions that resist definitive answers. If observa-tions of blacks can be credited, however, it would appear that many Negro physicians dealt sharply, and sometimes harshly, with patients in matters of fees. Peter Murray told groups of doctors in the Carolinas that their pa-tients were "not satisfied with the services rendered when contrasted with the prices demanded."[82] Negro doctors, in fact, could be just as hard on poor black people as white doctors. It seemed to Septima Clark of Charles-ton that if you did not have money black doctors soon stopped coming to your house.[83]

In fact, financial squeezing of patients was most apparent in the South's black hospitals. When in the 1920s the Duke Endowment began to support Negro hospitals in the two Carolinas it was struck by the harshness with which its clients dealt with patients—usually out of necessity. "Our hospi-tals," said a Duke official, "often collect from patients who are not able to pay and who should not be forced to pay, but the hospital had to exist. . . .

Hospitals actually take mortgages on . . . cows, pigs, and homes of poor farmers as security for hospital bills."[84]

In some cases harsh policy was aimed at more than just survival. A few hospitals, the Endowment discovered, sought to defraud both patients and the Endowment. The two most questionable operations, uncovered in the early 1930s, were those associated with the Waverly Fraternal Hospital and the Good Samaritan Hospital in Columbia. Those facilities padded their indigent rolls in order to maximize subsidies from Duke. Money not absolutely needed for patient care — and each had a large number of the chronically ill who required little looking after — was then split among hospital owners, trustees, and certain doctors.[85] In addition, Duke's contacts reported, many hospital physicians "were collecting professional fees from Negros who were treated in the hospital as free."[86] One of Duke's investigators was Bousfield. He talked to staffs of both hospitals, and even before evidence of fraud came to light, he reported that "he had never seen a place where Negroes were so exploited by their own race as they were in these hospitals."[87]

There was considerable evidence, then, to suggest that black doctors in South Carolina and throughout the South did less than they might have to keep themselves up to date and meet the health needs of their people. Yet how should one understand and judge that performance? Should all have striven for progress and change as did Matilda Evans and L.W. Long? Or was that an unreasonable expectation? Paul Cornely put the issue in proper perspective, perhaps, when he said that "one must not blame the victim."[88] And victim the Southern black physician surely was, for the racism that blighted his professional preparation also stalked his career as a practitioner.

Furthermore, the unremarkable performance of the average Southern black doctor, especially in the area of public health, was a function of more than social environment. As was the case for the average white physician, the black doctor's training conditioned him to be conservative in his approach to his art. It taught him that treatment of individual patients was his primary task. Grappling with broader social questions or challenging restraints on professional growth was not his role. By its very nature, professional education (for white and black, alike) encouraged individualism and a disregard, if not disdain, for preventive medicine. In addition, Negro medical students, even at black schools, were often subjected to the view that the Negro race was a sick race and that its ills were grounded either in wasteful living or in some inherent physiological weakness.[89] The chances of changing circumstances such as these were slim, at best, and so the black doctor often began his practice with the kind of fatalistic attitude that killed real effort.

Finally, there was a feeling among black doctors that if they were to have the social and financial success to which their training and sacrifices entitled them, they must not antagonize the white medical establishment. Success for the black doctor depended on the maintenance of relationships with white physicians that could be broken easily if they stepped outside agreed-on roles.[90] A black physician who looked at his career in that way could find good reason not only to accept social and professional practices that were medically counterproductive but also to bear down on those people (his black patients) whose patronage was crucial to his expected success.

Given their circumstances, it is in fact impressive that a significant number of black doctors did not view matters so narrowly and managed to rise above self-serving motives and work diligently for change. Yet it was not only black doctors who were seeking to upgrade the health of black people in the early twentieth-century South. Their efforts were seconded by numerous civic and corporate ventures—whose work forms the subject of the next chapter.

CHAPTER 5

Civic Crusaders and
Corporate Reformers, 1900–1940

A strong case could be made that while physicians and health agencies were best equipped in terms of training and resources to promote the advance of preventive medicine in the early twentieth century, actual progress came as much at the hands of laymen as experts. One thinks, for instance of the contributions of the certified milk movement, anti-TB associations, the Rockefeller Commission to Eliminate Hookworm, settlement houses, and various child health organizations.

The case for the importance of lay influence is strongest perhaps for work among Southern blacks, who had fewer doctors of their own to consult and who could expect less help from public health agencies. In the period from 1910 until the late 1930s (when an infusion of federal money permitted a dramatic expansion of government services), a number of valuable projects were launched among Southern blacks to provide the health care that underfunded public agencies were unable or disinclined to offer. Ranging from basic services, like home sanitation and immunizations, to more venturesome projects such as erection of hospitals and training and employment of public health nurses and physicians, private programs fell mostly into two categories, each with a distinct mission and leadership. On the one hand there were the corporate undertakings, such as the health work of the Rockefeller Foundation, the Rosenwald Fund, and the Duke Endowment, which rested on the secure basis of vast private fortunes, undertook large-scale projects, and served a regional clientele. In contrast to these were programs started by Negro laymen and laywomen, which depended primarily on the small contributions of the black community, plus whatever money — conscience or otherwise — could be prized from the white social and political structure. Necessarily limited in scope, these projects were nevertheless an important complement to the bigger foundation programs: their leaders had a first-hand knowledge of the problems of black communities, enjoyed their trust, and were thus able to reach them as no other group could.

In an era when black people were virtually shut off from participation in white society, promotion of the health and welfare of the race offered one of the few outlets for black leadership (along with education and religion) which had sympathy if not support from whites. Aware that their people could make no progress unless they first survived, black leaders across the South, a large proportion of them women, strove to curb sickness and death from such ills as tuberculosis and venereal diseases and to reduce the awesome mortality rate of mothers and infants.

Measuring the effectiveness of such self-help efforts is difficult for the historian. Certainly the Southern Negro death rate dropped steadily during the first four decades of the twentieth century (though never as fast as the white). But that was surely due as well to a gradual improvement in blacks' economic and educational status, a slow growth in the availability of hospital care, and a halting expansion of public health services. It would probably be accurate to say that private efforts, limited monetarily and geographically, played no more than a minor role in reducing overall Negro mortality. But for the people they did reach, those essentially populist health programs made a life-and-death difference, simply because the services they gave were usually unavailable elsewhere. Until such time as governmental agencies redefined their mission to include more of those who fell through the cracks in the private medical system, the great majority of Southern blacks would get no public services at all. Thus the private health care projects that black laymen and laywomen undertook were achievements of no small worth.

Programs came in various shapes and sizes. Some were ambitious and attempted to marshall the resources of large communities. The best-known program, one which sought to reach the great mass of American blacks and thus make some dent in the problem of needless deaths, was the National Negro Health Week movement. Launched in 1915 by Booker T. Washington and a coterie of national black groups and institutions such as the National Business League and Howard University, the Tuskegee-based movement was patterned on a program begun two years earlier in Virginia. The Negro Organization Society of Virginia, a general-focus, self-help group, had in 1913 proclaimed a "Clean-up Day," aimed at motivating Virginia blacks to upgrade sanitary conditions of homes and schools. The response was so enormous (130,000 blacks reportedly took part) that the Society and its president, Hampton Institute head Robert Russa Moton (a black), sponsored in 1914 a "Clean-up Week." That idea attracted the attention not only of the American Public Health Association but also of Washington, who saw its national possibilities. Washington died (in 1915) before he could develop the plan, but the slack was taken up by Moton, who came to Tuskegee as new president and brought with him a similar enthusiasm for a national self-help movement.

From then on the Health Week idea enjoyed steady growth and popularity (aided by Public Health Service sponsorship starting in the 1920s), until by the 1930s every county in the nation with a sufficient black leadership to take charge was devoting a week in April to making blacks think about better health. Besides attention to school health, home health, and sanitation, there were sermons on health, nightly meetings, end-of-week rallies, and efforts to persuade local health establishments to give more attention to black needs.[1]

In terms of enthusiasm, public exposure, and mass participation, National Negro Health Week was an astounding success. Unfortunately, there was little evidence that the movement produced significant changes in actual health care or condition (though it did heighten individual awareness). As with religious revivals, interest was avid while the show was on, but when the tents were struck people fell back into the old ways. More effective in actually improving people's lives were the various *on-going* black projects — even those having limited scope and only a handful of backers.

In the 1920s, for example, Septima Clark, then a young black teacher on John's Island, South Carolina, became a sort of medical missionary to the isolated Negroes on that sea island, whose only recourse when illness struck was to sing and pray and take home remedies. Beginning with ringworm treatment and diphtheria immunization, Clark first got funding from her social sorority, which was seeking ways to help the underprivileged. In 1929 she interested a white Presbyterian women's group in an expanded program. Thanks to Clark's initiative and the leadership of a dedicated white Charlestonian, Mrs. Ashley Halsey, the island's water system was improved, families were taught to upgrade diets, and landowners were convinced to screen tenant houses. Elsewhere, black women's groups were equally active. In the 1930s the national Negro service sorority, Alpha Kappa Alpha, channeled its resources into the establishment of a clinic in rural Mississippi. There, for a number of years, Howard medical graduate Dorothy Ferebee provided primary medical care and health education to area blacks.[2]

It was not surprising that many of these programs were spearheaded by middle-class black women. As Carl Degler has most recently shown in *At Odds*, white females in the late nineteenth century were still expected to function within a "separate sphere" of home and family, and while that idea limited their reach, it also encouraged involvement in outside activities aimed at preserving the home and its values.[3] When a black female middle class emerged in the South in the early twentieth century, its members seemed to follow a similar pattern. As was true of Murray, Bousfield, and their colleagues, the activity of many black women also belied the image of an insensitive black middle class.

Few stories better illustrate the activism among middle-class black females than the work of Lugenia Hope of Atlanta and Modjeska Monteith Simkins of Columbia, whose sustained dedication and administrative skill produced two of the most effective voluntary health organizations in the South. If the groups they created were exceptional in performance and longevity, the problems faced were fairly typical of those confronting other such efforts to render health care in a segregated society.

Lugenia Hope was the wife of Atlanta University president John Hope. Along with a number of other women whose lives centered around the several black colleges clustered on Atlanta's west side, she had long sought to find ways of "making the colored colleges of Atlanta inspire the masses of colored people."[4] In 1908 the unattended death of an old black woman in a nearby neighborhood so struck Hope and her friends that they resolved to create neighborhood organizations in each of Atlanta's sixteen black residential areas. To enhance their effectiveness the several chairwomen would be linked together in a federation christened the Neighborhood Union (NU).

The NU's first project was the establishment of a playground on the campus of Morehouse College. Its success, and the experiences gained from it, convinced Hope that what was needed was a comprehensive approach to neighborhood problems on the model of Chicago's Hull House. Impressed by Hope's plan, a number of white businessmen in the city agreed to provide initial funding, and in 1911 Neighborhood House, the country's first black settlement house, opened its doors.[5]

Like Jane Addams before them, NU leaders were concerned about the sorry state of the schools. In 1913, following a survey documenting overcrowded and unsanitary conditions, they brought those facts forcefully to the attention of Atlanta school commissioners. Thanks to added pressure from influential white women and church leaders whom the NU convinced to visit the schools, city government in 1914 moved to correct the more glaring deficiencies.[6]

It was inevitable that the Union would next turn to health, for the school survey revealed significant problems of home sanitation and illness. Tuberculosis was the major problem, and in 1914 Hope brought officials of the local anti-TB association together with various black groups to discuss some sort of combined effort. The NU had already done a house-to-house survey, which confirmed its worst suspicions, and Hope proposed the establishment of a Union clinic to provide health education and free medical treatment to indigents. The anti-TB association was in full accord and agreed to assist funding. Hope gathered additional money from several Negro insurance firms, and in 1916 the NU opened its center free of debt and with sufficient staff to offer a full range of services.[7]

Thanks largely to Hope, the clinic expanded rapidly and became a model for black communities in other Southern cities. In 1919 Hope assumed the added post of colored educational agent for the anti-TB association. Using the clinic as her base she instituted a program to train neighborhood workers in home nursing, child welfare, and care of the feeble-minded. One of the Union's original purposes had been to identify residents needing help. Hope now went a step further, furnishing neighborhoods with trained personnel to supply such aid. In 1922 she arranged for students of E. Franklin Frazier's School of Social Work (at Atlanta University) to earn course credit by assisting at both the clinic and Neighborhood House.[8]

What made the clinic effective, setting it apart from most public programs, was Hope's realization that it was not enough for health workers simply to make services available for drop-ins. Her staff went into the community and sold the program — and not just by appearing in churches, schools, and lodge halls. Where people were poor, uneducated, and largely defeated by life, workers had to do more. As Hope explained, "too many of our greatest health offenders are those whom you can reach only by going into the home, as they are not usually found in any other place, not even in the church."[9]

In making grass-roots contacts, student interns helped immeasurably. Used as a home visitation force, they kept on the lookout for sick people and paid special heed to the welfare of children and to home sanitation.[10] Whether the need was clinic care or screening of windows, the students' mission was to meet it. One girl assigned to work in a mobile clinic found no customers because the local preacher had forgotten to announce it during his service, so she "got out in the street and asked all the children who were out there playing to come in and let us weigh and measure them and to let the doctor examine their teeth, tonsils, and adenoids. I had in all fifteen persons examined."[11] Where patrons needed further attention, follow-up calls insured that patients complied with doctors' instructions.[12]

Naturally, staff and budget limitations prevented the NU from reaching everyone in need. But a useful model was provided for any public health department willing to notice. And on occasion the Union and its clinic came impressively close to 100 percent coverage. In 1919, as part of her anti-TB program, Hope sent 143 visitors into 5400 homes. Their contacts, plus those of Hope and her assistants in schools and elsewhere, reached 45,000 people, nearly three-fourths of Atlanta's black population.[13]

Ironically, the success of the NU ultimately undercut its effectiveness. In 1923 the newly established Community Chest (cc) of Atlanta, impressed by the NU record, invited the black group to become a supported agency. The offer was attractive to Hope because it meant an assured and possibly substantial operating budget. But in return, the NU had to abandon all programs except those dealing with infant and child health. Although discontinuing the settlement house would be hard, it was true that health activities had come to dominate the NU. Moreover, money problems had grown critical. Local government had underwritten (and would continue to fund) part of the Union program, but on the whole, Hope noted, "city officials . . . have not been sympathetic."[14]

So, the NU agreed to the proffered terms and joined its fortunes to those of the cc. On balance, that was an unfortunate decision, for it soon became clear that the politics of organized charity were not going to work to the Union's advantage. Once it gave up its independent identity, the NU could no longer solicit money on its own but had to associate with the general cc drive. When the revenues declined in 1924 and 1925 the NU was forced to accept a shrinking budget. To add to its woes, the National Urban League began trying to lure the NU away from the cc, to make it a League branch. Hope and her executive committee refused the offer, but the Urban League let the Chest think that negotiations were still underway. Suspecting the Union of disloyalty, and facing its own financial problems, the cc in late 1925 dropped the Union on the ground that it would be able to stand alone. At that juncture, even with no prospect of revenue for 1925, Hope was unwilling to go to the black community again because it had already given to the cc drive, and a new solicitation might result in the cancellation of Negro pledges to the Chest. That, Hope feared, would shock "our Atlanta plan of race relations," which Hope wanted "nothing to disturb. . . . "[15]

Fortunately for the NU, other black Atlantans were not so concerned about offending whites, and they began a separate fund-raising effort which did indeed cause widespread cancellation of earlier cc pledges. Alarmed, the Chest quickly came to terms with the NU, offering to reinstate the black organization if it would halt its drive. Although some Union members were bitter and counseled permanent disassociation, Hope believed that the best, long-run chance for financial stability lay in re-affiliation. Also she had it on good authority that if the Union re-joined, it would be given charge of a greatly expanded program for Negro health.[16]

That program never materialized. And while the NU performed an important service in succeeding years and vital relief work in the early Depression, the organization never reached its potential. Whether or not it would have flourished had it remained outside the Community Chest is uncertain. Most members were convinced that the cc connection had only

Lugenia Burns Hope, founder of Atlanta's Neighborhood Union, and a group of NU leaders, c. 1920. Hope is in the front row, second from the right. Courtesy of the Division of Special Collections and Archives, Atlanta University Center Library.

crippled growth, and eventually Lugenia Hope agreed. In 1934, the year before she ended her long association with the Union, she noted with some bitterness that its health program was "to a certain extent limited" by affiliation with the Chest. Because of the "meagerness of the Chest contribution" and the "increasing isolation from additional funds which this contribution entails," the organization had not been able to work effectively.[17]

Doubtless that was true, but the wonder was that the Union was able to achieve what it did in the face of institutional neglect and considerable black apathy. Not only did the NU improve and extend the lives of thousands of Atlanta blacks and touch the indifference of many whites, it also taught Atlanta's Negro leadership that much could be achieved, even within a demeaning social system, by concerted, collective action. And it was Lugenia Hope, more than anyone else, who provided the opportunity to learn that lesson. Russian immigrant reformer Mary Antin summed up Hope's achievement: "In every case," she wrote Hope, "the communal authorities will do nothing unless civic crusaders clamor for their rights." It was therefore "good to know that where there is need there do arise agents to meet that need."[18]

Antin's tribute might also have been paid to South Carolina's Modjeska Simkins, who began her work about the time Hope was bringing hers to a close. Simkins's contribution was at once narrower and wider than Hope's. Though an organizer of talent, she never created organizations, as such, but worked through established institutions. During the 1930s when Simkins was most involved with health issues, those problems alone absorbed all her energy. On the other hand, while Hope limited work to one urban population, Simkins addressed the health needs of all South Carolina blacks — and on occasion blacks from other states as well. The two women differed, too, in personal style. Hope, the wife of a black minister and college president, was a member of Atlanta's black elite. Though not condescending toward the lower class, she approached them with an air of *noblesse oblige,* and there was more than a little of the moralist in her. In her relations with whites, whose support was vital to the NU's success, she could be firm, but she was always careful not to offend.

Simkins came from a different mold. She also served in different times, when the grip of segregation was slowly beginning to loosen. The daughter of a bricklayer who taught his children to fear no one and who kept a loaded gun at hand to defend his family, Simkins never shared the resignation of those blacks who put their hope in the white man or the hereafter. "I'm a believer in confrontation," Simkins once said. "I don't believe in pussyfooting. I believe in the rights of all, and I don't mind raising sand to protect anybody who needs it."[19]

She began her career as a health reformer in 1931 when she became director of Negro work for the South Carolina Anti-tuberculosis Association. The Association had created a separate Negro committee several years before but had given it little attention or support due to lack of funds. But in 1931 it received a substantial grant from a soap company to employ a black health educator, and Simkins, who had a deep interest in medicine (an uncle and a brother were doctors) and who had recently lost a teaching post because she had married, got the job. Association director Mrs. D. McLaughlin MacDonald (a white) defined her duties: Simkins was to promote the prevention of TB among blacks, primarily in those South Carolina counties that lacked public or private health organization.

Simkins, however, set a different role for herself, and her independence would put her in conflict with the Association the whole twelve years she served it. As South Carolina's only full-time, statewide black health worker she decided that she could not limit her efforts to TB but must deal with the whole spectrum of health problems facing South Carolina blacks, a range of ills which included maternal and infant mortality, VD, malnutrition, insanitation, *and* TB.

Director MacDonald was able to accommodate most of that agenda. But the idea of anyone speaking publicly about syphilis and gonorrhea was unacceptable. In the years before the appearance of Surgeon General Thomas Parran's *Shadow on the Land* (1939), open discussion of VD seldom occurred outside doctors' offices and professional meetings.[20] MacDonald's view, like that of most of her generation, was that syphilis and gonorrhea were "diseases of sin, and we should not bother with them at all."[21] But Simkins had her own ideas, one of which, she said later, was that "if I was the director [of Negro work], I would direct." Whatever MacDonald thought about the fitness of discussing certain topics, "we just went ahead and did it."[22]

In her efforts to alter the health habits of South Carolina blacks Simkins followed two lines of attack: she sought to ally with as many groups as possible, and she sought to raise as much money as she could to pay for educational campaigns and nursing services for TB victims. The first group pursued were Negro teachers. State law mandated instruction in health education, but there was no requirement that teachers be trained for the work. Simkins attempted to bridge that gap. Immediately after assuming her position she enrolled in a summer health education program at the University of Michigan. On her return she began a series of two-day institutes for teachers to groom them in effective health education and give them rudimentary skills in diagnosing childhood diseases. The first institute was held in Saluda County, and though teachers had to attend over a weekend and without extra pay, sessions were well attended. A nurse from the state TB association gave clinical demonstrations using children from the local school; Dr. R.W. Mance of Columbia gave teachers free physical examinations; and Simkins taught a course in educational methods. Each institute featured an inspirational talk by Simkins at an evening public meeting. Her speeches were spellbinders, direct, pithy, and filled with the oratorical flourishes of the black preacher. At her first talk, before an audience of two hundred, she stressed the preventable nature of most illness and took special pains to convince her largely rural audience that there was nothing to fear from vaccinations.[23] Besides the institutes, Simkins's program also included two-week summer courses for teachers, held first at South Carolina State College (Orangeburg) and eventually expanded to all six Negro colleges in the state.[24]

Except for objecting to attention to VD, MacDonald was generally supportive. She did quarrel with Simkins, though, about scheduling. Too many meetings, MacDonald complained, took place on Sundays. Sunday was the Lord's day and should not be an occasion for business. Why could Simkins not hold her programs on weekday mornings, as MacDonald did with her women's meetings?

"How do you think the women you work with get to the 10:00 meetings?" Simkins asked. MacDonald replied that she had not the least idea. Simkins enlightened her: "'cause they got some Negro woman cooking the dinner and changing the babies while they come to the meeting. We have to take our people when we can get them, and that's at night and on Sunday."[25] The Sabbath meetings continued.

Besides teachers, Simkins also sought to reach black physicians and preachers. The first, she felt, needed to be kept abreast of new (and old) techniques for TB management. To that end she organized periodic conferences, often at the state sanatorium, to which she brought pulmonary specialists to demonstrate methods of early detection and discuss new treatments. Attention was also paid to the most routine diagnostic procedures, such as the tuberculin test. Simkins was convinced that some black doctors had never used it.[26]

Preachers were the most important agents for change in the black community. But they needed special handling. The notion that they should be concerned with the physical as well as spiritual welfare of their flocks had not occurred to many, and Simkins was convinced that they had to be seduced into following that course. So at her meetings with black clergy in South Carolina and elsewhere, she took pains to create just the right atmosphere of piety to put her audience in a receptive mood. In helping plan a health education institute for Southern ministers at Dillard University in New Orleans, she advised: "since most of these men will be provincial and ultra-religious in their reactions, I would suggest that we . . . open each day with a ten or fifteen minute devotional period or hold a daily assembly," combining a devotion and a health message. In the evenings, after supper, the preachers would expect a vesper service, and again the opportunity should be seized to weave the secular with the spiritual. Topics, she suggested, "might be 'The Religion of Health Protection and Christian Service' —or something like that—having the purpose of showing how health instruction and health behavior may be . . . correlated with the . . . activities of the church."[27] Apparently her tactics worked. After completing a number of meetings in South Carolina, North Carolina, and Maryland with black clergy of the Methodist Church, Simkins won strong praise from the church's director of Negro work. Simkins had not only awakened their interest in health but had "sent them back to their communities to do some definite work. . . ."[28]

All those gatherings required considerable funding. As the Anti-TB Association did not provide any, Simkins had to raise money in the black community. Although funds were never abundant, Simkins proved an effective money raiser during her eleven years. Her major feat lay in awakening —annually—concern over TB. The Negro press, largely ignored by state and county health departments in the South, was her prime vehicle. Deluged by her copy, editors and feature writers paraded the horrors of TB and gave the impression that the race faced virtual extinction if blacks did not help their local TB committees in their fight. For two months at the end of each year, TB attained the status of a major issue in Negro papers. As a result, collections rose dramatically. When Simkins took up her post in 1931 blacks' Christmas seal campaigns netted $1026; by 1940 they were bringing in over $11,000.[29]

There were also occasional white contributions. Once Simkins wangled an invitation to meet Northern millionaire Archie M. Huntington, who wintered on the South Carolina coast below Myrtle Beach. Simkins impressed him with her knowledge of Spanish architecture and eventually steered the conversation around to a contribution. Nothing was given that day, but the next week she received a check for $2000. MacDonald was astonished.[30]

By 1935 the Negro TB committee had its own mobile X-ray unit and was employing two nurses to give chest examinations, health instruction, and home care for the sick, dealing not just with TB but all illness. When Simkins met problems that her group could not address, she referred them to those who could. Thus in the late 1930s when she encountered a large pocket of pellagra among low-country blacks, she pressed the state health officer to include them in its distribution of dried yeast, which by then was a recognized pellagra-preventive.[31]

Dollars and programs were important, but perhaps Simkins's major achievement was to help her people throw off their passivity and fatalism about health and consider more effective ways of preventing needless debility and death. New ways of thinking came slowly, but by the late 1930s when a host of new public health clinics began for the first time to offer primary medical care, South Carolina blacks were ready, even eager, to take advantage of the new opportunities. Simkins could take some credit for that.

In Modjeska Simkins, black South Carolinians also had an advocate to voice their needs to the white medical and health establishment, with whom she was in frequent contact in planning physician conferences, TB clinics, and midwife training. As MacDonald had to concede, Simkins was "thoroughly acceptable and pleasing to both races," and it was that acceptability — and her push — which enabled her to widen understanding among whites of black health needs.[32]

Despite such effectiveness, in 1942 Simkins lost her job. Two years earlier she had become visibly active in the South Carolina Conference of the NAACP. MacDonald, who had never come to terms with the way Simkins ran her division, found it impossible to harbor a racial militant in her midst as well, and she convinced her board to hire another director.[33]

For her part Simkins had cause to welcome the termination. During the whole period, she and other black health workers had been routinely excluded from Association conferences and social occasions, even from meetings between local white officials and visitors from the national TB organization. Although Simkins said she "gave Mrs. MacDonald Hell" for shutting her out of professional meetings, the practice went on, and eventually Simkins had had enough.[34]

While Modjeska Simkins is remembered today more for civil rights than health work in South Carolina, her work in the health field did not end in 1942. At the close of the war she was instrumental in raising private funds for black hospital improvement. A few years later she played a key part in convincing state officials to make a special allotment of federal money for such needs. And in the 1960s she was a contentious but effective advocate for the desegregation of white hospitals (chapter 11).[35]

Black lay leaders like Hope and Simkins did not have a monopoly on black health projects. There was also an assortment of "white" organizations in the South in the 1920–40 era that sought to initiate change. Churches were often active. Besides the Presbyterian women who were at work on John's Island, the Episcopal diocese of South Carolina in the 1920s put nurse-midwife Maude Callan to work among the fifteen thousand unserved blacks of Berkeley County. More ambitious were the projects of the women of the Southern Methodist Church which that same decade supported settlement houses for blacks in Nashville and Augusta and for three years paid the salary of a traveling public health nurse in South Carolina. Interracial commissions, which sprang up in most Southern states following World War I, likewise devoted some energy to health improvement. In Georgia and

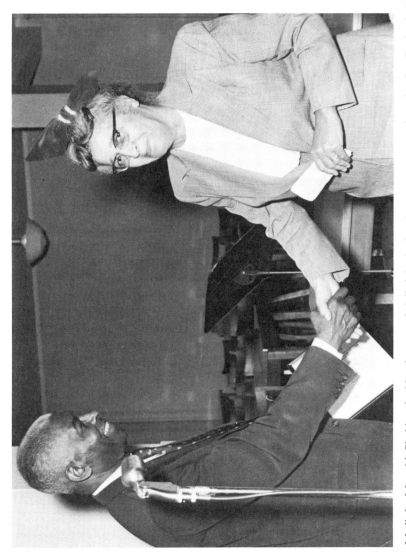

Modjeska Monteith Simkins, health reformer and civil rights leader, shown at a program honoring Dr. Benjamin Mays (left), c. 1950. Courtesy of Modjeska Monteith Simkins.

South Carolina those groups were effective in convincing state health departments to use part of available federal monies to hire a few Negro nurses for maternity and infancy work.[36]

Most of those ventures, though, while they might have relieved suffering and improved the health of considerable numbers of black Southerners, had little impact on segregated (and discriminatory) medical institutions. More effective in that regard were the large corporate endeavors of the period, whose ultimate objective was the creation of institutions and coteries of professionals sufficient to give blacks the health care they needed. Of the corporate ventures focusing primarily on the South in the pre–World War II era, the two most ambitious and successful ones were the Julius Rosenwald Fund and the Duke Endowment. Although each organization chose, perhaps wisely, to work for change within the confines of segregation, both challenged the racial status quo at key points and thus helped prepare the South for the demolition of its segregated health and medical system in the post-war period.[37]

Rosenwald, the Jewish merchant who made his fortune with Sears-Roebuck, began his long venture in support of Negro welfare in 1914, when, after talks with Booker T. Washington, he set up his first Rosenwald Schools. Pleased with initial results of his effort in rural education, the Chicago millionaire soon after established the Rosenwald Fund, which over the next two decades would construct some five thousand primary schools for Southern black children.[38] Inevitably educational support involved the Fund with black health, for it became clear that sickness posed severe obstacles to learning. Equally obvious was the considerably higher mortality of black youngsters. In 1926 Rosenwald became personally interested in such questions when a chance meeting with a Southern health officer opened his eyes to the seriousness of black ill health. Over the next two years the Fund studied the dimensions of black morbidity and mortality and considered possible ameliorative steps. One solution advocated by many was a wider use of black nurses, who could reach their people in ways no white nurse could. However sensible the idea, the realities of segregation and racism had largely prevented its realization. At the end of the 1920s only twenty-nine black public health nurses were at work in all the South.

One, however, had been employed in Durham County, North Carolina, as part of an experiment undertaken by the North Carolina Board of Health to improve the performance of black children at local Rosenwald schools. When Rosenwald traveled there in early 1928 to dedicate his one-thousandth school, he received such encouraging reports of her work that he directed Fund trustees to develop a plan to induce other Southern counties to follow Durham's example.[39]

In April 1928 trustees responded with a twelve-thousand-dollar gift to aid six county health units in North Carolina and Tennessee to bring black nurses onto their staffs. With that allocation an involvement with Negro health began that would extend over the next fourteen years and see the Rosenwald Fund invest some $1.7 million in all manner of projects. To manage its health services division, created in 1928, as well, trustees brought in Michael Davis, a medical economics expert who had also had several years' experience with the Rockefeller Foundation in New York. From the beginning Davis had the assistance of a succession of physicians assigned to the Fund by the PHS (the first was Taliaferro Clark) and, beginning in 1933, the aid of Midian Bousfield, who became Director of Negro Health.

Although the Fund chose its targets with care and always required recipients to bear part of project costs, the decision to provide one kind of aid often forced attention to other, related problems to insure success of the initial investment. Such was the case with the plan to increase the number of black public health nurses. From the outset Rosenwald trustees recognized that no private foundation could supply health services to even a fraction of the nation's 13 million blacks. The most that could be done was to demonstrate the effectiveness of black nurses and urge Southern boards to put them on staff. Obviously, the first would have to be highly skilled, if other health departments were to be persuaded to hire them. But it was soon apparent that few such nurses existed in the South. And there was little prospect of their appearing. With no demand for high-grade black professionals, first-class nursing schools had never developed in black hospitals. So the Fund had to begin by upgrading the quality of nurse-training programs, which it did in 1928 with a $25,000 grant to Meharry to help it improve both its medical school and hospital.[40] In the next two years ten other Negro hospitals received similar assistance, most of it going to Providence Hospital in Chicago, Flint-Goodrich in New Orleans, and John A. Andrew Memorial at Tuskegee. Soon the Rosenwald effort was paying dividends. By the end of 1934, 148 Negro nurses were working on city and county health department staffs in the South and another 26 were serving private agencies.[41]

The Fund was equally interested in opening public health staffs and hospital residencies to black physicians, a tricky business because it struck at a core segregationist credo that only whites should be in supervisory positions. But Davis and Bousfield believed that the effort must be made, for a breach in segregation's wall at those points would pay large dividends in terms of increased attention to black health problems. As with Negro nurses, success was partly a matter of upgrading the hospital training of Negro interns to insure their ability to compete with white applicants for agency and hospital posts. Thus the Fund had another reason to encourage black hospital improvement. In addition it established a number of fellowships for Southern black doctors to give them the special training they needed to qualify for positions.

Besides seeking to enhance the supply of black doctors, the Fund also tried to create a demand for them by working quietly but directly with health and medical administrators. In 1932 Davis convened a national group of hospital and health agency heads from both public and private sectors to discuss greater black representation at upper-level staff positions. Not only was the conference supportive of Davis's proposals, but it instructed its chairman to undertake negotiations with the American Medical Association toward the opening of internships for blacks in white hospitals.[42]

The Fund exerted greatest leverage via its willingness to pay (temporarily) all or part of the salary of black doctors added to state and local health department staffs. Ultimately state boards in Texas, Louisiana, and North Carolina (which suggested the idea), and city health departments of Baltimore, Louisville, and High Point (North Carolina) took advantage of the offer. Shortages of candidates and money restricted the number of agencies the Fund could help, but the low level of response from Southern departments was a greater problem. All needed additional personnel, but segregation had such a hold on thinking that few stepped forward.[43] Even those agencies that did add black doctors often restricted them to serving black patrons in administrative set-ups that gave them little contact with other, white health officers. Thus North Carolina's first black physician, Dr. D.A. Dees, was put to work in 1930 in a special syphilis treatment project in a heavily black county. Later, in 1935, when North Carolina hired a black doctor on a permanent basis with Rosenwald help, the state board restricted his educational efforts to black groups and kept him in the field and away from the center of decision-making in Raleigh. But even these tentative steps aided later progress, and of course the pairing of black doctors with black patrons had enormous advantages in selling health programs to apathetic black communities.[44]

Also successful were the Fund's efforts to encourage greater action against VD and TB. In 1928 Davis agreed to underwrite a substantial part of a PHS project aimed at demonstrating the effectiveness of mass methods for syphilis control in the rural South. The first PHS program to focus on rural blacks, over the next four years the project reached thirty-five thousand blacks in six Southern counties (including ones in Georgia and North Carolina) and provided treatment to 70 percent of those found infected. Although not all were cured, the disease was for a time substantially reduced in those six areas, and mass screening and treatment approaches were vindicated. (It was only decades later that the nation learned that the PHS, but not the Rosenwald Fund, had continued on in Alabama with its infamous Tuskegee experiment, which used black syphilitics as guinea pigs to study the disease in its untreated form.) One of the things that sponsors learned was that most blacks had no inhibitions about reporting for treatment. Unlike whites, few blacks associated syphilis and gonorrhea with immorality or any loss of social standing (though they did recognize VD as a health problem). Most simply concluded that they had "bad blood," which they felt was as treatable as bad teeth. In the late 1930s techniques developed in the 1928–32 Rosenwald-assisted demonstrations were extended throughout the South with passage of the LaFollette-Bulwinkle Act (see chapter 7).[45]

The Rosenwald Fund joined forces with another group in its battle against TB. Up to the late 1920s the National Tuberculosis Association, while it had an interest in blacks, had no money to finance special work in that direction and found most of its Southern affiliates disinclined to do anything either. In 1928 the Fund made a substantial contribution to the National Association, permitting it to create and staff a special Negro committee. Over the next decade and a half the Fund continued to back that work. As a result the national organization became an effective lobbyist for black TB victims and a valuable technical resource for state sanatoria and boards of health.

In addition Rosenwald made important direct contributions to TB diagnosis and treatment. Because early detection procedures, such as tuberculin tests and X-ray exams, were fairly costly to implement, many poor communities could not afford them. The Fund helped by financing research aimed at developing less expensive diagnostics. Some success was achieved with routine fluoroscopic examination, and the Fund invested additional monies to pay for physician training in the procedure. Economic barriers also made lengthy sanatorium confinement unfeasible for most blacks. To ease that problem, Rosenwald held demonstrations throughout the South to introduce the surgical procedure known as lung collapse therapy (induced pneumothorax), which not only was more effective than simple bed rest but enabled patients to become ambulatory sooner.[46]

Not all was smooth going. The Depression struck just as programs were getting underway, forcing president Edwin Embree to discontinue or delay funding for many new ventures. North Carolina health officials, eager to take advantage of Rosenwald's nurse fellowships, were chagrined to learn in 1930 that the Fund had decided to cut back on grants. The health board's Raleigh office had just convinced an additional five counties to make outlays necessary to attract Rosenwald money. North Carolina's health officer also found that he had gone ahead too fast in encouraging employment of more black physicians. Doctor M.L. Perry had an assured position at the L. Richardson Memorial Hospital in Greensboro (black) and a chance to work into the state board of health program—if he could get a Rosenwald fellowship to prepare himself in urology. But by October 1930, economic conditions were severe enough to force the Fund temporarily to discontinue all post-graduate awards. By 1932 the Chicago foundation, like many similar organizations, was at a virtual standstill. As Bousfield told a colleague, "now . . . you couldn't get streetcar fare to Evanston."[47] Within a couple of years the situation would ease; meantime it proved crippling.

The Fund also faced strong criticism of some of its programs. Sharpest attacks came from a number of Northern black doctors who were dissatisfied with the foundation's hospital development policies. Unlike its professional employment program, which sought to integrate the white medical establishment, hospital building posed no such challenge to segregation. Accordingly, a few physicians assailed the Fund for underwriting medical discrimination. As discussed previously (chapter 4), one critic was Louis Wright of the black Manhattan General Medical Society, who in 1931 hit the Fund for planning a segregated hospital in New York City. By going along with the prevailing pattern, claimed Wright, Rosenwald was actually helping to "extend segregation to areas that did not yet have it."[48]

The majority of black physicians, however, had as yet no quarrel with hospital segregation, provided that they could have their share of facilities. What disturbed some black doctors more was that the Fund was moving the profession forward too fast, not too slowly. Embree had insisted, as a matter of policy, that blacks be given full charge of the medical side of any hospitals built or enlarged with Rosenwald money. A number of black leaders like Bousfield and Murray regarded Embree's view as visionary: far from bringing about professional growth, forcing blacks forward prematurely only wasted foundation money and gave rise to professional jealousies.

One example of Rosenwald's alleged wrongheadedness was the Negro hospital in Savannah, which received funding in the early 1930s. Expansion of facilities and separation of financial matters from physician control won general applause, but the selection of a local black physician to manage the medical side was a fatal mistake, according to one black insider. "I endeavored to explain to Mr. Embree," the critic wrote Peter Murray in 1932, "that it was utterly impractical and almost impossible to efficiently operate a hospital to the full advantage of the institution and the patients" with a staff of doctors of the "limited education and medical preparation as furnished by the Negro doctors in Savannah."[49] What was needed was competent white direction. Although Embree "emphatically disagreed," the critic was convinced that Rosenwald's plan "has not worked to the advantage of the institution and the Negro doctors are today more jealous of their 'rights' than . . . at the time of the [hospital's] reorganization."[50] In the view of one segment of the black medical profession, the Savannah situation reflected a too common shortcoming of Rosenwald support: "moderately ample funds," but few results.[51]

The issue of black leadership was never resolved because, about the time of the Savannah episode, the Fund ended its hospital construction program, primarily for reasons of economy but also because it decided that hospitals were more properly the responsibility of local communities and the state. Besides, the Duke Endowment had entered that field by then, and Rosenwald was happy to yield to Duke and concentrate on other things.[52] Whether or not Rosenwald was misguided in pushing responsibility on Negro doctors was anyone's guess. Certainly, Embree's position was defensible, and critics of the Fund were not without their own delusions — one being that suitable white physicians would even consider black hospital superintendencies.

Yet critics of specific projects applauded the overall program, for in an era when those responsible for public health chose to ignore the Negro, the Rosenwald Fund was a godsend to black people in the South. Not only did it play a role in healing, but more important, it energized those public agencies in the South and in Washington on whom much of the black populace ultimately depended. "Without the prodding and stimulation of the Julius Rosenwald Fund," wrote Paul Cornely, "many federal, state, and local health agencies may still have been lukewarm concerning the health of the Negro."[53]

In many ways, the Rosenwald Fund was very much a part of the post–Civil War stereotype of the rich, Yankee "do-gooder" coming South to raise up benighted Southerners from the depths of ignorance, meanness, and illness. The fight of the Rockefeller Sanitary Commission against hookworm, the contributions of Andrew Carnegie to Tuskegee, and the charitable work of the Laura Spellman Rockefeller Foundation among Negro girls were also squarely within that tradition. By the 1920s, in fact, Southern blacks were accustomed to look primarily to the North for the help (many local whites would call it "meddling") which they could not get from their own region or government.

It was against that tradition that the appearance of the Duke Endowment came as such a historical surprise. Duke money was Southern money, amassed in the first instance from production of cigarettes and augmented, later, by investments in hydroelectric power. That such a fortune should be built up and controlled by a Southern family was itself a novelty. That a substantial portion of it should be given over in the Yankee manner to advance the welfare of poor Southerners — black as well as white — was breathtakingly new.

In December 1924, James Buchanan Duke, reigning patriarch of the family, announced that he was giving Duke Power Company securities in the amount of $40 million to create a new foundation, the Duke Endowment. Its primary purposes would be to establish and maintain a new university and medical school bearing his name and to create orphanages and hospitals for poor people of the two Carolinas.[54] In allocating 32 percent of available income to the construction and operation of hospitals, James Duke's aim was to bring hospital care within reach of the rural poor, who for reasons of income and geography had never enjoyed such opportunity.

The task of implementing Duke's vision of available, affordable hospital care fell primarily on the two senior officers of the hospital section of the Endowment, director Watson Smith Rankin and assistant Graham Davis. North Carolinian Rankin was surely an excellent choice for director. A physician and former dean at the Wake Forest Medical School, and for sixteen years state health officer of North Carolina, Rankin was the chief reason why his state enjoyed such a high reputation among Northern foundations and within the PHS. Besides large administrative talent, Rankin had also shown an uncommon sensitivity to the problems of blacks and a willingness to battle for the needs of all poor, even against the interests of his own profession (see chapter 6). Graham Davis, another native "Tarheel," was the son of a country doctor and like Rankin a strong advocate of the small, rural hospital. His knowledge of hospital conditions in the two Carolinas and his experience in hospital management would make him another valuable asset to the Endowment.[55]

The two men and their associates spent most of 1925 getting ready. After surveying hospital needs in the two states, they turned to definition of policy. The first aim was to make hospital care more widely affordable, and to that end they decided to give all supported hospitals one dollar a day for each charity patient. At that time a dollar was substantial aid, as average daily cost per patient usually ran no more than three to four dollars. A second objective was to construct hospitals—either new hospitals or additions to old, whichever served the community better. Although there were no hard and fast guidelines, Endowment officers agreed that all money not used for charity beds would be available for construction. Convinced of the importance of local support to hospital success, awards from Duke would be contingent on each community raising substantial monies itself. To insure sound and sensibly planned construction, Duke also arranged for a leading architectural firm to prepare a number of model plans for use by local builders.[56]

Finally, Rankin and associates decided that the Endowment had responsibility to assist, and if necessary compel, supported hospitals to upgrade the quality of their operations, whether on the administrative or medical side. If professional service were allowed to decline, consequences

would be as undesirable as they would be inevitable: first a poor community reputation, then a drop in bed occupancy, followed by a rise in per
capita cost, and ultimately an end to the institution's ability to serve.[57]

With policy set, funding began on January 1, 1926. First awards were
shared by thirty-four hospitals in North Carolina and eighteen in the lower
state. Of total distributions, $206,000 went for maintenance of charity beds
and about $110,000 for construction and equipment. Understandably, the
Endowment wished to move cautiously with capital grants. As Rankin and
his staff learned more about local needs, strengths, and weaknesses in the
Carolinas, those awards would rise, hitting a high of nearly $675,000 in 1930.
By contrast, charity care provision in 1930 was only $437,000, with 55 per-
cent going to North Carolina. But except for the early 1930s, when depression conditions virtually eliminated other sources of capital, operating grants
always exceeded those for bricks and equipment.[58]

Whatever the use of Endowment dollars, they met a critical need for
blacks and whites alike. Mill hands in the two Carolinas were among the
beneficiaries. Although it is not possible to determine to what extent textile
workers used Duke-supported facilities, the Endowment aided hospitals
throughout the textile region. In North Carolina in the 1930s Duke assisted
in the construction and operation of some 2500 new beds in 80 primarily
white hospitals (a 70 percent increase in space). Of that number about 1050
(or 42 percent) of new beds were in locales easily accessible to mill workers.
Moreover, as of 1940 about one-third of all patients in Duke-supported hospitals in North Carolina were treated free. In South Carolina the support
of facilities in textile counties was, proportionally, even greater.[59]

To blacks, Endowment aid was more crucial. When the foundation
started up, North Carolina blacks, though one-third of the state's population, had use of only 20 percent of its general hospital beds, at least one-half
of which were in all-black facilities. In South Carolina inequities were even
sharper, and Endowment money helped close the gaps. By 1930 Duke was
assisting the operation of nine black hospitals in North Carolina and six
in South Carolina, providing not only revenue but sound administrative
and professional advice, aimed at making black medical service equal to
that at white hospitals.[60]

More important in that day was the support Duke gave to hospitals
that accommodated blacks in segregated wards. There was never any question of using Endowment funding as a weapon to undermine segregation.
In fact, Duke aid to all-white facilities grew substantially in the 1930s, especially in North Carolina. But aid to facilities which served both races increased far more. In North Carolina in 1930 forty segregated hospitals with
2550 beds got Duke money for charity care, while in South Carolina the
figures were fifteen facilities with 1257 beds. At decade's end the Endowment

was aiding fifty-nine such hospitals (with 4200 beds) in the Upper State and twenty-six facilities (with 2540 beds) in the Lower. Not only did black patients benefit from the additional beds and the upgrading in care that Duke support required, but the Endowment funded a significantly higher rate of charity care in all-black and segregated facilities than it did in all-white hospitals. In South Carolina in 1940 average percentages of free days in those three classes of hospitals were, respectively, 55, 47, and 17.[61]

Although all hospitals were eager to receive Duke money, they frequently resisted restrictions attached to it. As a result, upgrading hospital care for the poor in the two Carolinas was not always as easy as it might seem. The problems encountered by the Endowment in dealing with the two competing all-black hospitals in Columbia (Waverly and Good Samaritan) might be offered as an illustration of the inherent snares in the way of doing good, even where need was generally conceded.

In terms of the malfeasance involved (see chapter 4), Columbia was fairly unusual. Only in a handful of cases, involving black *and* white hospitals, did Endowment-supported facilities falsify records in an effort to get more money from the Endowment than was due. Marshall Pickens, who joined the Endowment in the early 1930s, recalled, in fact, only two cases of excessive wrong-doing in his fifty years with the Endowment. The financial irregularities that occurred in the Waverly-Good Samaritan case, he thought, was due to the rare circumstance of two (competing) black hospitals in one city.[62]

What was not unique to Columbia, however, was politics — in this case the politics of hospital care in a racially segregated society not much given to public welfare. The entry into that situation of a foundation bearing large gifts touched off a scramble for funds among existing (white and black) hospitals that in broad outline probably occurred in many communities.

When the Duke Endowment first surveyed Columbia's needs, it found two black hospitals competing not only for custom and status from the black community but also for money from the white, for the city's white hospital (Columbia General) had control over the public fund for care of indigent blacks. Although the black facilities played the least admirable part in the chase for funds, the white hospital, which had financial problems of its own, was not above pitting Waverly and Good Samaritan against one another in a kind of bidding war to secure the indigent care fund.[63]

To the Endowment, such a situation was intolerable, especially for poor blacks of central South Carolina. Besides the need for increased revenue for charity care, medical services in the black hospitals needed improvement. But to Rankin and Davis one thing was clear: blacks, both paupers and propertied, would not get the care they should have until Columbia had a new, modern black hospital. In pursuing that goal Rankin had two options: he could assist with construction of an all-black hospital owned and staffed entirely by Negroes, or he could help underwrite the building of a black wing at Columbia General. Even though it had never accepted black patients, Columbia General assured Rankin that racial sentiment was changing and that there would be strong public support for such a unit.

Duke's preference was for option one, for it would most benefit black patients and physicians. But the existing black hospital situation was a major obstacle. It was not that the two hospitals were reluctant to be transformed, Cinderella-like, into modern, well-equipped facilities. The problem was that each wished to develop at its rival's expense. But erecting a new hospital on the foundation of just one of the old was unacceptable. Neither facility, alone, could provide the medical talent for a solid program. If the Endowment chose one hospital over the other, it would split the city's black physicians irrevocably. Before Rankin and colleagues would even consider funding a new black hospital, Waverly and Good Samaritan had to merge.

In short, Duke was committed to long-term reform above short-run gain. That position would be put to stern test as the foundation sought to develop a more favorable hospital setting for central South Carolina blacks. In 1929, Kirkman Finlay, Episcopal Bishop of upper South Carolina, was looking for a way to "show more completely the [Church's] sense of responsibility to aid the . . . [Negro] race," and late in the year he made contact with Edwin Embree to see if Rosenwald might aid his Church in acquiring and operating the Good Samaritan Hospital.[64] Certainly the proposal was one which had appeal for the Fund, and Bishop Finlay's initiative might have succeeded but for one thing. Rosenwald had earlier agreed to consult with Duke before supporting any hospital project or making any fellowship awards in the Carolinas. Such an arrangement not only made good sense in terms of avoiding duplication, but from Duke's perspective it was advantageous in another way, in that it gave the North Carolina foundation additional leverage in implementing its policies. So when Bousfield asked what Rosenwald should do about Finlay's proposal, Rankin's advice was to reject it. Trying to build a hospital on Good Samaritan's foundation would be throwing good money after bad.[65]

Shortly after turning back the bishop, Rankin sent Graham Davis to Columbia to talk to black physicians, to make certain that they understood the Endowment position: no capital funds until the hospitals merged. But Davis took pains to strike a positive note as well. The Endowment staff had already discussed the situation with Rosenwald, and in the event of a merger they were prepared as a joint venture to provide two-thirds of the cost of a new black hospital, if blacks could raise one-third.[66]

If Rankin and Davis were hopeful that Columbia's black physicians would now follow the Endowment lead they obviously overestimated the ability of the two hospitals to work for the common good. For two years Duke awaited signs of cooperation. One man who the Endowment hoped would move matters forward was Good Samaritan's superintendent S.R. Green, who had had considerable training in hospital administration and understood the need for merger. When Good Samaritan's board dismissed him in 1931, apparently for refusing to go along with questionable accounting procedures, the Endowment knew that it had no choice but to pursue its second option, the construction of a segregated black wing at Columbia General.[67]

By December 1931, Rankin had a concrete proposal to offer: if the city would bear about one-third of the costs Duke and Rosenwald would assist in building a modern, seventy-five bed Negro ward. Although the plan seemed unobjectionable to Rankin, it quickly stirred up a hornet's nest in Columbia. Some in the white community, including the editor of the influential *State* newspaper, approved the offer as a way of allowing whites to do their duty by blacks at bargain-basement cost. Others favored giving the whole white hospital to blacks and getting the foundation to apply its aid to building whites a new facility. Recently retired Columbia General chief of staff Pinckney V. Mikell felt that the city's black community was "by all rules of justice entitled" to the old hospital. It had a bonded debt of $300,000, but whites could pay that. After the transfer, Mikell said, white Columbians could then construct the kind of hospital their physicians and surgeons deserved, at a more "suitable location."[68] Colonel George McMaster, prominent son of a prominent family, fully agreed with Mikell's argument and was convinced that Duke and Rosenwald stood "ready to cooperate to their limit. . . . "[69]

Even if white leaders were willing to make a $300,000 gesture of interracial generosity, which was doubtful, Duke was having no part of the plan. It had no interest in investing in a new white hospital in Columbia just then. Moreover, it was determined to push the black medical community into a more professional stance, before allowing them any such reward as a hospital of their own. For the present, a black wing in an established facility was a suitable compromise between long-range goals and short-run needs.

To Mikell that position seemed sheer arrogance: "I for one think the Duke Foundation is doing fine work, but I am not willing for them to dictate as they are doing the policies of where, when, and how we should run our hospital affairs." But as usual, he deplored, money spoke louder than principle.[70]

Columbia's black community was even more avidly up in arms. In fact, the hospital issue prompted an assertiveness not seen for decades in

Columbia. In mid-December, 1931, four hundred people packed the auditorium of Allen University to demand the abandonment of plans for a black hospital wing. Most of the group's anger was directed against local white leaders who had, blacks claimed, promised blacks a hospital of their own years before. Having reneged on that, whites were going forward with the proposal for a black wing, which not only would exclude black doctors from practicing in the new ward but would be totally inadequate for black patients' present and future hospital needs. The meeting ended with blacks demanding to share in the making of city hospital policy and threatening to take their opposition to the foundations if Columbia General trustees did not abandon the current plan.[71] The local black editor was delighted to see such a show of backbone: it said "in no weak-kneed terms that Columbia Negroes know what their rights are and from now on intend to seek them."[72]

The editor, though, knew better than the meeting's organizers why there was no adequate black hospital in Columbia. Foundations like Duke and Rosenwald were interested only in supporting communities whose physicians "got along and would cooperate," and who could keep "personal problems and conflicts in the far background." Obviously that description did not fit Columbia's black doctors, and he openly challenged them to get their house in order. "A Negro Hospital must soon be established. Shall it be a hospital manned by Negroes or an adjunct to some existing hospital where Negroes will have but little say?"[73]

Whether Rankin would have changed course had black doctors suddenly joined forces is not known. The fact was they did not, and as a result they threw away their one good chance to have the kind of facility that they and other Southern black physicians badly needed. Not until 1939 would the boards of Waverly and Good Samaritan agree to merge. By then Duke, which had gone ahead with the segregated wing, was not prepared to make its 1930 offer again. Moreover, the Rosenwald Fund was out of the hospital construction business by then. Duke did put a little money into the combined facility but only enough to allow it to solve the most glaring structural problems and equipment needs.[74]

Meanwhile Duke did what it could to insure that Columbia's black physicians would have more than just a "little say" in setting policies for the new Negro wing (opened in 1934). One condition Duke imposed was that the hospital must give black doctors the right to care for their own patients, rather than surrender them to some white resident or intern. Only after a fashion did the hospital live up to that bargain. After waiting nearly a year to give the city's Negro doctors any word, the superintendent wrote each black physician telling him that he could practice in the new wing but only on private patients. Charity cases were reserved for white interns. As

90 percent of the new beds were occupied by indigents, that ruling signifi-cantly limited the practice of black physicians. Black doctors were so an-gered that most decided that they wanted no part of professional "integra-tion" on those terms, and for a number of years they restricted their prac-tice and what patients they could control to the second-rate conditions of Waverly or Good Samaritan.[75]

Although racial politics often hindered the Endowment, that was not the main barrier to Duke's establishing the hospital service needed by Caro-lina blacks. The main limitations, Rankin noted in the 1940s, were Duke's inadequate resources and lack of local community interest. Even so, the foundation achieved a great good with its money, which was hardly insub-stantial. By 1940 it was supporting 90 hospitals in North Carolina (10 of them all-black and most of the rest, mixed) and 40 in South Carolina (5 all-black and 26 mixed), a substantial percentage of all hospitals in the two states. Contributions for charity care that year — $550,000 for North Caro-lina and $382,000 for South Carolina — represented 30 percent of the total cost of free patient service delivered by those 130 facilities. As for capital contributions, Duke's gifts of $187,000, represented about 6 percent of all such monies.

As the capital investment figure suggested, the full measure of Duke's impact lay beyond dollars given. It also included dollars generated. Although it was impossible to measure the ripple effect, it would be reasonable to say (for 1940, for instance) that a large part of the "other" $2.2 million spent on charity care in Duke-endowed hospitals and a major part of the $3.1 used to build them was spent or paid over because of seed money provided by the Endowment.[76] Yet Duke aid always meant more than bricks, equip-ment, and operating capital. It meant sound guidance for small communi-ties that were attempting to establish or improve patient care. It meant, said long-time South Carolina (white) hospital administrator Robert Too-mey, showing hospitals "how to maximize the use of that one dollar [a day] when it meant something."[77]

Provision of medical services was the most visible and, in the short run, most valuable result of private health efforts such as those set in mo-tion by James Duke, Julius Rosenwald, Modjeska Simkins, and Lugenia Hope. For the black (and white) populations who were served, added hospi-tal beds, nursing care, TB diagnosis, and VD counseling were not only cru-cial, they were usually available from no other source. But there were other less obvious benefits of private health activity, and in the long run they may have had greater significance for Southern blacks. In brief, they can be iden-tified as health awareness and medical opportunity.

The educational work of civic crusaders like Simkins and Hope made their black publics far more aware of the requirements of good health and disease prevention than before. Awareness, in turn, encouraged a habit of seeking professional treatment when serious illness struck. But it was not just needy individuals who were awakened to new possibilities — public bodies were, too. By providing the services they did, corporate and community activists, together, demonstrated to somnolent public health agencies that black people acted like anyone else once they understood the rules of healthful living: they took advantage of medical services, so long as they were made reasonably available and offered in a way that did not compromise dignity.

By expanding services and resources, the large foundations at the same time increased opportunities for blacks to enter the health care professions — on a level with whites and sometimes side by side. Wittingly or no, as Duke and Rosenwald opened those opportunities and provided those services, they also set in motion changes in professional and patient expectations that would eventually be a factor in toppling the whole structure of segregated medicine.

CHAPTER 6

Blacks and the Southern
Public Health Establishment,
1900–1932

In contrast to the efforts of private parties, the final group with responsibility for the welfare of black Southerners — the region's state and local public health directors — did little either to challenge patterns of segregation or to address black needs. As constituted guardians of the health of the whole citizenry, these public servants bore greatest responsibility for the health of the black population. Yet the fact remains that until the infusion of federal money and larger purpose into Southern public health operations in the New Deal era, they failed their black patrons by a wider margin than any other group.

That failure, however, was not theirs alone. Many times, health officers wanted to do more but were checked by other forces. For example, state legislators and county commissioners in the South had never accepted the idea of substantial public taxation for social welfare — especially when major beneficiaries would be black. As the province, possibilities, and cost of public health activity expanded, those lawmakers gave ground only reluctantly.

White medical establishments were implicated as well. From the start of coherent public health activity in the South — about 1910 — private physicians opposed for economic reasons any health program which approached too close to their domain of curative medicine. Dominating the policy-making bodies of state and local health departments, physicians were always in position to make sure that public programs did not go too far outside desired bounds — and accordingly did not provide black people the kind of help they most needed.

128

If the failure of Southern public health officials had to be shared, it was also true that not all programs failed equally. And what distinguished one agency's record from another was often the element of personal leadership. Where a state health officer was himself insensitive to the needs of black citizens or took a narrow view of the scope of public health work (limiting it, say, to immunizations and environmental sanitation), that state would do well merely to hold the line against rising black morbidity and mortality. But an official who understood the social and economic basis of ill health, was racially fair-minded, and had some command on outside sources of funds could often put together a health program which came far closer to addressing blacks' major problems. In the period from 1900 to the beginning of the New Deal—when the federal government gradually came to set the standard for local health programs—South Carolina offered an illustration of the first kind of public health operation, while North Carolina afforded an example of reasonably solid performance. Georgia's program lay somewhere in between.

Before turning to those accounts, however, it is necessary first to examine the origin of the Southern health establishment's interest in the Negro. In doing so, one sees the same racism, easy optimism, and over-confidence in experts that characterized other Progressive-era reforms. And just as those features frustrated the aims of the Progressive Movement generally, their presence also helps to account for the failings of the Southern health establishment.

Southern health officers, along with a few socially conscious private physicians discovered the "Negro health problem" in the years just before World War I. A variety of things brought that problem into focus. Most Southern states began about 1910 to turn serious attention to collection of vital statistics. That, along with the employment of full-time state health officers around that time, enabled Southern states to watch more carefully for any trend which seemed to threaten the public welfare.[1]

One particularly alarming development was the growing black migration from rural to urban South (chapter 1). As long as they had stayed on plantation and farm, blacks had suffered and died relatively unnoticed, for organized health work and statistical reporting in rural America were virtually nonexistent. But in the city their high rates of morbidity and mortality became matters of public notice, comment, and concern, not just to health officers but to some private physicians as well. Thus, by about 1910, Southern professionals were having to reflect on the social and economic determinants of Negro health—on such issues as housing, life-style, and preventive medical services. With the formation of the Southern Medical Association (1907), interested private physicians had a forum for discussion of such matters and the "Negro health problem" was occasionally the subject of debate at annual meetings of Southern doctors. Health officers had a forum too—the American Public Health Association (APHA, organized in 1872). In 1914 the APHA held its annual meeting in Jacksonville, Florida, where the ill health of Southern blacks was the major focus.[2]

Health officers who met in Jacksonville were of two minds about Negro health, and their discussions revealed in microcosm the shifting attitudes that prevailed among whites in the health profession. All were agreed on the magnitude of black problems. Where they differed was over interpretation. Some took the position, extensively developed by Prudential Insurance Company statistician Frederick L. Hoffman, that "in the struggle for race supremacy the black race is not holding its own." The inevitable result of blacks' attempt to live as a free people, Hoffman asserted, could only be their extinction as a race.[3]

That process seemed to be accelerating with blacks' move to the city. There they were encountering new diseases for which they had little resistance and were living under the most appalling sanitary conditions. Already the black urban death rate was rising and the birth rate falling, and there seemed little hope of reversing those trends. As one frustrated health officer lamented in 1914, blacks did not respond to sanitary instruction as whites did. "When . . . we try to apply these same methods in preventive work among the negroes, it is almost as if we had entered a foreign land. . . . "[4]

The implications of such views were dire. If the race were destined to die out, it was wasteful to spend public funds to shore up its health. That view was summed up by one Southern health administrator who frankly advocated a policy of neglect: "The ultimate extinction of the colored race," he said, "was just a matter of time. Why seek to check the effect of the forces of nature?" The Negro was obviously not in his element on the American continent. Leaving him to his "predestined fate was a simple and effective method of solving a vexing question of race adjustment."[5]

Happily, advocates of a Spencerian solution were a minority. The bulk of Southern health officers who took part in the 1914 discussions believed that by implementing proper sanitary, housing, and social policies, the Negro's health decline could be halted. In fact, it had to be attempted in order to secure the health of whites. As Savannah's city physician put it, one could not keep "half of the community clean with the other half dirty . . . half healthy with the other . . . riddled with disease. . . . It is necessary that the whites, out of their own pocket, in order to protect themselves, furnish the negro with . . . better public charities than exist at present."[6]

Few regarded the task as one that would be easily or speedily achieved. It might take generations, for the Jacksonville conferees were con-

vinced that "negroes will not better themselves. . . . Their nature is such
that benefits . . . have to be given to them, almost forced on them."[7] Indeed, according to some health leaders, only stern policies would suffice.
"Somebody must get behind the negro with authority," a Kentucky official
advised, "and tell him that he must do so and so or 'git'."[8] Galveston's health
officer was prepared to use draconian measures, particularly against blacks
who could not restrain their sexual appetites. "The vagrant negro . . . is
a menace to white health and white security. He is nearly always a criminal
degenerate of high or low degree. I believe that he should be emasculated."[9]

Although racist assumptions underpinned every discussion, a growing number of public physicians were looking beyond so-called Negro traits
to what they regarded as the more basic cause of black ill health: their physical environment. Mobile's city physician noted that blacks were restricted
to the worst neighborhoods—sections that drained poorly and had im-
proper water and sewage. "Who is to blame for that I would like to ask?
. . . These are the conditions the white people provide for the negroes. It
is no wonder we find these unsanitary and unhygenic conditions, and until
they are remedied it does not seem to me that we can accomplish much
. . . . "[10] His Savannah counterpart agreed and insisted that "if they wanted
to help themselves they could not do it." In fact, "it would be just the same
result with the white race if they lived in the same environment."[11]

Although agreeing on a need for environmental reform most public
physicians believed that significant advances were possible in the short run
through health education and better nursing. Over and again they stressed
that the black nurse was best equipped for those tasks. Hospitals and health
departments could not do any better than to employ Negro nurses, because
they "can get at . . . [the Negro patients] when white nurses can't."[12] A curious blend of condescension and concern lay back of this and other proposals for black uplift. Jacksonville's health director summed up a common
attitude: "this race, so recently removed from savagery, is by nature imita-
tive, a characteristic which can be used to advantage in their sanitary education. They are, however, suspicious of our own race . . . and they will, in
many instances, receive instruction and assistance more readily from one
of their own color."[13]

But nothing would happen unless someone made it happen. Among
all but race fatalists the feeling was virtually unanimous that Southern
health officers were the ones who must shoulder responsibility for stopping
the decline of black health and improving the future. As one Louisiana
health officer and admitted white supremacist put it, it was the least whites
could do. "Now that the negro is removed from the plain of political action
[by constitutional disenfranchisement in the 1890s], his social and political
status as a child race thoroughly understood and settled forever in the' South,

we are confronted with a sacred duty . . . of improving his material welfare and especially his health."[14] That task was enormous, but a Virginia physician believed that Southern doctors were equal to it. "It is up to the physicians in the South," said John Lloyd, "to get in behind this movement and see if we can't shove it across. Now, it takes a long time, but the doctors, if they will work together, have a tremendous power in legislation, and legislation is the only way that we can meet this demand."[15]

To an extent such pronouncements merely reflect the high self-esteem common to all professional groups. On the other hand, assertions of responsibility were voiced so often and so sincerely that one suspects that white public physicians in the South really did feel a duty to help blacks. Whether their commitment would last and whether they realistically appraised their ability to effect needed reforms in the midst of intense white opposition to costly black welfare programs, only time would tell.

In several respects, the pre–World War I era did not offer a fair test of those officials' ability to act on their good intentions. For one thing, Southern states had only recently committed themselves to maintaining full-time health departments; and pre-war health budgets, yet unsupplemented with federal money, remained miniscule by contrast to those of many Northern states. In the Carolinas in 1915, state government allotted only about two cents per person for health programs, while Massachusetts spent three times as much. Except for North Carolina, which got an early start, county health work was still poorly organized in the South (and elsewhere) in 1915, despite the impetus from the Hookworm Commission. In North Carolina 7 counties (out of 100) spent $125,000 to maintain full-time health departments. South Carolina had 3 units (among 46 counties), all in urban districts, while Georgia with its 169 counties had none.[16]

Work at the state level was mostly focused on vital statistics and control of such contagious diseases as smallpox, typhoid fever, and diphtheria. There simply was not money, staff, or will for problems striking hardest at blacks—such as maternal and infant mortality, malaria, TB, or VD (whose dimensions were not even known). Pellagra also hurt blacks more than whites, although mill hands bore the heaviest burden. But even had sufficient funds been available, little could have been done to contain it, for until the 1920s its cause, prevention and cure remained mysteries. Thus, pre-war years were spent mostly putting out fires and laying administrative foundations.[17]

The era's only real test of professional determination to respond to black health needs centered around TB control. On that issue the verdict must be that white health officers failed the challenge. Most Southern states had built TB sanatoria for whites by 1915 (North Carolina in 1908, Georgia in 1911, and South Carolina in 1915).[18] But blacks were not even considered when plans were laid. The tacit understanding was that, in the face of limited resources, whites came first. Only in penitentiaries or mental hospitals could tubercular Negroes get adequate treatment. That, said a Virginia doctor, meant that a black "had to commit a felony, steal a horse, or break into a house before he had any chance to get well from consumption. The law-abiding darkey . . . could only die."[19]

There was of course a limit to what private and public physicians could do to reduce TB. Not only was medical intervention of limited value (by comparison, say, with economic status), but sanatoria questions were decided by legislative assemblies, not medical societies or state boards of health. Yet there was no indication that physicians even took exception to exclusionist plans when these were first laid. Not until 1917 did the South's organized physicians raise a protest to such policy, motivated in part by the example of Virginia and Louisiana blacks who, in the face of public indifference, built their own sanatoria.[20]

With the advent of World War I, some of the conditions which had frustrated earlier good intentions — lack of resources and a health focus limited to community sanitation — began to change. By 1918 in all states, health money was available in unprecedented quantities, and in the South there was a growing willingness to spend it in ways that had not been contemplated before — even on projects where blacks would be major beneficiaries. What happened was that the war suddenly awakened the nation to its poor state of health. To a people who prided itself on its strength and vigor, Selective Service examinations delivered a painful shock. In South Carolina one-third of 1917 draftees failed to pass induction physicals. Ten percent were syphilitic, and thirteen of every one thousand were labeled feebleminded. The repetition of that appalling record in every state (with the South in the lead), coupled with the vibrant patriotism of wartime, produced a national determination to eliminate underlying causes.[21]

In addition to revealing unsuspected problems, war also gave the entire South its first chance to see the results of adequately funded health promotion. Beginning in 1917, areas around military camps, many of them in the South, were subjected to intensive cleanup campaigns. The main objective was to safeguard troops. But as that could not be done without giving attention to surrounding civilian areas, many long-standing Southern health problems, such as malaria and VD, got attention for the first time. By no means were war-born projects pointed at blacks, but in several cases the focus was on those citizens unable to afford private services. Where that was so, blacks benefited substantially.

What happened in South Carolina was fairly typical, in terms of both specific projects and changes in popular attitude. In 1917 the Palmetto State became the site of three major Army camps, established near Greenville,

Spartanburg, and Columbia; and a primary concern was to protect soldiers against malaria, which was prevalent in all three areas. The largest of the new posts was Camp Jackson, located on a swampy site just to the east of Columbia. What the Army and PHS did there would be repeated later at Camps Wadsworth (Spartanburg) and Sevier (Greenville).

Beginning in July 1917, and continuing over the next year, local government and the Red Cross and, later, the PHS began draining marshy areas and oiling streams, not just at the camp but in the surrounding community. The effect was immediately apparent. At Camp Jackson only one soldier contracted malaria during the year, and in Columbia an examination of two thousand children in 1918 failed to produce a single case.[22]

State health officer James A. Hayne saw the work in broader perspective. South Carolina, he told Governor Richard Manning, had many areas "that are very fertile and yet are uninhabited or sparsely settled on account of malaria." If the Camp Jackson work could be extended statewide, the economic possibilities were enormous, and in the years after the war Hayne would promote anti-malarial work as a major goal, stressing its potential for opening rural South Carolina to white settlement.[23]

Equally valuable (and instructive) was the wartime attack on VD. The assembling of a massive draftee army forced South Carolina — and every other state with a military base — to confront a major problem whose very existence had been ignored. For strategic and political reasons, Secretary of War Newton Baker was determined to hold syphilis and gonorrhea in the camps to an absolute minimum. Doing that required cleaning up near-by civilian populations as well, and in fall, 1917, the PHS (cooperating with the Red Cross) opened civilian VD clinics in each cantonment town, where infected individuals could report for free treatment.[24]

Then in April 1918, as a result of federal pressure for more comprehensive action at the local level, South Carolina's General Assembly passed the state's first VD control law, requiring reporting of cases and giving strong regulatory power to its board of health. The first regulations required medical tests for suspected carriers, as well as anyone arrested or convicted for sex-related offenses. Treatment was mandatory (but free), and all persons not complying would be reported to authorities. To help states pay for such programs and extend the battle nationwide, Congress, in May 1918, passed the Chamberlain-Kahn Act, which provided $1 million a year to help states fund VD control programs. To snare the federal bounty each state had to appropriate matching funds and create a permanent VD division within its board of health.[25]

Not until early 1919 did South Carolina meet those requirements (and collect its $16,440), but thereafter its VD program expanded rapidly. Inside a year division head C.V. Akin, a PHS officer assigned to the state, increased its major clinics from three to eight and laid plans for facilities in all counties. Clinic clientele grew apace, and signs were that infected individuals were accepting treatment willingly. In 1918 clinic patients were mostly prostitutes or other lawbreakers whom the courts ordered to report. A year later 90 percent of them (mostly blacks) came voluntarily, a situation that would not have developed had not the twenty or more treatments of arsphenamine and bismuth been free. Surveying progress Akin and health officer Hayne grew confident that South Carolina was on the way to eliminating a long-ignored disease.[26]

One other important area that began to receive attention during the war was that of infant and child health, a field South Carolina had also previously overlooked. At the national level interest in child health had already developed owing to impetus from the Progressive Movement. The creation of the United States Children's Bureau in 1912 was one reflection of that interest, and by the outbreak of war it had proven the connection between infant deaths and low family income.[27] But it was the war's terrible toll on adults and its revelations of widespread deficiencies among youth that gave the greatest push to the child health movement. State board of health president Robert Wilson knew that most defects could have been corrected had a physician recognized them earlier. The fact that no doctor had done so, he added, "emphasized the great need" for child health work.[28]

Although no program emerged during the war, Wilson and his fellow board members used the period to good effect by conducting a state-wide speakers' campaign to convince fellow physicians and state and local political leaders of the need for funds. They were helped by Ruth Dodd, a public health nurse whom they had chosen to head any new bureau, and by the Children's Bureau, which in 1918 launched a much-publicized "save the child" campaign.[29]

Thus when South Carolina legislators convened in January 1919, the health board's request for ten thousand dollars to start a bureau of child hygiene won easy approval. With those and added monies from counties and the Metropolitan Life Insurance Company, Dodd was able to put twelve nurses in the field. Besides prenatal and infant care, they held sick baby clinics, taught classes of mothers and midwives, and examined school children. At year's end the board also finally began to address the problem of Negro midwives, by adopting an examination and licensing requirement based on that of New York.[30]

One reason for the continuance of South Carolina's health reform zeal beyond 1918 was military demobilization. The public was eager to cater to the expectations of its ex-servicemen, and good health was one of them. As Hayne explained, "the returning soldiers . . . had been taught how dependent was each individual upon the proper conduct of every other individual if a camp or community was to be kept free from disease. Their sanitary conscience was awakened, and they demanded the same paternal care from the State that had been provided by the U.S. government in safeguarding them from preventable disease."[31] A grateful nation would want to satisfy that demand, Hayne believed, and indeed South Carolina seemed as optimistic about health prospects as he was. State appropriations for health work, which had climbed slowly from $32,000 to $43,000 between 1915 and 1918, in 1919 vaulted to $77,500. "All you had to do," Hayne enthused, "was to shake the money tree and the money dropped."[32]

Even South Carolina blacks, whom the board of health had never singled out for care, benefited from the mounting interest. Besides attention received from VD and child health projects, in 1919 the General Assembly, at Hayne's urging, agreed to erect a black pavilion at the state TB sanatorium. The number of beds was pitifully inadequate, and the legislature required blacks to raise about one-third of the cost, but South Carolina had at least finally recognized its responsibility to help blacks contend with their major health dilemma.[33]

In neighboring North Carolina and Georgia the war sparked similar expansion. North Carolina established its child hygiene bureau a year before South Carolina. Although there were not sufficient public health nurses available, due to military needs, the board of health formed a nucleus of experienced practical nurses who in turn trained a coterie of laywomen in each county to carry needed instruction in infant care to state mothers. As in South Carolina, the general assembly in North Carolina also authorized a TB sanatorium for blacks, allotting $100,000 for the facility (compared to the lower state's $20,000). Georgia would eventually move in the same direction, although not until 1927, when the opening of a new facility for whites finally freed the old sanatorium for blacks.[34]

Thus, as the 1920s began, the two Carolinas and Georgia were taking their first tentative steps toward resolving the most serious Negro health problems—TB, VD, and threats to maternity and infancy. But the ability of state boards to expand their efforts into programs that could substantially improve black morbidity and mortality would hinge on several factors. Among them were the state of the economy, availability of outside aid, willingness of whites to continue projects whose major beneficiaries were black, and the pace of development of the county health units that would deliver actual services.

In the 1920s and early 1930s that constellation of factors proved on the whole unfavorable to the development of health programs for blacks in those Southeastern states. For one thing the national economy in 1920–22 experienced a serious post-war depression. The downturn was particularly severe in the deep South, for added to the collapse of cotton prices was another invasion by the boll weevil (a troublesome pest since the late nineteenth century), which hit hard at the South's principal money crop for several seasons.[35]

In partial response to weakened economic conditions, the national government, in 1919–20, ended assistance for malaria control and four years later terminated the Chamberlain-Kahn program of VD control. Maternal and child health, however, seemingly presented a different story. In 1922 Congress passed the Sheppard-Towner Act, the nation's first social security program, which provided grants to the states to meet health needs of expectant mothers and newborns. Yet the law (and an adequate program) required the states to provide matching dollars. In the face of a depressed economy, that was hard for Southerns states to do. South Carolina did not do it, and Georgia's legislature was only slightly more responsive.

Even had there not been economic constraints, racial calculation would have made it hard to attract money for any public programs operating primarily or even largely in the interest of black health, as Negro tuberculosis sanatoria and VD, malaria, and maternity and infancy projects would clearly do. The majority of lawmakers felt an inbred aversion to such proposals. Legislators less bound by bigotry still found it necessary to register opposition, but for a more practical reason: there was no advantage to be gained in aiding a segment of the population that had no votes to give in return.[36]

Programs seemingly as unobjectionable as those aiding mothers and children got tangled in racial calculation. The problem was that while such efforts would help whites, they would unavoidably shower benefits on blacks. Accordingly, any legislator recommending too lavish support risked public censure. Columbia University historian Frank Tannenbaum in *Darker Phases of the South* (1924) suggested why: "Whites are in fear of being outbred. They could not look with favor upon a large-scale program of child care and child saving. The fecundity of the colored race is so great in comparison to the whites that there would immediately arise an underground pressure of public sentiment against any program of basic health activity . . . which would, as it must inevitably do, cut down the death rate of the Negro also."[37] As a result, observed black sociologist E. Franklin Frazier, "it has been well nigh impossible in the South to get communities to adopt health programs when it was thought that the Negro would share the benefits." Even where disease among blacks posed a clear menace to whites, they "hesitated between the evil of sharing the ill health of the Negro and giving him a better physical basis of propagation."[38]

An additional barrier to the delivery of services to blacks was the slow growth of county health units, which was tied closely to economic conditions and to some degree to race feeling. However elaborate the intentions and plans drawn up in state health offices, unless there were medical directors, sanitarians, and public health nurses at the local level, sick people did not get help. At best, growth in county health organization was slow. In North Carolina the 32 organized counties (of 100) of 1924 expanded to just 36 by 1930. Lamentably, if understandably, it was the poorest counties, often with the heaviest black populations, which were usually without such organization. In Georgia the situation was nearly hopeless. Next to Texas, Georgia had the nation's largest number of local government units (169). Most were small, isolated counties without resources to support a full-time health officer and with a private physician population who regarded public health as a socialistic encroachment on their right to substantial income. As of 1915 Georgia had still not organized its first county health unit.[39]

It was not surprising, therefore, that many of the programs begun with such high hopes in the war period and just afterward foundered in the early and middle 1920s, as wartime idealism receded. The decline was most evident in South Carolina and Georgia. In the former, anti-malarial work continued a couple of years beyond the war, but only with the aid of grants from the (Rockefeller) International Health Board and the PHS. Their aim was to demonstrate the effectiveness of low-cost mosquito control and thus entice the state to extend the work into the more diseased rural sections. Effectiveness was duly established, but neither state nor local governments were willing to bear the cost after outside funding ended in 1921.[40]

In the maternal-infant area South Carolina continued funding through most of the decade, encouraged by the availability of federal money under the Sheppard-Towner Act. But after the mid-1920s the state program relied increasingly on federal money alone, and in 1928 (two years before termination of the national law) South Carolina ended its contributions. Never did the state take advantage of supplemental federal grants, for that would have meant more local money. Thus, maternal-infant work was always a bare-bones operation, concentrating not on primary care of needy clients, as Washington envisaged, but on midwife training, school inspection, and infant care instruction, all delivered from the state level. Only one staff member (of eight) was black, a field nurse, who in the nine years of the program was only able to cover each county once.[41]

The TB sanatorium program was similarly deficient. By the end of the decade the facility in Columbia was able to hold about 230 patients, but 90 percent of them were white. Even white children outnumbered blacks (by 50 percent). Although Hayne and his board continually pleaded for money to expand the number of beds for blacks, nothing was done. As a result of their long wait (plus the susceptibility of blacks to miliary TB), by the time blacks entered the sanatorium most were seriously ill. Consequently, hospitalized blacks died at about four times the rate of whites. Instead of serving the black community as a place of first resort, as it did whites, South Carolina's sanatorium tended to be a site for holding black incurables until death claimed them.[42]

Venereal disease control simply stopped in South Carolina in 1924. Earlier, Hayne had argued that by banishing VD the state could substantially eliminate its high welfare bills, for it was syphilitics, he told the legislature, who filled "our insane asylums, our poor houses, our TB sanatoria and all other places that demand the taxpayers' money. . . . " But with the termination of federal assistance in 1923, the promise of long-run economies no longer seemed attractive to lawmakers. The next year state aid dried up, and all VD work ceased. Hayne and board president Robert Wilson appealed strongly to the legislature to resume funding, but to no avail. The next year even the appeals stopped, and it was not until fourteen years later (when, again, federal money became available) that the state board again moved against VD.[43]

Georgia's legislature was equally reluctant to fund programs giving substantial (or even any) benefits to Afro-Americans. Sanatorium care became available only when whites were able to vacate their old facility for a new one (1927).[44] Control for VD failed to receive much support from the state even in the flush post-war period. What funding there was did continue through the decade, but Georgia health officer T.P. Abercrombie, for example, never had enough to set up clinics and had to concentrate on health education, a work of dubious benefit without free treatment. The state maternal-infant program also got off to a slow start, for the assembly balked at the notion of matching funds. As a result, Georgia, like South Carolina, lost considerable Sheppard-Towner money. But unlike its neighbor, Georgia increased its commitment somewhat as the decade wore on, attracting additional federal funding, which enabled the state to offer medical services to at least a few. The main innovation was a fully equipped health-mobile, which traveled through rural Georgia in the late 1920s giving free medical examinations as well as instruction in sanitation and nutrition, often in regions beyond the reach of local health units or doctors. Administrative supervision of both VD and maternal-infant programs was seriously handicapped, though, by having one director oversee both divisions.[45]

If it is generally true to say that the Southern states failed to meet the pressing health needs of black citizens in the 1920–33 period, they did not all fail to the same degree. In North Carolina, in fact, attention to black health problems was remarkable, given the constraints of a separate-but-unequal social order. That was not to say that North Carolina had a model program. VD work, for example, after a strong beginning in 1919, was defunct by about mid-decade, so far as any semblance of a statewide program was concerned. But overall, North Carolina gave more attention to Negro health than any other Southern state.

Although Negro TB failed to get adequate attention, by contrast with neighboring states North Carolina did reasonably well in terms of both budget and program. Its initial (1919) investment in black sanatorium care was larger; there were more TB beds for North Carolina blacks; and by 1929 sanatorium trustees—who constituted a body distinct from the board of health—could boast thirty-one diagnostic clinics across the state, serving both races.[46]

The state's relatively strong commitment to Negro health was apparent, too, in maternity and infant work. Unlike Georgia, a state of comparable total population, North Carolina took full advantage of the federal fund in the early 1920s, and in the later half of the decade, while South Carolina was gradually abandoning its commitment, North Carolina's services were on the rise. What particularly set its work apart was the willingness of the board of health to expend substantial money on curative medicine, notably in statewide surgical clinics for correction of tonsil and adenoid problems among children of indigent families. Although black children probably merited more attention, project staff allotted at least one of every four clinics to them, a number roughly equal to the proportion of blacks in the population (29 percent). If fairly administered, the program was also unprecedented in that it represented an invasion by the state into the field of curative medicine. That was apparent in 1921 from the angry protest of one county medical society which objected that the "treatment of disease as instituted by the state board is looking toward socialistic medicine and is a step toward state paternalism."[47]

Another undertaking unique to North Carolina in the South was a separate and quite amply funded bureau for medical inspection of schools. While all Southern states paid lip service to the idea of school examinations, North Carolina alone committed large funds and staff to do a fairly complete job. According to first director George Cooper, "the Negro schools have been visited just as the white schools and the Negro child given the same examinations that are accorded the whites."[48] Moreover, Cooper decided early on to use as many Negro health professionals as he could. In 1920 North Carolina became the first Southern state to put a black dentist on its board of health staff, and virtually every county health department, thanks to prodding from the state office, employed one or two black nurses.[49]

Discovering *why* different arrangements prevailed in North Carolina is more difficult than showing that they did. The Tarheel State suffered the same kind of economic malaise as its neighbors in the early 1920s, and the extinction of federal programs was felt just as keenly there. Moreover, the kind of racially biased thinking that dominated other Southern states was also present in North Carolina. On the other hand, the relatively small proportion of blacks in the population (29 percent, contrasted to 37 and 45 percent, respectively, in Georgia and South Carolina) perhaps acted as a brake on the kind of Negrophobia pervasive elsewhere in the deep South.[50] White North Carolinians, not feeling quite as overwhelmed by the black presence as their embattled neighbors did, could thus afford to deal a bit more generously with their black fellow citizens.

In addition one could argue that North Carolina did more for black people because it had more to work with. State and local governments, as well as outside agencies like the Children's Bureau, the PHS, and the International Health Board, were far more generous to North Carolina than to South Carolina or Georgia. In 1930 the North Carolina legislature, historically a more progressive body, provided a health appropriation averaging 6.5 cents per capita, while the general assemblies of the other two states gave about 25 percent less. Likewise the Rockefeller Foundation in the 1920s spent some $150,000 in North Carolina, compared to $111,000 and $78,000 in South Carolina and Georgia.[51]

But to argue that greater resources explained the differences in performance begs the question, for it leaves unexplained *why* North Carolina attracted more funding in the first place and why it utilized those resources more effectively. All other things being equal — and in the deep South they were more or less equal from state to state where blacks were concerned — the volume of services provided Southern blacks in a particular area was primarily a function of local leadership. And that meant chiefly the state health officer, for it was he who provided impetus for the total program, represented it to legislators and the public, and acted as contact with outside funders.

Nowhere was the influence of the state health officer more apparent (and crucial) than in the two Carolinas, whose public health programs, up to the Depression, were in large part reflections of the two men who directed them, James A. Hayne in South Carolina and Watson Smith Rankin in North Carolina. On each man fell essentially the same tasks, and in the final analysis Rankin's (and North Carolina's) success in reaching blacks far exceeded Hayne's (and South Carolina's), not just because of the former's larger abilities and more enlightened outlook on race, but also because Rankin proved much more adept at pushing back the restrictions which hemmed in every health officer who sought to improve the lives of Southern blacks.

In the South of the 1920s even the most skilled, well-intentioned health officer had to face up to certain limits when it came to race. Until the late 1930s when federal funds lifted much of the burden of health protection off the states (and simultaneously diminished the influence of local leaderships), no health officer could realistically hope, or dare to ask, for legislative support for programs designed primarily in aid of blacks.

The combination of economic and racial barriers would have discouraged the most aggressive and reform-minded health leader. For South Carolina's James A. Hayne (1872–1953), they proved virtually paralyzing. Descendent of an old and honored South Carolina family, Hayne was largely the product of a South Carolina upbringing and education. With the exception of a final undergraduate year at the University of Virginia, his schools included the Citadel, the University of South Carolina, and (for medicine) the state medical college in Charleston. In 1911, following some seven years with the PHS and the Army in such far-flung posts as the Panama Canal Zone (where he assisted in yellow fever eradication) and Fort D.A. Russell in Wyoming, Hayne was chosen as state health officer of South Carolina, a post he held until 1944.[52]

As an administrator Hayne's approach was exceedingly cautious. Although he was the health leader of a state with mammoth health deficiencies and although he enjoyed near-unlimited tenure, Hayne nonetheless hesitated to take even a small step beyond the line of broad public acceptance. He viewed his role, in fact, much like that of a political representative who strove to reflect the will of constituents — and nothing more. His was "an elected office," he once said, which meant that he "would not act until he felt the voter wanted the action."[53]

Yet even had Hayne been willing to take a more independent course, he would not have sought to implement programs carrying substantial benefits to blacks. Though by no means a racist of the stamp of "Cotton Ed" Smith, Cole L. Blease, and other South Carolina demagogues of his day, Hayne was a white supremacist. To him, the Negro, especially the sick Negro, whom he blamed for South Carolina's poor showing in national mortality tables, was primarily an embarrassment, not a challenge. In fact, it was questionable whether Hayne took black ill health seriously as a board responsibility. On several occasions he stated that, but for the black, South Carolina would have had an enviable health record. When the black birth rate exceeded the white, Hayne was dejected; when the opposite happened, Hayne rejoiced.[54]

To be sure, he was in the forefront of those pressing for more Negro beds at the state TB sanatorium, and it was largely his efforts which initiated reform in midwife practice. But Hayne's primary motivation was his desire to protect the health of whites, who might come in contact with Negro tuberculins or South Carolina's mostly black midwives. On the latter danger he confided to a national health meeting in 1924 that "in my state 80 per cent of the colored population are attended by midwives." That was "bad enough," but even worse was the fact that "20 per cent of the white population are also attended by the dirty, ignorant midwives."[55]

Hayne's notion of an ideal state was South Carolina without blacks. That was why he took such comfort from any statistics showing relative decline in their birth rate. That was also why he viewed with pleasure the steady drop in the percentage of blacks in South Carolina's population, which led him once to quip before a national meeting that "for a long time we had more Negroes than whites, but that distinction has passed to Mississippi at present."[56]

Although he would have regarded as reprehensible any attempt to exclude blacks from on-going programs, Hayne took a particular interest in those projects which favored or accorded a special advantage to whites. His enthusiasm for hookworm control prior to World War I and, later, his great concern about pellagra were partly the result of his belief, correct in the first instance and misinformed in the second, that those two maladies were primarily white afflictions.

Race played an even greater role in inspiring Hayne's interest in malaria control, which was one of his abiding passions, along with sanitary privy construction. Malaria was particularly a problem in South Carolina's coastal lowlands, a region whose population in 1920 was nearly two-thirds black. Though malaria struck hardest at blacks, Hayne's primary interest in controlling the disease lay not in improving their health but in making the area more attractive to whites, who he hoped would migrate into the low country in sufficient numbers to displace blacks. As he told state legislators in 1921, "we must get rid of malaria if we are going to have white immigrants." It was the threat of disease that had driven whites away, he argued, but an investment in malaria control could reverse that outflow, and "many counties . . . which are now given over to negroes and negro tenants will be occupied by white people and the fertile soil of these counties properly utilized." Not until whites replaced blacks could that area enjoy prosperity, because the "low country negro is usually incapable of the highly specialized knowledge necessary for truck farming" which "thrifty white emigrants" alone could undertake.[57] Although Hayne never secured the funds needed for effective malaria control, he kept up the effort, for he remained convinced that "when you remove that black belt then you wipe out the blackening of that part of the country. The Negro will live where he has malaria, but the white man will not."[58]

In fairness to Hayne, it must be added that prejudice was not the only basis of his policy priorities. He gave relatively less attention to such measures as VD control and maternal and child health partly because he was less attuned to the newer (post–World War I) thrust of public health, which put primary stress on personal health services rather than more traditional environmental protection. Hayne was a product of the old school of public health. His first field experience — in the Panama Canal Zone helping combat yellow fever — marked him deeply. Throughout his career his interests centered about community sanitation and the fight against epidemic disease. As public health approaches shifted, Hayne found it difficult to change with them, partly because the newer emphasis on individual services would invade the sphere of private doctors and partly, perhaps, because it would bring greatest benefit to blacks. That was not to say that he was uninterested in VD and diseases of mothers and infants, but as supporting funds dwindled in the 1920s Hayne accepted the collapse of those projects without much protest. Had he been able to attract outside funding from Washington or private foundations he would have happily continued such programs. But he did not energetically seek such aid.[59]

Even had he done so he would likely have failed, because among outside funders Hayne and the South Carolina Board of Health were held in low esteem. In the 1920s the PHS, for one, regarded South Carolina as a poor risk for the rather limited funds it had to invest in the states. Hayne, himself, seemed the major problem. Owing his appointment as health officer (in 1911) partly to the intervention of his well-connected and politically powerful family, Hayne was seen in Washington as an inept administrator and a man of questionable professional standing and little political influence. As a PHS field representative reported in 1926, "the health administration in . . . [South Carolina] is seemingly a hopeless conflict. To be successful one must be a native and a relative of those in authority."[60]

A persistent difficulty concerned Hayne's use of federal funds. In the 1920s the PHS looked on its state grants as seed money to assist local health officers with demonstration projects that would be used to convince legislators to take over programs on their own. Hayne, whether because of his reluctance or his inability, seldom succeeded in getting South Carolina's legislature to make such a commitment. Consequently, he was often pleading with Washington to extend support beyond the time agreed on, because "the total health appropriation [in South Carolina] must not be increased if it can be avoided lest it draw the lightning of economizing politicians."[61]

In response the PHS came to regard South Carolina as a "burden," and Hayne as someone who was willing to let Washington do his work for him.[62] As a result South Carolina found the PHS less and less generous. Once, when Hayne failed to find the local monies he had promised to support the work of a Service bacteriologist, Surgeon General H.S. Cumming ended federal support. Perhaps, he told Hayne, "the withdrawal of the Public Health Service will be a real assistance to you in that it may enable you to make clear to the state legislature the vital necessity of adequate appropriation. . . . "[63]

Dr. James Adams Hayne (c. 1922), state health officer of South Carolina from 1911–44. Courtesy of the South Carolina Department of Health and Environmental Control.

By the end of the 1920s South Carolina was finding it hard to get funds from Washington even when needs were pressing. In 1930 Hayne appealed for a PHS officer to assist him in educating the public about the importance of diet in preventing pellagra. The situation was bad in South Carolina, he reported, and there was neither money nor staff to do what was needed. If only the Service could help, "many people would be prevented from dying or going insane. . . . "[64]

After a month's consideration Cumming replied that, regrettably, he could not help: the PHS did not have an officer to spare. Privately, Cumming and colleagues stated their conviction that because of its leadership South Carolina would be a "poor selection" as a place for a demonstration in pellagra control. "The state health officer, along with two or three others high up in medical and public health councils, have spared no effort to oppose and obstruct the views adopted and proven by surgeon [Joseph] Goldberger and, with the state health officer, as leader and principal spokesman, have waged a continuous campaign of distructive criticism." Before any fruitful cooperation was possible, attitudes (and perhaps leadership) in South Carolina would have to change.[65]

A quite different set of attitudes prevailed across the border in North Carolina, largely due to the leadership and influence of Watson Smith Rankin (1879–1970). A North Carolina native, Rankin received a medical education that was a microcosm of the changes underway in the profession in the early twentieth century. He began at tiny North Carolina Medical College (the school would later fall victim to the Flexner Report) but transferred to the University of Maryland at Baltimore for his degree in 1901. He added a nice finishing touch by taking a post-graduate year at the Johns Hopkins, returning home to engage in private practice for several years in a rural community in the North Carolina piedmont. In 1904, distressed by the intellectual stagnation that he saw awaiting him as a rural practitioner, he accepted a pathology professorship at the Wake Forest College of Medicine, becoming its dean in 1905. Then in 1909, motivated by a growing interest in preventive medicine, notably in hookworm eradication, Rankin joined the North Carolina Board of Health as its first full-time health officer.[66]

As a health administrator Rankin differed fundamentally from Hayne and in ways which bore directly on the quality of health services available to North Carolina blacks. First and foremost, he exhibited little of Hayne's racism. Privately he might have shared the outlook of other white North Carolinians, accepting segregation as a given, but, unlike Hayne, his personal views did not affect his professional outlook. As a medical officer, strongly imbued with the research ethic, he was interested only in biological facts. The primary fact was there were a great number of people in North Carolina who were sick and in need of primary and preventive medical care. That some were black and some white made not the slightest difference. To Rankin, there were problems to be solved and people to be helped, and that was the end of it. He did recognize that blacks suffered to a greater degree than whites, and while he made no special appeals in their name, he strove consistently to improve delivery of services to them. To that end, when sizeable funds became available for VD control in 1919, Rankin and members of his board met with black leaders to plan the most effective means of utilizing the money. As a result of these consultations, extremely rare in those days (whether with white or black laymen), black churches and fraternal organizations in North Carolina took a lead role in VD work.[67]

Although no special pleader for blacks, Rankin did not shy away from programs which would bring them substantial benefit. Unlike Hayne, Rankin was convinced by war's end that health work could no longer be focused primarily on sanitation and contagious diseases — to him an overly narrow view that defined health merely as the absence of serious illness. For Rankin health also embodied wellness, and achieving that goal required increased public attention to preventive medical care, even if that meant entering the treatment field.[68]

Two new projects reflected this line of thinking. One was a program of physical examinations for adults, initiated in 1918 under the auspices of county health departments and in cooperation with local physicians. Called the Life Extension project, its aim was early disease detection, and it was modeled on the Life Extension Institute created in 1914 by the insurance industry to reduce mortality among policy holders. Although, owing to loss of key personnel, the project survived less than two years, some four thousand physicals were administered in four counties before its demise. The other effort, which was started about the same time and continued through the 1920s, was the medical inspection of schools discussed earlier. Conducted in all hundred counties, the North Carolina program was unique among Southern states in mandating that all children with serious defects be taken to health clinics for free or reduced-price treatments if their parents could not afford private care.[69]

Treatment of individuals by public health physicians was — for North Carolina and the nation — a radical departure from the tradition of fee-for-service medicine. That such a program was initiated in North Carolina was, again, a result of the larger view which Rankin had of public health. Sounding a note which would be widely voiced only in the 1930s, when national health insurance proposals began to win strong backing, Rankin estimated that "but one-fifth of the diseases of adult life which needed medical treatment are receiving it" from the private sector. Moreover, 30 percent of expectant mothers got only scanty prenatal care and no medical attention at time of delivery. Physicians might claim to be giving adequate service to indigent and isolated segments of the population, but Rankin knew otherwise: "the field of medicine that is occupied is not more than one-third or, more probably, one-fifth the field of existing and urgent medical need."[70]

The question demanding immediate attention was who was going to meet this need. Rankin frankly despaired over the likelihood that private medicine would take necessary initiatives, at least in the foreseeable future. Physicians had made admirable progress in acquiring scientific knowledge necessary to combat disease, but in the process of developing as scientists they had allowed their "social outlook" to atrophy. Until the profession rediscovered its social vision, which Rankin hoped would be achieved by reforms in medical education and re-direction of AMA leadership, responsibility for taking the necessary "social action" would have to be shouldered by those in public medicine.[71]

That Rankin was able to convince North Carolina physicians to support a few public programs in curative medicine was partly due to wartime enthusiasm for national fitness. But that faded rather quickly, as witnessed in South Carolina, and could not have given North Carolina programs much beyond initial impetus. More important as a motivating force was Rankin's personal prestige and influence. Victor C. Vaughan, an internationally known physician long associated with the Rockefeller Foundation, once called Rankin one of the three best health officers in the nation and the North Carolina Board of Health the "most alert, wide-awake, efficient and progressive health department in the country."[72] It was that prestige that Rankin called upon when he appealed to North Carolina physicians for support for innovative programs.

The tonsil and adenoid clinics, started in 1918, illustrated his ability to get private doctors to go along with projects they would normally have opposed. Able to show that many children were not being treated because of parental poverty, Rankin got the North Carolina Medical Association to endorse the public program, even though it meant a direct, state invasion of private medicine. So sure was he of his ground that when the Guilford County Medical Society attacked the program as being an entering wedge of socialized medicine, Rankin gave dissident doctors a stinging rebuke. They claimed that the clinics reflected poorly on their willingness to treat patients in their region. Rankin replied that the profession's "willingness or its unwillingness has little to do with the matter. The fact exists that these children are not treated and that fact by itself accounts for and necessitates the position of the state."[73]

The kind of respect Rankin enjoyed in North Carolina extended also to Washington and to national foundations. As a result, the North Carolina

Board of Health emerged in the 1920s as a kind of pet of such groups as the PHS, the Children's Bureau, the Rockefeller Foundation, and the Rosenwald Fund, all of which looked on the state as a pacesetter and were willing to invest substantially more money there than in other Southern states. Though strong programs were what won North Carolina its glittering image, Rankin's close personal contacts with outside agencies surely helped maintain it. For example, John A. Ferrell, the associate director of the Rockefeller Foundation and head of its cooperative program in the states, had been a county health officer in North Carolina during Rankin's early period.[74]

An added measure of Rankin's influence and a further explanation of North Carolina's progressive approach to the black health issue was the administrative staff he assembled to help conduct state and county programs. Where questions of race intersected those of health, individuals like John Ferrell and George Cooper showed themselves to be broad-gauged professionals who, like Rankin, set personal views aside and focused attention and energy on facts alone. As one of Rankin's early county health directors, Ferrell was color-blind when it came to meeting black health needs. Years later, after he had moved to the Rockefeller Foundation, he told an APHA audience that "any program for the improvement of health and the lowering of death rates in the South must afford [the] negro health protection."[75]

George Cooper spent his entire professional career with the North Carolina Board of Health, serving as Rankin's director of maternity and infancy work. In 1931 he was asked to address a group of white North Carolina clergy on black health problems and the board's response to them. Presented in a private session, Cooper's remarks could be considered a frank and honest assessment of not only the board's performance, but his own as well.

Cooper admitted that North Carolina "has not done all for the advancement of the health of its Negro population that it should do." But the board had not fully lived up to its responsibilities to whites either. The important thing was that progress "is being made all the time." Cooper, in fact, defied anyone to prove that North Carolina's health department had consciously discriminated against Negro citizens:

> "In all the . . . work since I have been a member of the staff . . . there has never been any difference in the work that the Board has endeavored to do among the white and Negro races. Naturally, the white people, being better organized and having better facilities for carrying on preventive work, have had most benefits from much of the public health work. At the same time, in all the great preventive efforts sponsored by the board, . . . the Negroes have had their full share of all such efforts."[75]

Although M.O. Bousfield and other outspoken Negro physician-activists would have taken issue with the "full share" claim, Cooper read the record right when he emphasized that the state board "has no prejudices to live down and no fallacies to support."[76]

Another health professional, whose work touched closely the needs of North Carolina blacks and who also mirrored Rankin's outlook, was L.B. McBrayer, who became head of the state TB sanatorium in 1913. Though his agency was separate from Rankin's, the latter had input into McBrayer's selection. Brought to Raleigh after several successful years of sanatorium direction in Asheville, McBrayer recognized the greater threat that the disease presented to blacks and was determined that the state should offer more than token attention to the problem. Insufficient beds meant not only more Negro deaths but also the inability of untreated TB victims, outside the hospital, ever to find jobs to support their families. Many states used cost as a reason for not acting decisively, but McBrayer did "not agree for a moment that any state in the South could not put up a sufficient amount of facilities to care for the white and the Negro races." Ample care for blacks was crucial to protecting whites, but it was also a matter of elemental fairness: "We as guardians more or less for the colored race have no right to send them out to be treated worse than we treat our lower animals."[77] Although McBrayer never obtained the legislative support he desired, his commitment to equality of treatment won for North Carolina blacks more ample care than they received at the hands of other Southern administrators.

Although Rankin stepped down as health officer in 1925 to take over hospital development at the Duke Endowment, North Carolina's reputation for health leadership continued, as did its willingness to move in new directions. One program begun by Rankin's successor, Charles Laughinghouse, had special relevance for North Carolina blacks. In 1928, at the invitation of the Rosenwald Fund and with its help, North Carolina became one of the first two states to employ black nurses as a permanent part of state and county health department staffs. By the early 1930s recruitment of black nurses was an integral policy, and Laughinghouse and his successors pursued the matter diligently, cajoling county commissioners to make appointments and then pursuing private and public funds for their support. Finally, in the mid-1930s those efforts culminated in North Carolina's board being the first in the South to hire a permanent black staff member.[78]

If black health problems were far from being solved in North Carolina, Rankin, his associates, and their successors at least demonstrated that it was possible for white health officials to do their job without prejudice. Facing black health problems squarely and making an honest effort at redress—those were the traits of Watson Smith Rankin that made him and his program unique in the South, if not in the nation. The state's contrast with South Carolina's record of health administration was striking, and

Dr. Watson Smith Rankin (c. 1950), *state health officer of North Carolina from* 1909 *to* 1925 *and, after* 1925, *director of the Hospital and Orphans Section of the Duke Endowment. Courtesy of the Duke Endowment.*

more than anything else topmost leadership seemed to be the factor deter-
mining the difference.

Taken together, the records of the North Carolina and South Carolina boards of health also provide at least a partial answer to the question
posed at the start of this chapter, which was whether Southern health officers would fulfill their early twentieth century pledge to resolve the health
problems of the region's blacks. Judging from performances in the two Carolinas, the verdict must be that some professionals (as in North Carolina)
honored that earlier commitment fairly faithfully while others (as in South
Carolina) did not. What seemed to tip the balance one way or the other
was the willingness and ability of the state health officer to keep the health
problems of the poor in the forefront of public and private discussion. Certainly the support of private physicians and state legislators was crucial to
the success that North Carolina enjoyed, but in the final analysis it was Watson Smith Rankin, largely, who convinced them to give that support.

Whatever the effectiveness of Southern programs in meeting the
needs of poor citizens—black and white—the continuance of any program
at all was put in doubt in the early 1930s by an economic depression so severe that it threatened to topple the South's entire public health structure.
In 1930–33 the cotton economy collapsed, private groups and local governments defaulted on financial obligations, and legislatures made drastic cuts
in agency budgets. In consequence, health boards not only had to scrap
surviving remnants of projects initiated in the 1920s; they faced the prospect of having to gut programs basic to the public health enterprise.

It was not just Southern boards that faced that dilemma. The APHA
in 1931 got reports from all over the nation of budget and staff reductions,
and by the next year two hundred local departments had sustained moderate to sharp appropriation cuts. But the Southern experience was the
harshest, what with the region's weaker economic base and more tenuous
commitment to social programs. The situation in Georgia and South Carolina was typical. In late 1930 Georgia health officer T.F. Abercrombie appealed to the PHS to help prevent the dissolution of his whole county health
program: "Owing to the low economic conditions in this state, we are losing
. . . two counties with the probability of the loss of several others during
the first six months of the year."[79] The Depression's effect in Washington
County illustrated what was happening generally. A cotton county with a
population of twenty-five thousand and a high malaria rate, Washington
had had a full-time health department for three years and was doing everything possible to continue the work, but the burden had become too heavy.
If outside aid was not secured, Abercrombie warned, the county "will not
be able to carry on."[80] Though the state legislature had never supported
county health work, Abercrombie hoped it would do so in 1931; but as the

state "is heavily involved . . . in [collecting] more than $5,000,000 in arrears," favorable action was remote.[81]

South Carolina faced similar difficulties. Because taxes were virtually uncollectable in 1930, the 1931 state budget was $2 million larger than revenues, necessitating drastic cuts in appropriations. The effect of retrenchment on the board of health would be shattering, Hayne predicted. Already funds for purchase of immunizing sera had been slashed by $20,000, and, as in Georgia, many county units faced a doubtful future. Dillon County had one of the oldest health departments in the state, but "on account of . . . the failure to collect taxes, unemployment, and the failure of three banks the [Dillon] legislative delegation have indicated that they must withdraw funds from the county health unit."[82] By summer, 1931, cuts were seriously affecting the state board's ability to control disease. Requesting emergency assistance from the PHS that July, Hayne told Cumming that "there is no doubt that there is a very serious menace in the typhoid situation in South Carolina. . . . " Owing to the reduction in state aid, the board had not been able to purchase enough anti-typhoid serum to cope with the disease, and Hayne believed it imperative that the "federal government assist us in this emergency by supplying the typhoid bacterin from the Army Medical School."[83]

Even in North Carolina, whose legislature had supported the idea of an expanding health program, the Depression had a destructive effect. In 1930 lawmakers reduced appropriations by 20 percent. Health officer Laughinghouse regarded that as a crippling blow, for it caused the departure of key people. Surgeon General Cumming found the cuts "especially regrettable in view of the fact that North Carolina at one time set a standard of public health progress and advancement for all the Southern states."[84] Laughinghouse hoped that future legislatures would be more generous. But the downward trend continued, with the result that the board's appropriation fell 55 percent between 1929 and 1933. In the face of shrinking tax revenues, some cuts were necessary, one PHS officer admitted, but "the reactionary group in the . . . North Carolina General Assembly . . . are adamant on reducing the state's activities to the point of crucifixion."[85] Unless North Carolina got some relief, county health departments would have to revert to part-time work and local health services would atrophy.[86]

Denied adequate support, Laughinghouse, Hayne, Abercrombie, and other health officers sought relief from those outside sources which had helped in the past. The response was discouraging. Private foundations had revenue problems too and were unable to offer much more than sympathy. In some instances they had to trim commitments already made. Rockefeller, which had long aided county health work in the South, in 1931 substantially curtailed local programs. Some work continued under a cooperative arrangement with the PHS, but the Foundation's chief objective after 1931, according to one spokesman, was "the saving of units which reasonably could be expected to survive." Weaker counties would have to be sacrificed.[87]

Rosenwald, too, had to cut back. North Carolina's board, after convincing six county units to add black nurses to their staffs was distressed to learn in 1930 that the Fund could not support the work as promised. Later, Rosenwald had to terminate post-graduate fellowships for Negro doctors.[88]

The federal government was in better position to respond to state appeals, but even its help was limited. As the conduit for special congressional appropriations of 1931 and 1932, the PHS made several emergency grants to state boards, but for the most part its funds only partly filled the gap (and by 1933 even national allotments were drying up). The 1931 appropriation was for the relief of those Southern counties hit by severe drought. Among Southeastern states, only North Carolina derived significant benefit. There, seventeen counties were able to maintain at least minimum health services. When funding stopped in 1932, five assisted counties gave up their health units.[89]

In 1932 the PHS got its second congressional appropriation for local work. Along with some money from the Rockefeller Foundation, the congressional funding was available to all states, but was so hedged about with restrictions as to be of little aid to the South. Small county health units (those with fewer than three on staff) and units lacking assurance of continuing local or state support were automatically excluded from assistance. Although the basic purpose of saving the best county organizations was laudable, the project was self-defeating, for it decreed that only those departments which did not really need help could get it. Georgia got only a little assistance. South Carolina got none. Although the state did obtain a $9000 loan in 1933 from the Reconstruction Finance Corporation to aid county programs, it replaced only a small portion of the $32,000 lost that year in federal and private money.[90]

Hence, from 1930 to 1933, health work in the South followed the same path to stagnation and bankruptcy as American business. In 1933, the fear of all health administrators — an upturn in mortality — finally materialized. In South Carolina, whose experience was representative, there was an increase in infant mortality and in TB for the first time since 1915. In maternal mortality, where there had been frequent fluctuation, the rise was the greatest in eighteen years. While it would be wrong to attribute increased deaths solely or even largely to cuts in health services — in the past, after all, mortality had steadily fallen without such services — most additional deaths were preventable and could have been reduced had adequate help been available. Unhappily, what occurred was that an increased number of people who had relied on private medicine found themselves in the position of needing public care at the very time that health agencies lost much of their capacity to provide it.[91]

The burden of increased death and sickness was borne mainly by the poor and, among them, by blacks most of all. In the 1930s blacks moved to the city in record numbers, yet it was in cities where their health was most endangered, not because the urban environment was necessarily more physically threatening but because in cities they were least able to sustain themselves financially. As a writer for *Opportunity* noted in 1932, blacks "are being forced off jobs to make places for unemployed white men —by intimidation, coercion and murder."[92] The Neighborhood Union's 1931 house-to-house survey of black sections, painted an appalling picture of the medical consequences of economic collapse. One family of twelve had had two deaths that winter. One was an expectant mother whose husband had died earlier in Chicago. She had come home to Atlanta to nurse a sick relation. The relative died and shortly afterwards the woman, herself, perished in childbirth. The remaining family, with a newborn infant and an imbecile child in its care, then lost its home.[93]

Even when hospital facilities were available to blacks, they were strained to the point of collapse. A Mississippi administrator reported that if he did not find additional funds soon, his facility would have to shut its doors. "To date, I have turned no one down, for there is nothing more distressing than for people to bring their child to a hospital for an emergency operation dressed in tatters and rags and when you know that there cannot be a cent paid, and it simply is not human to turn a patient like that away, knowing that they will die when a few dollars would save a life. As a result of this the hospital is in the verge of bankruptcy. We are . . . at the end of our cable."[94]

CHAPTER 7

The Federal Rescue
of Southern Health Programs,
1933–1955

In March 1933 the South's tortuous search for help in saving fading health programs finally ended with the inauguration of Franklin Roosevelt and the beginning of large-scale federal aid. The opening of the federal tap did more, however, than rescue faltering programs. It also brought about a basic shift in the control of public health work in America from the states to Washington. Before 1933 federal agencies like the Public Health Service and the Children's Bureau had been active in the states, but nearly always in an advisory capacity only. The 1930s began a new pattern. Washington was not only sustaining state and local programs financially (meeting up to 50 percent of total expenditures), but setting overall direction as well.[1]

And as it did so, earlier and sharp distinctions between states in the quality of their health programs began to dissolve. Although regional emphases remained, federal funding—and the guidelines and regulations that accompanied it—tended toward a uniformity in local health programs and procedures that erased the kinds of differences formerly seen between such states as North and South Carolina. Local health leadership remained important of course and was a factor in making one state more (or less) successful in carrying out an increasingly standardized program. But no longer could a man like Watson Smith Rankin or like James A. Hayne imprint his outlook and values on a state health program for better or for worse, as had been possible in the pre–New Deal era of local initiatives and local (or private) funding. Now the shape of things was increasingly directed by the PHS or the Children's Bureau in Washington. Health initiatives and policies continued to be the product of discussion and consensus between local and national leaders, but the framework for such discussion tended more and more to be defined at the federal rather than state level. Thus, the focus of a study of Depression-era health activity in the South is most properly centered on what emerged from Washington, not from Columbia, Atlanta, or Raleigh.

Among the social goals of the New Dealers, few received more attention than that of improving the public health. In August 1933 relief director Harry Hopkins, that rising star of the New Deal, told state governors and relief administrators that "conservation and maintenance of the public health is a primary function of government."[2] That health protection was a major goal of the new administration, no one doubted; what was uncertain was how federal health and medical care money would be administered. In March (1933) Congress had included substantial sums for health relief in the law creating the Federal Emergency Relief Administration (FERA). For the next nine months Hopkins groped for the proper vehicle for spending it.

His initial approach was to turn over a large portion of the fund to local hospitals, who had convinced him that they could get the best return on the relief dollar. The case set forth by South Carolina's Berkeley County Hospital was typical. Distributing funds directly to indigents or to medical practitioners was no solution, the hospital argued, because there were only six doctors to cover the whole of that largely black county. But if relief funds were pumped into the hospital, it could turn itself into a county-wide clinic. Persuaded, state relief officials started the hospital on a $1700 monthly allotment.[3]

However effective hospital-centered relief was in theory, the capital drain was so great that the FERA fund was soon threatened with bankruptcy. So in June 1933 Hopkins ended the arrangement. Thereafter state relief directors were only to pay for home care and treatment in physicians' offices.[4]

To make that plan work Hopkins turned to the PHS. If state boards of health would take on part of the job of medical relief administration, such as identifying the medically needy and arranging for care, they could tap FERA funds for their preventive programs. The surgeon general's office was interested in the plan, for it would help the public health establishment guard its turf. As the assistant surgeon general, C.E. Waller, told new North Carolina health officer J.W. Parrott, "if we do not seriously consider assuming the direction of this [emergency relief] movement . . . we may find ourselves being pushed aside with only a relatively small job to perform." But state officials in North Carolina and elsewhere were chary of the proposition. Much as they needed the money they did not want to become welfare offices. Their suggestion was that FERA aid be used to expand existing programs such as school health, home sanitation, and public health nursing, many of which could be focused on indigents.[5]

Ultimately Hopkins struck a compromise. Part of the FERA emergency medical fund remained in the hands of state relief administrators to be paid over directly to physicians and dentists who cared for FERA clients. In response to pressure from black medical leaders, including Peter Murray and M.O. Bousfield, Hopkins told his state directors that black doctors were to be given an equal chance to participate in medical relief work. The FERA and its state offices, however, made no effort to steer black patients to these doctors. As a result, a number of black relief patients sought out white physicians and dentists. This led some black professionals to complain of discrimination by the FERA, but for the most part black (and white) physicians were happy for the added income the federal program brought.[6]

The rest of FERA medical relief went to the PHS and state boards of health. Hopkins's sole condition was that nurses be sent into homes only on the orders of private physicians, as he did not want to step on the latter's toes. Otherwise, he was eager to promote home nursing and sanitation projects, for they would be labor intensive and would thus meet the other FERA goal: reemployment.

Thus, in February 1934 substantial federal funds became available to state boards of health for the first time since passage of the Maternity and Infancy Act of 1921. For the Southern states, the money came just in time. Hayne reported in June that FERA dollars had literally sustained the board of health in the last half of the fiscal year. More important were the expanded services that the new funds made available to Southerners. Besides thousands of sanitary privies built with FERA money in 1934 and 1935, it also enabled Southern states to establish for the first time a reasonably effective public health nursing service. Georgia, which had been without any program, was able in 1934 to add ninety nurses to its state staff for general home nursing and TB control.[7]

Substantial grants were made to Southern health boards for antimalarial work, as well, and not just by the FERA but also by the Public Works Administration and the Civil Works Administration, which were created to promote recovery through large-scale construction projects. In North Carolina between December, 1933, and March, 1934, CWA project workers drained 56,000 acres and dug 566 miles of ditches. Nowhere was malaria a greater threat than in South Carolina, which led the nation in mortality. But in 1936 Hayne could report that thanks to federal aid South Carolina was finally subduing its old foe, and by 1940 the contest was essentially over. Since 1935 whites had enjoyed an 80 percent drop in mortality. But the deadline among blacks was nearly as spectacular: their death rates fell 75 percent.[8]

In 1935 the FERA was replaced by the more amply funded Works Progress Administration (WPA), and health projects of the earlier agency underwent sizeable expansion. Besides bedside nursing, which in most Southern states was now extended to every county, WPA money paid for medical and dental inspection of schools, care of crippled children, improvement of child nutrition, and delivery of prenatal and postnatal care. Many counties, in the South and elsewhere, used their federal grants to set up free medical clinics. Virtually every county health department got the chance to launch a new program of some sort: Washington's only stipulations were that local programs get endorsement from the state board and try to avoid competing with local doctors. Even counties without organized health work got government attention. In late 1934 Congress provided the PHS with a "million dollar fund" to be spent by the states in areas which had not yet benefited from the new federal interest in health. In North Carolina thirty-seven counties received a $54,000 share of that allotment.[9]

Not all federal health relief was channeled through the public structure. Funds from the WPA created a host of new projects in the area of nutrition. Most American communities had their federal canning projects, which gave employment to nutrition teachers and important new skills to homemakers. In Gastonia, North Carolina, a textile town with crippling unemployment, the project director reported that 1825 families had canned 143,363 quarts of vegetables, most of them grown in government garden projects. Not only had vegetables "never been canned before," but many women did not know how to can anything. Now they were learning to "prepare in time of plenty for the non-productive seasons."[10] Pellagra deaths would drop because of such activity (see chapter 8).

The WPA school lunch projects had a larger, more immediate impact. Like all relief activities these too served multiple goals: child nutrition, reemployment, and disposal of surplus crops for American farmers. Though monthly school menus were largely determined by available commodities, considerable attention was paid to nutrition. The menu one week in April 1936 for the 203 children at the Four Miles School in Charleston was fairly typical: They had hot lunches prepared from apples, canned beef, flour, tomatoes, corn, string beans, and other vegetables.[11]

Yet what was good for the body was not always good for the soul. Given the feelings about welfare among Southern whites, participation in free lunch programs often carried a stigma. Will Campbell, Baptist minister, writer, and 1960s civil rights activist, recalled the torture he faced as a rural Mississippi schoolboy. Each day the lunchroom manager took a head-count of children intending to eat the noon meal. After recording those who were exchanging cash or produce for lunch, she would demand: "now, all the little relief children hold up your hands." The ordeal, said Campbell, was "almost more than I could bear."[12]

Despite such insensitivity the program reached large numbers of Southern children, black and white, with obvious good effect. In South Carolina,

A WPA-sponsored day nursery for black children in South Carolina, c. 1936. Such federal programs provided employment for adults and nutritious meals for children — black and white. Courtesy of the South Caroliniana Library.

by 1938, WPA lunch projects operated in all but one county, furnishing meals to forty-five thousand undernourished youngsters. According to school principals, lunches improved both attendance and health. One remarked that absence rates had fallen since the program started and another stated flatly: "there are no pale, puny children in my school now."[13]

Any review of New Deal health work must also pay attention to the in-house medical programs that several relief and reform agencies maintained for their own clients. Among those that put a special premium on good health as a precondition for client success were the Civilian Conservation Corps (CCC), the Farm Security Administration (FSA), and the National Youth Administration (NYA).

The CCC put some two million young men to work in the 1934–42 period (10 percent of them black) on a variety of projects in the field of resource conservation. Work, itself, was one spur to health because for most CCC boys a job in the "C's" was the only alternative to vagrancy, or worse. But health also got attention in its own right. In CCC camps boys enjoyed simple, nutritious meals, something that most badly needed. The CCC "chow" was in fact a source of envy to many outside the program. One camp in Oregon played baseball every Sunday against a visiting team of reservation Indians, who had to travel fifty miles to play a game they invariably lost. The reason they came was the camp's noonday meal. As a result of its emphasis on nutrition, CCC officials estimated that on average their boys gained twelve pounds in weight and one-half inch in height during their tenure as recruits.[14]

Medical services were also provided. The Army ran the camps, and every recruit got a scaled-down version of the induction physical. Although examinations were brief (three minutes on average), medical treatment and even hospitalization were provided, if needed. The very real value of such services was pointed up by the tooth-pulling caper of 1940. That year extractions among Southern enlistees were so numerous that the Army dental chief suspected staff dentists of going on a tooth-pulling spree to justify their existence. Ordering dentists to send all extracted teeth to him, the chief received eight thousand the first month. On examination he found them in shocking condition and concluded that every extraction was justified.[15]

The NYA was equally attentive to health. Begun in 1934, the program provided jobs (and medical care) to high school and college students to enable them to continue schooling. Under direction of Alabama-born social worker and New Deal veteran Aubrey Williams, the NYA gave substantial support to Negro youth, who by 1940 made up about 14 percent of male enrollment and 20 percent of female. Although the NYA never received the level of funding needed to carry out its more elaborate medical and health mission, Williams always considered health as important as jobs in securing the future of the nation's young.[16]

One of Williams's more venturesome ideas, which got considerable funding, was the establishment of residential centers located close to NYA projects and providing room, board, and routine medical care for NYA clients. By the end of 1940 South Carolina led the nation in the number of centers (75) and their total population (2611).[17]

In early 1941 Williams sought to expand the NYA's ancillary medical services into a comprehensive program. In each center a clinic would be set up to provide health education, laboratory tests, immunizations, X-rays, and dental services—in short, a program of socialized medicine for the nation's teenagers. But the ambitious scheme had almost immediate problems with funding and popular acceptance. In South Carolina, where physicians examined six hundred persons in the first three months, rumors spread in one town that girls were having to undress before lewd, male onlookers. Local physicians issued a quick denial, but suspicions and hostility remained.[18]

In North Carolina, the state NYA health director felt the effort was almost a total failure, due to lack of interest on the part of work-project supervisors and state physicians. The only good he could see had been the "considerable improvement in professional and public understanding of the health situation of the youth."[19] By 1942 the NYA was drying up even in those states where there had been a high level of activity. Defense needs were claiming a higher priority, and the health program was one casualty of the competition for funds.[20]

An agency with a far more successful health program was the Farm Security Administration. Launched in 1937, as an expanded version of the earlier Resettlement Administration, the FSA's chief aim was to salvage the economic and human potential of the nation's rural poor. Headed by Southern clergyman-activist Will Alexander, the FSA gave primary attention to tenant farmers of the South—black and white. Through a program of low-interest loans, the FSA sought to assist the improvement of both farm and home.[21]

Recognizing that poor health and unsanitary conditions were major barriers to economic progress, Alexander saw to it that rehabilitation loans also included money for nutritional and sanitary improvement. Besides stoves, pressure cookers, and canning instruction, goverment funds paid for privy construction, window screens, and improved water. By 1940–41 fairly substantial numbers were being helped: in North Carolina 1750 rural families in thirty-five counties had gotten sanitary funds, while in Georgia the figures were 4350 families in fifty counties.[22]

Nor were sanitation and nutrition the only problems addressed. By World War II four hundred thousand rural Americans—many of them black—were enjoying what amounted to a socialized medicine program.

In return for contributions to a group health fund, participants were able to receive physician and hospital services as needed. To staff the program, the FSA hired local doctors on a contract basis and, where possible, included black physicians — though in that effort black medical leaders thought that the FSA did less than it might.[23]

Agency efforts and health-related relief work played a crucial role in meeting the health emergencies of the Depression. But as historian Roy Lubove has noted, "from the viewpoint of national health needs . . . , their efforts were hopelessly inadequate."[24] The beginning of a truly national health program came only with passage of the 1935 Social Security Act (SS), which became the foundation for a sprawling edifice of federal health initiatives carried out by local officials. Yet Social Security meant more than merely an increase in programs and services. It also signaled what Lubove called a "new era in the history of American health and medicine," an era characterized by a shift of public health leadership from the states to Washington and a quest for a comprehensive national health program.[25]

Maternal and infant programs enjoyed substantial new support thanks to SS. Compared to the Sheppard-Towner Act, which gave states only $1.25 million a year for such projects, SS held out the prospect of a fantastic health bounty: $3.8 million for maternity and infant care, $2.8 million in aid crippled children, and $8 million for other state and local health services.[26]

But to snare that aid, states had to meet certain requirements, the most demanding of which was a dollar-for-dollar match by state and local governments (combined). That Southern states, the nation's poorest, were able to participate at the level they did was due in part to Washington's willingness to bend that rule. Southern activity was also facilitated by a special feature of the act which allotted certain SS monies solely on the basis of financial need, a provision that was clearly intended to benefit the South. "The North and the West aren't going to like it," assistant surgeon general C.E. Waller confided to a North Carolina contact, but this was "as it should be, particularly on account of the large Negro population. . . . "[27]

The act offered state boards of health two classes of aid. One — categorical grants — gave special attention to particularly serious problems. Initially, categories were maternal and child health, environmental sanitation, malaria control, and industrial hygiene. The other kind of help came from unrestricted funds, available for any use which state boards deemed proper, subject to PHS approval. States put that money to work chiefly in expanding county health programs. At the start of SS funding, fewer than 600 of the nation's 4000 counties had full-time local health departments. By 1939 that total had climbed to 1371. Of the three Southeastern states under review, Georgia felt the greatest impact from SS. Before 1935 few counties were willing to make the financial sacrifice needed for local health organization. But with

A physician examining members of a North Carolina black family who were clients of the Farm Security Administration, 1940. The FSA provided virtually free medical care to its borrowers. Courtesy of the Library of Congress.

federal help, interest mounted, and by 1940, 55 of the state's 169 counties (with 61 percent of the population) had created local units.[28]

The PHS, which administered most SS health funds (the Children's Bureau dispersed the rest), saw its role as more than mere money agent. While conscious of a need to maintain good relations with the states, the PHS also aimed to use its new authority to lift boards to a higher performance — by encouragement if possible, but by coercion if necessary, as Southern region director C.L. Williams frankly conceded. The PHS, he admitted to Thomas Parran, would be hard put to refute the charge of meddling in the states. "As a matter of fact we are constantly and earnestly endeavoring to influence state health departments in many ways, to our way of thinking to improve them." Williams believed that that was only proper and that the "Service should accept without question the fact that it is the leader of the public health movement in the United States."[29]

The basic power accorded the PHS was the requirement that state boards get Washington's approval before spending federal money. But for the most part, the Service sought to upgrade state standards by encouragement rather than veto — by meeting with state officials to explain, cajole, and plan.

Experienced personnel were obviously a key to program success. Building on a precedent established in the 1920s by a cooperative venture with the International Health Board, the Service called on state health officers to begin hiring division heads and county directors on the basis of prior field experience and an advanced degree from an accredited public health school.

At the time of Social Security's passage the only degree programs were at Harvard, the Johns Hopkins, Yale, and Columbia. But in the spring of 1935 events were unfolding in North Carolina to add an additional school there. Health officer Carl Reynolds, aware of the growing demand for trained professionals in the South, wanted to put North Carolina in position to provide them. The retirement of celebrated public health pioneer Milton Rosenau from Harvard's deanship gave Reynolds his chance. In conjunction with North Carolina's medical school dean, Reynolds invited Rosenau to come South and build a new school in Chapel Hill. To their surprise and delight, Rosenau accepted and in the spring of 1936 began teaching his first students. With the help of a special legislative appropriation and a PWA grant (the former helping secure the latter), Rosenau's program soon had a building of its own. Growth in faculty and students followed rapidly, and in 1940 the program became a fully accredited, degree-granting school of public health. As Reynolds predicted, the North Carolina institution also quickly became the school of choice for young Southerners seeking health careers. In its first decade and a half 55 percent of resident students at the North Carolina School of Public Health came from outside the state.[30]

There was also strong federal concern to build up the number of trained nurses in the South, especially black nurses, and to that end the PHS set up a degree program in cooperation with the University of Virginia. But even though training cost them nothing, Southern states tended to leave black nurses out of their manpower plans unless prodded — something the PHS often did. In 1939 when the Virginia program program was facing collapse because Southern states had sent no black students, Parran pressed each health officer to reconsider. The appeal worked: South Carolina's Hayne responded with a request for ten places, explaining that at first he had only asked for money for white nurses because they were the only ones with sure jobs.[31]

Private physicians (black and white) got attention from Washington too, especially obstetricians and pediatricians, who were crucial to improving maternal and infant mortality rates. In their cases the Children's Bureau provided funds which enabled state boards to pay doctors' way to special post-graduate seminars. White doctors were usually supportive of such programs, except when the PHS forgot the prevailing etiquette and tried to mix whites and blacks in the same program. In 1937 that happened in Georgia, and the state medical association immediately protested that it did not want Negro physicians participating in the course and asked that "only members of the [medical] Association be given places."[32]

White physicians were also sensitive to federal intrusion into the domain of curative medicine. To make sure that the public-private boundary was respected in its state, the South Carolina Medical Association in 1937 resolved that there should be no public treatment for syphilis except in extreme cases of indigency and only then where the family doctor approved.[33] Normally health officers were careful to observe these boundaries: North Carolina officials admitted to "bending over backwards" to avoid alienating doctors.[34]

Even with these sorts of checks, by the late 1930s newly expanded public health operations in Southern counties were doing vital work in salvaging and securing the health of many thousands of the region's poor, white and black. One example was the response of the Georgia board to a case in Newton County, a poor and heavily black district without organized public health services. In September 1941, state health officer T.F. Abercrombie got word of an abandoned, desperately sick black man in the county. Abercrombie sent a regional medical director to investigate, and nine miles into the Georgia countryside he found the man "in an old unfurnished house lying on a comfort on the floor. . . ." Besides having syphilis, the man was "covered with ulcers from his groin to his lower torso."[35] He had stopped treatment because he could no longer walk the nine miles to the doctor. After arranging for the invalid to get home care, the health officer told the county manager about the state's low-cost nursing service and stressed its vaue not only in controlling VD but in providing a range of health services that would help avoid "a repetition of such an unfortunate circumstance."[36]

Newton County eventually set up a nursing service, but more significant than trouble-shooting episodes were the preventive health services that local departments were initiating on a regular basis. The most important of the new programs were traveling maternity and infant clinics, which sought to halt the needless and worsening loss of life among Southern mothers and infants. South Carolina had the nation's highest infant death rate, and now that federal funds were available its health officials were determined to reduce that "extremely humiliating" statistic.[37]

Although benefits from the thousands of two- to three-day clinics were available to both races, black mothers took greatest advantage of them, partly because of greater need but also because of a tightening of state midwife regulations. Negro midwives still delivered about 80 percent of Southern black mothers, and by the late 1930s state boards of health were pressuring them to get their patients to a clinic before the sixth month of pregnancy.[38]

As a result, prenatal clinics became rather quickly a Negro service. South Carolina's first facilities (1936) registered 189 black mothers and 97 white. Thereafter the clinic population grew rapidly, as did the black-white ratio, rising to ten or twelve to one and sometimes more. In neighboring states volume and ratios were similar. North Carolina's first prenatal clinics (established in 1936 also) served nearly 11,000 Negro women but only 2100 white. In Georgia a few years later 14,000 black mothers sought help compared to about one-tenth that number of white.[39]

Soon, clinics were reaching a sizeable portion of the South's black maternal population. South Carolina's board of health estimated in 1940 that about 30 percent of expectant Negro mothers annually sought its help, while the number of Negro infants seen was perhaps as high as 15 percent. Sadly, white women were apparently more concerned about maintaining segregation than maternal health, for only when their condition was manifestly serious did they consent to visit what was increasingly regarded as a "colored" institution. On the other hand whites did not worry as much about racial stigmas where their infants were concerned, for in well-baby clinics in the Carolinas and Georgia, the ratio of black-to-white infants was nearer three or even two to one.[40]

In addition to providing new services, SS improved the health of blacks and poor whites in another way, by offering Southern boards an independent source of capital not tied to local will and whim. As long as blacks had to depend on local welfare offices and private charity to meet their needs,

A WPA-sponsored typhoid clinic for South Carolina blacks, 1938. The clinic, in Charleston, was directed by health officer Dr. Leon Banov, shown inoculating a woman in the center of the picture. Courtesy of the National Archives.

they were subject to the tyranny of the segregationist mentality, with the result that services were often used to enforce conformity to white concepts of race and morality.

The plea of a Pickens, South Carolina, black mother, who took her problems to Eleanor Roosevelt, was a common one. "Please help me," begged Amealie Brown. "I have five little children to support and I cannot get any help for them." Mrs. Brown had vainly sought assistance from her county welfare office, but "they tell me to make the children daddy help me with them [.] I am not married to the children daddy and he won't help me. . . . We is all raggy and bare feets and have a very little to eat. . . ." Brown wanted domestic work, but she had syphilis and could not get a health card. "Please help me," she ended, "before we starve to death."[41] In Johnson County, Georgia, there was a seeming conspiracy to deny care to indigents — be they white or black. According to an investigator, the county ordinary (local government administrator) "refuses to give aid to any individual regardless of conditions or circumstances. I have tried a number of times to discuss with him the need for medical care for indigents, and he always laughs at me and does nothing."[42]

The preference for segregation over health was sometimes made startingly clear. In the early 1940s Georgia Governor Ellis Arnall scotched health department plans to house tubercular Negroes on the top floor of the state's white sanatorium. Health officer Abercrombie had explained that the thirty-six-year-old building used for blacks was literally falling down and a fire hazard too. To prevent contact between white and black patients in the white sanatorium, the board had had a separate stairway and elevator installed. But none of that satisfied Arnall, who rationalized, "while I favor giving adequate health attention and facilities to negroes, . . . I think it would be a tremendous mistake to place negro patients in the white unit. . . . If you do this . . . you will play right into the hands of those who would like to discredit our health work in Georgia."[43]

By providing alternative sources of health funding SS freed the poor Southerner from similar tyranny by local welfare officials and others, who often made medical decisions on the basis of race or social acceptability. Yet that was not to say that expanded health systems in the South worked effectively and without bias. Never was there enough money from federal or, particularly, state and local sources to meet even the most basic needs of the region's poor. In Georgia, as of 1940, though gains had been made, still 114 counties with 39 percent of the state population refused to create health departments. In South Carolina the state legislature, year after year, was unwilling to give the level of support that the SS law required. Accordingly the state lost considerable funding that it otherwise would have garnered—though never as much as Washington, by rights, might have withheld.[44]

A fairly typical instance of public discrimination was the distribution of crippled children's services, one of the categorical programs of SS. According to a 1940 NAACP study, only Alabama among Southern states made fairly even-handed use of such monies. A more characteristic distribution was that in rural Georgia, where nearly 40 percent of crippled white youngsters got hospital treatment, while only 2 percent of blacks did.[45]

The objection could be (and was) made that Negroes were hypercritical and had unreasonable expectations. But it was also unarguable that most state and county health departments in the South did not make an earnest attempt to reach the black community. For one thing boards of health, North and South, made little use of black newspapers in their health education work. When officials did send releases to the black press, material was not suitably written. Health releases aimed at the black community never capitalized "Negro" and usually addressed readers in the dialect of a black sharecropper. Illiterates could not read them, and educated blacks only took offense. Paul Cornely summed up the situation by noting that among whites the attitude "all too often prevalent" was that "Negroes can get along with less. . . ."[46]

There was also the problem of discrimination at the individual, personal level. Just after the Second World War Cornely investigated the delivery of health services to blacks in several Southern cities. He found that physicians and nurses frequently carried over into their professional work the same sort of racist thinking that guided their private lives. In many clinics, "Negro patients were often treated with condescension, lack [of] sympathy, without respect and dignity, and without attention to many of the minor details for personal comfort and privacy . . . ."[47] Charleston black leader Septima Clark recalled Sunday immunization clinics where white health workers acted "like they were afraid to push up the sleeves of those black children." On one occasion, their disdain was so obvious that a group of visiting Midwest college girls "took over and did the clean-up."[48]

The cost of such attitudes went beyond the mere giving of offense. At best, they blunted efforts of health agencies to get blacks to take initiative for personal health improvement. At worst, they created overt antagonism toward all health programs and lessened the cooperation of black communities.[49]

Of course racism did not always and everywhere get in the way of professionalism. In the 1930s Modjeska Simkins worked closely with county health officials, and she described relations with them as good. Dr. William Fishburne, a South Carolinian and health officer of heavily black Berkeley County, was courageously open on the race question. Each time he and

Simkins completed a TB program, they would return to tea at his home in race-conscious Moncks Corner. Later, Simkins would joke: "that was like going to heaven without dying."[50]

Yet even if racism prevented rejuvenated and expanded Southern health programs from serving black clientele as they should have, perhaps expansion and rejuvenation, after all, were what was most important. That was certainly true of the effort launched against venereal diseases in the late 1930s, a program that more than any other symbolized the new concern for black health in the South, as well as the continuing problems in securing it. Previously some good work had been done, notably the cooperative project of 1928–32 (chapter 5). But over the next five years momentum flagged, and by the mid 1930s most state VD programs were barely holding their own.[51]

Then came SS and the availability of federal funds for VD control. National interest was largely attributable to the zeal of the newly appointed surgeon general, Thomas Parran, who had returned to Washington after a stint as New York City health officer. To Parran, eradication of syphilis, especially among Southern blacks, was almost an obsession. For years he had been lobbying for a national effort in such magazines as *Reader's Digest, Survey Graphic,* and *Ladies' Home Journal.* As surgeon general one of his early moves had been to convene a national conference on VD, which drew a thousand delegates and generated a demand for major congressional funding for long-term control.[52]

Once SS funds became available (1936), local activity increased. In Georgia the harried director of VD control was able to hire an assistant and send him to Washington for training. In South Carolina physicians and health officers adopted a plan for syphilis control, and by 1938 state doctors were manning public diagnostic and treatment centers in forty South Carolina counties.[53]

The most important project to follow in the wake of SS, however, was a cooperative, federal-and-state treatment program launched in 1937 in the same southeast Georgia area as the 1928-32 effort (Glynn, Camden, and McIntosh counties). To reach the thousands of blacks, whose syphilis rate was as still high as in 1928, the associated health departments used a two-pronged strategy. First they sought the involvement of black preachers, who would announce the times of blood-testing clinics (often on Sundays) and rally the congregation to take part.[54] Second, to those who reacted positively, doctors sent simply written, official-looking letters inviting a return visit to the clinic. Health officials were keen on letters, for they were convinced that blacks "like to receive letters, just as we all do and particularly in a large official looking envelope. They show it to their friends. They carry it around with them for weeks."[55] More important, the letters usually brought patients back to the clinic.

By 1938 the project had tested 80 percent of area blacks. Amont those with positive blood tests, 77 percent were convinced to begin the long chemotherapy that was then the only known syphilis cure. The problem lay in getting patients to continue, for treatments sometimes stretched out as long as eighteen months. Yet project staff were persistent. Ultimately 68 percent of lapsed patients returned. Usually the threat of quarantine was enough to bring them back. If it did not, sterner measures were available. The mayor of Brunswick (the area's urban center) gave "incorrigibles" a choice of going to jail or the clinic. Most chose the latter, and the few who did not got treatment behind bars.[56]

However questionable some of its methods, the success of the project was undeniable. In the draft physicals of October 1940, area blacks showed a drop in syphilis infection of about 40 percent from 1937. Moreover, the rate of stillbirths had fallen by more than 50 percent, a reduction that Parran attributed largely to anti-VD work.

But the project had significance beyond the three Georgia counties. Its early successes convinced one wealthy Georgia planter in 1937 to launch a similar work in his native North Carolina. Thus was born the Z. Smith Reynolds Foundation (the creation of tobacco magnate R.J. Reynolds, as a memorial to his son), which provided the North Carolina Board of Health with earnings from a $7 million endowment. Its support for syphilis control would continue until 1947, and besides yearly grants Reynolds added an extra $25,000 to help the board retain talented personnel.[57]

The most important spin-off of the Georgia demonstration, however, was the LaFollette-Bulwinkle Act of 1938. Impressed by the Georgia results Wisconsin Senator Robert LaFollette, Jr., and North Carolina Congressman Albert Bulwinkle won passage of a bill creating a $7 million yearly fund for state VD control.[58] Within a year the measure was giving large impulse to Southern programs. In 1934 the number of treatment centers in South Carolina, Georgia, and North Carolina had been, respectively, 0, 17, and 34. By 1939 facilities had multiplied to 81 and 89 in South Carolina and Georgia and 221 in North Carolina, which, because of Reynolds support, had the most clinics of any Southern state. Equally impressive (and alarming) was the rise in number of reported cases. Between 1935 and 1939, in the three-state area, it varied from 200 to 300 percent. In Georgia the number of syphilis cases reported rose from 9600 cases in 1935 to nearly 27,000 by mid-1939.[59] Not entirely a negative sign, the case increase meant that Southern states were finally uncovering the full extent of syphilis among blacks. With identification came the possibility of treatment and the prospect of an end to the long-time scourge.

There were, though, reasons for questioning whether the South would ever reach that goal—or even bring syphilis under control. In none of the three states were lawmakers willing to provide the level of support (50 percent) mandated by law. Although Washington was tolerant, local health departments occasionally lost funding. There were also defects in administration. Federal law required the creation of state VD advisory committees. Though clinic clientele was predominantly black, advisory groups were invariably white. Also only four Southern states (North Carolina was one) in 1939 required syphilis tests before marriage and during pregnancy. Moreover, case finding and holding procedures were often woefully inadequate. In South Carolina only one of four new cases received a follow-up visit, and as a result few syphilitics returned for the number of treatments needed to cure their disease.[60]

Besides the racially motivated disinterest of clinic staff, professional incompetence was sometimes a problem. The first chief of South Carolina's VD division was PHS officer Sedgwick Simmons. During his whole tenure Simmons was sharply critical of most private physicians and county health officers, who had little understanding of modern diagnostic techniques and as a result often failed to find the disease. Moreover, South Carolina clinics practically ignored gonorrhea despite strong PHS warnings about its greater prevalence.[61]

Then came the war, with its urgent insistence on health and fitness. Under that pressure many problems of VD control simply disappeared.[62] The change in the VD situation in Columbia, site of a major infantry training base (Fort Jackson), symbolized war's impact. Before 1941 the city's only VD clinic was a private facility whose directors were the mayor, a local printer, and a clergyman. Staff made little effort to hold patients for treatment or ferret out contacts. One discouraged military health officer called the clinic the "pumping station" for Columbia's infected population.[63]

In late 1941, however, the transformation began. The county health officer opened a major VD center to treat selective service rejects and all contacts of Fort Jackson patients. To assure adequate staff, the PHS added a VD specialist and a dozen nurses. Existing capabilities were strengthened and new facilities set up. The most important were PHS quarantine hospitals built in the vicinity of military posts, which confined female patients suspected of infecting servicemen. By summer 1943, South Carolina had three such hospitals.[64]

New programs reflected a substantial increase in funding. South Carolina's $97,000 federal appropriation in 1939-40 rose 40 percent the next year (to $136,000) and jumped 80 percent in 1942 (to $242,000). All the while, however, state legislators refused to raise their contribution, holding it to the $30,000 they had offered in 1938. But federal increases allowed both a boost in clinic activity and an education program aimed at blacks.[65]

Unquestionably, the major wartime contribution to VD control was penicillin, for with it came a real hope for the elimination of syphilis and gonorrhea. By the last months of the war enough was available for civilian use. For the first time states could contemplate compulsory treatment of all cases, for with penicillin a complete syphilis cure was possible after only a few days' hospitalization. Gonorrhea was eliminated with just one treatment.[66]

To utilize the new "wonder drug," in 1945 Southern states began concentrating patients at what were called "rapid treatment centers" (RTCS), similar in size to the earlier quarantine hospitals and funded almost entirely by Washington. By 1946 South Carolina had two, "Camp Victory" near Columbia, and a second at a former Air Force hospital in Florence. North Carolina had two as well, in Durham and Charlotte, where twenty thousand patients had received treatment by July, 1946. By then 80 percent of North Carolina's federal health money was going for VD control. But the results were astonishing. The thirty thousand new cases of syphilis reported in 1939 had plummeted to 8100 by 1945.[67]

If the war's impact on VD was particularly dramatic, its effect on other diseases and associated control programs was no less important. Strong impetus was given to Southern anti-malarial work. Although mosquito eradication had been vigorously pursued by the New Deal, only during the war was the disease virtually eliminated in the South. In addition, wartime manpower needs put new life into anti-TB work. In 1944 the PHS set up in the states a wide-ranging and reasonably well-funded program of TB control. To blacks, for whom the disease remained major killer, that was an important step, for boards of health were able for the first time to undertake thoroughgoing searches for early TB cases.[68]

The work also worked changes in popular attitudes toward health, just as it had in 1917-18. For the first time in memory, millions of young Southerners of both races received medical and dental care, housing, clothing, and food of first quality. Not only were they the more healthy for it, but their war experience accustomed them to regard such care and living standards as a norm, which they would expect their communities to continue after the war.

One specific service for which the war produced large demand was hospital care. More than anything else it was the wartime Emergency Maternal and Infant Care program (EMIC) which produced the new hospital consciousness. Created in 1943 EMIC was the nation's response to a medical care crisis in the vicinity of its military bases. As a result of a sudden concentration of service dependents in those places, thousands of young wives, expectant mothers, and infants were unable to find or afford needed medical and hospital care. The problem was particularly critical in the South, because of its disproportionate number of camps and its woefully inadequate obstetrical and pediatric services. As early as 1941 some hospitals were so over-crowded that women and newborns were being discharged twenty-four hours after delivery—unheard of in that period.[69]

In 1942 the Children's Bureau began discussions with states to find the best mode of response. As finally worked out, EMIC was to provide not only free hospital, maternal, and infant care for dependents of servicemen in the first four pay grades but also an upgrading of hospital OB-GYN services. As EMIC administrators, state health departments had authority to select participating hospitals and thus the leverage to bring each one up to minimum standards. So that health officers could control services, the Children's Bureau decided that payments would go directly to providers. When EMIC got underway in early 1943, the two Carolinas were among the earliest starters and Georgia trailed closely behind.[70]

But like all best-laid plans, EMIC was at first beset with large problems. The most immediate was how to cope with a sudden near deluge of applicants. State health offices in the South were literally overwhelmed by the manifold tasks of processing thirty to thirty-five daily applicants. As North Carolina's health officer reported, each one involved finding a doctor to take the patient at the agreed-on fee and an approved hospital to give "first class ward care," at the agreed-on rate. At year's end, instead of subsiding, problems seemed to be "growing bigger and bigger."[71]

Difficulties arose, too, with the AMA, which suspected the Children's Bureau of trying to push "the socialization of medicine in this country."[72] So great was its dread that it tried, unsuccessfully, to get EMIC shifted to the more manageable PHS. Doctors had other grievances as well. They objected to receiving payment directly from the government, arguing that EMIC was interfering with doctor-patient relationships. But more than medical ethics was involved: doctors also wanted a bigger fee than initially set. Where possible, state officials met physicians' objections about fees, for broad participation by doctors was critical to EMIC's success.[73]

Complaints also came from hospitals and patients over approval and eligibility rules. When states made initial hospital surveys they found that many fell below minimum obstetrical standards. In Georgia, where few hospitals passed muster, facilities for premature babies were often so primitive that infants were actualy safer at home. Substandard hospitals willing to upgrade facilities got on the approved list; those resisting change did not; and for sticking to their guns health officials were hotly criticized. There were complaints, too, when states refused payment for patients who had deliveries at uncertified hospitals. A Georgia woman, misled by the Red Cross about the need to use approved hospitals, took her case to her congressman, but Georgia's EMIC director refused to yield.[74]

Although EMIC never settled down to a smooth operation and was perennially near collapse, it got the job done. In the process it helped avert a national scandal. Had Congress not acted, North Carolina health officer C. V. Reynolds argued, thousands of Service wives would have been unable to get physician and hospital care during confinement. By the end of 1946 EMIC had handled over 19,000 maternity cases in South Carolina, nearly 21,500 in Georgia, and almost 38,000 in North Carolina, which topped even Massachusetts's total. The number of infants cared for, though only 7 to 15 percent of maternity cases, added more beneficiaries.[75]

Largely because of EMIC, Southern women underwent a major conversion to the idea of hospital deliveries. In South Carolina the war saw an increase from 52 to 68 percent of births. Home birth of course could be safe and was certainly more compatible with the naturalness of the event. But given that many new hospital patrons were women from pinched circumstances and unsanitary homes who would have gotten little rest from normal tasks if at home, hospital confinement was surely an improvement. How much black women benefitted from EMIC was not clear. Hayne estimated that most hospital newcomers were white. On the other hand Cornely considered EMIC "one of the best programs ever developed" for mothers and infants. And it aided black women, he thought, proportionally more than white women, for there were proportionally more blacks in the lower ranks.[76]

Surely an equally important long-term effect of EMIC was its impact on Southern (and national) hospital standards. Although earlier surveys had pointed up deficiencies in hospital care, none were as thoroughgoing as state EMIC evaluations. Those inspections provided exhaustive documentation of deficiencies in OB-GYN services and impressed national political and medical leaders with the need for broader, long-term reform. Surveys were also a spur to immediate improvement, for only if a hospital got EMIC approval could it receive a share of what ultimately became a $122 million federal bounty. And the changes were impressive. As the *American Journal of Public Health* put it in 1949, EMIC's emphasis on quality care raised standards in whole areas where, before the war, standards were low.[77]

Yet for all the good it did, EMIC was only a temporary expedient, which ceased in 1947. If the nation was to preserve and expand recent gains, a permanent national hospital program was an evident need. In 1946, just as EMIC was flickering out, such a policy emerged, with passage of the Hospital Survey and Construction Law—popularly know as the Hill-Burton Act.

Its origin lay in another and wider hospital crisis: by war's end demand (and need) for general hospital beds was far outrunning supply. Nineteen forty-four saw a record 16 million admissions, 2 million of which were maternity cases, which had tripled since 1930. Hospital crowding was so terrific, said *Modern Hospital*, that "beds scarcely have time to cool off between patients."[78] The overload was partly due to population growth—8 million more 'Americans since 1939. Also Americans had begun to get the hospital habit as a result of EMIC and the ending of the Depression. Then there was the growth of group hospitalization plans, which the AMA had been eagerly promoting since the late 1930s as a deterrent to "socialized medicine."[79]

Worse than crowding was the absence of any hospital at all for millions of rural (mostly Southern) Americans. If available they tended to be grossly substandard. End-of-war estimates were that 40 percent of American counties, with 15 million people, were without adequate hospitals.[80]

By 1944 several groups were urging a national solution. The American Hospital Association wanted the federal government to continue and expand its wartime construction program. About the same time the PHS, taking the Duke Endowment as its model, was calling for a national survey of total hospital needs and a plan of public construction and supervision. That summer (1944) the Senate held hearings on the question, and by their end a consensus was building for federally sponsored hospital construction. Finally in August 1946, a bill offered by Senator Lister Hill of Alabama and Congressman Harold Burton of Ohio passed the Congress.[81]

The most venturesome step yet taken by the nation in the health field, Hill-Burton authorized a five-year $75 million program of grants-in-aid to the states. The fund would help erect a national hospital system and a grid of public health centers, distributed in such a way as to provide care to every American. To qualify, states had first to agree to match federal dollars on a two-to-one basis. In actual dispersal of the fund, however, need would also be a factor. States with lower per capita income and fewer hospitals would get a disproportionate share of aid (up to two federal dollars for every state dollar) which meant that, again, Southern states would be Washington's chief beneficiaries.[82]

Next, states had to assess hospital needs. Surveys must not only identify counties with insufficient hospitals and centers but also determine whether existing facilities met minimum standards. For hospitals the criterion was 4.5 approved beds per thousand people, and for health centers (slated to get 25 percent of monies), one facility for every thirty thousand. Where urban and rural areas had equal need, rural Americans were to have first priority.[83]

Finally, states were to exert continuing supervision over construction programs by empowering some agency—usually the state board of health—to approve construction proposals. To aid those decisions governors were to name advisory councils to review each project in detail. Final authorization came from the PHS. As national administrator it would keep pressure on the states to serve their neediest areas first and to do it by building primarily small hospitals of fifty to one hundred beds.[84]

Certainly, the South's neediest were its blacks, whose hospital bed ratio (1:1000) was less than half that of whites and whose hospitals were nearly all unaccredited.[85] Hill-Burton recognized these problems, yet its handling of hospital segregation was ambivalent. The Act's "non-discrimination" clause mandated that hospitals must provide service "without discrimination on account of race, creed, or color. . . ." But there was a hedge: states that already had "separate hospital facilities . . . for separate population groups" could ignore the non-discrimination proviso if they supplied blacks with enough facilities and services "of like quality" to meet assessed need.[86] Hill-Burton, then, was open-ended where blacks were concerned, leaving it to Southern states (and the surgeon general as final arbiter) to decide how much blacks needed.[87]

Although, traditionally, white control meant racial injustice, Hill-Burton brought black patients (if not black doctors) substantial benefit. A few critics like black physician-editor Montague Cobb deplored the fact that the act strengthened segregation. But even separate wards were a novelty — and godsend — to rural blacks. Further, the evidence indicated that for the first time since *Plessy v. Ferguson* (1896), separate in this case was almost equal.[88]

The story of Hill-Burton in South Carolina was a fairly typical one, and blacks there benefited about as much as they did elsewhere, which was to say that they did much better than before but not as well as they might have. The state's first task was to survey resources and needs. Right away there was conflict. The state medical society wanted its appendage, the board of health (the Hill-Burton administrator) to do the job. But the hospital association and legislature insisted that a new, broader-based agency do it. Ultimately a survey group was formed of representatives from health, medical, and pharmaceutical interests, along with two "consumers." It would remain in place as the all-important advisory council.[89]

Completed in early 1948, the survey revealed a dismal picture. South Carolina had just 50 percent of the beds it needed, and about one-third of its counties had no hospitals at all, many of them the heavily black counties such as Clarenden (72 percent black) and Allendale (73 percent). The survey also revealed outright racial bias. Despite a provision within the Act for giving blacks special attention, the report concluded that there were "no special population groups or areas with special problems . . . that require a special allotment of beds.[90]

Thus the implementation of the initial stage of Hill-Burton did not augur well for South Carolina blacks. Part of the problem was that the survey-advisory council was all white. Black medical leaders, who pinned large hopes on Hill-Burton, tried to change that. In 1947 Charleston physician Carr McFall and Palmetto Association leader L.W. Long asked Governor Strom Thurmond to put a black on the council. But Thurmond turned them down, explaining that council make-up was already set. The best blacks could do, Long told colleagues, was keep in touch with proposed projects and try to block those that did not deal fairly with Negro patients.[91]

Prospects for fairness dimmed in 1948 as advisory council members turned to spending South Carolina's five-year, $9 million appropriation. Whereas the expectation was that it would go mostly for rural hospitals and health centers, the first proposal called for diverting $1,550,000 (with more to be added later) to build a teaching hospital for the Medical College of South Carolina, in Charleston, a project having strong backing from the executive committee of the board of health.[92]

The primary reason for the proposal was to safeguard the College's accreditation. As dean Kenneth Lynch revealed in a confidential letter to new health officer Ben Wyman (Hayne retired in 1944), the College could not maintain it without soon getting a new hospital. But that was not Lynch's only—or his public—justification. A major new facility could deal with complicated diseases beyond the scope of any community hospital. Moreover, two-thirds of patients, mostly black indigents, would receive free care. Thus Lynch thought it appropriate for the council and executive committe to give the Medical College a special priority rating.[93]

The executive committee agreed and instructed its advisory committee to set an early public hearing on the issue. The turn-out was poor, most testimony coming from College spokesmen who stressed the advantages of the facility. Apparently captivated by the idea of a high-powered hospital for South Carolina, the council gave its approval, and that spring a funding schedule of $500,000 a year was authorized, to begin in July.[94]

But the decision met immediate protest. The main objection was that construction of the College facility would subvert the purpose of Hill-Burton by delaying erection of smaller hospitals badly needed elsewhere. The most outspoken critics were South Carolina hospital administrators. One of them, C.L. Guyton, charged that the plan would eliminate up to 10 percent of allotted beds from every county, while a second, George Holman, accused the executive committee of betraying the goal of Hill-Burton, which was to put hospitals in counties with fewest resources. Joining those critics was a contingent of doctors from Greenville County, which had a far higher priority than Charleston and whose $2 million grant was derailed by the spring decision. Their leader was J. Delchard Guess, who, like most of his up-country colleagues, was incensed by what he regarded as aggrandizement by the Charleston medical clique. Despite low country claims, he said, only Charleston County would really benefit from the projected facility. The executive committee should reconsider its decision.[95]

Pressured by hospital administrators and by physicians whose altruism was mixed with professional jealousy, in fall 1948, the advisory council and executive committee rescinded their decision. Despite continued appeals from the medical school, plus the threat of legislative coercion, the advisory council continued to deny funding to the College until 1952, even though the executive committee wanted to relent. The council held firm partly because it decided that it had badly erred in its first decision and that local hospitals must have precedence. But its opposition to the College also stemmed from the fact that in 1949 its eyes were opened for the first time to the seriousness of black needs, which could be met only if the Charleston proposal were delayed.[96]

Here was something unprecedented in South Carolina history: a group of influential whites (the advisory council) joining the black cause, even to the extent of urging preferential treatment. Credit for the council's surprising conversion was due to one man, Charleston black physician Carr McFall. In September 1949, in response to repeated petitions from black doctors, Governor Thurmond named McFall to the council, making him one of the first South Carolina blacks of the century to be put on a state policy-making body. By his dignified demeanor and determination to make his colleagues aware of black needs, McFall created a climate of sympathy and willingness to act that would not have existed without him.

One of his first moves, made in December 1949, was to get the council to agree to meet occasionally with citizen groups. Presenting them as a way of building local understanding of the council's role, McFall apparently hoped that community meetings would also open an avenue for community lobbying. At least such was the result of his action. Starting in March 1950, a string of hospital delegations appeared before the council to seek help in meeting needs of black patients. Though most were from white-owned institutions, the first were trustees of the Waverly-Good Samaritan Hospital, who laid before the council their desperate need for funds to enlarge and upgrade equipment and facilities.[97]

Following their presentation, McFall delivered a speech that gave his colleagues some views most had probably not entertained before: Better hospital facilities were a critical need for black patients and doctors. Problems for patients were obvious; there was a crying need for improved medical service. In South Carolina not a single black hospital and only a few Negro wards of segregated hospitals could meet Hill-Burton's licensing standards. For doctors, problems were more subtle but equally pressing. If the black profession were to survive, it had to have full access to improved facilities. Besides places for private patients, the black doctor must "be allowed to work on charity patients, to follow through on autopsies [and] to hear staff discussions on difficult and rare cases. . . ."[98] If something were not done, black doctors were simply going to vanish from South Carolina. At present there was "nothing to induce Negro doctors to want to practice or to return to South Carolina after they finished their education."[99]

In the end McFall and the Waverly-Good Samaritan spokesmen were so persuasive that the council voted that day a special priority rating to enable trustees to complete a seventy-five-bed addition (the one contemplated in talks with the Duke Endowment twenty years before). Within a month the board of health executive committee approved a $130,000 allocation.[100]

McFall's influence was even more apparent the following year (1951), when the council urged an emergency diversion of funds for construction of four new Negro hospital units. Three were to be segregated wings of existing county hospitals and the fourth, an enlargement of Charleston's black hospital. None of the counties had a high enough priority to merit new construction. But testimony convinced the council that the situation for blacks deserved special consideration.[101]

Conditions in the Conway Hospital were typical. They were also of long standing, but recent pressure from black doctors and community leaders there had pushed hospital trustees into making the appeal. According to board chairman E.E. Whitsett, there were eleven Negro beds in a ward having space for six. Two additional beds lay in the hallway. "There were no isolation quarters, no private rooms, and only one toilet. . . ." When Negro babies were born, they arrived in a crowd. Yet in that environment doctors in 1950 had treated 825 Negro patients and delivered 125 babies. And numbers were growing as more and more black purchased hospital insurance.[102]

The major barrier in the way of approval of the four requests was funding: it would have to come from already approved projects. Ultimately, the council agreed that that was justified, and the project tagged for largest sacrifice was, again, the Medical College, which had finally gotten approval for the first-stage of a $10 million grant. Shortly after the council vote, in November 1951, the executive committee, with some misgivings, assented to the change.[103]

A white medical school having to step aside so that hospital problems of poor blacks could be addressed — could that actually happen in South Carolina? As it turned out, the answer was no. But it was not the Medical College that blocked the plan; it went along with the additional delay with surprising lack of fuss. Ironically, it was the PHS which forced the council to rescind its recommendation on the ground that it was unfair to address black needs in four South Carolina counties without allowing the other forty-two to present their special problems.[104]

To fathom that decision, one had to look past hospitals into the labyrinth of South Carolina politics. The PHS was not concerned about forty-two coun-

Charleston physician T. Carr McFall, a leader of the state's black physicians and a catalyst in getting Hill-Burton Funds for black hospital care, c. 1955. Courtesy of Mr. John A. McFall.

ties but only about one of them — Barnwell. Poor, heavily black Barnwell County had a large claim on Hill-Burton funds: no approved hospital, plus an expanding population, owing to the opening of the Savannah River plutonium plant. And Barnwell had something else that no South Carolina county could match: political clout — in the form of the two most powerful legislators in the state, Senator Edgar Brown and Representative Sol Blatt. In 1951 they decided that Barnwell would wait no longer for its hospital, and they told the advisory council that in pointed terms.[105]

Initially, the council resisted the Barnwell pressure and voted to delay its hospital for another year in order to move ahead with the black projects. But the council underestimated Brown and Blatt, who finally took their case to the PHS in August 1952. Bending to the greater force, the PHS refused approval for the Negro units and instructed the advisory council to proceed with the Barnwell facility and the Medical College hospital.[106]

In retrospect, November 1951 represented the crest of South Carolina's interest in using Hill-Burton money to close the racial gap in hospital care. After 1952 and the wrist slap from the PHS, special priorities for blacks were no longer given. Original plans were faithfully followed, which meant the diversion of funds to the Medical College, which by 1956 had gotten $6 million for its hospital, a sum only $1.5 million less than that given to all other hospitals in the state combined.[107]

Did that mean that Hill-Burton was of little benefit to South Carolina blacks? One participant thought so. Jacques Norman, administrator at Greenville General Hospital and member of the advisory council, charged that the executive committee shamelessly favored the Medical College over those counties with a large need for Negro beds. In July 1952, Norman sought a large cut in the College grant, and when the executive committee rebuffed him, he resigned.[108]

Norman had a point. But his view was overly negative, for it failed to take into account the number of heavily black counties which got Hill-Burton hospitals. By 1954, of nineteen new facilities, twelve were in counties with black population majorities. One of the twelve was in Barnwell County, and, although political chieftains Brown and Blatt had used political muscle to get it, that hospital served a county that was over 60 percent black. There were, to be sure, a number of heavily black counties which got no hospitals in the first decade of Hill-Burton. But they got the next best thing: public health centers. By 1954 fifty-eight clinics had been built, 70 percent in majority black counties.[109]

Equally significant was the fact that hospital care in the South, if still separate, was finally moving toward equality, for the number of new Negro beds was at least proportional to the black population percentage. And the quality of service for those patients — at least in Hill-Burton facilities — was also nearly equal. Thus a 1952 Georgia study of seventeen Hill-Burton hospitals reported that every facility served blacks, and all seemed to be giving a "reasonable amount of care to indigents."[110]

In North Carolina the situation was more favorable. Although Governor R.G. Cherry refused to appoint a black member to that state's Hill-Burton agency (the North Carolina Medical Care Commission), North Carolina's legislature was far more generous than others in the South in supporting federal projects, and the planning agency showed more foresight in its use of state and federal monies.[111]

In fact, North Carolina initiated its state-wide hospital program before Hill-Burton. Duke Endowment veteran Marshall Pickens sat on the North Carolina Medical Care Commission in the early period. He recalled that North Carolina blacks enjoyed access to all Hill-Burton hospitals. Moreover, North Carolina, Pickens believed, was more successful than any other Southern state in extending hospital care where it was needed. Although North Carolina did not quite succeed in putting a hospital in every county, each was served by at least a regional facility. Yet the state had not built hospitals "where they weren't needed and where they couldn't survive," as Pickens felt had happened in Florida and Georgia.[112]

In nearly every case the solution to Southern black hospital needs was not an all-Negro facility but a new wing of a segregated institution. Hence, by 1950 only four of 218 Hill-Burton projects, nationwide, involved all-black hospitals. Since the 1880s they had been the only feasible response to the problem of racial segregation, but Hill-Burton clearly marked the beginning of the end for them. All-black hospitals would endure well beyond 1950, but they would find it increasingly difficult to compete for patients and staff against better-funded Hill-Burton facilities.[113]

From the viewpoint of the black patient, however, that mattered little, for during Hill-Burton's first decade Southern states built segregated facilities on a generous scale. That was because per capita funding was higher in the South than elsewhere. In the initial five years, six of the ten most heavily endowed states were in the South (including North Carolina and Georgia). And at the end of Hill-Burton's first decade, half of all completed hospital projects (3500 of them) lay in the South.[114] The typical hospital was a small facility of fewer than fifty beds (56 percent of projects), operating in a community with fewer than five thousand people (53 percent). Such a profile indicated that Hill-Burton was fulfilling its primary objective of providing hospitals to rural Americans—especially to those living in the South, who had greatest need.[115]

It was equally clear that Hill-Burton was altering traditional patterns of hospital use among the poor of both races. Before the 1950s hospital admissions varied directly with patient income. By 1963, however, one medical sociologist could note that admission rates were virtually equal across incomes.[116]

If Southern black patients received large benefit from Hill-Burton, the same was not true for black physicians. Their most important gain was the ability to accompany their private patients into local, public hospitals, a right provided by law but secured only by the persistence of black physicians. In 1949 South Carolina doctor W.H. Young reported to his Palmetto Association colleagues that he had contacted "several heads of county supported hospitals on . . . Negro doctors administering services to their patients. . . ." He had also seen the president of the South Carolina Medical Association to get his support. "All saw no reason why this should not be done," and Young urged colleagues to push "this important question."[117] Carr McFall found that the main barrier had not been white physician opposition, as much as white ignorance. "Many white medical community groups were surprised to learn that Negro physicians could not treat their patients in local hospitals." Knowledge, alone, "often resulted in corrective measures."[118]

But acquisition of courtesy privileges did not lead to other gains. Through the 1950s the South's Hill-Burton hospitals remained closed to black interns, refused to employ black residents, and generally denied black physicians opportunity to treat black charity patients. And of course hospitals lying outside the Hill-Burton system — the majority in the south — did not have to admit black doctors *or* patients. Changing that situation was beyond the ability of black doctors alone. As Georgia physician and NMA president Ralliford Smith observed in 1958, opening up hospitals involved the elimination of the whole structure of segregation. And black voting power was the only force strong enough to do that.[119]

Although blacks' ability to get the training, public health services, and medical care that they needed would await the civil rights movement of the 1960s, much progress was made in the earlier era of segregation. Federal health programs of the 1930s and 1940s were primarily responsible for those advances, for the creation of emergency relief agencies, local health clinics, and hundreds of new (or enlarged) hospitals provided Southern blacks with preventive and curative medical services that only a few had enjoyed during the earlier period of the state funding and control.

Yet the contribution of black physicians, community leaders, and foundations like the Duke Endowment and the Rosenwald Fund had also been important. If smaller in scale than the work of federal agencies and programs, these private individuals and groups raised the consciousness of many black and white physicians and health officers. In so doing they helped prepare them for the next step in the struggle for equality in health and medical care.

PART III

Problems Addressed

Mill Hands

CHAPTER 8

Mill Owners and the Village Health Environment, 1900–1950

Before any examination of the post–World War II phase of black health history is undertaken, however, the threads of the mill workers' story need to be regathered and attention focused on the efforts that were made to respond to their health dilemmas. In making that inquiry, the historian is aware of both continuities and discontinuities with the black story. Parallels emerge in the way that class bias and economic absolutism (in the case of mill hands) and racism (as directed at blacks) affected the health of each group — first, by contributing to the onset and spread of illness and, second, by impeding its prevention and cure.

Equally clear are the dissimilarities between the two accounts, which emerge in the present chapter's survey of community responses to textile health problems. By contrast to the many-sided effort to aid blacks (see chapters 4–7), few helping hands were extended to ease the burden of ill health among mill families. While it was true that the Duke Endowment was active in most textile counties and New Deal health and work relief programs benefitted a fair proportion of mill workers, none of those private and public efforts — excepting possibly the Rockefeller Hookworm Commission — singled out textile hands and their families as a population with special health problems and needs. And except for the efforts of Joseph Goldberger, Charles Wardell Stiles, and their colleagues against pellagra, permanent federal agencies like the PHS and the Bureau of Labor did little beyond the surveying of mill village conditions. Public agencies at the state level were even less active than those in Washington — even after the infusion of New Deal purpose and money — partly out of an unwilling-

ness to challenge employer authority and partly due to the distraction of
a multitude of other health problems.

What was more, few if any physicians emerged from textile communities to push their people's interests as black doctors did theirs. The South's
racial history provides ample explanation for this disparity, that is, a segregated society would need to produce black doctors to treat its black patients, but would probably assume that textile hands could rely on the
white middle class to supply their physicians. Even so, the inability of textile villages to throw up their share of doctors — or lawyers, poets, and art-
ists, for that matter — speaks pointedly to the lack of opportunity in these
villages and the dispiriting effect that they had on families trapped inside
them. Not even the occasional layman emerged to take the lead in health
reform, as happened in black communities.[1] Those physicians who did minister to mill hands frequently harbored a strong aversion to them. A South
Carolina physician, following the exit of several mill patients from his office, fumed to his next visitor, "'God damn it, I hate these mill people.
They're the dirtiest, nastiest people in the world.' The doctor then raised
his window to 'let the air clear.'"[2]

The only parties who professed a special and continuing interest in
the well-being of the textile hand were the owners of the villages. Yet these
expressions of concern more often than not lacked substance and were offered chiefly, if often unconsciously, to firm up support from local elites,
dissuade workers from joining unions, and disarm outside critics.

Interestingly, these critics mainly attacked owners for the health dangers that they allowed to exist inside their mills. Yet in responding to such
charges, employers and their supporters chose to ignore critics' points and
to proclaim instead all the things they were doing to safeguard health inside
company-owned villages. Like politicians, owners chose to play from their
strong suit and emphasize company welfare programs, the latter a fairly
common feature of mill village organization from the outset.

Hence the debate between Northern critics and Southern textile owners that ran on fairly continuously until the Depression took a curious
form. Antagonists tended to talk past each other, with neither responding
directly to the charges or claims of the other. As a result, it is difficult to
obtain a clear, overall picture of attempted solutions to the health problems
of mill workers. One finds only two distorted (and largely unchallenged)
views that address separate facets of the whole issue. To get an accurate
understanding of what was being done (or not done) in the hundreds of
Southern mills and their associated villages, the historian needs to examine
each realm separately. Since village health problems received attention well
before those of mills, owners' efforts to protect the living environment of
Southern hands will be examined first.

Owners made large claims about the extent of their benevolent activity in mill villages. Partly these glowing reports of their own doings sprang from their need to attract labor. But most textile leaders also believed that a system of village paternalism was raising significantly the living standards of tenant families drawn into the mill orbit.

To promote a sense of community and order, owners commonly built churches and schools, and furnished their staffs as well. But employers were particularly fond of drawing notice to their efforts toward providing worker housing. In the early twentieth century the typical Southern mill was either an isolated factory set in the midst of a farm district or one located on the outskirts of an established town or city. In either case, owners had to provide housing for employees to insure a ready supply of labor. Rented at a nominal rate (about twenty-five cents per room per week), dwellings varied in size according to the number of workers in a family.[3]

No matter their size, all houses, according to owners, were constructed with modern sanitary practice in mind, as homes reportedly were provided with pure water and the latest in waste removal. Frequent reference was made to a village's natural drainage, which minimized the risk of malaria. One early help-wanted flyer, distributed by South Carolina's Pacolet Mills in farm communities near Greenville, painted a beguiling picture. "We furnish you good, comfortable houses at fifty cents a room per month," said the broadside. "We furnish you wood, coal and provisions laid at your door at market prices. Pacolet mill houses are located on a hill and the place is noted for its health and free from all malarial diseases. . . . We have good water, a splendid system of free schools . . . ; in fact everything that appeals to one who wishes to improve the condition of his family."[4]

Charles Wardell Stiles, the PHS zoologist who "discovered" hookworm in the South and helped lead the early crusade for its eradication, was convinced that mill owners were generally doing great work in home sanitation. By 1910 Stiles had toured mill villages in the Southern textile states, and he reported that every one he had visited had privies for its families. Furthermore, most owners also saw to it that they were regularly cleaned, about once a week. Unglamorous and undramatic work, that, but Stiles saw it as significant. Not only were mills "bettering the condition of the rural whites"; they were also offering those one-time farm people the "opportunity to outgrow" the hookworm infection that they brought with them from their farms.[5]

The generally acknowledged ill health of Southern tenant farmers prior to their becoming mill hands, in fact, provided the mill owner his best defense against attacks by those who pointed to large numbers of emaciated, woebegone villagers as proof that the textile baron was stealing the health and even the life of workers. The owner's rebuttal was that mills had not produced such people—they had simply inherited them. Indeed, credible observers like Stiles testified that newly arrived farm families had sanitary habits little better than animals. Many had not only never seen a privy but refused to use one, preferring instead to squat under their houses. So bad was the problem that some mill owners refused to house new hands among the older workers, installing them instead in outlying houses for two to three months until they were properly broken in.[6]

Instead of abusing healthy workers, then, mills claimed to be rescuing sickly ones. Textile labor was in a transition stage, and the appearance of pallid faces and worn-out bodies should cause no surprise. It would take time for decayed farm workers to be made into robust mill hands. Meantime, mill supporters argued, "the best thing that can happen" to poor white farmers—man and boy—"is for them to go in the cotton mills," for only there could they find the good food, shelter, and sanitation needed to shake free of their anemia and broken-down condition.[7]

Besides sanitary improvements, a fair proportion of early twentieth-century mill owners also were offering their hands a chance to obtain regular, professional medical care for the first time. The mill schemes, called physicians' clubs, involved a regular deduction from workers' wages and the payment of this money to one or more local practitioners, who were obligated to treat participating families on demand. According to mill publicists, the system worked greatly to the advantage of the hands. Monthly deductions were small (about ten cents per family member) largely because the mill used its influence to keep fees low. Participation was usually voluntary, and mill families were free to choose among cooperating physicians.[8]

It was not just mill owners and their spokesmen who were touting the health benefits of textile work. By the time of the First World War, Southern physicians and industrial development agencies were proclaiming a health renaissance in the region's mill villages. The South Carolina correspondent for the *Southern Medical Journal* reported in 1916 that both owners and operatives were cooperating fully with the state board of health in eliminating typhoid and other preventable diseases.[9] The state's industrial development department paid particular tribute to mill management. Executives, said the 1916 annual report, understood that paying attention to sanitation and water supply was good for profits, because operative efficiency and health were closely linked. And department inspections in South Carolina amply confirmed management's high degree of health awareness: Aside from workers' overconsumption of patent medicines, health in the state's mill villages was as good as in any other center of population, reports stated. In all, the expanding health campaigns of South Carolina mills were a "great and needed adventure. . . . " Due to such activities, the department proclaimed, the growth of textiles was nothing short of "wonderful."[10]

Although workers would not have called it wonderful, one development common to larger villages that particularly impressed the state officials in the South was the creation of settlement houses. Modeled after those in Northern cities, they stressed such subjects as improved nutrition and food preparation, better child care (aided by the creation in some villages of child clinics), and home sanitation. Such welfare programs appeared in Atlanta, at the Fulton Bag and Cotton Company, and throughout South Carolina, where large mills dominated the industry. Often those programs were begun under YMCA auspices, as owners felt that a religious organization had the best chance of "reaching the operatives."[11] Later, as federal funds became available through the Smith-Lever Agricultural Extension Act (1914), some mills set up settlement houses in partnership with land grant colleges. Winthrop College in Rock Hill, South Carolina, ran such a program with several mills in its region. College sociologist and project administrator Mary Fraysor let it out that more than just home and hygiene was on the agenda. A strike was then on (1915) at Brogan Mills, and Fraysor's hope was that her night meetings would give adults "something so big to think about that they will not brood over real or fancied grievances."[12]

If a number of owners were making substantial efforts to upgrade employee health, it was equally true that no owner was totally to blame for what problems existed. Employees bore some responsibility as well. Much of their hookworm, whose rate of incidence ranged as high as 85 percent in some early twentieth century villages, they brought to the mills themselves; and their primitive sanitary habits often frustrated the most earnest efforts to introduce a more modern mode of toileting. In addition, the almost fanatical independence and suspiciousness of newly minted factory hands made such routine medical interventions as smallpox and typhoid vaccinations occasions for flight to some other mill that was less interfering. Of course the manner of such intervention often added to employees' resentment and terror. In Newberry, South Carolina, in 1903 not two but three segregated smallpox clinics were held—one for blacks, one for whites, and one for mill workers. And in nearby Union that same year, the town constable accompanied the vaccinating physician (at the mill owner's request), both to compel compliance and defend the doctor.[13]

But the more common failing of owners was not that they ruthlessly imposed better health practices. Rather, too many virtually ignored employees' medical problems and needs, rendering the official picture of a high level of benevolent owner activity both illusory and self-serving. As one 1920s survey of mill health programs in North Carolina showed, management's involvement with preventive and curative medicine varied widely and was governed by the personal interest of individual owners or superintendents. In the early twentieth century, unless an owner encountered a production-limiting problem such as malaria, most did little beyond the minimum needed to attract and hold workers, which usually meant the construction of often shoddy houses and a few simple structures for schools and churches. Since an ample supply of workers was nearly always available — save for the years during and just after World War I — most owners generally had no cause to give more than minimal attention to the health of their "people." At the same time that some owners were imposing smallpox vaccination on their help, for example, others were opposing the practice out of fear that "shots" might unfit their operatives for work.[14]

Most owners, in fact, were blissfully ignorant of the health needs of their villagers. Comfortable in the belief that hands were already enjoying improved health simply by the act of moving to a mill, few saw any need to put that assumption to the test. In the pre–World War I period virtually no mills had physicians in their employ. Only a small minority hired resident nurses, and almost none kept any records of illness and death. Moreover, few villages had the benefit of services from a public health agency. Most workers, then, lived in unincorporated villages, and in South Carolina, at least, the state board of health was not empowered to appoint a local health officer for them unless petitioned to do so by 25 percent of voters. During the first decade of the century, only one or two such petitions came forth. As a result, health conditions in most textile villages were as much a closed book to their owners (and to state officials) as life in black neighborhoods was to the South's urban whites.[15]

Then, in World War I that situation began to change, as many more owners started to take steps that gave their claims of benevolence some substance. In part the new interest in village health and sanitation was a product of discomfiting wartime disclosures of national unfitness, the awful experience of the 1918 influenza pandemic, and the health idealism of that period (see chapter 6). But it was also the result of pure calculation. The war years saw the imposition of a high surplus profits tax. Rather than pay more money to Washington, most owners put it into village improvement, much of it health-related.[16]

Nurses were the most common new addition to the village scene, and they appeared in a number of guises. Occasionally, the village social worker was competent to provide home care and health education, but most company nurses were just that — professionals, hired on specially for the work. Others were not in mill employ at all. A few were on staffs of city or county health departments, while some had a private, non-mill employer. After the war, group life insurance became more common in the industry, and one major insurer, Metropolitan Life, saw economic and social advantage in providing nursing to mill policy holders. Finally, there were cooperative schemes in which a single nurse worked for a group of mills. Although no program provided care to more than a few families in a given year, use of nurses was moderately widespread. A study in North Carolina in the middle 1920s found that 81 of 322 mills hired nurses under one arrangement or another. On the whole, hands responded favorably and eagerly to the nursing work, despite occasional instances of mill families who tried to exploit nurses as domestic servants and others in which nurses bullied people into altering health habits.[17]

Besides employment of nurses, textile money was also used for certain capital improvements important to health. Village sewer systems, for example, were installed at an accelerated rate in both Carolinas after 1918. Health implications were obvious: more indoor, flush toilets and fewer unsanitary privies. By 1925 in South Carolina only about 30 percent of mill village houses still had foul, open privies, in sharp contrast to a decade before, when about two-thirds of families had relied on primitive-type disposal. Not all the new sanitary toilets were indoor, flush type, but that was the trend. Just before the decade's end, a survey of twelve Greenville villages revealed that ten had indoor facilities in every home, while in the remaining two, modernization was soon to begin through a special bond issue. Besides that, each home also was equipped with running water and electricity, and a few with bathtubs. Management remained a bit leery of the latter innovation however. Too many tenants, owners said, echoing a familiar charge thrown against blacks, used tubs to store potatoes and coal. So most mills held back on bathtub installation until the family showed that it was "ready" for one.[18]

A final post-war health development was the provision of group insurance. Though most policies provided only death benefits, a fair number paid disability income (in the range of ten dollars a week) in case of sickness. Initially, premiums tended to be borne by employers, but after about 1923 costs came to be shared with workers. In North Carolina around 30 percent of textile corporations offered workers some sort of group insurance. For South Carolina the proportion was probably larger, given the greater average resources of its mills. In addition, coverage there may have more regularly included sickness benefits. In 1925 Saxon Mills, an industry leader, began providing life and health insurance to all employees, the whole package paid for by the company.[19]

Collected together, mill health programs, along with the clinics and hospitals erected in the 1920s, seemed an impressive testament to management's new concern for employee welfare, especially in view of the fact that many programs were begun after the ending of high wartime taxation. Yet in the face of owners' long record of previous indifference, historians might be excused for wondering if more lay back of such spending than human solicitude.

And other motives have not been hard to find. In the case of group life and health insurance, University of North Carolina sociologist Harriet L. Herring found that the primary reason why mills offered the policies was to hold workers. Begun during the post-war boom of 1918–20, group insurance was seen as a way to reduce high labor turnover. But the turnover continued, and, as mills realized it, many abandoned the insurance idea. In North Carolina nearly 56 percent of plants which had offered policies dropped them by the mid-1920s.[20]

What was true of insurance was, according to another industry-watcher, Broadus Mitchell, even more so for other health and welfare programs. Virginia-born economist Mitchell, a Johns Hopkins professor and a man who pinned his hopes for social reform on economic development, believed that by the 1920s corporate welfare was aimed strictly at advancing management's interest. It had not always been that way. Mitchell, who was bewitched by the New South mythology, believed that the nineteenth-century founders of Southern textiles — a race of giants, he felt — were truly concerned with workers' welfare. But after the turn of the twentieth century, in his opinion, a lesser breed of owners had begun to assume control, and by the end of World War I mill paternalism had assumed a new and uglier guise. Instead of keeping management's and labor's interest in balance, owners were attempting to advance themselves at workers' expense. "Paternalism, which for many years was generous," Mitchell claimed, "at length became calculating." The calculation was simply that if the owner provided visible signs of concern in the form of nurses, kindergartens, sanitary improvements, and insurance policies (but not higher wages), workers would not listen to the siren song of union organizers. If Southern cotton manufacturing began as an altruistic venture, Mitchell lamented, "now [1925] it has become a tyranny, . . . a device for delaying democracy," and a weapon to use against higher pay, shorter hours, and more independence of life for mill operatives.[21]

Of course, owners and their supporters could reply that it did not matter why health improvement was made, so long as it was. Actually, it mattered greatly. By offering nurses, better sanitation and insurance in lieu of higher pay, owners deprived operatives of the one sure solution to problems of ill health. Just before the war, in a study of 750 Southern mill families, PHS investigators had demonstrated the direct relation between low income and debilitating illness. Only when an average-sized family earned an income of about $900 a year (a level attained by only 25 percent of South-ern textile families) did the sickness rate drop to that of all American households.[22]

Using health improvement primarily as a way to reach objectives be-lieved good for business (eg., holding workers, keeping unions out) was to put that improvement on a shaky footing. If business soured, there would be little compunction about jettisoning health programs. And that indeed proved to be the case. In the first half of the 1920s there was just such a downturn in cotton textiles, and in response a large proportion of mills abandoned fledgling health projects. The discontinuance of nursing pro-grams was a case in point. In the middle 1920s, at least a fourth of Southern textile companies dropped the services, for reasons ranging from a claim that the work had not fulfilled expectations ("We did not think that it paid," one manager cryptically put it) to a feeling that "people did not take to it. . . ."[23] One close observer of textile welfare in North Carolina believed that the primary cause was economic. When times were flush, as they were for about three years after World War I, management saw health programs as indispensable. But when economic conditions took a downturn they were soon seen as fringe programs, whose cost could safely be trimmed away. One mill owner in Gastonia who withdrew from a cooperative nurs-ing program in 1924 put it simply and candidly: "That was when times were better; cannot afford it now."[24]

But Broadus Mitchell would probably have replied that that was not the whole story: programs were ended not simply because they were an added burden in a difficult time. Owners discontinued them because they no longer served strictly business objectives. With the advent of hard times, mills did not need to go to special lengths to keep workers on and unions out. Scarcity of jobs and general employment insecurity would by them-selves accomplish those goals.[25]

A more critical measure of the depth of owners' concern about the health issue was their response to the upsurge of pellagra in the 1920s (chap-ter 2). Recurring with frightening suddenness and shattering effect (for the South thought itself rid of the disease), pellagra's comeback posed a health crisis whose dimensions were both emotional and biological. Yet the re-markable thing was not pellagra's reappearance, but how little the South did to contain it. This time inaction was not due to ignorance. Southern doctors, health officers, and many mill owners had been mindful of its seri-ousness since before the war. In the early 1920s, as a new wave of pellagra cases hit, the PHS launched a major effort to publicize the growing danger and urge immediate preventive steps. When President Warren Harding voiced his hope in 1921 that not a day would be lost in saving Southerners from what he implied was "plague and famine" in the region, pellagra became, overnight, major news.[26]

In part, it was the wide publicity given pellagra that shaped the South's response. For the first time the connection between pellagra and poverty was being publicly made, and Southerners felt insulted, particularly by the president's willingness to join those maligning the South. Put on the defensive, region leaders expended energy, not grappling with the malady, but denying its existence. Health officers, physicians, businessmen, and politicians all protested that the South was being unjustly portrayed. Even progressive Watson Rankin derided the PHS claim of food scarcity and accused the surgeon general of being afraid to admit a mistake. Business leaders rejected Washington's claims of a pellagra increase out of fear that bad news would hurt profits. Goldberger's Spartanburg supporters felt compelled to explain that having a pellagra hospital in their midst did not mark their area as a center of disease. Also, owners insisted, mill wages were good in Spartanburg. To the degree that pellagra existed it was not poverty that caused it, but workers' ignorance of proper diet — a familiar management rationale for worker ill health.[27]

Not all owners shut their eyes to the strange sickness. Spartanburg's Saxon Mills cooperated fully with the PHS, and the superintendent of Hanes Knitting Mill in Winston-Salem began an annual ten-acre planting of green vegetables for workers' use. But the bulk of owners took no steps to prevent that eminently preventable disease. Owner inaction became all the more remarkable after 1925 when Goldberger discovered, and the PHS publicized, the almost magical restorative qualities of brewers' yeast. Although the PHS proved that yeast could effectively eliminate pellagra at a cost of only about $1.70 per patient, there was no evidence that mill owners made any use of it.[28]

More than any other episode, the pellagra crisis of 1920–30 demonstrated the hollowness of mill management claims of concern for the well-being of "our people," the mill working families. For certain, blacks and white sharecroppers were also hard hit and needed much attention. But the mill owner had never promised to aid them. He had, however, often proclaimed his solicitude for his hands. And as victims of a sort of semi-captivity they were dependent on that aid. Owners could of course point to the depressed economic conditions as a reason for their inaction in welfare matters. Even so, in the face of all of their claims that they were exercising an enlightened paternalism, owners' unwillingness to respond to pellagra in the 1920s stood out as a glaring example of a responsibility undischarged.

But if mills were ignoring the threat of pellagra (and at the same time cutting back sharply on general health protection), other developments were taking shape by the mid-1920s that would work in a more positive direction. One was the move by Southern cities after the war to incorporate satellite communities into urban jurisdictions. The new arrangement was satisfactory to all parties: cities got tax revenues, while outlying populations got a variety of urban services such as water, sewage, and preventive medical care. Mill workers were particular beneficiaries of the incorporation movement because the cities which had most to offer in the way of health services included many of the textile capitals of the South, such as Atlanta, Columbus (Georgia), Greenville, Spartanburg, Columbia, Charlotte, Winston-Salem, Greensboro, and Durham.[29]

Besides incorporation, another promising post-war trend was the growth of county health departments, largely catalyzed by the work of the Hookworm Commission and spurred by the sanitary zeal of the war. In North Carolina in the 1920s the number of organized counties grew from seventeen to thirty-six and, in the lower state, from six to twenty-three. Not all textile counties gained a health department, but in North Carolina twelve of nineteen mill counties could count a fulltime health director by 1930.[30]

Of course proximity of services did not insure their delivery. County budgets remained low, and sometimes the added mill population, located on the county or city fringe, got short shrift. As one North Carolina mill executive complained, "we are the stepchildren of the county down here, for the [health] workers like to stay up at the county seat."[31] Thus, like the black population, mill hands were often neglected by official agencies, who in the interest of augmenting slim budgets sought primarily to impress (and serve) more influential elements of the community.

Even so, work was being done by public agencies that had not been contemplated in the pre-war years. Epidemics were brought more swiftly to a halt, as in 1923 when typhoid flared out of control in the Pacific Mills community, near Columbia. The state board of health simply took over and soon had the disease contained. Five years later when pellagra was peaking in South Carolina, state health officer Hayne, realizing that his resistance to Goldberger's ideas was hurting his standing with Washington, swallowed his objections to the diet theory and initiated a major campaign to contain the disease. One feature was the distribution through county health offices of about six tons of brewer's yeast, enough to cure some thirty-four thousand adult victims. As a result, by 1929, deaths were down in South Carolina for the first time in eight years.[32]

And the surprising thing was that the death rate continued to decline — all across the South. In a period of worsening economic depression, pellagra deaths should have, by all prediction, continued upward. But the utter collapse of cotton prices had the effect of encouraging diversification in Southern agriculture and a greater availability of vegetables and dairy products. That, plus an increase in yeast distribution and vigorous nutrition education work by health and Red Cross officials (who convinced Southern families to supplement their stark diets and to become spring gardeners), appeared to be the basic explanations behind the taming of pellagra. By 1940, though hunger continued a problem, total Southern deaths from pellagra had fallen 77 percent below the 1928 level.[33]

But if the beginning of national economic depression in 1930 eased the burden of pellagra, that was the only comfort Southern mill hands and their employers could find in that decade. To the handicaps of low revenues and wages was added the problem of unsteady work. Mills that did not close often went on short time, forcing employees to accept a fraction of the fifty to sixty hours that they had worked in the 1920s. Management at South Carolina's Springs Mills would later (and justifiably) take pride in the fact that they were able to keep all their operatives working half-days.[34]

Many were not that fortunate. W.A. and Susie Crede, a mill-working couple in Columbia, had taken advantage of better times at the start of the 1920s to buy a home of their own outside Olympia village. In 1930 their mill cut work to half-time, and on top of that Susie became seriously ill. Their only option was to sell their home and return to the village. But with half-wages and one earner ill, the sale money melted away. As Crede lamented, "there was too many hospital and doctor bills. And Susie was helpless so long."[35] By 1934, hands in Gaston County, North Carolina, which boasted more cotton mills than any place in the world, were getting in a bare twenty hours a week. A local business leader frankly admitted that "no satisfactory living standards can be maintained under such conditions."[36]

Faced with reduced revenues, mill companies, too, had to tighten belts. Just how much the new cost-consciousness affected primary medical care programs is difficult to assess. One could assume that the 1920s trend toward their elimination accelerated with the Depression. Almost none of the Federal Writers' Project narratives, which were replete with accounts of mill workers' ill health, mentioned a company nurse or clinic. Moreover, if sanitary conditions inside the mill were any indication, management gave scant attention to health needs on the outside. A 1930s inspection of industrial health safeguards in South Carolina reported that "the lack of such features in some cases is rather appalling." Even soap and towels were "very rare."[37]

The one positive step which some owners did take was to revive physicians' clubs, which had become defunct after World War I. In the Depression, doctors' income had plummeted like everyone else's, and a working arrangement which might not have looked attractive a decade before

Mobile clinic used to combat pellagra in Spartanburg County, South Carolina, in the early 1930s. The clinic provided medical examinations, nutrition education, and pellagra treatment (yeast) and represented the kind of effort which eliminated most of South Carolina's pellagra by World War II. Dr. Hilla Sheriff, future director of the state's maternity and infant program, is at left of woman's group. Courtesy of Dr. Hilla Sheriff.

seemed much more so in the 1930s. One Columbia mill worker remembered his employer starting such a service. At a cost of only twenty-five to thirty cents a week per person the plan proved highly popular, so much so that, if anything, workers often took advantage of the doctor, going to him for the slightest injury or illness. Yet such arrangements did not seem to be widespread. Mill hands who told WPA writers of their Depression-era health problems spoke instead of fee-for-service arrangements and high bills. Winston-Salem hand Lacy Wright had to use a private surgeon for his wife's appendectomy, and he was two years paying off the bill, at a rate of $1 a week.[38]

As Wright's experience suggested, life for a great many Southern mill workers in the 1930s became a fight for survival. With wages down and health-related welfare programs disappearing, not only did illness rates rise but victims in most instances suffered alone, without professional attention. About 1936 Dr. James Hughes started a practice in Greenville, and he saw among mill patients a great deal of malnutrition, plus a lot of malaria. In his estimation the average blue collar worker was in "bad shape."[39]

Exactly how heavy the burden of illness was in the 1930s is impossible to measure. As in the 1920s, those who should have known did not. The chief sanitary inspector of the South Carolina Board of Health only occasionally visited mill towns.[40] And the state's mill superintendents had little better idea of how their families were faring. They held doggedly to the notion, expressed by one welfare director in 1938, that Southern cotton mills were making not one product but two: "cotton cloth and citizens."[41] Yet the state's textile industry was then keeping sickness records on just 19 percent of its employees and giving pre-employment physicals to but half that fraction.[42]

Thus, in trying to gauge the level of ill health of Depression-era mill families, the historian has to rely on impressionistic evidence — notably Federal Writers' Project interviews of the late 1930s. But these sources all point to the same conclusion: if textile families were not actually sicker in the 1930s than in the 1920s, they found their episodes of illness more difficult to bear, emotionally and economically.

Whether the cause was poor diet, too many pregnancies, inadequate medical care, or something else, nearly every family interviewed in South Carolina had had a serious health problem in its recent past. Mr. Huffstetler had been on the verge of giving up his job because of the painful aggravation of an old hernia (a step he had avoided thanks to a loan from his mill to pay for surgery).[43] Bill Johnson had developed TB in 1938 just months afer his marriage, and his brother (in the mill) and sister also had it. All had probably gotten TB from their mother. She had been sent to the state sanatorium but fled home after only a few weeks. There, despite her constant coughing and spitting, she went "right on about the house-work, cooking and everything."[44] Then there were the Prossers, both of whom had poor teeth. Mr. Prosser's were so bad that he had been in misery a year. Mrs. Abel Stearns had an illness that required three operations. Susie Crede was so helpless that her husband had to hire a black woman to look after her while he worked. Fanny Miles lost an eye to cataracts and glaucoma. Sara Taylor also had failing sight. Mr. Padgett was felled by a stroke in 1938.[45] And so it went: of all South Carolinians interviewed only the Tally Smiths reported an ample diet, a past free of serious illness, and a happy outlook on life.[46]

But there was more than just pain and fear in those households. There was a feeling of desperation, as well. Like Southern blacks, textile hands in the 1930s, while they might be ill, could not afford to be sick. Money was simply too scarce for any to be able to miss work. Moreover, being absent from the job meant risking unemployment. After several days' absence Carrie Johnson's father found that the mill had no place for him. Faced with such a prospect, men and women gritted their teeth against pain and labored on. Huffstetler worked for fourteen years with his hernia until lifting finally became too much for him. John Prosser, though his "old teeth was just ruinin' me with poison," kept at his job for a year before a relative came to his aid. Mr. Padgett could not afford to stop work either, even though he knew his blood pressure was high. The stroke that he had been warned about finally took his life — at work.[47]

South Carolina conditions were hardly exceptional. A study of one North Carolina textile town suggested that in the upper state, too, health was in near collapse. That inquiry was important for another reason as well: it suggested that contrary to long and general belief, mill families were less healthy than similarly situated rural Southerners (blacks excepted).

Undertaken in 1939 as a joint venture of the Rockefeller Foundation, Duke University Medical School, and the North Carolina Board of Health, the study examined the nutritional status of a rural mill town in the North Carolina piedmont. The town, with its all-white population of four hundred (nearly all of whom were reliant on the local mill), was seen as typical of most small North Carolina textile communities. Although a few residents grew their own food, most purchased provisions from nearby farms with wages averaging about twelve dollars per week. Area farmers, who worked a region of "rather low soil fertility," were about two-thirds white and one-third black.[48]

After careful measurement of vitamin and mineral intake during consecutive fall and spring seasons, investigators concluded that the mill community "was in general . . . moderately malnourished and in this [it] was probably representative of quite large similar groups in the state."[49] In contrast, rural whites enjoyed slightly better nutritional status, while area blacks fared worst of all.

In the course of their inquiry, scientists noted a strong seasonal variation in nutrition. In the spring, after the "long winter of partial privation," vitamin levels were at their lowest point for all population groups. But then, after fall harvest, levels rose considerably, and most people were able to make it through the next lean period without clinical signs of disease. Yet the passage through was a narrow squeeze, and the study suggested that, but for yeast distribution, pellagra would have been a clear and fearful possibility. As the researchers reported, "borderline adequacy is an unsatisfactory level; any accident, sickness, or fever would greatly increase the need and throw the individual promptly into a deficiency state."[50]

Much of the danger that mill villagers faced from vitamin deficiency was avoidable by using modern methods of pressure cooker canning or rapid freezing. But North Carolina's mill people (and its blacks) were not using those methods. They were still caught in the "stone age cycle" of summer abundance and winter scarcity. It was true that textile families were only "slightly anemic," managed to get just enough vitamin A, and showed only a few cases of clinical scurvy or other deficiency diseases (as pellagra). But if they were not obviously ill, researchers doubted that they were healthy either. At best North Carolina mill hands were probably contending with chronic ill health all year long.[51]

Yet at that very time events were unfolding which would shortly begin raising the living standard of all Southern textile families, until by the 1950s they would be almost indistinguishable from the great bulk of American industrial workers. The magic leaven was money—that major determinant of health and quality of life—and its source was that last card in the New Deal deck, the Fair Labor Standards Act of 1938. The Wages and Hours Act, as popularly named, not only ended employment of children under sixteen, but set a twenty-five cents per hour minimum wage (scheduled to rise to forty cents by 1945) for all workers making goods for interstate commerce. Under the touch of the new statute the lot of the lowest-paid mill workers improved immediately. Just before the law passed some 13 percent of all Southern textile hands (the proportion was far higher in South Carolina and near that average in North Carolina) earned less than the new minimum. Nine months later the proportion had fallen to 1.5 percent.[52]

Then came the war, with its upward pressure on jobs and pay, causing wages in Southern textiles to advance well ahead of those mandated by law. By 1940 workers had already achieved an average wage of forty cents an hour. That average rose to fifty-eight cents in 1944 and to seventy-five by spring, 1946. For the lowest paid textile hand improvement was equally swift. By law the War Labor Board had authority to jump the minimum wage ahead of schedule where substandard living conditions existed. In the textile South that was done several times between 1941 and 1946, until by the latter year the minimum wage stood only about ten cents behind the average pay rate. To be sure, cost of living rose as well, by 35 percent from mid-1939 to mid-1946. But pay for textile hands climbed faster, leaping some 132 percent during the same seven years.[53]

Equal improvement occurred in hours. By law the maximum work week had to be cut to forty hours by late 1940, with time-and-a-half for overtime. Of course during the war many textile hands labored above forty hours, but they were paid extra. The important point was that between 1938 and 1945 a transformation occurred in the amount of labor required of the average mill hand. In the middle 1930s a full-time employee put in fifty-five hours over a five-and-one-half-day week. A decade later his work had fallen to forty hours, with two days off.[54]

The health benefit of such changes was obvious. By war's end, textile hands could eat better and afford more medical care than ever before. And as nutrition improved, they moved back from that border of ill health where they had stood prey to both infections and the effects of short-term nutritional deficiency.

It was true that not all workers moved ahead equally. A 1954 study of a South Carolina mill county revealed higher than average illness rates, a pinched life-style, and backward health attitudes (such as the belief that polio was God's punishment for sin). But thanks to a post-war decade of high textile profits, increased unionizing activity (forcing management into a defensive position of benevolence), and government-mandated wage boosts, new life was born in Southern mill villages. One sign was the disappearance of those very villages, as company entities at least. In the late 1940s, largely for reasons of economy, management began selling houses to workers. And because they were able to afford middle-class aspirations for the first time, workers began buying the houses.[55]

As they acquired homes, higher wages, and middle-class tastes, textile hands also became less and less distinguishable, not just from the general Southern white population, but from the Northern work force as well. Merger with the national norm had clear implications for health. Mill hands still fell ill in their homes and communities, but no longer could they be singled out by statisticians and health officials as an exceptionally benighted group. They now had only the normal health problems of the American industrial work force, which for Southern textile hands represented significant improvement.

Yet normalization left one coterie of health problems still unresolved: occupational illness. As in most American industries, the major industrial hygiene problems in textiles — problems stemming from excessive heat, humidity, noise, fatigue, and dust—had only barely been identified by the start of World War II. Even more discouraging, the one group in position to take action against industrial conditions in textiles, the mill owners, refused to recognize the problem. Until they did so, cotton hands would continue to be silent victims of the workplace.

CHAPTER 9

Textile Owners and the Problems of Occupational Health, 1900–1970

While touting his health work in company-owned villages in the early twentieth century, the Southern mill owner said little about meliorative efforts in the mill itself. And with good reason, for nothing was going on there in the period before World War II except for the making of cotton yarn and cloth, often under conditions inimical if not ruinous to health.

In part, managerial inattention was due to ignorance of sources of danger. Work was by nature hard, dirty, heavy and hot; and operatives, glad merely to have jobs, did not often ask for relief. Besides, occupational illness in textiles seldom assumed an acute form and was almost never specific enough to be traced to the workplace. In addition, when operatives were sick they were mostly sick at home, which made it easier to disassociate ill health from work.

Nevertheless, any plea of ignorance on the part of owners was also self-serving, for labor and health agencies outside the South issued fairly frequent warnings about the health hazards of mill work. But Southern owners chose not to listen, or if they did, not to pay heed. No one, after all, was requiring them to do so (and would not until the century was about three-fourths over). Until workplace changes were mandated by economic considerations, Southern hands had little choice but to labor, and suffer, in silence.

From the start, the strategy of Southern mill owners when accused of harboring serious health hazards in their factories was either to ignore the charges, deflect them, or defame those who raised them. One of the first such attacks on Southern owners came from prominent Indiana Progressive Senator Albert Beverage, one of the national spokesmen for child labor reform, who in the early twentieth century singled out Southern textiles as particularly villainous offenders. In 1907 during Senate debate on a child labor bill, Beverage lashed the Southern textile industry for tolerating inhuman conditions in its mills. Painting a ghoulish picture of psychotic foremen driving exhausted children in dust-filled factories, Beverage and his medical sources agreed that the consequence was seriously impaired health, especially from TB. But that was not the worst of it. While the South was abusing its white children, it was sending its black children to school. It was "enough to wring the heart," this Progressive lamented, "to think that day by day you are permitting a system . . . which is steadily weakening the white race . . . and steadily strengthening the black. . . . "[1]

Southern textile leaders could not allow that assault to go unchallenged, and one of the most elaborate responses came from South Carolina. In answering Beverage, industry spokesmen largely ignored his critique of conditions inside the mills, choosing to fight on their own ground by parading owners' welfare work in mill villages. The main reply took the form of a published tract, issued by the South Carolina Department of Agriculture, Commerce, and Immigration, the public arm of the textile industry. Written by veteran Charleston reporter August Kohn, the pamphlet had one chapter entitled, "the Health of the Help," which extolled the work being done in mill housing and sanitation.[2]

But Kohn did not completely ignore the mills. One of his arguments was an updated version of what slavery apologists had said a half-century before: mill conditions could not possibly be as bad as alleged, for no sane man would allow injury to those who were the source of his wealth. A mill superintendent was judged (and paid) according to how well he retained his help, and the brutal or harsh man could not have held his workers. Mill presidents knew that and were insistent on healthy work conditions because "the healthier anybody is the more anxious and the more willing he is to work. . . . " Consequently mill owners went to considerable expense to provide the "very purest water" to the mill and keep it always clean. Kohn was only sorry that statistics were not available to prove that "health conditions in the cotton mills are as good as they are elsewhere." If data had existed, they would have demonstrated that "there could be no more kindly or considerate treatment given to any class of people than is accorded the help in the cotton mills."[3]

It was easier, of course, to defame critics than rebut them, and here textile spokesmen drew heavily on arguments that had long been used against those championing the Negro's cause. Dean William Few of North Carolina's Trinity College (later, Duke University) was closely allied to state mill men, and in 1909 he told *Atlantic Monthly* readers that all criticisms of textile conditions came from outsiders who did not understand the South. In view of the backwardness of most mill families, "much remains to be done," but it would not be done by "crude, unfair or evil-minded agitators or by well-meaning but ill-informed sentimentalists." Rather, the hard problems of factory life would only be solved, step by step, by those with "actual experience" of running mills.[4] With mill hands as with blacks, the South knew best how to handle its own problems.

To note owners' determination to ignore or sidestep criticism is not to say that there were no improvements in working conditions. Changes occurred when it was obvious that they would enhance productivity and profits. One problem that received management's attention was excessive cardroom dust, which all recognized as an obstacle to worker efficiency. When vacuum strippers were first introduced in Europe about 1905, American owners rejected the innovation, arguing that the suction would cause too high a breakage rate in the fragile sliver. By about 1912, however, experience and improved strippers were proving otherwise, and the devices were rapidly introduced in American mills. Dustiness was further reduced in many Southern mills in that period when owners shifted from coarse goods production to manufacture of fine cottons, which were milled from higher-graded, less dusty fiber.[5]

Elimination of the sanitary hazard associated with the "suck shuttle" was also a consequence of the introduction of new equipment, though health improvement had no part in the decision to install it. Mouth-threaded shuttles were a minor bottleneck to production, and, when self-threading ones became available about the end of the First World War, newer, more progressive firms readily adopted them.[6]

Where a health problem had no clear economic dimension, owners ignored it. Such was the case with noise. Neither medical nor industrial literature of the pre-1930s gave the problem more than barest notice. One of the few times when *Textile World* (the industry's major trade journal) alluded to the problem was when it published a letter from a mill manager complaining that vibrations and noise from a nearby card room made it hard for his office staff to concentrate. He wanted to know if there was any way to insulate his section to keep the noise out.[7] Whether those white collar workers got relief was not reported, but for the hands noise was one fact of mill life which no one questioned.

In the post–World War I era the Southern textile industry was in much better position to address job-related hazards. Except for a downturn in the early 1920s, profits were strong until the Depression. Moreover, the industry was beyond the pioneering stage and enjoyed a heightened stability and confidence.[8]

Not only was the industry in better position to act; it was once again facing considerable pressure to do so. This time criticism came from both outside the region and at home. If child labor had been the focus of earlier "Yankee" criticism, a drive to unionize adult workers underlay most later attacks. In 1920 the Bureau of Labor Statistics reported (and *The Survey* publicized) a study showing that mill operatives were 50 percent more likely than other workers to die before age forty-four, largely due to "wear and tear" on the job.[9] The next year brought a harsher, more explicit indictment: addressing a convention of Northern textile workers on the need to unionize the Southern industry, American Federation of Labor president Samuel Gompers painted a picture of "weary women carrying babies in arms into the mills" and charged that murder was being done there.[10] Then came the report of the union-related Workers' Health Bureau of New York, which documented higher illness rates in textiles and claimed that it was the "occupational factor"—the heat, dust, and fatigue of work—that was most responsible for the greater morbidity.[11]

But not just outsiders found fault. The attack which most angered Southern owners came from fellow Southerner James Cannon, teetotaling Methodist bishop of the diocese of Richmond and soon-to-be-exposed manipulator of the stock market. In 1927 Cannon read a collection of articles by left-leaning journalist Paul Blanchard, touching on mill conditions and deploring workers' long hours, low pay, and lack of unions. Cannon's response was to organize a committee of forty-one prominent Southern churchmen to work with mill executives to ameliorate conditions and help end the isolation of mill villages from the life of surrounding communities. Their first step (1927) was a published appeal to Southern textile leaders to take corrective steps.[12]

Industry reaction to Cannon's move was stormy. Resisting even the suggestion of workplace problems, owners used the 1928 meeting of the Southern Textile Association to respond publicly to the Richmond bishop —and to suggest who and what really lay behind his charges. Georgia mill president W.D. Anderson led the counterattack. Cannon, said Anderson, was a Judas. "Living here among us," he should have known "what has been done, what we are now doing, and, if really interested [he] could have found out what we hope to do."[13]

What was more disturbing about the bishop's attack was the comfort it gave to the industry's real enemies, "the professional labor agitators, the trouble-makers, the socialists, the Reds. . . ."[14] Socialist journalists like Blanchard (Cannon's tutor) were men "who have sinister designs on the conditions that exist down here, . . . who would like to throttle our development, [and] . . . who have no love for us, except to despoil us. . . ."[15] In the embattled South the "red herring" strategy was still the preferred defense: outside criticism, whether lodged against Southern mills or Southern segregation, was unworthy of notice because it came from those who wished the region harm.

If Southern owners were deaf to criticism, there were other groups emerging in the region from whom workers might perhaps anticipate a more constructive response to the issue of occupational health. The 1920s saw the beginnings of a major shift of New England mill corporations to the South.[16] That migration brought south people who had kept abreast of public efforts to define health dangers in textiles and who had participated in state-mandated programs to eliminate the most obvious ones. Some had even initiated health improvements voluntarily so that, as one said, "employees may be able to give their best service for the common good of the organization."[17]

But anyone hoping for progress from Yankees-come-South was only courting disappointment. Although the migrants lacked the paternal mindset governing Southern thinking, they had an equally strong reason for opposing health improvements. Expenses of that kind would have defeated their purpose for coming South in the first place, which was to reduce costs of labor. About that they were quite candid, at least within textile circles. When New England's Pacific Mills acquired a chain of South Carolina plants from Colonel Leroy Springs in 1923, the firm's representative pointed to "longer hours of work and a lower wage scale" as the main factors in his company's decision to move.[18] From that perspective, spending for dust control and heat and humidity regulation would have been patently irrational acts.

Northern mill owners were not, however, the only potential force for change in the South. A more likely impetus for reform was the budding occupational health movement, which by the 1920s was commanding allegiance from public and private health groups in the North. As early as 1906 Massachusetts's health board had begun surveying conditions of work and mortality among operatives and was soon trying to meliorate the worst conditions by promulgating standards for water purity, ventilation, and humidity. Interest quickly spread beyond Massachusetts. In 1910 the American Association for Labor Legislation, which would soon propose the first national health insurance measure, convened a national conference on industrial diseases, and two years later Congress passed the first significant occupational health statute, the Esch Law, taxing manufacture of white phosphorous matches. Equally important in providing a national forum for the new movement were the American Public Health Association and its *Journal* (begun in 1904).[19] Encouragement came, too, from the Public Health Service, which in 1914 received a mandate from Congress to study occupational disease. But it did more. At annual meetings with state health officers PHS leaders discussed industrial problems and urged their state counterparts to get busy in the field.[20]

Yet for all the zeal and interest in the North, little enthusiasm for "industrial hygiene" was transmitted to Southern health agencies. That was not to say that state boards had no interest. In 1908 South Carolina's first health officer, C.F. Williams, carried out investigations of stale air and bad sanitary conditions in South Carolina mills. However, in the first case he was willing to accept management's arguments that windows had to be nailed shut to control humidity, and, in the second, he put the blame for poor sanitation on workers. A few years later James Hayne would report to fellow state health officers that South Carolina was requiring reporting of occupational diseases. But the claim had little substance: twenty-five years later South Carolina's first industrial hygienist complained that state doctors virtually ignored reporting regulations.[21]

Public inaction was partly due to the absorption of Southern hygienists with other dangers, such as pellagra, hookworm, and a medley of infectious diseases. But the ignoring of industrial hygiene was a result of more than a need to attend to other priorities. State boards had little interest in, nor understanding of, industrial health.[22] To some extent that was because health officers, like other public servants, realized that the textile industry was virtually a law unto itself. Knowing that it was both futile and politically hazardous to press the industry to face unpleasant facts — for there would be no back-up in state legislatures — health officers had little motivation even to learn what major problems were. Yet health leaders were not merely reformers on a tight leash. They also held back because they believed, in New South fashion, that if health risks did exist in the workplace, such was the unavoidable cost of progress. Even North Carolina's Watson Smith Rankin was dazzled by the prospect of industrial growth and downplayed the health challenges it posed. In 1913 Rankin was an expert witness for a Durham chemical plant which was being sued by area residents for polluting the environment and endangering workers. Rankin felt the suit lacked merit. The odors and gases were not harmful to health, he reported. Even if they were a great nuisance, "we must accept such conditions as part of the program of modern civilization with its many advantages offsetting its disadvantages."[23]

But boards of health were not the only agencies in the South with responsibility for industrial hygiene. Virtually every Southern state had an industrial development office, which claimed an equal devotion to interests of employees and owners. The record, however, belied any such impartiality: capital, not labor, was the true constituency. Primarily, development agencies sought to do two things: shield industry from unreasonable demands of labor and assist management in creating an image of industrial benevolence. As for improving conditions in the workplace, an Oklahoma mining inspector once gave clear if pungent illustration of how official favoritism inhibited action. About 1920 this worthy told a business audience: "when I go into a mine and find a lot of things wrong and the owner tells me that if he has to put in all those changes he will go bankrupt, I just say 'well, brother, forget it.'"[24]

In the textile South, state industrial agencies were equally slavish, none more so than South Carolina's Department of Agriculture, Commerce, and Industry (ACI). Created in 1908 out of the older Bureau of Agriculture, Commerce, and Immigration, the department contained a labor division whose avowed purpose was to safeguard the physical and moral well-being of workers. To that end it was authorized to implement the state's first factory inspection statute, an approach that was also undertaken in Georgia about the same time.[25]

Those initiatives, however, turned out to be more illusion than substance. Georgia's law, which focused primarily on fire safety, provided no control over sanitation or ventilation. Similarly, in South Carolina, factory inspection until the 1930s was concerned almost exclusively with keeping underaged children and blacks out of mills and in upgrading toilets. The ACI department could have done much more. By 1915 it had legal authority to control humidity in weave rooms, but that mandate must have been accorded for public relations. In the next twenty-five years it was never exercised.[26]

That was not surprising, for the primary mission of ACI was not industry-supervision but industry-boosting. The various ACI commissioners were always careful to picture mill owners as generous patriarchs, work conditions as steadily improving, and unhealthy situations as exceptional.[27] The department's 1925 annual report showed how far self-deception could go. That year its commissioner heralded a major modernization program in South Carolina mills. It featured installation of costly sanitation and health equipment, such as germ-proof humidifier systems and modern vacuum cleaners, which had "eliminated as far as possible" dirt, dust, and waste from textile machinery. Altogether, sanitary conditions in mills had improved "at a wonderful rate."[28] Yet thirteen years later the state's first comprehensive industrial hygiene survey reported that cotton dust, high temperature, and humidity endangered the health of at least three-fourths of South Carolina's mill population.[29]

Of course the textile South was not unique in ignoring worker health. In 1925 Ohio State University scientist E.R. Hazelhurst reported that, nationwide, factory inspection and industrial health programs were mostly a sham. Standards were lacking. Inspections were perfunctory. Interest focused on toilets and seats for females. Yet Southeastern states, said Hazelhurst, were especially backward. In the Carolinas and Georgia, "very little" was being done to supervise industrial health. There was no reporting of industrial illnesses, and personnel were not only "quite unqualified" for the work but preferred to "side-step it."[30]

One issue that state agencies were not able to side-step in South Carolina was the stretch-out. In March 1932, having heard long and loud complaints from constituents, legislator J.C. Williams of Spartanburg proposed a board of health investigation of the effects of the stretch-out on the "mill boys." Williams's resolution cleared the general assembly by a wide margin, but it was evident that election-year politics was a major reason. Hearings did not begin until the day after elections and got little press coverage. The independent report, which became available in December, was disappointing from the workers' vantage point, for it concluded that there had been insufficient time for an accurate study of the health question. Moreover, workers were reportedly divided over the amount of stress that the stretch-out caused.[31] For its part, the executive committee of the board of health seemed as much relieved as disappointed by the study. With but one exception members gave it their endorsement, adding that "it will require not less than three years, probably longer . . . to reach any conclusions of value."[32] Actually there *was* one conclusion to be drawn: South Carolina workers had no one to whom they could turn to protect them from dangers at work.

Yet behind the seeming hopelessness of the situation, changes were taking place at the national level which would soon provide an advocate, not just for Southern mill hands but all industrial workers. In 1933 Roosevelt launched his New Deal, and its concern for the national health was clear from the outset. Besides blacks, youth, and mothers and infants, industrial workers also fell within its range of interests. With the Social Security Act came funds for industrial hygiene divisions in every state board of health.[33] Though the new divisions would work no overnight miracles in the textile South—in fact they would be almost as subservient to industry as earlier agencies—they would nonetheless increase awareness of problems in textiles. They would also transform the industry's negative stance toward occupational health issues to one of responsibility for on-the-job health, provided of course that improvements did not cost too much.

The two Carolinas were among the earliest beneficiaries of new federal funding (Georgia would not start industrial health work until late in the War). Both in fact had been pointing toward an intensification of effort even before Social Security passed. In South Carolina, Hayne got his first exposure to actual textile conditions when he accompanied the stretch-out investigation into a number of mills. Over the next couple of years he paid increased attention to scattered reports of mill hazards, and in 1935 he reported to the legislature that nothing was being done to safeguard the state's 145,000 industrial workers, of whom 80,000 were in textiles. Hayne judged the problem severe enough for immediate state and federal help. State legislators ignored the request, but the next year federal money let Hayne start work.[34]

In North Carolina, interest was keener but also focused more narrowly on problems of silicosis and asbestosis, whose etiologies had been recently worked out and which involved 155 plants (only five of which were asbestos mills, with 500 workers). Even before the SS law, the North Carolina General Assembly passed an occupational diseases law, covering siliceous and asbestos workers and dividing authority between the state department of labor and a newly created industrial commission. The availability of SS money enabled the state board of health to become involved, by creating an industrial hygiene division whose main function was to provide data and services to the industrial commission. They included setting standards for target industries and administering pre-employment physicals and X-ray examinations to endangered workers.[35]

One of the first tasks of all the new hygiene divisions was to survey state industries to find out what and where hazards were. In North Carolina that meant discovering the number and location of workers exposed to silica and asbestos dusts. In South Carolina the state's two newly hired industrial hygienists (North Carolina had a force of five) undertook a broader survey. They reported findings in March 1937, and they confirmed that health problems were legion in textiles and elsewhere and that concern and control were practically nonexistent.[36]

In South Carolina textiles, for example, nearly 90 percent of hands were exposed to organic dusts and about 50 percent to high humidity and heat. Among those endangered groups only 21 percent and 32 percent, respectively, worked in mills which tried to set some controls. About 17 percent of hands handled toxic chemicals and none got protection. Some 4 percent worked amid siliceous dusts, but only one-fourth had protection. Overall, a high proportion of South Carolina wage earners were exposed to conditions known to produce diseases elsewhere. It was "only natural," said state hygienists Bob Brown (a chemical engineer) and Harry Wilson (a physician), that "these same conditions and materials will cause identical results in South Carolina."[37]

Not only was South Carolina's textile industry ignoring patently dangerous conditions, but employers had little more inkling of their employees' state of health than they had in the pre-war era. Sickness records and pre-employment physicals were still a rarity, and periodic medical screening was unknown. South Carolina mills were not even "prepared to care for the most trifling injury," as most were unwilling even to bear the cost of a first-aid room.[38]

Corporations in most states scrimped on the money allotted to health and safety, but South Carolina firms did worse than most. In 1938 a study of industrial health services (such as sick benefit assistance, sickness records, and a full-time plant physician) in fifteen states, including six in the South, found South Carolina in last place in five of the seven categories and next to last in a sixth.[39] At its best, Brown and Wilson observed, South Carolina did "not even measure up to the low marks made by industry in other states. . . . "[40]

Armed with such findings, industrial hygienists in the two Carolinas were determined to alter prevailing conditions. North Carolina's division announced that it aimed to "bring the benefits of preventive medicine to the million and a quarter of North Carolinians who are engaged in industrial pursuits. . . . " New manufacturing processes had been introduced with "little thought being given to their possible effect. . . . " In textiles, manufacturing methods long in use and long unsuspected now appeared to carry risks of pulmonary infection and degenerative changes.[41] Those sorts of threats would be the focus of the division's coming attack.

In South Carolina, division hygienists had higher expectations: to use the power of the state to work a basic change in owner-employee relations. Epidemic diseases were controlled only when government agencies got power to implement broadly based preventive measures. The industrial hygiene division was created to take the same strong steps "to protect and preserve the health of the industrial worker."[42]

Even with their new mandate, if these public servants truly thought they were going to effect a health revolution in textiles and other Southern industries, they formed their hopes without considering ruling political and economic realities. The textile industry, as the largest employer and most potent economic force in the Carolinas, exerted enormous influence on local political leaderships, who willingly accorded it full sovereignty over its domain. Besides, industrial hygienists were upstarts who had yet to establish their legitimacy. Until they did so, management would continue to set all industrial priorities.

A General Electric health and safety director about this time sketched the limits under which his public counterparts—even in Northern states— would have to work. Industrial health agencies must take special care to see that recommendations "are sensible, practical, and economical." But state health officials must have a care for more than just industry profits. They also had to consider employee morale. Workers were by nature "curious and possibly suspicious" when a health inspector entered a plant.

He was therefore under special obligation not to arouse their fears unnecessarily, for "a careless word," even if said in jest, might "excite or worry" them. Besides protecting workers thusly, industrial hygienists had an equal "responsibility to try to improve relations between employees and their management."[43]

Zerbst, Brown, and other industrial hygienists quickly learned these limits and scaled down their hopes accordingly. When they actually began to make calls on mills, they put on the garb of supplicant and assured industrialists that they came as friends, not intruders. In South Carolina the division's first report announced that its role would be investigative and advisory only.[44]

James Hammond, who took over industrial health work from Bob Brown in 1942, argued that there was no alternative. "It would not have been a wise and effective way to have attempted to be a policeman. . . . Conditions were set for you, and the terms on which the game had to be played. You had to play on the basis that the employer was the person responsible for the plant, and you had to work with him and his philosophy. . . . "[45]

The same tone was heard in North Carolina, whose industrial hygiene division made a virtue of its powerlessness. Said division head H.F. Easum: the agency "has no police authority; it is purely a fact-finding organization." But that was "probably advantageous in that the results of investigation will not be prejudiced in favor of either capital or labor. The intent . . . is to remain strictly neutral with respect to such interests."[46]

State labor organizations also got support from the New Deal, and they aimed for a stronger health regulatory role as well. But their activity was just as circumscribed as that of the industrial hygiene divisions, and for the same reasons. In North Carolina the labor department's mission was to promote the "health, safety, and well-being" of workers, and to that end it was empowered to order mills to "provide suitable respiratory devices to strain the dust from the air taken into the lungs." Yet that same empowering legislation excused employers from compliance should it "work a hardship on them."[47]

Just how much this accommodationism improved unhealthy conditions is difficult to assess. Certainly the voluntary compliance approach netted some gain, both in terms of management attitudes and improved conditions. Even though industrial hygienists were admitted to industrial facilities on sufferance, they were admitted, and once in the mills they pointed out existing health hazards and sometimes persuaded management of the value of preventive steps. For most supervisors and managers, contacts with state hygienists provided their introduction to the subject and their first realization that worker ill health was not just a matter of poor living habits. South

Carolina's Brown saw some signs of change, even in the 1930s. "Accomplishment during my period could not be measured statistically," but he was certain that "we established an awareness of industrial hygiene and a mild recognition of its value in the industrial . . . community."[48]

At the same time there were serious limitations to the volunteer approach. First of all, it created a client relationship out of what needed to be substantially an adversarial one. Stressing the creation of industrial good will, health and labor agencies soon fell into the old habit of praising manufacturers, publicly, for their cooperative spirit and progressive outlook. Management was flattered so often that it soon had an exaggerated notion of the progress it was making. Worse, regulators often believed their own rhetoric. In addition, making too much of little gave workers a false sense of security, in the mistaken belief that the state was safeguarding their welfare.[49]

Yet far from that, a sort of partnership developed between regulators and regulated that worked to the benefit of employers far more than operatives. Even surprise mill inspections were conducted at the sufferance of industry. It was true that management seldom refused to open their gates, but that was because they were usually tipped off in advance. A South Carolina mill hand, whose work career began in the 1930s, recalled that when the department of labor made inspections "they always let them know they was coming." He knew this, he said, because "I've done the cleaning." A fellow worker confirmed that claim: we "swept the floor, blowed down, cleaned up and [inspectors] said, 'Oh, what a wonderful place. Fine'"[50]

North Carolina's industrial hygienists avoided falling into a subservience to textiles only because they avoided that industry almost entirely. The division's primary, absorbing interest lay in preventing asbestosis and silicosis. Admittedly, they were deadly diseases, but they also involved relatively few workers, employed by companies with little political clout. On the few occasions when textiles came under investigation, it was chemical contamination or worker nutrition that got attention, not heat, humidity, noise, or cotton dust. Some thirty years after inauguration of occupational health work, the North Carolina Board of Health admitted that it had gotten its priorities wrong where textiles was involved: an industry employing 85 percent of state wage earners had commanded over the years only 1 percent of staff time.[51]

For South Carolina's Brown the slow pace of change finally palled. In 1942 he left his post to take a similar position in St. Louis. As for his reasons, he felt he was "'dead-ended' technically and professionally and was advised by friends in the Public Health Service that I could better my career and advance more responsibly if I would move to another [non-textile] state."[52]

Yet at the same time that hygienists like Brown were struggling uphill to educate mill executives to give some attention to workplace health, events were building in another quarter which would put an unprecedented premium on worker productivity. Out of those new economic concerns would come fundamental changes in the operations of textile mills, which in turn would lead to substantial health improvement. That most of the health gains were only side effects of economic calculation does not lessen their importance, but it does suggest one of the main routes by which occupational health reform has come to American industry.[53]

Once more, the catalyzing event bringing on all these changes was World War II, which challenged textiles to meet sudden new production goals (up about 90 percent between 1938 and 1942) and exacting new military specifications. Sustaining that sort of production increase in the face of a shrinking supply of experienced labor made management receptive as never before to the claims of government and medical spokesmen that worker efficiency and fitness were closely tied. What was more, a special urgency now surrounded the issue of industrial health. New defense workers were primarily the old, infirm, and female, whom war work subjected to heightened stress and fatigue, and in many cases to new chemical contaminants.[54]

According to the *Southern Medical Journal,* of 4 hundred million industrial man-hours lost in 1941, 90 percent were lost to illness. Over the next four years government, medical, and industry leaders told textile managers how they could reduce their share of lost days. One problem was dermatitis. As early as 1941 the PHS warned of an outbreak of skin problems associated with new synthetic resin finishes required by the military. By 1944 according to the leading industry journal, *Textile World,* the most serious problems had been solved by introducing mechanical handling devices and impervious clothing. To aid in the early identification of these and other diseases, government advisors also began to urge the hiring of industrial nurses and the initiation of a policy of employee physicals. Before the war ended initial steps were being taken on both these matters.[55]

A wide-ranging discussion opened, as well, about the industry's heat-humidity problems. A 1940 PHS survey pointed to South Carolina mills as being "responsible for most of the [industry's] exposure to high humidity."[56] Though industrial hygiene manuals of the period saw high humidity as unavoidable, managers began to discuss ways to limit its ill effects by providing employees with showers and time to acclimatize themselves to outside temperatures and humidity at shift's end.[57]

A few executives believed more could be done. During the war some turned to air conditioning as a way to improve both the work environment and production. In taking that step textile executives were following a trend well underway in the South. Already the larger movie theaters had adopted air conditioning, as had the region's trains; and by the war it was being tried out in major department stores. In fact, in the early 1900s a primitive form of air conditioning had even been introduced to the textile industry in several North Carolina mills. But cost and various technical problems had shortly ended the experiment. By World War II, thanks to such improvements as the invention of freon (1931), air conditioning was now safer and cheaper, and it seemed time to rethink its possibilities for textiles.[58]

Advantages to the industry were several. Air conditioning — and early installations were actually non-refrigrated, air-cooling units — permitted more precise temperature and humidity control, and that in turn allowed a reduction in the moisture required for a given relative humidity. In summer 1941, a Davenport, North Carolina, mill installed one of the nation's first modern systems. The results were gratifying: a lowering of the spinning room temperature to 80° and a reduction of humidity to 48 percent, as well as a sharp drop in "seconds."[59] By war's end, though air conditioning had been installed in just a few mills, *Textile World* was promoting it as a remedy for most personnel and production dilemmas. "Air conditioning of cotton mills," one executive wrote, "is the most human thing the industry could ever do." For those less interested in the "human thing," air conditioning also had advantages in reducing high summertime labor turn-over. And there were other business dividends: "better quality, reduced waste, better-kept and cleaner machines . . . , and all these mean more units per man-hour plus personal business contentment."[60]

Another change, which proceeded to virtual completion during the war, was the provision of nutritious, in-plant meals. By tradition, mill meals were eaten on the run and were usually nothing more than a poor quality bag lunch or a "dope" and a "dog" (cola and hotdog) bought from a meal-time vender. Employers knew that such meals were deficient, but they felt that what hands ate was their own affair. Besides lunches had no bearing on production.

The war challenged the conventional wisdom. With maximum production the number one priority, federal food and production agencies and the Armed Services sought to educate employers in all industries about the relevance of nutrition and to urge management to provide workers with hot noon-time meals, plus time to eat them. *Textile World* also joined in, assuring owners of pay-offs such as employee efficiency, good will, and better health. Any firm which ignored nutrition, said editor Thomas Ott, was foolish indeed: "there is no way to estimate the eventual damage done to a worker's health and the loss in efficiency and production — it is probably very great."[61] By 1944 several large mills, such as Beaumont Manufacturing of Spartanburg, were installing cafeterias, and at war's end textile leadership, at least, had accepted "in-plant feeding" as standard policy.[62]

Although the war period saw only limited action against actual health problems, top management's attitude toward occupational health underwent thoroughgoing change. Textile leaders now firmly embraced the idea that on-the-job health and comfort of workers merited serious attention. Sentiment and humanity played little part in the new calculus. In fact, workers were still no more important than machines. But for the first time they were *as* important and had to be kept in the same, good running order. *Textile World* was a barometer of changing outlook among progressive employers. In 1947 its editor boasted of a new day in textiles: "workers' comfort and health as well as high wages are now an agreed on means to achieve higher production."[63]

From the worker's vantage point, however, an agreed on outlook meant little until it was translated into visible workplace improvement. And the fact was that except for large, progressive firms there was little translation through most of the 1940s. Only big firms could afford such expensive innovations as company nurses, pre-employment physicals, air conditioning, protective clothing, and cafeterias. In the majority of Southern mills, and for the bulk of hands, working conditions remained just as harsh, unsafe, and unhealthy as ever. In fact the Department of Labor in 1945 expressed great concern about health in textiles. The major obstacle to human efficiency, it said, was the "heat and humidity conditions inseparable from satisfactory processing of the cotton fiber."[64] If anything, that problem worsened after the war. For one thing new high-speed spinning frames and looms, installed as a part of textiles' post-war modernization campaigns, generated more heat than earlier models. In addition the need for more pliable fibers to take the strain of faster machinery necessitated a higher humidity.[65]

Heat and humidity were just one set of problems though. In 1944 South Carolina proclaimed proudly that 27 percent of textile companies had industrial nurses. But a more important fact was that 73 percent did not. Near the end of the war a young Greenville physician saw the results of industry disregard of preventive medicine: nearly all men in the cloth-printing department of one local mill had chronic blood dyscrasia. The mill had a physician on contract, but he was an old man, not really up to date, and he never thought to test for anemia.[66] About the same time a South Carolina boy, then sixteen, had to leave school and go into the mill to save his family from eviction from their village. He, too, recalled a cursory physical: the doctor "looked in my orifices, thumped me a bit and pronounced me in good health."[67]

But just as the war spurred industry *recognition* of health problems, af-

ter the war other forces were at work to bring them under control. As before, economics was the spur to change: with business continuing to boom
in the post-war years, management was understandably interested in any
changes which could boost worker productivity. Predictably, changes came
first in larger firms and spread to smaller ones as the dollar value of innovation proved itself.

Although mills gave continuing and wider attention to sanitation,
medical services, and nutrition after 1945, the most important development
by far was the broad implementation of temperature and humidity control
by refrigerated air conditioning. To management its primary appeal was
still its impact on employee productivity and reduction of "seconds." Air
conditioning enabled a Pacolet Mills plant in South Carolina to solve a wor-
risome stoppage problem in a basement spinning room and to eliminate
a severe heat condition which had made it hard to hold workers.[68] Another
Pacolet facility in Gainesville, Georgia, reported with satisfaction that "better control over humidity and temperature is paying off in better weaving.
. . . Loom stops are [also] fewer with air conditioning."[69] Air conditioning
was soon being touted as the greatest boon to low production costs since
cheap, farm labor.[70] *Textile World* in fact urged it as "one of the first postwar
projects."[71]

Not only were there benefits in increased efficiency, but air conditioning was absolutely essential to successful milling of new synthetic fibers
such as nylon and rayon. Introduced commercially in the late 1940s, synthetics required both lower temperatures and precisely regulated relative
humidity. Obviously air conditioning was just what the doctor ordered.[72]

As suggested by the Pacolet experience, the new technology also had
relevance to certain labor problems. In the immediate post-war years workers remained scarce in Southern textiles, especially in summertime. That
was partly because of competition from new industries; but also with living
standards rising everywhere, labor was unwilling to abide the harsh conditions of before.[73] In 1945 the Department of Labor summed up textile's dilemma: "we hold no brief for the reliability of industrial prophets [who
were predicting a textile decline], but we agree with them that the cotton
industry will be faced with increased competition from other industries,
including synthetic textiles, and that its working conditions will have to be
improved."[74] Air conditioning was to be that era's "quick fix."

Unionization threats were another labor problem which played a role
in spurring air conditioning and other workplace improvements. In 1945
with its "Operation Dixie," the Textile Workers Union of America (TWUA),
a CIO affiliate, began to step up efforts to organize Southern textiles. To meet
that challenge the industry could no longer use harsh, union-busting tactics
of the past. It now resorted to a subtler form of anti-unionism that went

by the name, "personnel relations." For the most part personnel relations was "soft soap," not substance. Its guides, according to *Textile World,* were the "recognized findings of industrial psychology," whose aim was to "make the worker feel important and show the worker that his work is creative." Workers with good self-images would turn a deaf ear to union seductions.[75]

But the effort to put the worker in the "right frame of mind" had to involve more than rhetoric. Keeping unions out called also for an end to bad conditions. And so, beginning in the late-1940s, workers began to enjoy the comforts of restrooms, modern toilets, and smoking rooms—the last of which were sometimes enclosed with large glass windows to discourage loafing. In the area of direct health improvement, owners started to pay equal attention to pre-employment physicals, periodic check-ups, recreation programs, and in-plant feeding.[76] But again the major change was air conditioning, and its implementation was rapid. By the late 1950s the air-conditioning revolution was essentially complete. *Textile World* no longer gave the innovation any notice, and in 1958 South Carolina's labor department reported that "most all" textile firms had installed modern air conditioning systems.[77]

Still, not all hands shared the benefits of change. As late as the 1960s in smaller, out-of-the-way mills, conditions remained the same as in the 1930s. And there were some problems that resisted solution everywhere. One of them was noise, against which mills made no progress in the postwar era. Dermatitis was another concern. Addressed first during the war, by the 1950s skin diseases were again a problem as a result of chemical treatments required for the new wrinkle-, crush-, and crease-free fabrics. As for dust inhalation, the most serious hazard of all, no one even saw it as a problem until the 1960s (see chapter 10).[78]

Despite the persistence of problems, the trend by the 1950s was unmistakably toward elimination of unhealthy conditions. The contribution of the profit motive was evident and perhaps paramount. But was it the only force for improvement? What of the parts played by physicians, unions, and state regulatory agencies?

The role of Southern doctors is dispensed with quickly. At best it was minimal. Often it was obstructive. Until the 1960s most doctors had neither interest in nor knowledge of industrial hygiene. The subject was seldom taught at medical schools, and once in practice most physicians had no contact with textiles or any other industry. In fact, the majority of doctors regarded the fledgling field of industrial medicine much as they viewed public health work—as a refuge for failures, incompetents, drunkards, and other addicts.[79]

Apart from lack of exposure, the fee-for-service attitude was the principal barrier to physician involvement with occupational medicine. Medical associations might have supported the idea of pre-employment physicals, but when corporate physicians proposed health maintenance programs, they were often opposed as constituting an invasion of private medicine. In the 1940s the company physician at South Carolina's Sonoco Corporation suggested such a program, only to find local practitioners in opposition because of the Sonoco patients they would lose. A decade later when an imaginative North Carolina doctor, Logan Robertson, began marketing a health-maintenance program to various industries, including textiles, local physicians often raised strong objections for the same reasons.[80]

Textile unions were more forthcoming than doctors, but their influence was primarily limited to mills where they were recognized bargaining agents, and in the anti-union South in the 1950s less than 10 percent of hands worked in union shops. Even there, unions gave occupational health a low priority. It was true that by the late 1940s the TWUA was vigorously promoting group health insurance and heat-humidity standards in contract bargaining.[81] But later critics, such as relentless consumer advocate Ralph Nader, would hit the CIO-affiliated union for doing far less than it might have. Union leaders, said Nader, "with their swollen treasuries and shrunken imaginations have almost uniformly failed to equip their staffs with the skills to locate and detect the full range of job hazards and to develop strategies for prevention. . . . "[82]

That might have been true. Yet to its credit the TWUA did launch, early on, a nationwide campaign to eliminate what was then seen as the industry's most serious health problem, excessive heat and humidity. At their 1948 convention, delegates approved a plan to get textile management to adopt air conditioning in every plant. Besides bringing economic and health benefits to the attention of mill presidents, the union also drafted a model law (making air conditioning mandatory) and sought friendly lawmakers to introduce it in each textile-state legislature.[83]

It was a worthy endeavor but, in the South, a futile one. In North Carolina and Georgia the bill was never introduced.[84] In South Carolina it found a sponsor, representative John Long of Union, but it made no headway. Most assemblymen were afraid, as textile spokesmen and the *State* paper wanted them to be, that the bill would be a "$40,000,000 barrier to new industry" and would make South Carolina uncompetitive with other Southern textile states.[85]

Like state legislatures which created them, public regulatory agencies in the South were strong for the principle of industrial hygiene but cautious about challenging the textile industry on specifics. That was not to say that there was no activity at the state level in the post-war era or that there were no differences between states and between agencies within states. North Carolina's industrial hygiene division, for example, had done a good job protecting workers against asbestosis and silicosis. By 1954 asbestosis was completely eliminated and silicosis on a sharp decline.[86] Enforcement in those industries was so vigorous in fact that in the early 1950s one insurer withdrew from the state because "too many occupational disease claims have been filed, lately."[87]

The main problem in North Carolina was that hygienists still virtually ignored the textile industry. Only once before the mid-1950s had the industrial hygiene division given it attention. That was during the war. Even then, concern was limited to nutrition, sanitation, and chemical exposure. Although some hygienists were not happy with the situation, the passing years saw the division become more and more just a service department for the state industrial commission.[88]

Then in 1955 the North Carolina Board of Health, with legislative help, began to take the first steps to invigorate and expand its industrial hygiene work. The main impetus came from new division chief H. Robert Coler, who unlike his predecessors was willing to face up to agency nearsightedness and to demand change. In his first month on the job Coler told the state health officer just how bad things were. Not only did the section have "no real program to show," but its "whole medical service is not in accord with what a modern state health department should do."[89] By 1957 its program was expanding, as recognition grew that new industries had brought about new health problems. With legislative support the division began to test for radiation exposure and to initiate the state's first standards for industrial noise. In addition, it helped sponsor the first governor's conference on occupational health. Although the last two activities brought the division into some contact with textiles, hygienists would continue to overlook most problems in that industry for another decade — until the problem of byssinosis finally forced a shift in emphasis (chapter 10). [90]

In major respects South Carolina's industrial hygiene work in the postwar decades followed the opposite road. Attention remained focused on textiles, and even though hygienists Brown and Hammond had to go hat in hand, they did succeed in increasing industrial awareness of workplace health problems. Hammond, especially, was able to establish a close rapport with mill management, which he used to argue the economic value of a healthier work force. High temperature and humidity were to him the most serious problems. At a 1947 industry conference he warned of the 100° temperatures and 85 percent humidities that were common in summertime mill rooms. Although few workers, he admitted, became ill enough to stop work, chronic heat sickness was widespread and the cost to management, high, for it "steals production, quality and good morale."[91]

But one or two men could have only limited impact, and unlike the upper state, South Carolina had no program to compensate workers who

lost their health, whether in mills or elsewhere. In 1949 South Carolina legislators did pass an occupational disease law, but insurance and textile lob-
byists rendered it virtually useless to workers. Industrial commissioner James
Reid had drafted the bill and he recalled that mill owners "were afraid that
this was sort of the invitation to lower the flood gates. . . . " Governor
Strom Thurmond was also disappointed, said Reid, but signed the bill because it was "at least a first step."[92]

Actually it proved to be South Carolina's last step. About the time
North Carolina was invigorating its industrial health work, South Carolina
scrapped its whole industrial hygiene operation. In July 1951, the legislature
eliminated the hygiene division, and from then until the passage of the federal Occupational Health and Safety Act in 1970, South Carolina had no
program to safeguard health in the work place.

Accounts of why the state took such a retrogressive step vary, but
most involve South Carolina's elder statesman, James F. Byrnes, who resumed his legendary political career in 1950 as South Carolina governor.
One account had Byrnes dismantling the hygiene division to get back at
organized labor, which he believed had scuttled his vice-presidential bid
in 1944. Another saw the termination as an episode in a long-running feud
between Byrnes and state health officer Ben Wyman. A third explained it
in terms of a state fiscal crisis, coupled with Byrnes' scant appreciation of
public health work, which led him to mark several health programs (including industrial hygiene) for elimination.[93]

Whatever the real explanation, South Carolina's political leadership,
from governor down, was clearly unable or unwilling to concede serious
health threats in the industrial work place. What dangers did exist, they
apparently concluded, would be dealt with by corporate management, who
did not need to be coerced to do their duty by their employees.

Elimination of South Carolina's industrial hygiene division did not
end all public concern with worker health. There was still the labor department, which also had a mandate to protect wage-earner welfare. But that
mission was severely undermined by the department's continued narrow
definition of industrial hygiene and by its incestuous relationship with the
textile industry. For the department, occupational health remained little
more than clean toilets, potable water, and "good housekeeping."[94] That the
milling process itself could pose health risks seemed beyond its ken. Perhaps that was because the department was committed to speaking, hearing,
and seeing no evil about the textile industry and to maintaining what was
almost a doglike fealty to it. In a public expression of that loyalty labor department commissioner William Ponder insisted in 1955 that "the vast majority of *our people* [emphasis added] are anxious to comply with the law and
are disposed to correct noncompliance when the same is properly called

to their attention."[95] Given the leniency of South Carolina factory law, that might well have been true. Moreover, the weakness of the statutes relating to industrial hygiene, combined with the passive role of state regulatory departments, also explained how the regulated could actually outstrip the regulators in promoting workplace changes beneficial to health.

One problem, though, for which capitalist imperatives seemed to offer no solution was mill noise. Because hands simply became deaf, not less efficient, there was no economic incentive to correct the problem. Management's explanation for many decades of neglect was summed up by Springs Mills vice-president Francis Bell who said, "we pretty well accepted noise as part of the job." Workers, Bell remembered, were equally complacent. About the only time they complained was when they had to wear ear plugs.[96]

The main reason for the complacency of both was that hearing loss was gradual. Initial impairment was in the high frequency range, which had few practial consequences. Only after a decade's exposure to noise of 100 decibels or more would loss be apparent. In a textile mill, only weavers had to face noise of that intensity.[97]

Yet, despite appearances, hearing losses were widespread. One experienced mill hand estimated that at least 50 percent of weavers suffered hearing impairment. Many of them had to use lip reading outside the mill to help them converse. In the 1960s, hearing test studies confirmed that ten years of work in a 105-decibel environment (not uncommon in weave rooms) produced severe deafness in over 40 percent of workers.[98]

To make matters worse, noise intensity was on the increase after World War II. The cause was not just faster looms but changes in plant design. Starting in the late 1940s mill construction in the South expanded rapidly, as migrating New England owners began to refurbish old mills and erect new ones. What resulted, said one textile engineer, were "today's modern plants, windowless, with low ceilings and cement floors," which produced "even noisier textile operations."[99]

If management was not ready to respond, or workers to complain, the federal government decided that it was. In January 1969, as part of a national surge of interest in occupational health, the outgoing Democratic Labor Secretary ordered all mills doing business with the government to reduce noise to a maximum of 92 decibels. By 1971 levels were to be lowered to 85. The industry appealed to the incoming Nixon administration to set aside the Democratic standard. But Nixon, then in his bring-Americans-together phase, was not willing to do that, and in May 1969, the Democratic ruling went into effect. The one thing Nixon did agree to was to extend the deadline for initiation of action, and by the end of 1969 union leaders were complaining that noise levels in many Southern weave rooms were still above 100 decibels.[100]

If work areas were not suddenly quieter, employees were afforded more protection after 1970. Following all the publicity about rising deafness, workers took easier to wearing ear plugs and muffs, and management, to enforcing the regulations. Properly fitted, such devices cut noise by as much as 45 decibels, and even with mass-produced, soft plastic plugs, the din of crashing spindles was transformed to something no noisier than off-peak traffic. Yet the problem's long-term solution seemed to lie not with ear plugs, carpeted floors, or noise-absorbing ceilings but with quieter looms, which were entering the market by the late 1970s. The product of German and Japanese technology, air-jet and water-jet looms promised not only to speed the weaving process and make it less prone to breakdown but also to provide mill hands, at long last, a work environment more fit for human consumption.[101] Although the wait was long, once more the marketplace seemed able to produce its own solutions to problems of textile worker health.

Yet there was one problem, the deadliest one of all, for which the marketplace could offer no solution. That was the malady known as byssinosis, a disease acquired from cotton dust inhalation. Because elimination of dust was very costly, and the existence of the disease difficult to prove, mill management fiercely opposed even recognizing it as a problem. As a result, that recognition did not come until textiles' other occupational health problems were well on the way to solution. The story of what finally led industry to reverse its stance and to move against byssinosis is the subject of the next chapter.

CHAPTER 10

The Discovery of Byssinosis in Southern Textile Manufacturing, 1930–1970

The discovery of byssinosis, or "brown lung" disease, in the Southern textile industry progressed something like an eruption of "Old Faithful." As anyone knows who has seen the Yellowstone geyser, it begins with many tantalizing false starts. Only after what seems an eternity, does the great blast come that keeps on coming. It was the same with byssinosis. Several times after 1930, concern arose among scientists, physicians, health officials, and mill owners over a possible respiratory disease caused by cotton dust. But after periods of debate, the issue would vanish from the literature and private discussion, and long years of silence would ensue. After several such false starts, finally in the late 1960s a debate began which rather quickly moved to a consensus that byssinosis did indeed exist and was a problem of large proportions.

Several factors lay behind this final acceptance: an increasing sophistication in medical technology, a growing professional and public interest in occupational hygiene, a late-awakening health concern within textile unions, and a felt need on the part of mill management to improve the industry's image. But the primary determinant was the weight of British experience, which had the effect of forcing a repeated examination of the issue in America until it was finally recognized that "brown lung" existed on this side of the Atlantic too.

Although byssinosis (from the Latin, "byssus," meaning fine linen, flax, or cotton) had been the subject of occasional but inconclusive comment in both British and American medical literature since the early century, the British began to come to terms with the disease only in 1927. That

year the Home Office named a special departmental committee to investigate a reportedly high level of respiratory illness among Lancashire cotton
workers. Initial findings were baffling. Clinical examination had shown
mill rates of bronchitis, emphysema, and asthma at near epidemic levels,
suggesting some new and unknown disease. Yet when microscopic, radi-
ological, and post-mortem examinations were made, nothing was revealed
beyond the usual pulmonary pathology.[1]

Then British clinicians made some interesting discoveries. They found
that most illness was concentrated in the cardroom, one of the dustiest
parts of a mill, and particularly among that section's older operatives. They
noted too that respiratory impairment tended to be proportional to length
of employment. Finally, they detected that afflicted mill workers, unlike victims of asthma or emphysema, only had trouble breathing in, not breathing
out.[2]

By 1932 the Committee had decided that what the Lancashire workers
had was a distinct occupational disease, caused by long years of inhaling
cotton lint. To reconcile that finding with the lack of distinct clinical or biological evidence, the committee contended that it was "in the causation
rather than the character of the malady" that the disease could be differentiated from similar illness outside the mill.[3] As for what to call it, the committee opted to retain the name they found, to their surprise, in earlier literature: byssinosis.[4]

Almost immediately the British report got attention in America. In
1932, a PHS team was ending a general inquiry into the effects of cotton dust
exposure in a South Carolina mill, and they decided to test the Lancashire
findings against their experience.[5] Their verdict, given in two PHS *Bulletins*
in 1933 was essentially that "it can't happen here."

The alleged salubrity of American mills was based primarily on three
findings. One was that Carolina cardroom hands showed no greater breathing impairment than spinners or weavers, which led to the obvious conclusion that abundant dust had no "definite effect. . . . "[6] Second, those workers who complained of respiratory problems such as chest tightness showed
no abnormality on X-ray examination.[7] Finally, while cardroom hands did
have a higher rate of long-term absences than other mill workers, few of
the missed days were due to respiratory illness. As for short-term absences,
which *were* tied to respiratory ills and which were also more frequent, the
American team suggested simply that carders, who were easily replaceable
by extra hands, stayed home (with no pay) in order to "give the spare
hands a chance to work."[8]

For years the 1933 studies would be referred to as proof that American
workers were not troubled by byssinosis. But those studies were hardly con-
clusive. They were based on the experience of only one mill. Investigators

did not follow up with operatives who had complained of byssinosis-type symptoms. Nor did they explain why short-term cardroom absences showed a higher incidence of respiratory causes than absences in the general population.[9] Finally, signs were that PHS scientists knew their conclusions in advance. As one of them noted, "in view of the low concentrations of dust . . . [by comparison with British mills] it became apparent that no adverse effect on health was to be anticipated from this source."[10]

After the 1933 reports — and largely because of them — nothing more was heard of byssinosis in the United States for the next seven years. During this period several states (including both Carolinas) set up offices of industrial hygiene to safeguard worker health.[11] Yet none of those agencies sought to follow the British lead. In large measure, inaction was due to lack of awareness and information, but it was also a function of economic and political realities.

In the Carolinas, whether the threat was from cotton dust or some other possible hazard, regulatory agencies had to move with caution and deference when it came to the textile industry (see chapter 9).[12] In 1938 South Carolina's industrial hygiene division even urged that its findings be made immune from civil subpoena "in order that the way be fully paved for a full and complete cooperation with and from industry."[13]

To some, state industrial health programs were a farce. James Hughes, a South Carolina physician who got into industrial medicine in the late 1930s, held that the South Carolina agency "was set up as a tool of management, a cover up. . . . " When state hygienists visited a plant "they were told what to see and not to see." But often, "they wouldn't come in there. They were afraid to."[14]

Yet, inaction was surely less a matter of fear than legal authority. As noted earlier, in both Carolinas, education, tact, and moral suasion were the only weapons given to state industrial hygienists. In view of the uncertainty of byssinosis and the prevalence of other, more insistent problems, British claims were understandably ignored.

But in 1940 the issue suddenly resurfaced, and for the next seven years the disease was debated by health specialists in government and industry alike. What pushed it into view were two related but widely separated developments, one occurring in the South and one in England.

In 1938 M.F. Trice, an industrial hygienist with the North Carolina Board of Health, was called to a local mill to investigate a severe respiratory and intestinal illness in its cardroom. Noting that the sickness coincided with a recent run of brownish, trashy cotton, Trice searched the literature and found to his surprise that a decade before the British had met similar symptoms and saw them as signs of serious degenerative disease.[15]

Convinced — wrongly — that he too had evidence of byssinosis, Trice undertook in 1940 to alert textile management to its dangers. Finding the editor of *Textile World* willing to feature his article (but not to use the term, byssinosis), Trice warned the industry that it was heading for serious trouble if it did not get rid of excess dust. Although he conceded that trashy, brown cotton was seldom milled, Trice believed that even high grade fiber might contain the offending agent. To safeguard workers, then, the industry must be prepared to take quite drastic and costly steps.[16]

That same year the British took a step that heightened American interest and apprehension. In 1940 Parliament passed legislation providing compensation for all male byssinosis victims who had suffered complete disability after at least twenty years of cardroom work. What moved Parliament to act as decisively as it did were key research findings following the 1932 report.[17]

One of the most important developments had occurred in 1936 when a Medical Research Council scientist succeeded in identifying the stages of byssinosis (breathlessness first on Mondays, extending in succeeding years throughout the week), which aided diagnosis and cleared the way for disability awards.[18] By 1939 a second departmental committee had concluded that "where there was total incapacity . . . a medical board should be able to decide whether the disease was occupational."[19] In 1941 Parliament's action was reported in America, and within a short time the compensation scheme, along with Trice's alarm, was generating a rather strenuous debate over the possibility of byssinosis in American mills.[20]

The opening shot was fired in 1943, in the prestigious *Journal of Industrial Hygiene and Toxicology*, by Massachusetts physician Leonard Bolen. For several years Bolen had watched the health of two mill patients deteriorate from some kind of lung disorder. By 1943 one man's ailment had so advanced that he was able to breathe normally only at night and only then "if he held his head low with hands touching the floor."[21]

Bolen knew of the British work and was convinced that both patients had byssinosis, for they showed all the classic symptoms: At first their breathlessness had occurred only on Mondays, but had gradually extended through the week. Both complained of breathing constriction, as if an iron ring bound their chests, and for each man the *drawing* of breath was especially difficult. Although he was not willing to rank America's problem with England's, Bolen felt that the matter merited careful attention.[22]

The next study, arguing on the other side, was reported in 1944 by two Mississippi hygienists, Wayne Ritter and Morris Nussbaum. Ironically, their research was undertaken to prove the prevalence of byssinosis. The problem was that Ritter and Nussbaum could not find any, whether among retirees, ex-cardroom operatives who had been hospitalized in the state TB sanatorium, or working mill hands. Among the latter, inquiries were made about respiratory problems, but no one admitted to having any. Ritter and Nussbaum conceded that workers perhaps felt constrained by the presence of the mill foreman during questioning, but they were also willing to credit foreman testimony that most operatives who claimed breathing troubles were only faking to get off work.[23]

Ultimately, Ritter and Nussbaum concluded that "byssinosis as a clinical entity is without foundation in the cotton industry." That judgment held for Britain as well: British studies were "without clinching proof," and Parliament, they believed, had acted prematurely in giving compensation.[24]

The debate was soon continued in other quarters, and positions taken were often surprising. In 1945 the industry-sponsored Textile Research Institute convened a conference on cotton dust diseases. One presentation argued that the certain effect of cotton dust inhalation was byssinosis, and the speaker urged the industry to institute safeguards.[25] The same year, however, the Bureau of Labor Standards, which had traditionally been alert to possible dangers in the workplace, reported that the only dust-related problem in textiles was a "minor illness known as cotton mill fever."[26] Given textiles' good health record, the Bureau was sure that "nothing inherently unhealthful exists in the industry."[27] Less surprising was the view of industry physician C.L. Roman, offered the next year in the *Canadian Medical Journal*. After extensive testing of his Montreal firm's employees, Roman declared that whatever lung disorders had existed "have now been eliminated by . . . technical improvements which now provided clean, dust-free air."[28]

If any industry leader had decided at that point that the byssinosis question had been laid to rest, his decision would have been premature, for in 1947 appeared the most thorough, even-handed examination of the issue to date. A painstaking review of the literature, carried out by a group of PHS physicians under the direction of Barbara H. Caminita, this study sought to say something definitive about the likelihood of byssinosis occurring in American mills. Years later, when industry spokesmen and others were seeking to rebut byssinosis claims, they would often refer to the Caminita team's conclusion that " . . . the problem of serious dust disease . . . is hardly known to exist in the United States."[29] Virtually ignored, however, was the qualification that followed: it was entirely possible, said the PHS group, that the disease did exist and was simply unrecognized, ignored, or hidden by the fact that workers left the industry prior to becoming disabled.[30] Before America's industry could rest easy, said the PHS team, intensive studies were needed on every aspect of the problem. Until such researches were completed — and they had not as yet even begun — the byssinosis issue would remain unresolved.[31]

In the end, however, that warning went unheeded, and with the Caminita study, American interest in byssinosis fell once again into limbo. Not until 1967 would an American textile corporation give any attention to the possibility that it was harboring a killing occupational disease. In view of the publicity given byssinosis in the 1940s, two questions require answers: first, were Southern mill owners of the 1940s aware of byssinosis and studies done on it? Second, if there was awareness, why did it not produce at least an inquiry into the possible presence of the disease?[32]

Despite later claims to the contrary, there were signs that executives of major firms did know about the byssinosis debate and about the British experience. Throughout the 1940s the malady was occasionally noticed and sometimes featured in leading trade publications such as *Textile World* and *The Textile Research Journal*.[33] In addition, management would have learned of byssinosis from contacts with state industrial hygienists. In the 1940s South Carolina's James Hammond maintained close ties with mill executives. On occasion he spoke about byssinosis and the British findings and about the chance of the United States having the disease, a possibility he did not think likely.[34]

Some textile executives also learned of the disease in the course of normal business, which by the post-war period was truly international in scope. The experience of Hugh W. Close was probably typical. In the late 1940s Close, who was on his way to the top of Springs Mills Corporation, had his first introduction to byssinosis. "I happened to hear about it," he recalled, "from [company director] Robert Amory, whose family is part British. He said, 'you know, there is something that came on some time ago they call byssinosis . . . and this is happening in Britain.' And I'm sure I asked, what about over here, and he said, 'oh no, it can't happen over here,' . . . but it really wasn't treated as a problem. Whether or not we were turning our backs on something or not I couldn't say."[35]

As to why mill executives chose to accept only negative evidence and did, indeed, turn their backs on the possibility of byssinosis, the answer is more complex than that offered by demonological characterizations of Southern textile magnates. For one thing mill owners knew of the greater dustiness of British mills, and they had it on good authority—i.e., the 1933 PHS study—that there was a direct, quantitative relationship between visible dust and disease. As for cases that had been identified in the United States, they were easily explained away. According to South Carolina hygienist Hammond, those individuals were likely congenital asthmatics or people with a peculiar dust allergy.[36]

Of course, there was equally potent evidence on the other side, and to understand why it was ignored one has to note not only the high cost of dust control but also the entrepreneurial psychology peculiar to Southern mill owners. In piedmont mill towns, even into the post-war era, the mill owner or his manager was not only the community's dominant economic force but its social and moral arbiter as well. To most owners, the help were not just people, but "our people," for whom decisions had to be made as with so many children.[37] Over the years owners had come to the view that they and only they had the right to make those decisions. Accordingly, suggestions for change coming from outside were instinctively opposed.

Claims about dust disease and suggestions for costly protective measures fell into the category of outside meddling. Springs president Close recalled that he heard about byssinosis, not from the South, but "from theorists in the North" and that "nobody paid any attention to it in the textile industry in the United States until very much later."[38] Thus, if the Southern mill owner knew about byssinosis at all, he would be apt to view it as a fantasy of Northern physicians and federal bureaucrats, who were only trying to interfere with his long practice of running his own show.

Perhaps if Southern physicians had raised a warning, mill owners would have responded differently. But to have expected doctors to be more forthcoming was to have expected the impossible in the 1940s and 1950s. As noted earlier (chapter 9), the generality of American physicians had neither interest nor training in questions of occupational health. Those few who practiced industrial medicine mostly did so out of their own offices, on a retainer basis. Their practice was limited almost wholly to acute problems such as cuts, breaks, and burns, and they seldom had occasion or invitation to familiarize themselves with a mill's operation. In addition, any doctor in the textile South who came down on the wrong side of an issue like byssinosis, risked not only his professional status but his social standing as well.[39]

Added to their general disinterest in the issue of occupational medicine was the profession's ignorance about byssinosis. Periodically in the 1950s the editor of the AMA *Journal* got inquires about byssinosis. His replies mirrored the profession's understanding. To a Southern doctor who implied a causal connection between mill work and lung impairment, the editor replied that "it does not immediately follow that the conditions described resulted from exposure in a cotton mill. The conditions are common, apart from employment." Though byssinosis existed among cotton workers, the editor conceded, it was the result either of an allergy or some bacterial infection. While rather common in England, byssinosis was "little known in the United States."[40]

If that view reflected a medical consensus in the 1950s it was soon to undergo sharp change. During the very years when America was lapsing into inattention, the British were reconsidering the whole byssinosis question — not only in relation to their own country, but to America, as well.

Ironically, the British research, which was spearheaded in 1951 by

R.S.F. Schilling of the University of Manchester, did not begin on the trail of byssinosis at all. The general view among occupational health specialists at Manchester, in fact, was that byssinosis was no longer a problem. What Schilling and colleagues were after was an explanation for an apparent excess of cardroom deaths from cardiovascular-renal disease.[41]

After two years of diligent searching, the Schilling group found no CVR problems, but they discovered something more surprising: clear byssinosis symptoms among two-thirds of Lancashire cardroom workers, about 20 percent of whom were totally disabled but not drawing compensation.[42] To determine if the problem was as general as it appeared, they broadened their study to embrace other Lancashire mills. The second set of results fully confirmed the first.[43]

The Schilling investigations had broad significance. They forced a revamping of Britain's whole byssinosis compensation scheme.[44] They also added important new elements to the diagnosis of byssinosis and the understanding of its etiology, such as the finding that it was the trashy part of the cotton boll, not the fiber, that triggered breathing impairment.[45] Finally, and most important to American workers, Schilling's studies had the effect of catalyzing the third—and concluding—phase of the American discovery of byssinosis.

In 1960, after publishing his results in the American *Journal of Occupational Medicine*, Schilling decided that if Britain's problem was ever to be fully understood he needed to have a look at some American mills. Supposedly, Americans did not have a byssinosis problem. If that were true, he reflected, "it is important to determine why."[46]

That same year he got his opportunity. After suggesting to a party of visiting American doctors that no one had really looked for byssinosis in the United States, Schilling got an invitation from one of them, an Alabaman, to study mill conditions in his state.[47] Ultimately, Schilling and a colleague were able to examine a limited number of workers at two mills. An American specialist later claimed that the Britons were purposely shown two showcase mills to make certain that their findings would be favorable. If such a ploy was attempted—and Schilling doubted it—it was not successful.[48] Though the mills *were* less dusty than in England, Schilling found among nineteen cardroom workers one sure case of byssinosis and a significant loss of workday breathing capacity among all the rest.[49]

Published in 1961 in the AMA *Journal*, Schilling's investigation, the first clinical study of byssinosis since 1933, had two important results.[50] First, it put the Southern textile industry on the defensive. Second, it encouraged a small but growing band of American specialists in occupational medicine to look into other Southern mills. As Schilling himself put it two decades later, "this was the prelude to much more comprehensive epidemiological surveys in the United States. . . ."[51]

The first clash between Kennedy-era medical activists and textile conservatives took place in Atlanta in 1964. There, Arend Bouhuys, an established figure in European occupational medicine who had recently joined the Emory University Medical School faculty, was planning an investigation of Georgia mills.[52] But Georgia's Textile Manufacturers' Association was determined to stop him, and in June it alerted members to "another proposal by another professor" to hunt for byssinosis and suggested that since "this will be a *private* investigation . . . " they should refuse to cooperate.[53]

But Bouhuys succeeded in turning industry's flank. He obtained permission to study the mill in Atlanta's federal penitentiary, where he found an alarming 29 percent of cardroom workers with byssinosis symptoms. He also discovered what seemed a clear correlation between cigarette smoking and disease.[54] Though Bouhuys would not complete and publish his study for several years, early reports of his findings spurred other hunters.

Nowhere was there greater activity than in North Carolina, the nation's leading textile state. There, doctors Kaye Kilborn of Duke University Medical School and Leo Heaphy of Bowman Gray Medical School became convinced of the seriousness of the problem from the number of cases they had found among retired mill workers at Durham's Veterans' Administration hospital. In 1965 Bouhuys and Schilling, who were then both at Yale, came to North Carolina, and Heaphy had the chance to confer with them and, as he put it, "smuggle them" into a Winston Salem mill.[55]

Interest was also building in official quarters in North Carolina. In 1965 and 1966, state occupational health physicians found a disturbingly high percentage of "undetermined pathologies" during a mass X-ray screening in the textile industry. In 1966 the North Carolina Board of Health conceded that it had not paid sufficient attention to health problems in cotton textiles. In view of the recent X-rays, a reordering of priorities was a clear need.[56]

The next year that shift began. By arrangement with Fieldcrest Mills the board sent one of its hygienists, P.E. Schrag, into a company plant in Eden, North Carolina, to do a full-scale examination. Schrag found 29 percent of cardroom workers, plus 10 percent of weavers and spinners, with byssinosis symptoms. Though Fieldcrest refused to allow publication of results, the board alluded to them in its biennial report and for the first time labeled byssinosis a serious occupational disease.[57]

During the next two years additional studies were made. In 1968 the North Carolina board collaborated with Kilburn of Duke in making tests at two mills of the A.M. Smyre Company, of Gastonia, where approxi-

Dr. Arend Bouhuys (standing) giving a lung-capacity test to a Southern cotton mill worker to establish the presence of byssinosis, c. 1970. Bouhuys did more than anyone to demonstrate the presence and extent of the disease in America. Courtesy of Mrs. Fenna G. Bouhuys.

mately 25 percent of cardroom workers were found to be afflicted. Those results were published. The next year Bouhuys did a similar study in two other North Carolina mills, with similar results. What made his findings particularly striking, he reported, was the fact that they "were obtained in mills with modern textile equipment . . . and with relatively little [visible] airborne dust."[58] But the note which attracted greatest interest was Bouhuys's estimate that seventeen thousand American textile workers were literally dying on the job with byssinosis.[59]

Such claims were too much for many in the industry to take, and in 1969 they counterattacked. When Bouhuys aired his findings at a Raleigh meeting of a national engineering society, several textile executives in the audience were incensed. "No one," they said in later rebuttal, "has done enough research to decide anything about the disease, or its connection with the textile industry."[60] But the most venomous attack came from the editors of *America's Textile Reporter,* of Greenville, who viewed the whole byssinosis issue as a conspiracy on the part of radical doctors, "lousy . . . Northern Democrats," and the subversive textile unions to destroy an American industry. If byssinosis existed, it did so only among inferior races like blacks in Africa, who "are bound to be afflicted by new diseases more superior people defeated years ago."[61]

But that was a minority view. Most industry leaders decided that the sensible thing to do was to stop denying the problem and confront it squarely, even if that meant conceding its existence. Thus in 1969, when John Lumsden and James Merchant of the North Carolina Board of Health and Duke Medical School approached Burlington Mills vice president Charles McClendon about a major epidemiological survey of company employees, McClendon was eager to participate.[62]

Burlington, the nation's largest textile firm, acted in part out of what McClendon described as a sincere interest in employees' welfare. "If there is something wrong, we want to know about it," he told Lumsden.[63] Yet Burlington also had a more strategic objective in mind, it seemed. In the mid-1960s American textile leaders became extremely concerned about what they called their image problem. In a decade which saw most of the nation agonize over problems of poverty, discrimination, and injustice, textiles were seen as an industry which did not care about people and which came down on the wrong side of every issue. And that image hurt, not least in the recruiting area, as the industry sought to attract bright young engineers and business graduates. *Textile World* editor L.A. Christiansen expressed the general worry when he wrote that image "affects almost every aspect of . . . business. . . . "[64] To counter its bad press, said Christiansen, the industry needed to *do* more and to talk more about what it was doing.[65] Or, as

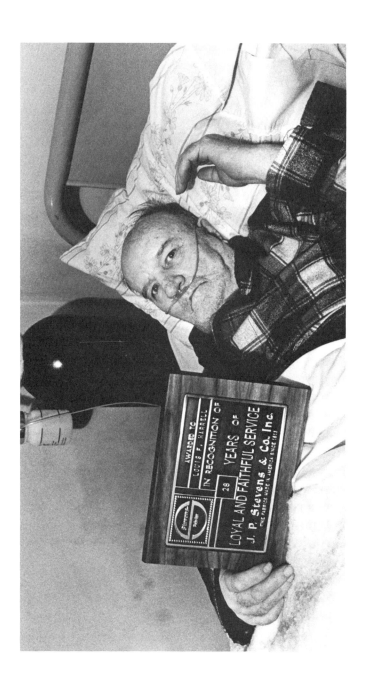

Byssinosis victim Louis Harrell, long an employee of the J.P. Stevens Co. mill in Roanoke Rapids, North Carolina. Harrell, who was then (1978) in litigation to get compensation for his disease, was in the last stages of byssinosis, confined to bed, and dependent on an oxygen tank. Mr. Earl Dotter, American Labor Education Center.

Hugh Close put it, "we need to make it easy for people to like the textile industry."[66]

Clearly, the Burlington study provided opportunity for the sort of image lift that Close and Christiansen were calling for. And in 1971, when the finished study turned up an awesome 38 percent of cotton cardroom workers with acute byssinosis symptoms, Burlington did not flinch.[67] In fact, vice president McClendon conceded publicly that "byssinosis can be clinically diagnosed and is attributable to cotton dust." Company medical director Harold Imbus went him one better, calling for a national program of disability compensation.[68]

Routine compensation has yet to be enacted into law, and money awards have thus far been few and difficult to obtain. The first federal dust standard (set in 1969 at one milligram of dust per cubic meter of air) was far higher than unions and most scientists thought was safe, and while a much lower standard (.2 mg. per m³) was issued in 1980, the Reagan administration began to give signs of wanting to relax it. Moreover, debate continues over the etiology, extent, and diagnosis of chronic-phase byssinosis (the deadly form).[69]

But 1971 at least brought industry's admission that a malady called byssinosis did exist. And hard on the heels of its discovery, the textile industry began to take its first (voluntary) preventive measures, which included the elimination of the offending agent in raw cotton, further reduction of atmospheric dust, and the beginning of routine pulmonary testing of workers.

That discovery and those measures, however, were nearly forty years in coming, and when industry finally began to respond there were those— including some in the industry, itself—who wondered why it had taken so long. Ronald Davis, an editor of *Textile World,* was one of them. In an article titled, "Diagnosis, Brown Lung. Prognosis, Misery," Davis conceded that while byssinosis had lately become a popular cause, "sufficient documentation of the disease was published in the past several decades" to have alerted owners to a problem.[70] Although most textile executives would probably have disagreed with Davis, the tens of thousands of mill hands then suffering from the malady would surely have said "amen."

At the same time that mill executives, reform-minded physicians, and others were struggling to define and subdue the last significant occupational health problem in textiles, black Americans were assaulting a major health problem of another kind, but one which for them was also a sort of final barrier. For Afro-Americans the issue was not one of proving the existence of a new disease but of gaining access to primary medical institutions—a crucial right if black doctors were to give, and black patients to receive, appropriate and equal medical care for diseases long known. Yet the fight over desegregation of medical societies, schools, and hospitals was easily as protracted as that surrounding byssinosis, for what was being challenged was racial self-interest, a force which in the South was easily as strong as economic self-interest. The story of this assault against traditional ways of training black physicians and caring for black patients is the subject of the next chapter.

PART IV

Problems Addressed

Blacks in the Era of Integration

CHAPTER II

Desegregating Southern Medicine, 1945–1970

In the popular mind the struggle for racial integration in the South after the Second World War is identified almost exclusively with education, voting rights, and public transportation and accommodation such as buses, hotels and restaurants. Yet concurrent with those very visible and highly charged campaigns, another quieter fight was going on, out of sight of newspaper reporters and television cameras, a fight that was to be as important to blacks as the more dramatic struggles for schools, ballots, and beds. That was the fight aimed at discriminatory practices in American medicine and health care, and it had as principal targets the all-white medical society and school and the rigidly segregated Southern hospital.

Unlike more celebrated civil rights battles, that contest was not carried out in the streets nor even, primarily, in the courts. It took place instead in pages of medical journals, at professional meetings, and in firm but generally friendly talks between black and white physicians and hospital administrators. When long-standing barriers in the South finally began to fall, progress was in no small part due to white physicians themselves. Although sharing the racist assumptions of other whites, as medical professionals they had also felt the counter-pull of a set of ideals having no relation to color. Moreover, they had had long and generally favorable contact with black physicians. Thus, as they began (in the 1950s) to grasp more fully the fictitiousness of "separate but equal" in their domain, they were able to set aside traditional racial practices in favor of a new order that was medically and ethically sounder than the old.

But if white doctors deserved credit along with the federal government, by far the major impetus behind desegregation was the persistence and energy of black physicians, who sought to create a climate of opinion in which change was not only possible but irresistible. Although many black doctors played important parts, the most influential figures were Howard University's Paul Cornely and Montague Cobb, two men who found activism as much to their taste as academe.

At the mid-1940s, however, only the supreme optimist could have found any reason to be encouraged about medical desegregation. Even among black physicians (North and South) there were scarcely any signs of a willingness to challenge the segregationist status quo. The Southern contingent of black physicians had improved its earnings over 70 percent during the war and were beginning to gain on their Northern colleagues. Few saw any reason to upset a system which was rewarding them ever more comfortably and with which they had long ago come to terms.[1] As for the few restless spirits, the always-present example of what happened to "troublemakers"—even in prestige professions—added a further check. Readers of the *Journal of the National Medical Association* recalled an episode in a little Louisiana town in 1944, in which a group of blacks, including the town's only doctor and only dentist, overrode the opposition of local whites to seek federal aid in creating a job-training school for black youth. They got the money and the center opened, but ten days later police seized the backers, beat them brutally, and threatened them with death if they remained.[2]

For Southern white physicians the idea of segregation was still so deeply entrenched that even moderate proposals met swift rejection. In 1946 when Paul Cornely visited Charleston under the auspices of the Urban League, one of his calls was on Medical College of South Carolina dean, H.C. Lynch, to explore prospects for improving the position of the state's black doctors. While Lynch was generally sympathetic he was unable to endorse any solution which would bring black and white doctors in closer contact. Cornely probed the possibility of access to the city's major teaching and charity hospital, a private facility owned by the county medical society. Lynch replied that society rules forbade it, and he held out no hope of their modification. Cornely knew that the College would not admit black medical students, but he wondered about nursing candidates, as well as the odd black physician doing post-graduate study. Lynch protested that College facilities were inadequate and suggested that the "only solution" was to create separate schools and hospitals. He could not even satisfy Cornely on the matter of blacks attending College clinics and seminars. The one concession Lynch offered was to convene separate conferences and seminars if black doctors wanted.[3]

At public hospitals and TB sanatoria, institutions subject to closer supervision by lay boards and elected officials, there were additional obstacles. Motivated by both personal choice and a need to keep an eye on voter reaction, Southern political leaders in the late 1940s resisted any weakening of segregation, even to meet humane goals. Georgia governor Ellis Arnall's refusal to permit black TB patients to be housed on a segregated floor of the white sanatorium (chapter 7) was only an exaggerated example of all officials' fear of arousing popular outrage.[4]

But to note the depth of black indifference and the strength of white resistance did not mean that there had been no improvement since the 1930s. After passage of Hill-Burton in 1946 Southerners of both races, but blacks particularly, began to enjoy an access to modern hospital care that they had never known before. Although segregation itself set limits on quality of care, all hospitals receiving federal aid had to make some provision for black patients. There were, certainly, a few black doctors like Cobb, who believed that Hill-Burton was only rooting hospital segregation more deeply. If Jim Crow was hard to eliminate, Cobb warned, "delux Jim Crow," posed even greater barriers.[5] Yet getting into previously all-white facilities at least moved blacks in position to strike for full equality. As a Florida black doctor said, "it will be easier for us to come from the basement to the other floors than it will be for us to come from across town."[6]

In fact, despite surface appearances that discrimination and segregation in Southern medicine were still intact, forces were building underneath which, given proper direction, might result in the destruction of traditional practice. Beginning with Gunnar Myrdal's *An American Dilemma* (1944), race relations earned increasing attention at the national level. Our enlarged international role accounted for much of the new concern. As tensions grew with the Soviets after 1945, America's relations with the race-conscious "Third World" became critical. In a Cold War climate, discrimination and segregation were suddenly more than just an embarrassment. They seemed now to threaten our very security. For that and other reasons the post-war years saw a myriad of conferences, seminars, and high-level commissions on the race question. From the health and medical field came reports detailing the burden of discrimination, and for the first time medical segregation itself began to come under attack from respected individuals and groups. In 1945 Surgeon General Thomas Parran asserted that the national welfare demanded an end to discrimination in medical education. Well-qualified Negro doctors and nurses were best able to care for Negro patients, so if black Americans were to receive the attention they deserved, "competent Negro men and women must be enabled to get first-rate professional training . . . [and] access to facilities. . . . "[7]

Two years later the Commission on Hospital Care, a joint venture of the American Hospital Association and the Commonwealth Fund, expanded on Parran's recommendations. Besides their professional obligation to black physicians, hospitals had a moral responsibility to black patients.

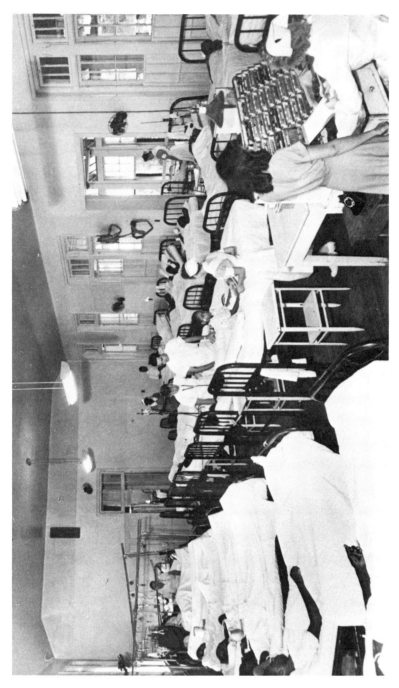

A black surgical ward in Charleston's segregated "Old Roper" Hospital, c. 1950. Although patients were all black, the professional staff here was all white. Courtesy of the Waring Historical Library, Medical University of South Carolina.

No one should be denied service for any reason—religious, economic, or racial. Where segregation was still a legal requirement, black patients should at least receive the same quality of care as white.[8]

Although Yankee rhetoric had little effect on Southern medical practices, as a broader civil rights movement gained momentum in the late 1940s, Southern doctors and hospitals were put on the defensive for the first time. Desegregation was capturing the thinking of many Northern professionals, and they began to charge Southern doctors with being out of step with the best traditions in medicine and democratic citizenship. As the editor of *Modern Hospitals* lectured, "there are thousands of hospitals and doctors, in hundreds of cities who are failing in their responsibilities as Americans and as healers by permitting the kind of segregation which results in inferior facilities and care, or no facilities and care at all, for the Negro population."[9] The tide of professional opinion was not yet running against the South, but with proper direction it might do so.

It was that task—building pressure against medical segregation in North and South—that Montague Cobb set for himself. Long an opponent of segregation, it was only in 1946, when he joined the NAACP and represented it at hearings on the national health insurance bill, that he began to voice his feelings. The next year he took over as editor of the *Journal of the NMA*. It was then, he said, that "we started raising Hell."[10]

Cobb recognized a growing disaffection with segregation in the white profession, but to capitalize on it he believed that he must first change the thinking of his own colleagues. Unless he could bring them to see that institutionalized discrimination was the greatest obstacle to black health and medical progress—and stir them to act on that belief—little would change. Doing that would not be easy, as most older black professionals shared little of Cobb's zeal. Their aim, Cobb lamented, was not to fight for principle but to get "what you can, when you can, and as you can."[11] When in the late 1940s blacks finally began to get more, through Hill-Burton and increased public health spending, conservative doctors discovered another reason for inaction: agitation might cause them to lose what they had gained.[12]

Cobb's strategy for loosening conservatives' hold was to encourage colleagues to look at medical segregation in a new way. Unlike earlier black doctors like Murray and Bousfield, he argued that it was naive to believe that segregated institutions could be improved. Segregation was inherently discriminatory. "It is just as well to realize that now as later and set our sights accordingly."[13] He also insisted that if they would honor the best traditions of American democracy and retain their self-respect, black physicians must be willing to forego short-run gains, whether of income or improved (but segregated) facilities, for the larger goal of integration. Labor unions had been able to "sacrifice for principle. Can the 'noblest profession' show less fortitude than the organized worker?"[14] Black doctors must give up their taste for "expensive automobiles and other forms of ostentation," tighten their belts, and prepare for a long struggle.[15]

Finally, he pointed out that segregation was a national not just a Southern problem. Although Northern manifestations were more subtle, they existed nonetheless, and as long as they did Northern black doctors would be held to second-rate status too. They needed to understand that, for they would be the key to influencing the federal government and the white profession, whose support in turn was all-important in ending segregation in the South.

Cobb opened his campaign the moment he sat down in the editor's chair, and he never let up. At the 1947 NMA convention he distributed reprints of a piece he had just published in the *Journal* in which he called on Association members to stop wrangling over internal politics and start attending to more important matters.[16] His emphasis was on the delusion that opportunity existed for Negro doctors outside the South. The reality was that Northern black doctors (and their patients) were trapped in medical ghettos of substandard, cast-off hospitals once belonging to whites. Larger, better-equipped white hospitals and medical schools might claim an open admissions policy, but really they accepted just enough black patients and students to give the appearance of openness.[17]

Cobb's first sallies met angry denial. He recalled getting "dark looks" at the 1947 meeting for revealing the "stark inadequacy of the Negro medical ghetto. . . . " For urging the NMA to "smash vigorously at the ghetto system," he and like-minded colleagues were regarded as "dangerous or visionary radicals. . . . "[18]

But gradually attitudes began to change. Thanks to Cobb's continual hammering, plus the backing of a number of influential NMA colleagues in Washington, like Cornely, the 1948 convention reflected a different mood. That year the NMA paid a special tribute to the NAACP, whose general secretary Walter White was on hand to deliver a main address.[19]

It was Cobb's success in linking the NMA to the strategy and purposes of the NAACP that more than anything else finally brought black doctors to connect their interests to the broader civil rights movement. As chairman of the NAACP's medical committee (and by 1950, an NAACP director), Cobb succeeded in creating a sort of overlapping directorate which resulted in each group's assisting the purposes of the other. For the NAACP the linkage provided a valuable ally in the fight for national health insurance, as well as a source of funds for civil rights litigation. The NMA in turn hoped to tap the resources and manpower of the civil rights group in pursuit of medical desegregation. By 1950 the NAACP was trying to implement a program of action at national, state, and local levels to break down color bars in hospitals, medical colleges, and professional associations.[20]

To sustain the desegregation commitment and remind doctors of their part in a broader movement, Cobb began a regular *Journal* feature titled, "The Integration Battlefront," in which he reported every skirmish and hero in the war on medical segregation. Occasional editorials on the broader civil rights movement also sought to spur action. When the Montgomery bus boycott got underway in 1956 Cobb applauded vigorously. "The walkers in Montgomery," he said, "have taught us all a great lesson. More and more the Negro doctor has come to see the common cause as his cause."[21]

With Cobb in the vanguard and his colleagues joining increasingly behind him, the black medical profession began about 1949 to move onto the offensive. Their first targets were all-white professional associations and schools, located almost entirely in the South. Ultimately both campaigns succeeded, but at varying rates. What determined the pace was the weight of (white) public involvement. In the case of professional associations, which function in virtual isolation from popular dictates, discriminatory practices ended rather quickly. For medical colleges, on the other hand, change was slower, for some were public institutions and all had to make concessions to (white) alumni sentiment.

As discussed earlier (chapter 4), membership in local, white medical societies was a critical need for Southern black doctors. Although physicians like Cornely and L.W. Long had realized that for many years, only in 1949 was a serious effort launched to open local associations. The AMA had long accepted blacks as members of the national body, and at the annual AMA convention in May, Peter Murray, the first black member of the AMA House of Delegates, urged it to put pressure on Southern societies also to accept blacks.[22] Although the AMA did not respond in 1949, partly because Northern members felt they needed more time to prepare Southern colleagues, physicians were optimistic about chances in 1950. As one said: if Southern states did not feel "they are stigmatized by the 'damned Yankee' they will get in line on the matter."[23]

But there was feeling among some blacks that the AMA was only hoping to strike a deal with the NMA over national health insurance. Earlier, AMA leaders had approached their black counterparts with a vague offer of recognizing black medical societies as AMA affiliates if the NMA would join against Truman's "socialized medicine" scheme. Cobb and others who believed strongly in the plan rejected the offer, and the projected bargain collapsed.[24]

In 1950, at the urging of Cobb, Murray, and the NAACP, the AMA finally reversed its sixty-year-old policy of accepting exclusion among member societies. Although its resolution dealt the mildest slap at discrimination, it did urge segregated affiliates to consider "taking such steps as they may elect to eliminate such restrictions."[25] Cobb applauded, but he continued to believe that the AMA acted primarily to court black physician backing for its anti-health insurance stance.[26]

Whatever the motive, the 1950 resolution was clearly not going to have much effect in the South, unless additional pressure was applied. Accordingly, black professional organizations across the region sought to exploit the opening by having members attempt to join white societies. Carr Mc-Fall directed the effort of South Carolina's Palmetto Association.[27] In 1951 McFall was in continuous contact with leaders of white dental and medical societies. Although he got nowhere with the dentists, he found physicians willing to negotiate. The eventual plan called for blacks to seek membership in county societies, while the white state association gave support from its end.[28] In June 1952, the wall of exclusion finally fell when Charleston county's society took McFall into membership. Shortly after, Greenville's society did likewise, and soon local associations over the state began falling in line, as white physicians came to see that desegregation was not disruptive after all. Apparently fairness was as catching as discrimination: "when the question of Negroes in the Anderson . . . Society came up," a black doctor reported, one member "cited the smoothness with which the Greenville society runs with Negro members," and that was all it took.[29]

Elsewhere, the pattern was much the same. Nineteen fifty-two also saw the end of segregation in state and county societies in Arkansas and Georgia, and in 1953 Alabama's medical association opened its doors. By 1956 every Southern state society but two had agreed to admit blacks to membership.[30]

One hold-out was North Carolina (the other was Louisiana), and the sequence of events there suggested that beneath the surface of white professional acceptance lay a wide stratum of prejudice. In 1954 North Carolina's society dropped the word "white" from membership criteria, but when black physicians attempted to join county associations they found that doors were only half open. The precise status offered was scientific membership, which meant that blacks could attend business and technical sessions but not strictly social functions. The black organization, the Old North State Medical Society, rejected the offer and censured two black colleagues who accepted it.[31] Although the black association brought immediate pressure on its white counterpart, the half-way offer stood until the early 1960s. Continuing pressure from blacks was mainly responsible for changing white minds, but a biting attack by the state's leading paper was also a factor. In 1961 the Raleigh *News and Observer* asked what, exactly, the North Carolina Medical Society was. Was it a "social organization with some scientific sidelines or a scientific society with some social sidelines?" When some doctors were social members and some, scientific members, "all may be confused as to which are the medical members and which are the dancing, dining, and cocktail party members."[32]

Gaining entry into Southern medical schools took far longer. As with the societies, the opening of white colleges was critical to the black profession — and its patients. By the late 1940s the supply of new Negro doctors and dentists was estimated to be insufficient even to replace the number lost each year to death and retirement. As a result the black patient-to-physician ratio, always too high, was mounting upward. The surgeon general estimated in 1949 that five thousand additional black doctors would be needed just to get the ratio down to 1500:1, which was still twice the national average. Northern schools could help, of course, by enrolling more black students, but it was more important to open the twenty-six colleges in the South (one-third of the nation's total). That was where 75 percent of blacks lived, and as of 1948 not one had accepted a black applicant.[33]

It was not that Southern states were unconcerned about the need for more black doctors or about aspirations of black youth. As early as 1946 North Carolina's Medical Care Commission gave considerable attention to those issues, determined "to make sure that each Negro boy and girl be given an equal opportunity to receive medical training."[34] The problem was that integration was outside all imaginable solutions. In North Carolina the medical commission devised four alternative schemes to meet its "obligation to the Negroes," and not one involved desegregation.[35]

One possibility which did attract North Carolina's interest and which became a primary proposal of the 1948 conference of Southern governors was the development of Meharry Medical College as the region's official black school. Under terms of the plan, which Meharry itself originated, Southern states would provide Meharry a 70 percent subsidy to train their black students. It was hoped that the scheme would put the South outside the reach of the 1938 *Gaines* decision, which threatened desegregation of Southern professional schools if states did not create separate-but-equal institutions at home.[36]

The plan never came to anything, but it might have had it not been for black doctors and the NAACP. Cobb did not learn of the scheme until Southern governors announced it, but he immediately hit it as a cynical racist move. He also criticized Meharry for being a willing dupe. "We do not find the Southern Governors' Conference recognizing the long-time injustice to their Negro population. . . . Instead, we see the deplorable spectacle, on the one hand, of an offer to keep Meharry alive by . . . [using it] to take the South's responsibility for training Negro medical professionals off its hands and to perpetuate traditional discrimination; and on the other, the Meharry Trustees offer the school as an outright gift."[37] In 1949 the governors sought to get Congress to aid the Meharry plan. The NAACP met them head-on, arguing that the compact was merely a dodge to maintain segregation where the Supreme Court had already said (in *Missouri ex. rel. Gaines v. Canada,* 1938) that it could no longer stand. Cobb and the NAACP emerged as winners in congressional committee by a one-vote margin.[38]

With his flank protected, Cobb turned attention to desegregating Southern colleges. He first surveyed existing attitudes. With the exception of the University of Arkansas Medical School, which dropped its color bar in 1948, every other school responding to Cobb's inquiry told him that no such step was possible. "Negro students will be acceptable," one dean explained in a choice bit of obfuscation, only "when environmental conditions in their states became more propitious."[39]

Seeing no opening locally Cobb sought to generate pressure from the national accrediting agency, the Association of American Medical Colleges and Schools (AAMC). At the same time he urged black physicians to sponsor enrollment of black students at all-white colleges.

His prodding of the accrediting association brought no result. In 1950 he started conferring with AAMC leaders, but he found them evasive. All assured Cobb that they personally opposed discrimination but that the Association could not interfere with policies of member schools. Five years later, with still no action, Cobb told AAMC leaders that the problem was fast being solved school by school and that if it did not move soon, the AAMC would have lost the chance to play any role at all. "The AMA has shown the way," he chided. "What does the AAMC lack?"[40]

As Cobb predicted, solution did come locally. Even by 1957, some gains were evident. Thanks to pressure exerted by black physician groups and a willingness of many school administrators to take new steps, fourteen of the twenty-six Southern colleges, mostly in the upper South, had opened doors to blacks. Fear of federal court action accounted in part for the response, but equally important was a growing appreciation by the white medical community of the handicaps facing the black profession. That appreciation grew as black and white doctors began to have opportunities to meet as equals in meetings of professional societies, an awareness that Carr McFall noted while serving on South Carolina's Hill-Burton advisory council.[41]

Yet, by itself, white openness was not sufficient to integrate Southern schools. Black physician groups had to put forward qualified candidates, for schools were not willing to take such initiatives. Where Southern colleges remained segregated—and several, including those in North Carolina, South Carolina, and Georgia had all-white student bodies until the mid-1960s—the reason was often that no black candidate applied.[42]

Such was the case in South Carolina. In 1951, the Palmetto Association first turned attention to desegregating the state medical college in Charleston. With the NAACP it began searching for a suitable student. A year later, though several prospects had emerged, none had enough money to finance medical studies. The black doctors thereupon agreed to provide a yearly scholarship of five hundred dollars, but even with that lure the Association could not turn up a candidate both academically qualified and willing to go to Charleston. Exceptionally able black students had opportunities to attend Northern colleges, all of which had financial aid to offer as well.

For those reasons, plus perhaps a flagging of Palmetto Association effort, it was 1965 before the first black student, Sara Prioleau, matriculated in Charleston. She did not graduate, however. The first black to obtain the degree was Bernard Deas, who enrolled two years later. In 1967, in fact, barriers finally fell at most of the hold-out institutions, for not only South Carolina but Bowman Gray Medical School (Wake Forest), Duke University School of Medicine, and the Medical College of Georgia all acccepted their first black students that year. Seemingly they had reached a mutual decision that if unprecedented steps had to be taken, they were best taken in concert.[43]

By contrast to medical societies and schools, hospitals presented a far more difficult and complex problem. It was one thing to desegregate associations and colleges and another to change traditional relationships in institutions serving a mass clientele. Many hospital administrators, North and South, might personally have favored abandoning segregation, but for economic reasons they feared to take initiatives ahead of popular opinion. And in the South, even after several years of Hill-Burton, opinion dictated that hospital care would be delivered on a segregated basis. In the post-war years, a sizeable number of blacks, in fact, were still accommodated in all-black institutions, which in Paul Cornely's view remained "only high grade convalescent homes. . . . "[44]

In the North the situation was not much better. White institutions claimed to be integrated, but actual practice was usually more restrictive than open. Commonly, hospitals either limited the number of blacks in wards, or put them in private rooms—or double-occupancy rooms, provided another black was already there.[45]

Hospital opportunities for black physicians and interns, whether in North or South, remained sharply limited. A growing number of black doctors did enjoy courtesy privileges at segregated hospitals, but only in connection with their paying patients. For the would-be black intern, the South remained a barren ground. Shut out of positions at accredited white institutions, his or her only options were an unaccredited black hospital or depar-

ture from the South. The outflow of youthful talent continued as before
the war, and in turn it affected the profession left behind. In 1951 McFall
could count only three black doctors in South Carolina under fifty, a result
of the fact that "there was no place in the state where a Negro physician
could get their intern training."[46]

With the coming of Hill-Burton, of course, prospects for Southern
black patients and doctors had brightened. In new federally sponsored hospitals black patients, if still segregated, at least had benefit of modern facilities
and enjoyed roughly equal treatment.[47] In 1950, when the new Hill-Burton
hospital opened in Greenville, black surgical and maternity patients were
accommodated for the first time in the county facility. Comparing blacks'
facilities with whites' at that time, hospital administrator Robert Toomey
admitted that while they were "now better" than before, they were "still
separate" and "scarcely equal. . . ."[48]

Yet as time passed, acceptance of the black presence became more
and more routine at Hill-Burton hospitals, and quality of service, less distinguishable by race. Savannah got its first federal hospital in 1957, and two
black doctors sat on its planning board. According to one, Henry Collier,
white physicians were easy about cooperating with blacks by then because
of long interracial contact at the city's two Negro hospitals.[49] Raleigh got
its Hill-Burton facility, Wake Memorial, even later (1961), and the next year
Tuskegee Institute dean B.D. Mayberry had occasion to inspect it while his
wife was receiving treatment. He later wrote Wake administrator William
Andrews that it was an unexpected pleasure "to visit your institution. In
the Admission Room, I found the personnel most courteous and prompt
to act." While his wife was convalescing Mayberry saw several other departments in the black wing and found them all "clean [and] orderly. . . ."[50]

White patrons, to be sure, were not always as eager to welcome black
patients, even in segregated wings. Wake Memorial nearly collapsed financially in its first year because white patients were unwilling to go to what
was popularly derided as a colored hospital. As Wake administrator Andrews admitted to Duke Endowment executives, "the continued low census
at Memorial Hospital has . . . forced us into some rather drastic measures."[51] Eventually, overcrowding in the city's other hospitals—Rex and
Mary Elizabeth, neither of which admitted blacks—plus a resurgence of
common sense deflated the boycott. A white patient reported that she had
received "excellent food and service" at Wake. Moreover, she "did not see
a Negro patient." Her conclusion, shared by a growing number of whites,
was that "having both races in the same hospital produced no problem."[52]

Black doctors benefited almost as substantially from Hill-Burton, for
new hospitals and hospital additions gave many their first chance to practice medicine as it ought to be practiced, with greater access to modern

equipment and technology, increased contact with specialists, and more high-grade clinics and seminars.[53] What especially impressed many black doctors was the ease of their entry. To be sure, the law helped considerably. But there also seemed to be, on the part of white professionals, a willingness to do the right thing. White physicians and hospital administrators (in federally funded facilities at least) sometimes welcomed black physicians so openly that the latter were startled. Greenville Hospital's Toomey said that the awarding of full privileges to black physicians (to serve *black* patients) in 1953 came out of a "sense of correctness and dignity. There was no other reason for it. . . . People within the hospital just felt that the continuation of [professional] segregation was wrong. . . . "[54]

Although Toomey's explanation downplayed the influence of the law, blacks remembered the same cordiality. About the time Greenville was according equality, in another part of the state black internist Ranzy Weston was seeking to join the Aiken County hospital staff. He was fully prepared to be rebuffed "because of the way things had been. . . . " When the administrator told him that all he had to do was "make an application," Weston was flabbergasted. It must have shown on his face because the administrator, "a Yankee," went on to tell him that "this hospital belongs to the county of Aiken, and we get Hill-Burton funds. . . . " Weston was a taxpayer, and if qualified, he had a "right to get on the staff."[55] Likewise, when Tuskegee's Mayberry visited Wake Memorial the thing that he found most surprising was "the extent of integration of hospital personnel." And the question raised in his mind was, "if it could be done here, why not other places in the South?"[56]

One answer was that many Southern places *were* doing what Wake was. In an earlier study Paul Cornely found that 25 percent of Southern general hospitals had blacks on active staff, 25 percent extended them courtesy privileges, and 12 percent accepted Negro interns. Further, in every category hospital staff integration in the South was substantially equal to that in the North.[57]

Yet Mayberry's question had merit: if upwards of 50 percent of Southern hospitals had opened their doors to black professionals by the late 1950s, an equal number still shut them out. As for black patients, discrimination was more evident. Despite Hill-Burton the patient situation remained into the 1950s near what it had been in the pre-war period. As of 1956 90 percent of Southern hospitals were white run, and of those, about one-third did not admit any Negro patients.[58]

Among the two-thirds that did, over half had gotten no Hill-Burton funds and were thus under no compulsion to accord equal treatment to blacks they did admit. In the late 1950s at Columbia General Hospital (not yet a Hill-Burton facility), there was no X-ray equipment in the "colored wing," and black patients needing that procedure had to be carried across a wide, open court to the main building. In the seven hospitals associated with the Medical College of Virginia, not only were no Negro physicians allowed as late as 1957, but black patients were quartered in "sub-standard buildings, with sub-standard equipment, [and] greatly overcrowded."[59] Hence, despite Hill-Burton, as of the late 1950s at least 60 percent of the South's public and private hospitals either did not admit black patients or still accorded them inferior care.

One group of hospitals in the region, though, had accepted patient integration by then. They were the South's Veterans' Administration hospitals, which in 1950 had opened their wards to black patients under pressure of a directive from the VA's chief medical administrator. Nine hospitals in the Carolinas and Georgia were affected by the new policy. Joan Kirshner was a new staff member in one of them, in Atlanta, and she remembered the order. It stated simply that henceforth new admissions were to be assigned to wards without regard to race. She also recalled considerable apprehension about problems that would arise, but worry was needless. Integration proceeded without difficulty. The same unexpected smooth transition occurred at the VA facility in Columbia: former chief surgeon Richard Ferguson recollected that there was "a little griping," but that "no one left the hospital because of it."[60]

But the relatively few VA hospitals offered no avenue of opportunity to the average black patient. For a growing number of black physicians, solutions (for doctor and patients, alike) were also not going to be found in more separate-but-equal Hill-Burton hospitals, nor even in new all-black structures. Opportunity and equity lay in the complete overturning of hospital segregation, and in the early 1950s a movement began within the NMA aimed at that goal. Initial leaders were Cobb and Cornely, but by the late 1950s they had help from a number of black doctors in the deep South. Inspired by the civil rights fervor of ministers and students, they were making their stand for justice too.

Yet for about a decade the hospital desegregation fight was a labor without issue — for black doctor and patient. The white medical establishment ignored the appeals of the Cobb-Cornely group. As for black physicians, until the later 1950s, most were unwilling to actively support them, while a sizeable number firmly, if silently, opposed desegregation. To that group, said Cobb, desegregation was a threat. It would destroy the fiefdoms they had built up in third-rate black hospitals and would also throw them into competition with younger, abler blacks (not to mention whites), putting their very careers in jeopardy.[61] Yet for all that, the few activist black physicians did have an impact. When hospital integration finally came, it was the earlier efforts of the Cobb-Cornely group which had prepared the way.

In challenging Southern hospital segregation Cobb saw that, just as in the fight against all-white societies and schools, he must heighten black doctors' awareness in order to make them an instrument for change. His approach was both to assail and inspire. As he wrote in one editorial, what were needed were "pioneer spirits," who rather than yield to the allure of "fundamentally insulting placebos" would "tighten their belts and continue the struggle for principle."[62]

Cobb gave *Journal* readers as many examples as he could of the fight for principle. Even where there was little occasion for celebration, Cobb found elements of victory. When the Memphis NAACP branch reversed itself and rejected a plan for a new, all-Negro hospital, Cobb applauded. He likewise congratulated blacks in Columbia and St. Petersburg when they helped defeat local bond referenda calling for improvement of black facilities. As he had done in the fight against segregated societies and schools, Cobb tried to link the energies of the NAACP to hospital desegregation. By 1953 the NAACP was urging state chapters to form local physician health committees to survey and report on the extent of hospital segregation. Touting the NAACP as the action arm of the NMA, in 1954 Cobb urged every doctor to contribute one hundred dollars to the group's anti-segregation fund, a substantial part of which would be directed at hospitals. By its 1954 meeting the NMA was able to give two thousand dollars to the civil rights group. Legal counsel Thurgood Marshall came to receive it and stayed to make the major address.[63]

By the mid-1950s a number of Southern blacks were also beginning to move against hospital segregation. Aroused not just by Cobb's editorials but also by the *Brown* decision, in 1956 three Wilmington (North Carolina) doctors brought suit against that city's large Walker Hospital to force admission of black doctors. Though they lost their case (they would win it in a second suit in 1964), the effort was significant. For the first time, Southern black physicians had challenged the status quo in the courts. After Wilmington, legal action was no longer unthinkable or unethical. One of the plaintiffs, Hubert Eaton, underscored the new possibilities: "if you don't know what to do, go to court; that is the only way we know of in Wilmington, North Carolina."[64]

Not many were ready yet to follow that advice. But a new militance was gaining ground, even if its object was so far only the desegregation of hospital staffs. Richmond black doctor Daniel Webster Davis had been trying for several years to get the Medical College of Virginia to open its associated hospitals. By 1957 he was tired of begging: "I shall recommend that our next battleground be the federal courts."[65] In Gastonia, North Carolina, George R. Watts began stirring up things as soon as he arrived in town. As a black he could not practice at the town's two white hospitals. So his first stop was at the larger facility, Gaston Memorial, where he intro-

Montague Cobb (left) and Hubert Eaton at the 1964 meeting of the National Medical Association. Cobb is recognizing Eaton for his role in the 1956 desegregation suit against a Wilmington North Carolina hospital, the nation's first such action and one which Eaton and two colleagues finally won in 1964. Courtesy of Dr. Hubert A. Eaton.

duced himself to a shocked white superintendent and asked for a tour of the building. Given access to the emergency room—apparently to forestall his asking for more—Watts soon found that it was open to him only if he did not use it. When the hospital refused his first emergency patient, Watts rebuked the superintendent for unprofessional behavior and made formal application for staff membership. By 1957 he was ready to go to federal court if the hospital turned him down.[66]

Inevitably, interest in staff desegregation led to a desire to desegregate wards as well. As Wilmington plantiff Eaton said, "we don't want a partially integrated hospital where everything will be integrated except patients; we want [a] completely 100 per cent integrated hospital or no hospital at all."[67]

But opening white wards to black patients would never occur as a result of black initiative alone. Federal government backing was critical, and to bring that about sizeable white professional support was essential. In that effort Cobb continued to play a lead role, but he got substantial help from his Howard colleague Cornely.

The primary focus of Cornely's effort was the American Public Health Association (APHA), a group largely in sympathy with black professional goals. Cornely was a member of the APHA's committee on medical care, and in 1954 he helped draft a resolution repudiating discrimination and segregation in its delivery. The next year, with Cornely playing a lead role, the APHA adopted it as the will of the Association. In 1956 he returned to the APHA convention to urge members to assume responsibility for putting the Association position into action. "Every public health worker, whether in the North or South, ought not to accept the patterns of his community as sacrosanct." Where they impeded the health of any group, the health professional should seek to change them. The dysgenic character of segregation and discrimination, Cornely insisted, was no longer in doubt: they "are environmental factors and are just as damaging to health as water pollution, unpasteurized milk, or smog."[68]

In the same address he called Association delegates' attention to a recent Illinois statute which denied tax-exempt status to any private hospital refusing admission on account of race. That ban should be widened, Cornely thought, and he urged his APHA colleagues to join him in recommending the addition of nondiscriminatory clauses to all federal and state health laws, denying public money to any hospital or health center maintaining separate facilities for blacks. If legislatures were unwilling to do that, Cornely warned, "it may be necessary to pursue this matter through the . . . courts until it reaches the Supreme Court," as was done in education.[69]

In the late 1950s, however, such an amendment had no chance of passing Congress. That body had only just reached the stage of enacting the weakest sort of voting rights act. Not until 1962, in fact, was New York Senator Jacob Javits, long a foe of segregation, willing to introduce a restriction on Hill-Burton funds in Senate committee.[70]

Mainstream medical and hospital associations, however, were not under such constraints and in carrying the hospital desegregation fight to them, Cobb, Cornely, and allies launched their most ambitious political campaign, the Imhotep Conferences of 1957 to 1963. Largely the brainchild of Cobb, but strongly supported by Cornely, the national meetings sought to assemble white and black physicians and hospital administrators for face-to-face discussions on hospital segregation. Imhotep (from the Greek for "he who comes in peace") reflected the hope that integration could be achieved voluntarily, without divisive court and legislative battles, which Cobb saw as a "waste of time, energy, emotional tension, and money."[71] Even if friendly persuasion did not move the white establishment, blacks would at least have a forum for presenting their grievances, plus the moral certitude that it was whites, not they, who had turned their backs on rational, peaceful solutions.

It was quickly clear that a forum was all Imhotep would provide. Not a single white medical or hospital association — not even Catholic or Protestant hospital associations — sent delegates to the initial 1957 sessions. The AMA sent only an observer. But the standoffishness of the federal government was the greatest disappointment. The Department of Health, Education, and Welfare, which also only sent an observer, would not even let the group use its auditorium, a facility regularly used for NMA meetings. As a consequence of the boycott, the first 175-delegate meeting was almost a solid phalanx of black faces. In all, thirty-two organizations from twenty-one states participated. Although no one came from Georgia, eleven traveled from North Carolina and one from South Carolina.[72]

Without whites to address, Cobb, Cornely and other conveners were in the position of having to preach to the converted. Cobb presided over the first session (as he would at all others) and used the occasion to lambast Hill-Burton and call for its revision. Cornely, too, urged action but cautioned that hospital desegregation would not come easily, for many private hospitals would rather close down than accept Negro staff and patients on all wards. But the session was not a total loss. Black delegates caught a sense of mission and common purpose which they had not had before. Richmond physician Daniel Webster Davis spoke the sense of the meeting when he said that "we have gotten great benefit and inspiration . . . , and I do hope that we will go on from year to year with these meetings until . . . we shall receive complete emancipation."[73]

They did continue, but so did the white boycott. At the next two conferences the delegates — their numbers shrinking — had to content themselves with petitioning Congress to amend Hill-Burton and with requesting HEW to block all federal monies going to segregated facilities. Between the

1959 and 1960 conferences Cobb sought to energize local hospital desegregation by getting the NAACP more involved. At his urging the NAACP asked its state conferences to initiate a broad attack on medical discrimination, including encouragement of physician activism and meetings with white hospital authorities. If nothing else, the sessions might sensitize whites to such offensive habits as labeling beds and linens with the word, "Negro," and addressing black patients by first names.[74]

But these approaches had no visible impact, and the fourth Imhotep conference (1960) shrank to thirty registrants. North Carolina's delegation dropped to five, and South Carolina (like Georgia) sent no one. In desperation, conference leaders sought to shift entirely to the grass roots, by creating local action committees which would press for desegregation at the community level.[75]

That did not work either, and in 1963 Imhotep held its final session, in Atlanta. After calling on churches to "eliminate unChristian attitudes" in their hospitals, Cobb, Cornely, and other backers ended the seven-year struggle with a rather hopeless appeal for a mass letter-writing campaign by black citizens.[76]

All were disappointed, but the principals did not think the venture futile. Cornely felt that it had heightened awareness of deficiencies in hospital care for blacks and perhaps also "helped to push the concept of equity in health services."[77] Cobb saw its influence working in another direction, on the thinking and, eventually, policies of national Democratic administrations — notably on passage of the 1964 Civil Rights Act. Beginning with the election of John F. Kennedy, Cobb made a practice of funneling Imhotep findings to the White House. There was little response to Imhotep alerts until 1962, when the administration began to press for Medicare. At initial hearings on that proposal, and subsequently, the Imhotep group in the NMA gave strong backing to the administration bill. They were, in fact, the only physician group to support it, and as Cobb interpreted events, the NMA thereby won both the gratitude of the White House and, as a sort of *quid pro quo,* its close attention to Imhotep recommendations concerning hospital desegregation.[78]

Even so, the impact of Imhotep on the 1964 Civil Rights Act was minimal. The law, which banned segregation in public accommodations and cut off federal funds from any state or local agency practicing it, affected many facilities and activities besides hospitals. Moreover, the most immediate stimulus came from Martin Luther King's 1963 Birmingham campaign, which shared the goals of the later law.[79]

Imhotep's likely role was to provide an added dimension to the picture of social discrimination, to which the administration of Lyndon B. Johnson was increasingly responsive. Apparently Johnson was eager to push ahead rapidly with hospital desegregation. Shortly after the law's passage he directed the surgeon general and the Justice Department to meet with hospital administrators and leaders of the NMA and AMA to make clear the requirements of the new law. Cobb attended the meeting and recalled that federal officials adopted the tone that everyone should "be good boys and girls and settle down and get this plan initiated." The 1964 Civil Rights Act was, after all, the law of the land, and "we might as well abide by it."[80]

And abide by it they did. Between 1964 and 1970 the large majority of Southern hospitals accepted desegregation of patients and physician staffs without the application of federal sanctions. Compared to the history of school desegregation, the story of hospital integration provided a chapter in Southern race relations of which the region could be proud. Hospitals were in fact the first vital social institution, apart from the armed forces, to implement full-scale integration — putting them ahead of schools, colleges, neighborhoods, and of course, churches. And they did it on the whole with surprising speed and unexpected good will.

That was largley because in hospitals the primary consideration was quality of care, not the color of patients on the floor. Of course professionalism could not assert itself until hospital administrators had assurance that racial tolerance would not cost them patients. As Savannah black doctor Henry Collier noted, hospital managers might have favored patient desegregation before 1964, but "everybody was afraid to do it." White patients "just didn't want to lay in the bed next to the 'nigger,'" and administrators were understandably unwilling to put them there.[81]

Therein lay the chief value of the 1964 act. By putting nearly all hospitals under the same requirement, previously inconceivable changes could now be made. When Greenville General announced in the mid-1960s that it was fully desegregating its wards, the hospital simply referred to the Civil Rights Act as the reason. As administrator Toomey saw it, the law gave hospitals the opportunity "to finish off the entire process of desegregation."[82]

But civil rights legislation was not solely responsible for the progress made in desegregation. The federal courts also played a key role. While the federal bench did not speak often to the issue of hospital desegregation, it did speak early and effectively. The most important case was a 1963 judgment of the Fourth United States Circuit Court of Appeals, which began to register its impact just as Congress passed the 1964 law. The case was *Simkins v. Moses H. Cone Memorial Hospital,* and according to former United States attorney Terrill Glenn of Columbia it was the "granddaddy of hospital desegregation suits," for it did what black medical reformers had been unable to do for fifteen years: eliminate segregation from the province of the Hill-Burton Act.[83]

The origins of *Cone* went back to 1962 when a group of black doctors, dentists, and patients in Greensboro, North Carolina, brought suit in federal district court to force the desegregation of the city's two private, all-white hospitals, Moses H. Cone and Wesley Long. Cone and Long had recently gotten Hill-Burton grants, even though both remained closed to black physicians and patients. In fact, the two institutions had admitted their discriminatory intent. Yet North Carolina's hospital regulatory body had approved the requests on the ground that a simultaneous award to Greensboro's all-black L. Richardson Memorial satisfied the federal requirement of equal provision for Negroes.[84]

Plaintiffs disagreed. Charging that Richardson Memorial was inferior to the two white hospitals in staff, equipment, and facilities, they protested that their exclusion from Cone and Long was a denial of constitutional rights under due process and equal protection clauses of the Fifth and Fourteenth Amendments. In December, District Judge Edwin N. Stanley ruled against the plaintiffs. Though agreeing that there was discrimination, Stanley found that he was unable to give blacks relief because, being private facilities, the hospitals were not bound by the Fifth and Fourteenth Amendments.

Four months later the black group appealed the ruling to the Fourth United States Circuit Court of Appeals. There, presiding judge Abraham Sobeloff and two of his four colleagues, Albert V. Bryan and J. Spencer Bell, did not feel stymied by the barrier of privatism. They decided that private hospitals which got Hill-Burton money were sufficiently involved with the state "to be within the Fifth and Fourteenth Amendment prohibitions against racial discrimination."

As for denial of protection, there was no doubt about that: exclusion of blacks from more modern, white facilities had helped impose "severe consequences" on Negro doctors and the black populace, for the latter had an infant death rate twice that of North Carolina whites and a maternal rate five times greater. Looking for a solution going beyond plaintiffs' petition, judges struck at the statute which had underwritten the discrimination. In November 1963, they declared that that portion of the Hill-Burton Act "tolerating 'separate-but-equal' facilities for separate population groups" was unconstitutional and therefore null and void.

In expunging racism from Hill-Burton, *Cone* revealed the broad influence that the 1954 school desegregation ruling had had on the Southern federal judiciary. In his majority opinion Sobeloff conceded that the two North Carolina hospitals had "accepted government grants without warning that they would thereby subject themselves to restrictions on their racial policies." In fact they were now being told to do what the government promised they would not have to do. "But in this regard the defendants, owners of publicly assisted facilities, can stand no better than the collective body of

Southern voters who approved school bond issues before the *Brown* decision. . . . "[85] Every white Southerner must be prepared to sacrifice for the larger good of justice.

As for what that sacrifice would entail, *Cone* was unequivocal: All hospitals which had accepted Hill-Burton money in the past (or would in future) were duty-bound to admit black doctors and patients on an equal footing without delay.

The new will in the Southern federal judiciary got prompt illustration in South Carolina. In 1962, a year before *Cone,* a black woman had been forcibly removed from an all-white waiting room of the Orangeburg Regional Hospital, a new facility built with Hill-Burton funds. Gloria Ratchley promptly sued the hospital, to force its desegregation. United States District Judge George Bell Timmerman, however, had ruled for defendants, accepting the hospital's argument that segregation was necessary for smooth operation, as well as for the physical and mental health of patients.[86] Two years later (after *Cone*) the Fourth Circuit Court of Appeals vacated Timmerman's decision and ordered a re-trial at the district level. That time new judge Robert Hemphill decided that integrated facilities were a right and that (white) patient health would not be jeopardized by them. In January 1965, he gave the hospital sixty days to desegregate fully or have the court do the job.[87]

White opinion was outraged. A month after the order, the *Charleston News and Courier,* the major low-country paper and a bastion of segregation, berated Hemphill for "forcing racial integration down the throats of patients. . . . " It was a prescription, said the paper, that ran counter to all laws of "spiritual and physical healing."[88] Considering the intensity of opposition Hemphill remained remarkably faithful to the mandate of *Cone.* The desegregation plan that he approved provided black plaintiffs (and patients) nearly all that they asked for. His two concessions were more loopholes for whites than restrictions against blacks.[89]

Thus by 1965 the federal courts and the 1964 Civil Rights Act were working in tandem to pull Southern hospitals toward integration. *Cone* imposed the new ethic on hospitals which had enjoyed Hill-Burton funding in the past. The public accommodations statute reined in those recalcitrant facilities that hoped for future federal assistance, whether from Hill-Burton (which continued until 1975) or any of a multitude of other medical programs and agencies, such as the National Institutes of Health, the National Science Foundation, the Kerr-Mills Law, and HEW.

Yet in practice it was more the prospect of federal enforcement than its actuality, which led Southern hospitals to abandon segregation. And in fact, it was neither federal agencies nor the courts that applied most of the pressure for change. That came, rather, from private associations and community groups which either threatened hospitals with punishment if they did not alter policy or promised reward and advantage if they did.

Chief threateners were civil rights groups. Early in 1965, just as HEW and other agencies were beginning to implement the 1964 law, the NAACP announced that it was requesting a HEW investigation of twelve Southern hospitals, all allegedly guilty of gross discrimination, but still getting federal aid. One, in the North Carolina piedmont, was found to be maintaining separate wards, dining areas, and operating rooms. Another denied Negros the right even to visit white patients.[90]

Local NAACP groups meantime threatened to take hospitals to court. Following Hemphill's ruling in the Orangeburg case, South Carolina NAACP head I. Dequincy Newman warned that he would soon initiate suits against other state hospitals, if they did not voluntarily integrate.[91]

Not all civil rights groups were so quick to look to federal authority. Some, like the Richland County (South Carolina) Citizens Committee, under the leadership of Columbia's Modjeska Simkins, tried first to gain voluntary compliance. As of summer 1965, Columbia General, a recent beneficiary of Hill-Burton funds, still maintained a segregated black wing, separate washrooms, and an all-white nursing dormitory. Having just revealed abuses of black patients at the state mental institution, Simkins and company approached hospital officials and urged them to take steps to end segregation. Only when that approach failed did she request an "on-site" visit from HEW officials in Atlanta. Ultimately (about 1967) Columbia General integrated without a court order or a shut-off of federal money.[92]

But desegregation came not only from the pushing of civil rights activities. It was also a result of *pulling* by mainline white groups, which had their own reasons for wanting to desegregate public institutions. In Columbia about the time of the 1964 act, mayor and insurance executive Lester Bates formed a Community Relations Council, composed of prominent black and white citizens, to work for peaceful, gradual integration of public facilities. In part the Council reflected the city's willingness to bow to the inevitable. But it was also evidence of new thinking among the South's urban white elites. To them segregation still had emotional appeal, but more important was a stable social climate, deemed essential to business. As one Columbian recalled, the feeling was that "federal legislation was in the wings, and . . . desegregation would go over better if citizens were led to do it gradually and voluntarily rather than have it forced down their throats."[93] In keeping with this policy, two physician members of the Council called on Columbia Hospital superintendent J.M. Daniel and sought his cooperation, arguing the wisdom of changing before change was forced. Simkins was applying her pressure about that time, and the push plus the pull was the combination which led hospital trustees to start dismantling more than a century of segregation.[94]

Nor was Columbia exceptional in witnessing that sort of pressure and response. In Greenville a similar blue-ribbon committee emerged in 1964. It promptly began to press for desegregation of such institutions as restaurants, stores, and hospitals. Agitation from civil rights groups was not a factor, there, according to Robert Toomey, who was part of the citizen effort. Not only was the NAACP nonexistent, but "the black leadership was working with us, and we were delighted."[95]

The same sort of elite apparatus was at work in Charlotte, although there black medical and civil rights activists also played a role. Though spurred by the 1964 law, the Charlotte Race Relations Commission owed its creation to the Greensboro sit-ins of 1960. Duke Endowment's Marshall Pickens was Commission vice chairman, and he and his colleagues had learned a lesson from Greensboro: "not to let the situation get out of control but to control it and do what you're supposed to do." Well before 1964, then, Charlotte leaders were calling on restauranteurs and retailers such as George Ivey to urge that "things should simply be opened up to avoid somebody coming in here insisting on having a seat."[96] After the Civil Rights Act, the Commission shifted its attention to hospitals and schools. "Hospital people would come talk to us," said Pickens, "and we told them to put the black doctors on the staff and put the black patient in the hospital." In Charlotte, Pickens noted proudly, integration was achieved without rioting in the streets, without even any conflicts. That was so because the leadership said, "we're going to do it, and let's just move it along. . . . [Don't] raise questions about it, just do it."[97]

The only cost of volunteerism was the inordinate length of transition. As Columbia physician and one-time mayor Frank Owens noted, there was "no overnight change."[98] Indeed, once hospitals showed signs of shifting away from segregation, HEW pretty much let them set their own pace. Such an attitude encouraged hospital stability and eventual community acceptance of change, but it also gave room for foot-dragging and outright flouting of the law. Columbia General did not integrate obstetric wards until 1969, and it acted then largely because declining births made two wards redundant. Before white women were put in once all-black quarters, however, the black section was remodeled and refurbished. On opening it, superintendent Daniel announced that the unit now stood ready to give patients the "best care possible. . . . "[99] According to the NAACP, evasion of the law was all too common, and the federal government did nothing to stop it. For years after the Act's passage, HEW continued to fund hospitals that "excluded Negro doctors and limited desegregation under so-called 'patient choice' policies."[100]

There was also the problem of hospitals that lay beyond reach of the law or the courts. Those were institutions which had never taken Hill-Burton money before 1964 and afterwards chose to forego federal funding rather than disavow segregation. Most were small, inconsequential facilities with little to offer patients of either race, but a few were large, modern facilities with sufficient financial resources (often provided by Southern Protestant churches) to resist racial equity. Of course many caved in with passage of Medicare (1965), whose funds—and patients—were denied to segregated hospitals. Raleigh's Rex Hospital was one institution integrated by Medicare. Denied funds early in 1966, Rex promptly accepted its first Negro maternity patient and shortly after assured the Raleigh black community that it "intends to comply with the Civil Rights Act so it can accept Medicare patients."[101] Over the next three months Rex desegregated further, and in 1967 a federal court judged the hospital sufficiently in compliance for Medicare funding.[102]

A few hospitals held out longer by rejecting Medicare patients, but even their course became increasingly difficult. For all their toleration of gradual desegregation, the courts showed little patience for overt discrimination, and by the end of the 1960s they were laying all manner of unforeseen snares in its way. The fate of Charleston's "new Roper" hospital (built in the 1940s) showed just how difficult being all-white had become. That privately-owned facility got tripped by its own cafeteria.

"New Roper," so named to distinguish it from "Old Roper" (which had closed in 1959), had never accepted black patients. When the issue of compliance had first arisen in 1964, Roper's chief of staff recommended that the facility open its 330 beds to Negroes so that it could qualify for federal funds. But the Medical Society of South Carolina, which owned the hospital, refused on the ground that federal aid would only mean federal interference.[103]

If permissible ten years before, such exclusion now raised hackles in the Democratic Justice Department. In August 1968, Attorney General Nicholas deB. Katzenbach brought suit against owning doctors to force them not only to integrate hospital facilities but to abandon discriminatory employment and promotion policies. Justice's case centered on the hospital's cafeteria and snack bar. Because they served visitors from other states, they and the hospital which housed them fell into the embrace of the Interstate Commerce clause and were thus places of public accommodation, subject to the 1964 Civil Rights Act.

In March 1969, United States District Judge Robert Martin accepted that reasoning and ordered an end to segregation and discrimination as they affected both patients and employees at Roper. But Martin went further and closed all loopholes that might be used to defeat the spirit of the decision. The hospital could not ask a white whether he was willing to share a room with a black. Nor could a white patient be moved from a room occupied by a black, unless a doctor attested to a compelling medical reason. Further, for the next two years the hospital had to give evidence that it was not discriminating against employees or patients. By the end of the decade the kind of judicial tolerance shown earlier by South Carolina judge Hemphill was no longer available.[104]

Seen in broader perspective, funding denial and court orders in the Rex and "New Roper" cases were the exceptions, not the rule. They were mostly characteristic of that group of hospitals with no black patients, even on segregated floors. Compulsion was the exception because the majority of hospitals, as they saw changes coming, moved forward voluntarily to accept them. Rarely had white hospital administrators and physicians — and the same could be said of most black doctors — agitated for change, or even invited it. But when it no longer appeared avoidable (and pressure from civic and civil rights groups prompted that conclusion), they accepted it willingly and with apparent good grace.[105]

Savannah's bowing to the inevitable might serve as illustration. As soon as it became apparent that Washington was serious about the 1964 act, the city's white hospitals wrote all black doctors, inviting them to apply for staff privileges. According to one, Henry Collier, hospitals were even willing to bend some standards to allow black doctors to perform minor surgery even though they were not certified to do so. By the 1970s, however, standards were being raised again, as more Negro physicians became board certified.[106]

Ranzy Weston of Augusta was another black doctor whose experience spanned both eras, and his story suggests the gains that desegregation brought to all black doctors, even those working in modern Hill-Burton facilities. Weston had had privileges in the county hospitals in Aiken, South Carolina, and neighboring Augusta, Georgia, since his arrival in the area in 1953. But he and his patients were isolated in somewhat second-rate black wards. Occasionally, he crossed the color line to treat a white patient, but he recalled with rueful humor that "they didn't want me to treat white women. . . . No matter how old they were they didn't want me to treat white women."[107]

With integration, things changed markedly. As Weston recalled, if a black doctor had the qualifications, he had equal access to the best facilities available and was admitted fully into the company of specialists whose help he had never totally enjoyed before. If the specialist, usually white, did not want to help, that no longer counted. He *had* to — that was the new ethic.

Most black patients, especially those in non-Hill-Burton hospitals, also moved up from second-class status. They, too, could now routinely gain access to a bevy of specialists generally unavailable before. Moreover, black cases came under review of the entire hospital staff. That was an important new dimension, for it insured that the black patient's well-being was not subject any longer to control by just one or two doctors of perhaps average-to-limited competence, as was often true in all-black and segregated hospitals. Black patient welfare was now guarded by the practice of case survey and review, long a tradition in white hospitals, but extended to most black patients only with integration.[108]

The only losers were the South's all-Negro hospitals. They had never taken sturdy root, and they had been overlooked, even weakened, by the Hill-Burton Act. With the 1964 law their end was at hand, for as Duke Endowment's Pickens put it, once integration came, "blacks preferred to patronize the local white hospital."[109] Not all black hospitals collapsed, certainly. The strongest institutions, such as L. Richardson Memorial in Greensboro and Flint-Goodrich in New Orleans continued on a strong course. But by the mid-1970s the great proportion had been absorbed into white hospital systems, collapsed utterly, or been converted to out-patient clinics.[110]

The fate of the Waverly-Good Samaritan hospital in Columbia, which had played such a large if sometimes troubled role in the medical care of central South Carolina blacks, illustrated the general trend. Recipient of a Hill-Burton award in 1950, the hospital enjoyed new vigor up to the 1960s. But with approval of a new county hospital by Columbia voters in 1967, Waverly's end was in sight. The large and fully integrated Richland County Memorial opened in 1972. Waverly closed the next year. By mid-decade the small black hospital sat abandoned and for sale, a home only for occasional derelicts.[111]

Otherwise, hospital integration in the South signaled a gain for everyone. And one fundamental reason why it proceeded as smoothly as it did was because white Southern physicians and hospital administrators, compared to school superintendents, for example, had no real stake in maintaining segregation. White patients might have been as touchy on the subject as white school patrons, but public opinion did not intrude into the hospital as it did into the classroom. Staff physicians and administrators were more in control of their publics than their counterparts in education. The main thing holding up hospitals was assurance that that public could not escape to some still-segregated facility across town. Once that was provided — by force of federal law and judicial decision and by pressure from white and black community leaders — the pace of change was rapid and certain. To Savannah black doctor Collier, the really amazing thing was how swiftly and completely the whole segregationist edifice collapsed. White doctors, said Collier, "acted like it was never any different, like segregation had never existed."[112]

CHAPTER 12

The Health of Blacks
after World War II, 1945–1970

The desegregation of medical institutions was unquestionably an important step in blacks' move toward equality in health care and status. Yet more (and better-trained) black doctors, wider access to hospital beds, and improved treatment could not by themselves do much to raise the health level of the whole Southern black population. For one thing, it took time to produce the needed black professionals. More to the point, increased professional care was only the most obvious determinant of health and arguably not the crucial one. As always, non-medical variables — life-style, nutrition, education, racism and especially economic status — had an influence too, not just on blacks' need for care but also on their ability to act on that need and to profit from whatever professional contact did occur.

The existence of so many variables, however, makes it difficult to generalize about the health of black Southerners after World War II. In truth, when one surveys the health of blacks in post-war decades, one cannot be sure whether to "point with pride" or "view with alarm." The historical record gives ample opportunity for both, and even contemporary observers could not agree on the direction events were taking. In 1946 new South Carolina health officer Ben Wyman reflected on the rapidly expanding program of indigent-care clinics and noted that doctors had given generously of time and skill to their mostly black patrons. As for clinic patients, Wyman was sure that they felt that they had gotten as good attention as they would have from a private doctor.[1] Yet one year later, *Southern Exposure*, the journal of the respected, interracial Southern Regional Council, pointed to the vastly higher death and illness rates of blacks and concluded that "those are but a few of the hazards incurred by being born black in a white man's country. 273

And when one asked, 'what is being done about it?' The answer is: damned little."[2]

Faced with the task of finding pattern amid diversity and confronted with evidence of both health progress and stagnation, the historian is tempted to fall back on the view that historical interpretation is mostly a matter of perspective. As in the parable of the optimist, the pessimist, and the half-full (or half-empty) pitcher of cream, one could focus either on the extent to which blacks were catching up to whites or on how far they continued to lag behind.

But such would not be the best formulation of the situation, for in this case there was not *one* pitcher–i.e., one Southern black population – but two, each with its own health history. One was an increasingly urban population, lying within reach of public health agencies and private physicians and fairly aware of the need for preventive medical care. At the core of that group was a slowly emerging black middle class, which by the 1960s was enjoying increasing economic opportunities. With rising income came all the other improvements – in housing, leisure, education, nutrition, and medical care – that would combine to produce health improvement. It was the mounting weight of that population in the period after the war, along with expanding health services, that accounted for the overall decrease in black morbidity and mortality rates, and improvements in other measures of health.

At the same time there was another black population – between 35 and 40 percent of the whole, and possibly more – who lived almost entirely outside existing health and medical systems and were practically untouched by educational and economic improvements of the civil-rights sixties. Mostly rural blacks, but including many urban poor, members of this population, if employed at all, were still trapped in low-pay jobs such as farm tenancy and domestic service. Their relative numbers changed little from the end of the Second War to 1970, and they lived increasingly in families headed by women, which added to their economic woes. On the whole they lived lives of such impoverishment and physical and social isolation that they were largely invisible to those health agencies, doctors, and political leaders who had the means to help them.[3]

The enormous medical needs of this black underclass came to the public attention only in the late 1960s, when an aroused national concern about racial inequities resulted in the "discovery" of vast numbers of hungry and malnourished Americans, not just Southern blacks, but people of all races and sections. Until this time, the black population of which medical and health establishments were mostly aware was the more viable – and visible – portion, which had both inclination and, increasingly, the means to improve and safeguard their health. Because of sharp gains made by that fraction of the Southern black population, there were many signs of average statistical improvement. Thus health officers like Wyman of South Carolina had reasonable cause for optimism.

Probably the major impetuses behind the health gains of the relatively more advantaged class of blacks were various changes in public attitude and awareness. As detailed earlier (chapter II), by the end of World War II a consensus was forming among the national leadership that second-class citizenship for blacks was no longer acceptable. As one major problem blocking Negro advance, ill health got considerable attention. For leaders in public health, in fact, its improvement became for the first time a major goal. Not only Thomas Parran, but his successor Leonard Scheele as well, was determined to expand health opportunities for blacks. As Scheele told Public Health Association colleagues in 1949, when one asked what Negroes needed, "the answer is simply one word: more."[4]

At the same time, a number of national health studies were measuring the precise dimensions of Negro ill health. Their results produced both a program for action and a wider recognition of how seriously handicapped blacks were. For many thoughtful Southern whites those studies, often the first such accounting to come to their attention, disrupted the comfortable illusion that blacks were able to make do with less than whites.

One of the most important was an investigation by the National Urban League. Launched in 1944 with funds from the (Rockefeller) General Education Board, the study sought to encourage local leaders to take a clear-eyed look at race relations and, after identifying major problems, to search for solutions. Focusing on a range of issues including health, Urban League consultants between 1944 and 1947 visited thirteen Northern and Southern cities, including Winston-Salem, St. Petersburg, and Charleston.[5]

The health expert was Howard's Paul Cornely, who had already done a similar study for Rosenwald, but without any reformist goals. Later, in Charleston and other Southern (and Northern) cities, Cornely found that whether the subject was VD clinics, TB beds, dental care, health education, or services for handicapped children, Negroes got least. Sometimes they got nothing. Nationwide, Cornely said, one of the elemental rules of public health practice was being abused: the delivery of services according to need.[6]

Recognizing that well-being hinged on more than just provision of services, Cornely helped local leaders identify major social and environmental barriers to health. White attitudes were one of them. In many clinics "Negro patients were often treated with condescension, lack of sympathy . . . respect, and dignity. . . . " Such treatment was itself a cause of ill health, for it "often prevented full utilization by Negroes of all of the services which are available to them."[7] Cornely also noted a persistence of the old habit of blaming the victim, as Charleston's Welfare Council (Cornely's local sponsor) seemed to do when it called on blacks to "exhaust their own ability and resources before appealing for public aid."[8]

But at least white officials were having their eyes opened to the size of black problems, and that led to a recognition of a need for expanded public responses. Even the most ardent segregationist was unable to resist that conclusion. As one leading Southern surgeon put it to the president of a black college: "you know, Doctor . . . , I've been thinking a lot about your [health] problems lately, and I really think . . . niggers ought to have something."[9] New thinking among the white health establishment was even conceded by a skeptical Montague Cobb, who noted in 1949 that change "is churning on these issues where it has never churned before."[10]

One important result of all the churning and discussion was a large-scale expansion of the embryonic network of clinics for low-income and indigent mothers and infants, which had first appeared with passage of the Social Security Act. Few of the early clinics provided continuing medical care. Rather, most were periodic and brief affairs, whose services were offered by a team who traveled out to some local site for a few days' visit. Now, with Hill-Burton providing principal funding, Southern communities began to get permanent health centers. Between 1949 and 1952 North Carolina began construction of thirty of them, offering mothers and infants the kind of on-going service theretofore enjoyed by only a few.[11]

Crucial to the flowering of the health centers was their (sometimes grudging) acceptance by private physicians, who provided their manpower. They accepted them because state health officers convinced them that the only way to head off large-scale government intrusion into medicine was to make more abundant and rational provision for the poor. Throughout the 1940s, with national health insurance bills simmering in Congress, intrusion was a real possibility. Consequently health officers like North Carolina's Carl Reynolds were persuasive when they told the state doctors that if they did not act to expand health services for the poor, "we will have superimposed upon us ill-advised schemes to which we could never subscribe. . . . "[12]

Expanded maternity and infant clinics continued to be a near exclusive preserve of black Southerners, offering a sort of public substitute for private medicine. In South Carolina by 1950 the number of black expectant mothers seen at the clinics was about fifteen times greater than the number of white. The latter were more apt to bring their infants to the clinic, although clinic staff still saw about twice as many black babies as white. In North Carolina and Georgia, ratios were similar.[13]

As before, there were racial reasons for the lopsided distribution of aid, but it was also due to a continued tightening of midwife regulations. By the early 1950s most Southern states were finally able to enforce the rule that midwives have their clients examined by a physician before the sixth month — or lose their licenses.[14] According to Georgia's midwife supervisor Miriam Cadwallader, "women came out of the bushes" with the regulation. "In some of the counties women who had ten babies and had never been seen . . . before checked in for an examination."[15]

Although most expectant women who came (or were brought) to clinics probably got only one or two professional examinations, those few contacts were for most their sole chance for qualified medical attention. In 1949 in South Carolina and Georgia, 59 and 55 percent of Negro women had no doctor present at delivery. In North Carolina the figure was over one-third. And if clinic patients got little of the personal attention associated with private medicine, examinations were as thorough as those done in a private office. Clinics tested for TB and VD, arranged free treatment for indigents, gave a basic series of immunizations, and advised mothers on diet. Succeeding years added red blood counts, and tests for cervical cancer and the Rh factor.[16]

The clinics also seemed to have a wide reach, at least in the first post-war decade. If directors' reports could be believed, virtually every expectant Negro mother in South Carolina, North Carolina, and Georgia made at least one clinic visit before delivery. Apparently the experience had value beyond that one visit: many black women learned to seek prenatal care earlier and to put a higher value on professional attention. In 1950 less than half of South Carolina's clinic patrons reported before their sixth month. By the end of that decade, the proportion had risen to about 75 percent. As for selling women on professional care, only 5 percent of South Carolina's clinic patrons in 1950 initially planned to use a doctor at delivery. Yet when that time came 40 percent actually did.[17]

None of this, however, is meant to denigrate the value of the midwife as a birth attendant. Before the 1940s unskilled midwives had perhaps endangered many black women and infants, but two decades of midwife regulation were having an effect. South Carolina reputedly had the nation's best program, and one midwife, Maude Callen of low-country Berkeley County, was the subject of a 1951 feature in *Life*. That piece not only attested to the skills of those dedicated women but also to the fact that it was not usually midwives who put maternal health at risk. The unsanitary environment of pregnancy and birth played a greater role. Callen seldom found even the simplest equipment or provisions at hand. At times there was not even a newspaper for a birth pad. For a crib she often had to use a fruit crate set on chairs near the stove. Mothers' grasp of basic rules for infant health and safety was often woefully limited: Callen frequently saw newborns laid in bed with other children.[18] Moreover, the physical condition

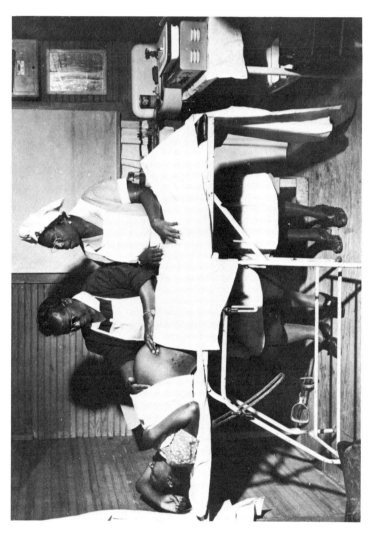

Berkeley County (South Carolina) nurse-midwife Maude Callan (center) examining a maternity patient of a local midwife, c. 1950. In 1984 Callan received the United Way of America's highest award for volunteer service. Courtesy of the South Carolina Department of Health and Environmental Control.

of many pregnant black women frustrated the efforts of even the best-trained midwife. In comparison with white women, expectant blacks were more frequently young, small statured, in poor physical condition, and burdened with an improperly formed pelvis, characteristics tied not just to low income but also to high maternal and infant mortality.[19]

Yet despite the handicaps of being born black in the South, the average health status of Negro mothers and infants improved at a fairly rapid rate in the post-war decades. Some of the early improvement was likely due to the recent growth of prenatal and infant care services, because before the late 1950s deep-South blacks had not begun to enjoy any significant rise in socioeconomic status, as better jobs, quality education, and improved housing remained closed to them.

The maternal death rate underwent a dramatic drop. In South Carolina, North Carolina, and Georgia in 1945 the number of black women dying in childbirth (per 10,000 live births), was 540, 490, and 525, respectively, contrasted to 175, 186, and 206 for whites. Twelve years later, figures for blacks had fallen to 175, 175, and 160. Although white mothers enjoyed a higher percentage improvement, the absolute drop in Negro mortality averaged twice as much as the white in the three target states (see figure 1).[20]

For Negro infants, the post-war decade also saw gratifying improvement, though for two categories (neonatal and infants under one year), whites gained ground faster. Where black infants made greater absolute (and roughly the same relative) improvement was in the fetal death category. But that was not surprising. The fetal rate was one reliable measure of the quality and availability of prenatal care, and its improvement confirmed the rising health status of expectant black mothers and tied it to increased public services (see figures 2 and 4).[21]

Improvement in maternal and infant health was most rapid among Southern urban blacks, a population that continued to expand in the post-war decades. The drop in infant mortality was one sign of improvement in urban health. In 1945, as in the past, black urban rates had been higher than rural in all three states (for whites the two rates had nearly evened up), with large cities having an excess of some twelve deaths per thousand live births. By 1957 the differential had reversed itself in Georgia and narrowed sharply in the Carolinas. By 1969, North Carolina cities, too, had a lower rate, while in South Carolina urban and rural rates were practically even. In part, improvement was due to the fact that city-dwellers (many of them recent rural migrants) found more health services available than before. As early as 1948 a North Carolina study noted that while only about 7.5 percent of rural children saw a public health nurse, over one-third of city youngsters got her attentions (see figure 3).[22]

But if a move to the city meant better life chances for black infants

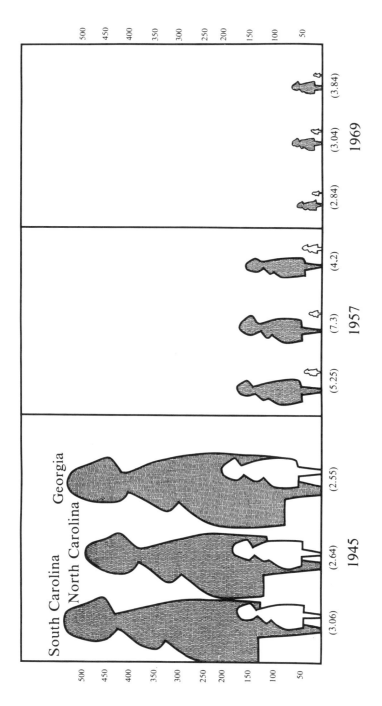

Figure 1. *Maternal Mortality by Race (per 100,000 population) for South Carolina, North Carolina, and Georgia: 1945, 1957, 1969. Black-to-white ratio in parentheses.* (Sources: *Vital Statistics of the United States, 1945, 1957, and 1969; Grove and Hetzel, Vital Statistics Rates in the United States, 1940–60.*)

Figure 2. Black Neo-Natal (under 28 Days) and Infant (under 1 Year) Mortality (per 100,000 population) for South Carolina, North Carolina, and Georgia: 1945, 1957, 1969. Black-to-white ratio in parentheses. (Sources: Same as Fig. 1 above.)

and women (and men, too) by the end of the 1950s, more than just increased services was responsible. Urban life also implied greater social, political and economic opportunities, thanks in large part to the successes of the civil rights movement, whose material benefits fell mostly on city-dwellers. As a recent study has shown, in the mid and late 1960s, especially, urban blacks in South and North made "major social and economic advances. . . . " There were gains in income, employment, education, and home ownership, and a sharp drop in the number of blacks in poverty.[23]

In the area of income, in fact, *Southern* blacks improved most. In 1964 black income in the South was 57 percent of that in the North. By 1974 Southern earnings had risen to 75 percent. Similar strides were made in the proportion of Southern black families earning above $10,000. Between 1953 and 1974 the Southern percentage increased nearly eightfold (from 4 to 31 percent). In the North it doubled. Progress made by South Carolina blacks was typical. In the 1960s high school graduates rose from 10 to 18 percent, while the fraction earning a comfortable living ($5000 to $10,000) vaulted from 6 to 33 percent. Better-educated families were more aware of the requirements of health—whether food, housing, medical care, or surgery—and better-paid families were more able to purchase them.[24]

The 1960s, then, because of several factors—expansion of services, urbanization, and increased income and education—brought the average Southern black woman and her infant the greatest health improvements they had yet experienced. They even began to close the gap on Southern whites. In South Carolina, North Carolina, and Georgia, for every measure except death among newborns, decreases in black mortality in 1957-69 were larger than those for whites. Greatest gains came in Georgia, where black maternal mortality fell 64 percent, while the white rate dropped only 12.6 (see figures 1, 2, 3, 4).[25] For expectant Negro mothers and their infants, the two groups most at risk in any population, a corner had been turned.

But what of the Southern black population as a whole? There, too, all measurements indicated that blacks on average made continuous and often rapid gain. To be sure, there were lapses as well as major stumbling blocks along the way. Negro housing long remained an incubator of disease rather than a barrier against it, one post-war study estimating that three-fourths of Southern Negro homes were "below the safety margin for health."[26] School environments, too, remained a worry. A 1949 Peabody College survey in Spartanburg revealed that every one of that county's fifty-seven Negro schools was in "poor" or "very poor" condition, whereas only half of white buildings rated that low. In a black school in Jasper County (South Carolina), children had to run with every flush of the toilet, and eventually filth from its overflow covered parts of the yard. Not until the early 1950s, with the

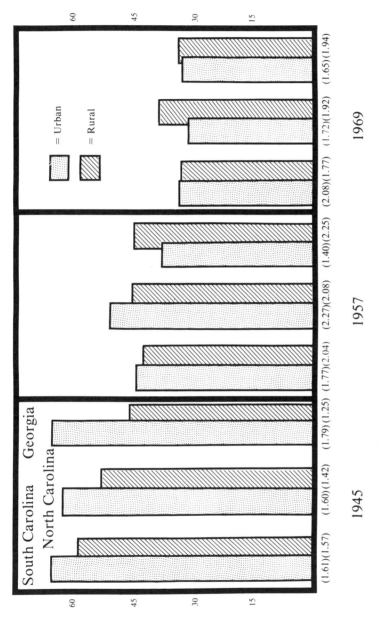

Figure 3. Black Infant Mortality, Urban vs. Rural (per 100,000 population) for South Carolina, North Carolina, and Georgia: 1945, 1957, 1969. Black-to-white ratio in parentheses. (Sources: Same as Fig. 1 above.)

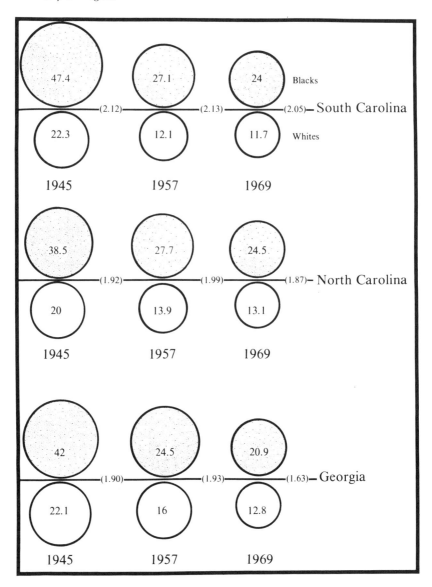

Figure 4. Fetal Death Ratio (No. of Still Births per 1000 Live Births) by Race for South Carolina, North Carolina, and Georgia: 1945, 1957, 1969. Black-to-white ratio in parentheses. (Sources: Same as Fig. 1 above.)

looming prospect of school desegregation, would public officials begin to honor the "equal" part of "separate but equal" in their school facilities.[27]

Despite such barriers, signs of overall health improvement were numerous. Mortality from TB, the particular scourge of black Americans, had been falling since the century's turn with little help from medical science. But it was only after the war that it finally lost its terror, owing to the provision of more sanatorium space and the introduction of effective chemotherapy. Federal aid helped pay not only for beds but also for TB control programs, which searched out cases of disease and got victims started on treatment when hospital care was unavailable. By the late 1960s that program and the sanatoriums were mostly benefitting black tuberculars.[28]

Although black TB continued a problem into the late 1960s, health department determination at least helped bring it to bay. A contagious disease, easily diagnosed and amenable to control, TB was the sort of malady that organized health forces battled best. By 1970, thanks to a large assist from rising living standards, the battle was largely won. In South Carolina in 1966 black mortality stood at 6.3 deaths per 100,000 (it was 55.8 in 1945). That was still three times the white rate, but for twenty years black progress had at least kept pace, the black rate dropping 88.7 percent and the white, 87.4.[29]

VD, especially syphilis, was another persistent problem for blacks, although the availability of penicillin in the post-war period shifted the odds in the victim's favor. As before the war, health departments used circus-like campaigns to motivate black citizens to seek tests and treatment, even resorting to soap opera-like radio shows ("Lips of a Strange Woman"). The one new ingredient was VD-control programs aimed at discovering victims and getting them into treatment.[30]

Ironically, the end result of all this activity was not elimination of VD. As more and more cases and their contacts were run to ground, incidence again rose sharply just as it had done in the late 1930s. In North Carolina a dramatic upsurge appeared as early as 1946. But if reported cases were on the rise, newly identified victims were now for the first time getting effective treatment. More important, blacks were no longer dying of syphilis. In 1945 it had killed 272 Georgia blacks and 217 in South Carolina. In 1970 those totals fell to 8 and 6.[31]

As the stories of TB and VD suggested, blacks got more and better professional care, generally, in the 1945-70 era. One measure of that was the dramatic increase in the number of black women giving birth in hospitals. In 1945, an average of 28 percent of Carolina and Georgia women still had babies at home or somewhere outside a hospital. By 1969, 92 percent of new mothers went to hospitals. Another index was the declining proportion of blacks listed as dying from "ill-defined" (or "unknown") causes — a designation that usually indicated an absence of medical care at death. In 1945,

58.3 Georgians and 87.5 South Carolinians (per 100,000 of population) fell in that category, making it the second leading cause of death in both states. Twenty-five years later, lack of professional attention was a sharply reduced problem. The rate from "ill-defined conditions" now stood at 18.9 and 49.4 in Georgia and South Carolina, lowering it to the tenth and seventh causes of death for blacks in those states. Whites died far less from unknown causes in that period, but signs were that blacks were closing the gap. By 1970 their rate of improvement was substantially more rapid than whites' (see figure 5).[32]

An equally important sign of the normalization of black health were changes in the known causes of death. In the 1940s the picture was still reminiscent of the 1920s. It was also in marked contrast to the white pattern. In South Carolina and Georgia in 1945, syphilis and homicide were among the ten leading causes of death for blacks but not whites. Though major killers of both races, pneumonia and TB were far greater menaces to blacks, relatively and absolutely. Whites, by contrast, showed a much higher rate of death from cancer and accidents (particularly auto), and only whites had suicide as a leading cause.

By 1970 mortality had been democratized: syphilis and TB had disappeared from the top ten lists for South Carolina and Georgia blacks, and deaths from auto accidents and cancer had now entered, at about the same level as for whites. The only major differences remaining from the 1940 list were the importance of suicide among whites and homicide among blacks, though murders among Georiga whites had increased faster than for blacks. The one new, important cause of death among whites was emphysema. Probably many of those deaths were really due to byssinosis, contracted over long years in cotton mills. Clearly, segregation had not worked to whites' advantage in every instance.[33]

Although for nearly every disease and among all age groups Southern blacks continued to die at a higher rate than whites, their overall, age-adjusted mortality not only fell sharply after World War II, it also dropped slightly faster than the white. Progress was particularly clear for black males. In South Carolina in 1940 Negro deaths stood 52 percent above white, improved to 47 percent in 1950, and to 44 percent in 1960. In Georgia the gap closed by about the same measure, from a 55 percent excess in 1940, down to 47 percent in 1960. In North Carolina black males lost ground in the 1940s but then began to gain it back in the 1950s, ending the decade with a mortality 44 percent above whites (see figure 6).[34]

For black females the overall picture was less clear. Certainly age-adjusted mortality dropped every decade, remaining always well below that of black males. But in some states white women did better. In South Carolina, between 1940 and 1960, black women narrowed the gap separating them

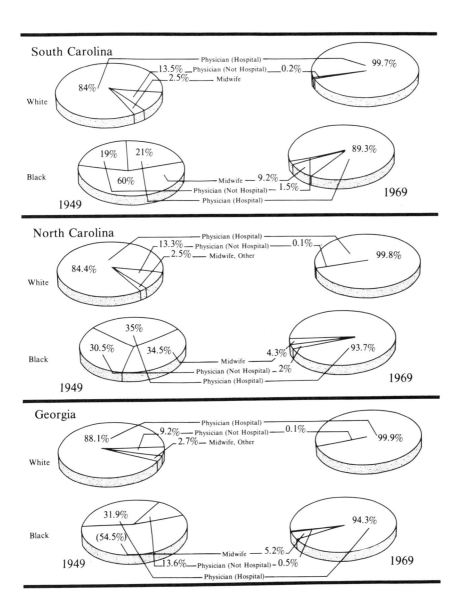

Figure 5. Attendant at Delivery, by Race, for South Carolina, North Carolina, and Georgia: 1949 *and* 1969.

(Source: *Vital Statistics of the United States,* 1949 and 1969.)

from white women, as they did in North Carolina. In Georgia, though, the opposite occurred, black female mortality standing 81 percent above the white in 1940, but then rising to 86 percent in 1950 and staying there over the next decade. But black women consistently closed one gap: that separating them from white males. By 1960 in North Carolina, South Carolina, and Georgia their age-adjusted mortality had nearly reached the white mark and was advancing fast (see figure 6).[35]

As important as mortality in measuring health improvement was life expectancy at birth. For blacks in the three target states it rose continuously during 1950-70, and except for one group (North Carolina males) it increased faster than for whites. Black females did best: in 1950 their life expectancies in South Carolina, North Carolina, and Georgia were 61, 63, and 61 years, respectively. White female infants that year could expect to live, on average, nearly 11 years longer. By 1970 blacks had increased their life chances at birth to 67, 68, and 67 years in these three states, which brought them to within 8 years of white females. Equally noteworthy was the fact that black women by 1970 could finally expect to outlive white men, giving black women for the first time the rightful biological advantage of their sex (see figure 7).[36]

On viewing such improvement a casual observer in the South might have concluded that blacks by the 1960s were on the way to health equality with whites. But such a view would not have been warranted. At the end of the decade it became suddenly clear that while the mythical average Southern black was living longer and healthier, a very large number of real black Southerners had gained very little in health since World War II. Many in fact remained in desperate straits, enduring conditions of hunger, malnutrition, and unattended disease more commonly associated with the world's underdeveloped nations. Evidence of such conditions was so overwhelming and unexpected that one Southern health officer made an unprecedented admission of failure. After decades of annual reports pointing with pride, South Carolina's Kenneth Aycock conceded that his state "stands in severe deficit in terms of the health needs of her citizens." Many blacks, in fact, faced massive problems of simple survival.[37] As poor people's advocate Ralph Nader put it, not just in the South, but all over the nation "there are people who simply never see doctors, who are not getting any kind of medical care, who do not have the money to get medical care, [and] are not tied in with any programs such as the public health service. . . . "[38]

That poverty existed Americans had long conceded, especially during economic depressions. But the general and comforting belief was that in normal times — particularly in the prosperous decades following the war — Americans always had enough to eat. If black and poor white diets were dull and unvaried, they at least provided ample nourishment, thanks to federal food-supplement programs.

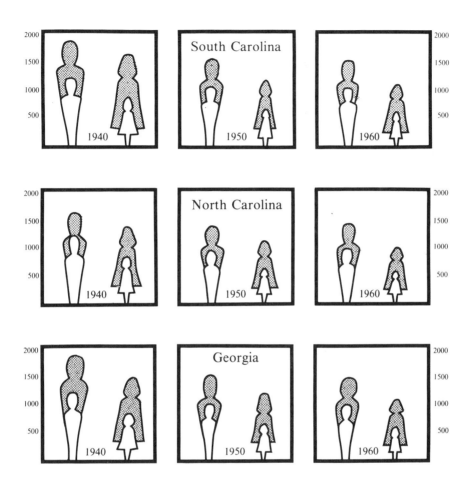

Figure 6. Age-Adjusted Mortality by Race and Gender (per 100,000 population) for 35 Causes of Death in South Carolina, North Carolina, and Georgia: 1940, 1950, 1960. (Source: Grove and Hetzel, *Vital Statistics Rates in the United States,* 1940–60.)

Figure 7. Life Expectancy at Birth, by Race and Gender, for South Carolina, North Carolina, and Georgia: 1949–51, 1959–61, 1969–71.

(Source: *State Life Tables, 1949–51, 1959–61, and 1969–71.*)

But that assurance was rudely jolted in 1967 when reports broke of upwards of 10 million Americans of all races living with the daily pain of hunger. As one distraught black mother put it, her children "get up hungry, go to bed hungry, and don't ever know nothing else in between."[39] For children, particularly, hunger and accompanying malnutrition were so serious as to imply actual starvation, and if not that, alarming physical and mental impairment at least.

The "discovery" of widespread hunger in a nation of the over-nourished occurred in the spring of 1967, when a United States Senate group traveled to Jackson, Mississippi, to inspect the workings of federal anti-poverty programs. In the course of the visit senators saw hunger so stark that one of them, Robert Kennedy of New York, literally wept in despair.[40]

Shortly after, a second "poverty tour" went South, sponsored by the Marshall Field Foundation and made up of a group of physician-activists such as Robert Coles of Harvard and Raymond Wheeler of North Carolina and the Southern Regional Council. Coles's report to the Senate Employment and Poverty Subcommittee was graphic. They had seen "hungry and malnourished children, children with swollen ankles, swollen bellies, widely infected skin, wasting muscles, and for practically each part of the body . . . significant illness. Hearts had murmurs. Percussion of chests indicated lung infections. Teeth were in awful condition. Children needed glasses, needed antibiotics, needed drugs that would rid them of worms. . . . Children had, almost universally, angry and unhealed sores and chronic sinus condition, and, in the words of one mother, 'colds, colds, colds; they never get over them. . . . '"[41] The net result of such conditions was a "mortality rate that is comparable, say, to the underdeveloped nations of Asia or Africa."[42]

But hunger was the most disturbing observation. Raymond Wheeler put it most starkly when he told a meeting of North Carolina anti-poverty workers: "we do not want to quibble over words, but 'malnutrition' is not quite what we found. The boys and girls are suffering from hunger and disease and, directly or indirectly, they are dying from them—which is exactly what starvation means."[43]

Although the hunger revelations drew immediate and wide press attention, there were many scoffers. On the face of it, hunger charges were difficult to credit, for government was subsidizing not only a generous commodity distribution program but since 1961 a food stamp plan that was offering low-income Americans in every state bonus food-purchasing power with only a small cash outlay.

The Southern congressional farm bloc was particularly vehement in rejecting the hunger thesis. Mississippi Democrat Jamie Whitten, chairman of the House Appropriations Sub-committee, seemed to see the issue as part of a liberal-socialist conspiracy to force integration on the South. He was sure there was little hunger among Southern blacks. Where it existed it was their own fault: "If they had the training and foresight of other people, they wouldn't be in a condition of poverty."[44] To get at the real motives behind the hunger claims, in 1968 Whitten got the FBI to send investigators to "question" the Northern reporters and their Southern informants who had started all the rumors.[45]

Whitten's House colleague W.R. (Bob) Poage of Texas, chairman of the House Agriculture Committee, did more. In 1968, in an apparent effort to smother the issue, Poage asked county health officers in the South and elsewhere to appraise the hunger charges. When their responses came in, Poage saw that they got wide media attention. The health professionals' basic contention was that there was no widespread suffering. Georgia county health officer C.B. Creagh struck a common note: He did not know of "any county in which serious hunger exists." In fact, he said, "it is of interest to note" that vitamin disease had almost totally disappeared from the South.[46]

Although several respondents reported the presence of hunger, as often as not it was explained away as the result of ignorance, coupled with loose living. According to Mississippi health officer Cecil McKlemurry, "the number one cause of malnutrition [is] absence of family structure." The solution was not more food for undeserving people, but measures which "make it worthwhile for adults to become married. As it stands now this promiscuous relationship is actually being financed and subsidized by welfare and give-away programs."[47]

Social philosophizing among health officers extended also to intestinal parasites, which were often found in conjunction with malnourishment. Some Southern public physicians felt that far too much was made over worms. Richland County (Columbia), South Carolina, health officer John Preston told one audience that worms were nothing to worry about. In his boyhood everybody had them. The thing really to be concerned about, Preston chided his dumbfounded listeners — a biracial group of about 250 people — was that their meeting had not opened with a prayer.[48]

Critics, however, did not have the field to themselves. By early 1968 a bipartisan coalition had formed around the hunger issue. It included not only senators like North Dakota's George McGovern but also foundations, churches, civic groups, and labor unions. To investigate the magnitude of the problem, by year's end McGovern succeeded in getting his senatorial colleagues to create a special subcommittee to gather testimony. Soon every periodical with any claim to a national readership was running a special on the hunger question. By mid-1968 and for the next two years, hunger and malnutrition were the nation's hottest domestic issues.[49]

Although the liberal position was soon enjoying greater credibility, largely because the civil rights movement had accustomed most Americans to believe the worst about black conditions, government could hardly be expected to move against the problem until someone spoke more authoritatively about its actual dimensions. Even so knowledgeable a figure as the surgeon general admitted that no one knew the extent of malnutrition in the United States. A great deal of evidence had accumulated to document flaws in existing food schemes (i.e., self-defeating food stamp purchase requirements, underfunding of school lunch programs, and a surplus food distribution scheme that gave scant attention to nutrition). But no one stepped forward with the facts showing how serious American hunger really was.[50]

No one, that is, until PHS nutritionist Arnold Schaefer came before the McGovern Committee. In 1967 Congress had given the PHS (and Schaefer) the task of measuring scientifically the extent of American hunger. For some months Schaefer's study was stalled by congressional inaction in the matter of funding. But finally in January 1969, after about eight months study of the poor in Texas, Kentucky, Louisiana, and New York, Schaefer was ready with preliminary findings.[51] They revealed, he said, "more malnutrition than I ever expected."[52] While few Americans were acutely starving, one-third of children had unacceptably low levels of vitamin A, and two-thirds lacked necessary iron. What was particularly upsetting was the discovery of conditions like *kwashiorkor*, a severe protein deficiency previously linked to undeveloped nations. In essence the Schaefer study concluded that the much-debated claims of massive hunger were not off the mark.[53]

The next month the McGovern Committee (and the nation) heard even more dramatic testimony — this time from a former South Carolina governor, who explained how and why the Southern states could fail to see the kind of suffering Schaefer documented. Ernest F. Hollings, then senator from South Carolina, admitted that as governor he had covered up the existence of widespread hunger and malnutrition, so as not to scare away new industry. "We didn't want the vice president of the plant in New York to know the burdens [of locating in South Carolina]. We told him only of the opportunities. You don't catch industry with [round-] worms — maybe fish, but not industry."[54] Although Hollings's soul-bearing stirred anger in some — a Greenville matron branded him the "new head of the 'whore corps'" — almost all applauded his stand and agreed that hunger was indeed a mammoth problem.[55]

The resolution of the quantitative aspect of hunger raised an equally important issue, namely its historic dimension. Millions of blacks, but also many Indians, Esquimos, and poor whites, were doubtless hungry and malnourished in the late 1960s. But how far back did the problem reach? Had great numbers also been suffering in the 1940s and 1950s?

Some argued not. They insisted that the kind of hunger discovered in 1967 was a relatively new phenomenon, unknown among earlier Americans save in time of serious national calamity, such as the Great Depression. Hence the nation, while it might have other crosses to bear, was innocent of having long ignored widespread hunger.

Anthropologist and social critic Margaret Mead was one who made that argument. Serious want had existed in the 1930s, but effective work by such federal agencies as the Farm Security Administration and the Bureau of Home Economics had practically eliminated it by the end of the war. But then Congress had foolishly allowed its hunger-fighting apparatus to atrophy. "We relaxed and went home," Mead told the McGovern committee. "Nutrition research turned to very elegant small problems . . . very important but not related to the problem of feeding people."[56] Thus, when a new population of hungry Americans reappeared, largely due to dislocations in the economy such as the displacement of tenants by farm machinery, the government lacked mechanisms and expertise to detect and solve the problem. As a result, hunger had multiplied until by the late 1960s it had reached alarming dimensions.[57]

Others were not as willing to treat an earlier generation so kindly, and they had the more persuasive argument. Although there were no broad studies of clinical malnutrition in the South in the first half of the twentieth century, a number of individuals in close contact with the poor recalled a long-running problem. Parasitologist John Lease came to South Carolina in the late 1930s and was later instrumental in demonstrating roundworm infestation among coastal blacks. He had witnessed hunger since his arrival, and he believed that South Carolina's "medical industry" had known about it too, but the problem had never "been taken before the public."[58]

South Carolina NAACP leader I.D. Newman recalled decades of malnutrition so severe and intractable that it was scarcely dented by any government program. "In spite of the New Deal, the Fair Deal, the comfortable Eisenhower years, the New Frontier, and the Great Society," blacks had continued "no better off than the poorest of the poor during the darkest days of the depression. . . . "[59] What Newman observed in South Carolina was equally present in the upper state. The 1942 nutritional study of the farming-textile community in the North Carolina piedmont (chapter 8) found levels of vitamin deficiency among white mill-hands and especially rural blacks that left those people little margin of nutritional safety.[60]

Thus, Robert Coles was dismayed by what he saw in Mississippi, but not particularly surprised. "We know that those conditions have persisted for years," he told Congress, and "have been responsible for thousands of stunted lives and premature death." Chronic hunger, in fact, had "been buried in the medical literature for years and years."[61]

Indeed, that literature had contained grim warnings of human tragedy at least since the 1930s. In the middle 1930s Howard's Hildrus Poindexter, writing from Mississippi, was upset not only by the malnutrition he saw among black children but also by local health officials who passed it off as their normal condition (chapter 4). By the early 1950s the situation had improved little. In 1951 the South Carolina Board of Health reported serious nutritional deficiencies among black mothers seen in clinics. A third seldom, if ever, ate meat, and 40 percent were deficient in calcium.[62]

Other reports of the 1950s told of worm infestation and vitamin deficiency. Still others revealed not just problems but public inertia as well. In poor, heavily black Edgecombe County, North Carolina, there was severe malnutrition, but the local health department had limited its response to urging black families to use more milk. In 1954 a local black teacher undertook more effective action. Each morning she fed her charges hot cereal cooked on the school stove. For most, that was the only breakfast they got, and the teacher felt that "even if I can't teach them to read and write, I'm going to teach them how to live." But her hope was frustrated. The county health officer, with regret, stopped the free breakfasts because "school facilities did not meet state sanitary standards."[63]

If America's political history since 1933 featured any principle at all, it was that government was responsible for meeting basic human need. If hunger was a long-standing problem, the question demanding answer was how the guardians of the national welfare — the political, bureaucratic, medical, and health leaderships — could have so long ignored this most basic need.

In fairness to the guardians, their long inattention was to some extent due to the unwillingness of the poor and hungry to come forward, thus hiding the magnitude of the problem. As medical sociologists explained (chapter 1), the poor hung back because sickness was something to delay, not give in to. Otherwise one took oneself out of the struggle for survival and incurred loss of vital income. In the early 1950s a Tuskegee study found ample evidence of such attitudes. For poor blacks in Alabama ill health had several gradations, ranging from "not-so-well" to "really ill," and only the latter merited care. Moreover, real illness was defined not with reference to how one felt but solely in terms of whether one could work. Even then, a sufferer did not necessarily seek professional care, for expense might be too great. Children were expected to bear up too. Adults saw childhood diseases as simply part of life, seldom calling for attention beyond home remedies. Just 12 percent of the families in the Tuskegee study went to physicians or clinics when their children fell ill, and they did so only after home therapy failed.[64]

In succeeding decades those habits persisted among the approximate 35 to 40 percent of blacks who remained in poverty. As late as 1970 a resident at Meharry's Hubbard Hospital lamented that "the average poor black adult . . . comes to the hospital only when he's on his last legs. He doesn't know anything about his medical needs or his right to medical attention."[65] A black doctor in Columbia noted a similar situation: most of [the poor] come in only when . . . they can't go to work. . . . Often they won't come back for about a year, or until they need medicine again."[66]

But in the final analysis it would not do to blame the victims. The primary causes of the nation's failure to respond lay elsewhere. And woven into every other cause was the same fundamental one: racism. Subtle and sometimes not so subtle, racism still imposed blinders where blacks were concerned and made acceptable the belief that blacks either did not need the kind of sustenance that whites enjoyed—or did not deserve it.

In the distribution of scarce health money racism was an invisible but major arbiter. Health and welfare directors still commonly gave whites (and white sensibilities) prior consideration. In Thomas County, Georgia, in 1949 the health commissioner vetoed a health center site in a "rather run down colored section" because it "would not attract white patients. Also the [white] nurse midwives would have to go to the center at night and they might be afraid."[67] Blacks commanded a goodly proportion of health spending, but as Paul Cornely frequently noted, it was never doled out in proportion to their share of problems.

Southern welfare departments remained overtly racist. As administrators of federal commodity distribution and—beginning in 1961—food stamps, relief agencies might have reduced hunger significantly. Yet too often county welfare heads were more interested in withholding than distributing food, especially to a clientele largely perceived as shiftless blacks. As South Carolina's Hollings put it, "some of your welfare officials . . . resent anyone getting onto the welfare rolls. They don't look upon it as an opportunity to clean up a problem, but rather they almost look upon it as their money, and they are not going to give it away. . . ."[68] From his long experience in the South, Coles found that welfare heads routinely used food assistance to control behavior, withholding it from blacks who in any way challenged white authority.[69] Sometimes welfare was harnessed to the protection of existing economic arrangements. As Hollings explained, the "main effort . . . is to make sure the food stamp program doesn't reach the attention of the hands . . . of certain influential farmers."[70]

Racism operated more critically at the national level, where it combined with bureaucratic politics and economic interest to frustrate efforts to meet—or even recognize—the needs of the hungry. It existed most critically in the various committees of Congress that controlled funding for national food supplement programs. Since the 1930s they had been under domination of powerful Southern congressmen with clear ideas of what blacks did and did not need. The fact that some of those congressmen coveted federal "hand-outs," themselves, never seemed to strike them as inconsistent. Mississippi's Whitten and the large farmers of his congressional district received enormous farm subsidy payments from the government, but they balked at the idea of approving food relief for those they saw as the lazy and shiftless.[71]

As administrator of national food supplement programs, the United States Department of Agriculture was in position to exert a countering influence. Unfortunately, secretaries of Agriculture also had to get along with Southern farm bloc congressmen. If they wanted adequate appropriations for basic Department programs, it did not pay to press too hard for increased food for the nation's poor. Even a progressive like Orville Freeman, a one-time Farmer-Labor governor of Minnesota and secretary under John F. Kennedy and Lyndon Johnson, was skittish about proposing more than a minimum food supplement. Robert Coles was dismayed to discover that state of affairs when he and his cohorts approached Freeman in 1967 about more hunger relief. Freeman and aides were frankly discouraging and advised the doctors "not to expect much change." The Department, they told Coles, "is beholden to the agriculture committees of the Congress. . . . In particular Mr. Whitten's name came up and Mr. Poage's. . . . In essence we were told we were wasting our time, and we were very discouraged."[72]

Even without the need to appease racially sensitive Southern congressmen, the Department, said critics, would not have taken a lead role against hunger. Its main goal since the advent of the allotment/price support policy of the 1930s was maintenance of high prices for American farmers, and by the 1950s powerful economic interests had coalesced around those programs. Though Agriculture secretaries had the power (since 1949) to declare crops in surplus and buy them for distribution to the needy, what they bought and distributed was decided primarily by farmers' economic needs. In the thirty years before 1969, fruits, vegetables, eggs, and poultry had made up 26 percent of surplus commodities purchased by the USDA. Yet according to one physician who investigated the program, few of those nutritious foods had been in the commodity distribution pool.[73] In 1966 the USDA had even returned (to Treasury) over $200 million in tariff receipts that it could have spent on food supplements.[74]

That same bias toward producers, charged Pennsylvania Senator Joseph Clark, marked even Freeman's leadership, and it was not right. As physician-activist (and 1967 Mississippi visitor) Alan Mermann of Yale put it, "the hungry should not be at the mercy of an agency set up to ensure an agreeable market price for suppliers of food."[75]

Perhaps it was visionary to expect the farm lobby, its Washington bureaucracy, and influential Southern congressmen to be more sensitive to needs of the hungry. But more might have been expected from those immediately responsible for the nation's health, its public health agencies and private physicians. Yet they, too, were blind to the problem of hunger, and the reasons for their long oversight explained much about the workings and constituency of the public health establishment in America.

Habit and tradition formed part of the problem. Earlier in the century when contagious and insect-borne diseases had been major and obvious dangers, heavy involvement with such matters as immunization and privy construction were proper activities for protectors of the public health. And health agencies had battled them effectively. But as those threats were mastered, new problems had come to the fore — or were more sharply revealed once contagious diseases were subdued. Some stemmed from dangerous workplace environments; others were personal health problems, originating in a substandard (or excessive) life-style. They included chronic diseases like strokes and heart attacks, plus all the problems associated with poverty and malnutrition. Though health agencies knew much about the prevention and elimination of such conditions, they gave them little attention and continued to concentrate on what had worked so well before.[76]

Conservatism in the public health bureaucracy was evident in its clinic programs, especially as they related to blacks. The traditional problems of expectant mothers and infants were fairly effectively dealt with, but many of those seeking help were hungry, infested with worms, sometimes mentally retarded, and burdened with diseases such as anemia and rickets.[77] Yet clinics gave little attention to those ills, Robert Coles observed. "The concept that the public health service sometimes had, as its function, is to give tetanus shots, to give diphtheria shots, but not to give . . . [black clients] the kind of comprehensive medical care that they need."[78]

Health-department inertia sprang from more than "old fogeyism." Agencies failed to respond to hunger, malnutrition, and other personal health problems not just because they were looking elsewhere but also because to have done so would have offended their main constituency — private medical practitioners. To put it simply: local, state, and national health departments did not grapple with personal health problems because organized private doctors, for economic reasons, did not want them to do so and if necessary were willing to block them from trying.[79]

Physician opposition, however, was seldom overt. It did not have to be, for health boards, North and South, generally shared private doctors' commitment to fee-for-service medicine — even for poor Americans. That harmony of view was not surprising. Although post-graduate work in public health administration had been a standard since the late 1930s, health directors had all received their primary training in medicine and were thus imbued with the private medical ethic. In addition, private doctors had supervisory authority over most state health departments, an arrangement which existed in the Carolinas and Georgia until the early 1970s (when consumerism and the rise of environmental concern finally forced a widening of the direc-

torship of state boards, adding lay members and eliminating or neutraliz-
ing physicians' voting majorities).[80]

A shared viewpoint also influenced health policy at the federal level —
though to a lesser extent. In the late 1940s a Washington lobbyist for national health insurance legislation lamented the lack of support for the
measure in federal health circles. But that was not surprising, she thought.
Top health officials in the states and Washington "are overly cautious to never
disagree with organized medicine's propaganda machine."[81]

Of course interests of health professionals and private doctors were
not identical. Those who worked day to day in public medicine came to
see at first hand the limits of the fee-for-service system in meeting the needs
of the whole population, and in some states they strove to expand preventive services. North Carolina's health officers continued to be willing to
challenge that state's physicians. Yet caution was always required, for even
modest program extensions often met strong opposition from organized
physicians who saw a financial threat. At their 1952 annual meeting North
Carolina doctors railed against the recent tendency in public health work,
which they believed "infringes on the field of private practice and leads to
increasing government controls." State health officer Roy Norton responded
that if doctors would only analyze the work of state and local departments,
"you will convince yourself otherwise."[82] But Tarheel State doctors were not
convinced. At its 1959 and 1960 meetings, the North Carolina Medical Society again voiced concern that the board of health was trying to replace
"our fine system of fee-for-service private practice" with a system of socialistic
medicine.[83]

American physicians, of course, have long mistaken social medicine
for socialized medicine. What has been less evident is the impact of that
thinking on the ability of state boards of health to meet the needs of the
poor. In the South, where notions of individualism and freedom enjoyed
wide popular support, physician conservatism was especially inhibiting. Those
activities which threatened to take away money or patients were often hedged
about with so many restrictions as to limit usefulness. The influence of the
fee-for-service philosophy varied, of course, from state to state. Where there
was a strong *public* health tradition and forceful, independent leadership,
as in North Carolina, programs were somewhat more responsive to the poor.[84]
South Carolina, however, lacked those traditions, and there public health
was more attuned to physicians' interests than to those of the needy.

Even in traditional areas of preventive medicine, South Carolina health
leaders and the physicians who guided their programs took care that only
the truly needy — i.e., the totally impoverished — got free treatment. In the
early 1950s state physicians approved a mass VD screening project, but only
on condition that treatment be left in doctors' hands. The only patients they

were willing to relinquish to health departments were those who could prove their indigency to a newly created and independent agency. Concern to weed out "welfare chisellers" was so great that the agency required applicants to sell their property before seeking certification for free care. According to field reports, physicians' charges were so high and board regulations so stringent that a large number of blacks went without treatment.[85]

Cancer clinics also illustrated the limits private medicine put on public health in South Carolina. Set up in the early years of World War II to offer diagnosis and treatment to patients unable to afford private care, South Carolina's program seemed as much concerned to discourage the ineligible as to provide care. To secure an appointment at a public clinic a patient had first to get a physician to make application for him to the county health department. That agency then called on the welfare office to investigate the client's financial status. If the patient proved to be indigent, the health officer next sought approval from the state cancer control division. If that were accorded, the officer petitioned a particular clinic for an appointment. Final arrangements were communicated to the originating physician, and he contacted the patient.[86]

Without question, clinics filled a critical need and served many blacks, who comprised a steady 40 percent of patients. Yet restrictive, complicated admission policies surely shut off care to many. Whites were also handicapped certainly, but it was more often the black who had no personal doctor to initiate admission. It was only suggestive, but in 1970, 718 new Negro cancer patients were identified by the state board of health, 471 at South Carolina's eleven clinics and the rest among private patients. The number of blacks dying from cancer that year, however, was 868.[87]

A health activity of particular relevance to the poor, also stunted by physician influence in South Carolina, was home nursing. In the post-war era such programs had atrophied, but in the early 1960s new plans contemplated a massive enlargement, aiming at a standard of one three-nurse team for every ten thousand people. In South Carolina that translated into three hundred teams, caring primarily for indigent families or those in isolated areas with no private doctors.[88]

It was soon clear that such programs had little behind them but good intentions. By 1968 South Carolina had put only thirty-seven teams to work, most of them appearing after 1965 and passage of Medicare. Lack of funds was not the only cause for the short-fall. South Carolina physicians apparently were more concerned to keep the program from serving the undeserving than they were in expanding its reach. Board of health sensitivity to that view was reflected in the state health officer's assurance in 1966 that home health care "is of no means an attempt to supplement that of the attending physician." Quite the contrary. Private doctors, alone, he reminded, had power to request such service, and it was they who controlled it.[89]

South Carolina doctors' objections to extensions of preventive medicine and their corporate blindness to hunger and malnutrition came out in the open in the face of criticism from one of their own number. When the critic was an outsider too, as was Dr. Donald Gatch of Beaufort County, fellow physicians were doubly hostile.

Donald Gatch had all the credentials of a "trouble-maker." Born and raised in Nebraska, he set up practice in South Carolina in the early 1960s following a residency in Savannah, which he found to be a pleasant experience and one which revealed a needed field of work. A dedicated doctor and civil rights activist, and a man with a talent for abrasiveness, Gatch was incensed over the medical neglect of blacks and was determined to do what he could to bring about change. In. 1962 he published an article in *Public Health Reports* on the high parasitic infestation in Beaufort County, an early warning of a problem that would later symbolize the hunger crisis. What brought him to the unfavorable attention of his colleagues, though, was his 1967 testimony on malnutrition before the United Auto Workers' hunger inquiry.[90]

Those particular sessions were in Columbia, and Gatch had the "bad manners" to go there and give his views about health conditions in the South Carolina low country. They were grim: over 19 percent of his mostly black patients harbored roundworms and showed serious problems of anemia, lassitude, and weakness. Sometimes if worm eggs made it to the lungs they caused pneumonia. Children suffered most: "they'll be weak, anemic, underfed, and living in those shacks. A freezing spell comes, and they've had it; a baby dies here, another one there, next door. And the worms, they go all over the body . . . to the eyes, the lungs, the stomach, the liver. The other doctors here never see any of these people; and then when I describe conditions like these, they turn on me and call me every name in the book."[91]

When Gatch returned home, they did that and more. First there was denial. Resident physicians at Beaufort County Memorial Hospital insisted that the few cases of infant malnutrition they met were all the result of "parental inexperience, indifference or gross neglect." Then came shock. Stung by Gatch's questioning of the state midwife system, physicians were incredulous that anyone could defame "one of the . . . most closely supervised midwife programs in the entire United States." Finally, they sought to get even. After the hearings, the hospital staff, with members hissing Gatch's name, initiated steps to take away his hospital privileges.[92]

Although Gatch, himself, ultimately left (supporters said he was driven from) the state, his fight with the Beaufort medical establishment in 1967-68

represented a kind of high watermark of the effort by those who would ignore or cover up problems of hunger, malnutrition, and illness among the
poor. Testimony from people like Schaefer and Hollings helped turn matters around, but what was most important in bringing the country to grapple with the hunger issue were shifts in public opinion. Fueled by civil rights
victories in voting, public accommodations, and housing, a national momentum was building to eliminate racial discrimination on all fronts. When
the "discoveries" of hunger and malnutrition were shown to have solid foundation, that momentum quickly propelled black health to the top of the
national priority list, forcing federal and state health offices to give attention to problems they had long ignored.

The turn-around on the part of North and South Carolina's boards
of health revealed the strength of the new pressure and the kind of action
it generated throughout the South. By 1968 North Carolina health leaders
had revised their whole outlook on nutrition. In shifting its program from
the personal health division to the community health division, the North
Carolina Board of Health served notice that it no longer regarded nutrition
as a problem of over-consumption, influenced by individual choices, but
as one of under-consumption, affecting whole populations and rooted in
conditions beyond individual control. As one of its first actions the reorganized nutrition section surveyed eight hundred families receiving food
stamps (or surplus commodities) to learn why such plans "were not reaching all those eligible" and were not "accomplishing their purpose." The survey revealed a number of previously unsuspected problems (e.g., the cost
of stamps, transportation difficulties, and limited operating hours of food-
stamp offices) and changed not just the board's outlook but also that of Governor Dan Moore, who soon after sent a top aid to speak before the McGovern
committee for food stamp reform.[93]

In South Carolina a new state health officer was in place in 1968, Dr.
Kenneth Aycock, a Carolina-born physician with wide experience in county
health work. Although the hunger issue had no bearing on his selection,
he proved far more sensitive to the issue than his predecessors, impressing
even Donald Gatch as a "helpful" administrator.[94] At the February 1969
meeting of the board's executive committee, right after Schaefer's preliminary
report, Aycock urged board physicians to accept a recent USDA offer to finance
an emergency nutrition program in Beaufort and Jasper Counties. In addition, Aycock advised that the South Carolina board would soon participate
in the second phase of the Schaefer survey.

That meeting also marked the first time the hunger question came
before the executive committee. Discussion proved lively and protracted
and focused on the McGovern hearings, the publicity surrounding a recent
Hollings "hunger tour," and defects in the food stamp plan. Some physician-

committee members had difficulty conceding that hunger was a real problem or was the board's responsibility, in any case. On the matter of food
stamp expansion, one worried that "it could lead to waste and contribute
to apathy on the part of the recipients."[95] But outside momentum and pressure
made such views suspect, at least on a public board. At the committee's
next meeting, Aycock met neither opposition nor reservation when he told
of the board's recent efforts to offer the poor of Beaufort County a comprehensive solution to their basic problems of housing, sanitation, education, and malnutrition.[96]

Of course neither South Carolina, nor any other Southern state was
remotely near the point of offering blacks comprehensive solutions. Yet the
last years of the 1960s finally did see significant moves against hunger — particularly by the federal government.

Key actions were undertaken by the USDA — under strong prompting.
The first, in the summer of 1967, was modest: reduction in the maximum
charge for stamps to five dollars per month for totally impoverished families.
That was far from the free distribution that Senators Clark and Kennedy
wanted, but it was as far as Secretary Freeman felt he could go. But pressures
were building to take him further. One revelation that aroused a great out-
cry was the report of 256 counties (mostly in the South) with no food programs but with massive hunger.[97]

Then in the spring of 1968, after an emotional CBS documentary on
hunger and after the murder of Martin Luther King, the "Poor People's
March" descended on Freeman. On May 23 leader Ralph David Abernathy
led a group of protestors into the secretary's office. The confrontation was
angry. Blacks demanded to know "how many more babies will have to
die . . . before you exercise the full power and authority . . . in feeding the
hungry?"[98] The time to talk was over, Abernathy insisted. Poor Americans
of every color "want action and they want it now. . . . " Those who were
"starving and dying in the world's 'richest nation' must have food — and not
as a handout but as a right."[99]

Angry at what he felt were Abernathy's distortions but aware of unmet
needs and the political explosiveness of the hunger issue, Freeman asked
Congress for a $100 million food stamp increase. When he had to explain
to Congressman Poage why just four months before he had agreed to a $20
million boost, Freeman said simply that he had since gotten a deeper understanding of poverty. He also promised to initiate federal stamp distribution
in all counties which refused to do it on their own.[100]

Pressure for program improvement continued at such a high level
(thanks largely to hunger coalition lobbying, Schaefer's report, and Hollings's testimony) that the incoming Nixon administration also felt compelled
to respond, though it owed little to black voters. New Secretary of Agriculture

Clifford Hardin agreed to the free food stamp trial in South Carolina's Beaufort and Jasper counties. In December 1969, at the urging of his Harvard nutritional advisor Jean Mayer, President Nixon convened a conference to consider long-run solutions. Although the much-publicized meeting produced nothing tangible, it did generate a presidential recommendation for a $270 million boost in food stamp funding for 1969-70, which was to rise to $1 billion the next year. The aim, said conference sponsors, was to insure that all of America's hungry got adequate food aid.[101]

Unfortuntately, that never happened. Like most American reforms, the hunger crusade enjoyed only partial success, leaving significant problem areas undisturbed. Perhaps because they responded to initial revelations with such emotional intensity, the public soon tired of the issue. One sign of that was the collapse of hunger as a media issue. In 1969-70, national periodicals published over thirty major articles on America's "nutritional problems." By 1972 the total fell to four, and the next year there were none, the focus having shifted back to "over-nutrition."[102]

Unsurprisingly, congressional interest fell off too. When Schaefer gave his final report to the McGovern committee in May 1970, only McGovern was there to receive it. Despite his sobering revelations about Southern children who were unable to bite or chew and were stunted in growth, Schaefer's appearance before the committee went virtually unreported. Moreover, the Nixon administration failed to honor its pledges. Instead of the $270 million increase for stamps by 1970, the president asked only for enough to continue the program at its existing level.[103] In 1971 Hollings reminded the nation that most of those who were hungry and malnourished before the 1967 discoveries were still hungry and malnourished. Nationwide, the senator lamented, "less than one [eligible] person in three now receives food stamps." Even adding in all other programs, "we still fail to reach about 50 per cent of the hungry poor."[104]

Happily, such gloomy reports did not accurately foretell the future. Owing to continued pressure from people like Hollings and the hunger coalition, as well as from anti-poverty lawyers who went to court to demand expanded food aid as an entitlement of the poor, the increases of the initial years resumed. Food supplement programs grew at such a rate, in fact, that by the late 1970s hunger among black and white Americans was largely eliminated. In 1977 Field Foundation investigators returned to Mississippi. They found far fewer hungry people than they had ten years before. Local black doctor Aaron Henry accompanied both Field visits, and while he found black families to be just as poor, children "are not as hungry, not as malnourished." The basic changes in their lives, Henry noted, were more food stamps and more school lunches.[105]

Those changes had begun even while Hollings was wringing his hands over fading concern. In North Carolina between 1968 and 1970 the number of counties having some sort of food program rose from eighty-three to ninety-seven (out of a hundred), and participation by eligible families went up 23 percent. During the next two years food stamp funding in the state rose from $34 million to $103 million, while the outlay required of purchasers fell about 16 percent. In neighboring South Carolina, by 1969, all forty-six counties had stamp plans in place, a 100 percent increase in one year. Within the next twelve months five of the state's poorest counties were also participating in a new supplemental food program for expectant mothers, infants, and children (WIC). It provided a free distribution of eggs, cheese, butter, milk, and other basic foods to safeguard the most endangered groups.[106]

Seen in broader perspective, however, food relief addressed just one health problem of the poor—and the one most easily dealt with. Equally troubling (and more difficult to set right) was their low access to medical care. As late as 1970 outreach workers of one grass roots health organization in low country South Carolina were "astonished" to discover "how many [black] people have been too poor, too far from doctors or simply too dispairing to hope for hospital care."[107] Medical histories were little different from those on the eighteenth-century frontier. One woman had a serious leg ulcer which had gone without treatment for twenty years. A second person suffering from second-degree burns had never returned to the doctor after her first visit. There were cases of untreated diabetic ulcers, which would not have occurred if a doctor or health worker had identified the disease in its early stage. Further, blood pressure rates were higher there than almost anywhere in the nation. Strokes and heart failure were common, as were worms and anemia. And reflecting the central place of hard, physical labor, there was a "tremendous amount of crippling arthritis in knees."[108]

But if illness problems of the black underclass were legion, they were also beginning in the 1960s to receive wide attention for the first time. Once again the public's awakening was partly the consequence of the broader civil rights movement, but it was also a result of President Lyndon Johnson's determination to close the remaining gaps in the nation's medical care system, a move which would aid Americans of all races. The end-product was a new program aimed at lowering the death rate and physical suffering of America's underclass by providing public medical, surgical, and dental care comparable to that available in the private sector.

The plan was Medicaid. Passed into law in 1965 and initiated in most Southern states in 1969 and 1970, Medicaid followed the pattern of its predecessor, Medicare, in drawing funds from the Social Security tax and in limiting focus to a single population group. Medicare helped the elderly. Medicaid aimed at America's welfare recipients.

But if Lyndon Johnson and the Congress intended Medicaid to plug the last hole in the nation's medical care delivery system, for the Southern poor, at least, the plan proved as much delusion as solution. Medicaid appeared to offer easy access: one merely had to certify that he or she was on public welfare. According to federal guidelines that would include all people living at or below the official poverty line, which in 1970 was set at $4,000 per year for a family of four. The problem was that Southern states set the welfare level much lower, so low in fact that the greater proportion of the needy (of both races) were left out of the Medicaid solution.[109]

In South Carolina, for example, federal measurement in 1970 suggested that 600,000 people should have welfare assistance. But by state reckoning, only 138,000 individuals were deemed eligible for welfare (and free medical care). Of the 462,000 families left out, some 120,000 could have gotten at least medical aid if South Carolina had opted to participate in the "medically-needy-only" provision of Medicaid, an option that extended care to those with incomes no more than 33 percent above a state's welfare cutoff. Because that would have encumbered South Carolina with added expense, however, the state refused the option. Certainly South Carolina was a poor state and funded public programs only with difficulty. But Medicaid did not drain South Carolina's (or any state's) economy. It enhanced it. One salient fact about Medicaid in South Carolina was that for every dollar appropriated by the state, Washington sent in three and a half dollars. That aspect of Medicaid, however, got little notice.[110]

One might, of course, take the optimist's route and focus on those Southerners who enjoyed Medicaid coverage. They were, after all, the largest fraction of those at the very bottom and had been long overlooked by private and public health providers. Yet even they faced so many additional, hidden hurdles that their pursuit of better health ended far short of the goal Congress had set. Again, South Carolina offered one of the best examples of a good idea gone bad, although North Carolina did little better.

The Medicaid law offered states sixteen additional (optional) services, such as the "medically-needy-only" plan and a dental program. After eight years of Medicaid, South Carolina had opted only for six services, which meant that clients sometimes got care so limited as to be self-defeating. For orthopedic patients South Carolina's plan would pay for braces and crutches but not for corrective shoes. South Carolina paid for extraction of teeth but not the cost of dentures. No reimbursement was permitted for immunization for tetanus, diphtheria, whooping cough, measles, rubella, and mumps, even though more than half the state's low-income population had no protection. For infant care, South Carolina Medicaid coverage did not begin until the moment of birth. Expectant welfare mothers had to arrange prenatal care and delivery at their own expense. Public clinics, of course, offered prenatal care, but by the 1960s they were not reaching the number of poor black women that they once had, perhaps because of the increasing fashion of using private physicians, even among those who could ill afford it. Greater access to private care might not have made much difference, but South Carolina chose not to test the possibility.[111]

Instead, the Palmetto State opted to use Medicaid partly as a device to impose moral behavior on the poor. For example, the state welfare department (Medicaid's administrator) withheld assistance from families with dependent children — and an absent father — until the mother had made an earnest effort to locate her spouse and make him pay child support. That was done even though the law said that aid was to be given *while* the search was on.[112]

Not all shortcomings originated in the states, to be sure. A major flaw — understandable politically, however self-defeating medically — was the law's refusal to permit reimbursement for generic drugs. Only brand-name items were covered, and that led to a cost problem severe enough that many patients did without. One public physician estimated that in 1968 half the state's Medicaid patients were unable to buy prescribed medicines. South Carolina added to the problem by denying coverage for any drugs not on the basic formulary, brand-name or not.[113]

In North Carolina, medical rights activists felt that their Medicaid plan was equally a failure, and their complaints pointed up other shortcomings in state programs. Hubert A. Eaton, the black physician who had filed the 1956 hospital integration suit in Wilmington, was 100 percent behind Medicaid initially. Yet after only a few years he became convinced that in North Carolina, Medicaid was only a "new name for the old system of humiliating and depressing clinic-style health care."[114]

What caused Eaton and other black — and some white — doctors to lose heart was the refusal of the state Medicaid administrator, the welfare division of the North Carolina Department of Human Resources, to allow physicians to provide services that they believed were necessary for quality medical care. Time and again, Eaton and his physician-son had Medicaid claims rejected or reduced — usually by laymen — until finally they concluded that the state's pinch-penny policies made it impossible for sympathetic physicians to serve the state's needy as Congress intended.[115]

In North Carolina, Eaton was convinced, the delivery of first-class care was never even the intention. Instead, the conscious goal seemed to be providing second-rate care. And that position, he believed, had tacit support (if not actual backing) from the state's white doctors, 85 percent of whom refused to participate in Medicaid in more than a token way. Even to its limited extent, their participation was often grudging. Emergency room staff at Eaton's local hospital made it difficult for Medicaid patients to locate a private doctor to take their cases. The hospital allowed them only one call to find a doctor on the participating list. If they failed, they were shunted to the free clinic. There, Eaton observed, they were frequently treated by nurses.[116]

In 1974, after several years of voicing concern about the plan, Eaton and his son had a conference with state Medicaid officials. The meeting, as Eaton recalled it, laid bare the bias he had long suspected. One of the state's consulting physicians, after listening to a string of complaints from the younger Eaton, stopped him with the remark: "After all, doctor, these are just poor people. We don't want them to have Cadillac work-ups."[117]

Ultimately Eaton brought another suit, that one aimed at forcing North Carolina to live up to the congressional goal of single-standard medical care. In late 1977 the state entered a consent decree. No wrong-doing was admitted, but the attorney general stipulated that North Carolina Medicaid administrators would henceforth insure free choice of physicians by every patient and in general see that Medicaid patients got a level of care equal to that available in the private sector.[118]

But afterwards, little changed. Charges for necessary services (immunizations, pap smears, urinalyses) continued to be rejected. Finally, about 1980 the Eatons had to curtail their own participation in Medicaid (it was bringing them only about $2 per hour return). Surviving financially while delivering good medical care to Medicaid patients was, regrettably, no longer possible.[119]

If the poor in the Carolinas and the rest of the deep South were deriving limited benefit from Medicaid, there was one group which seemed to have the opposite experience, at least in the initial years of Medicaid. They were the private health providers, such as hospitals, nursing homes and pharmacists. The South Carolina Council for Human Rights, a citizens' advocate group with a long and credible record, made a close study of the first four years of Medicaid in the Palmetto State. Its conclusion was that the program had gone off-track somewhere: "if it is true that few welfare recipients get the best health care possible . . . , it is also true that every effort is made to ensure that physicians, pharmacists, and hospitals get their money out of Medicaid."[120]

The Southern Regional Council, the Atlanta-based civil rights group whose work was likewise marked by careful research, reviewed health prospects of the poor over the whole South. Published in the late 1970s its findings agreed with those in South Carolina. The "massive infusion of money," said the Council, "has increased corporate profits in the health care industry far more than it has improved quality and quantity of medical services. Statistics show that the disparity between public care and private profits is still greatest in the South, as it was thirty years ago."[121] The South, for example, had the fewest number of health professionals (per capita), yet was the "prime market" for new, fast-growing hospital chains. In addition, while Southern hospitals offered the least out-patient and preventive care services, the region also had the highest proportion of hospital beds controlled by "privately-owned, for-profit corporations." And to its elderly, the South offered the fewest opportunities for adequate health of any region, but at the same time it had the highest percentage of for-profit nursing homes.[122]

Thirty years after the Second World War, the South still offered an observer the choice of the pitcher half-full or the pitcher half-empty, so far as the health of blacks was concerned. On the one hand, their average health performance had improved significantly against both the national norm and Southern white levels. Mortality had fallen dramatically, and black life expectancy was closing in on white. Most black women now had their babies in hospitals. And urban services had expanded and improved to meet the needs of a growing black population. The reasons behind these improvements included an improved economic status, increased public services, attention to problems of hunger and malnutrition, and passage of Medicare and Medicaid.

Meanwhile, a sizeable proportion of blacks — mostly those on the bottom rungs, who made up 35 to 40 percent of black society — shared few of those gains. In 1977 Raymond Wheeler, the white Charlotte doctor who accompanied the original Field visit to Mississippi, examined again the health status of those poorest of the Southern poor and found that for them "sickness in many forms is an inevitability. . . . " The nation might have been able to put a man on the moon, but "little has been done to make it possible for the poor of our nation to be able to walk and run with strong, healthy bodies."[123]

The continuing health lag was apparent even in North Carolina, the state that had long been the region leader in public health programs and commitment. In 1981 the North Carolina Board of Health published an accounting of the ten leading causes of death for whites and blacks. It revealed that with but two exceptions black men and women perished at rates that were consistently and significantly higher than white rates. The exceptions were chronic obstructive pulmonary disease and motor vehicle accidents, which pointed up unresolved problems for Caucasians. For all other categories North Carolina blacks died at a rate that was, overall, 45 percent greater for men and 60 percent greater for women. The persistence of such differentials into the 1980s was, as Wheeler said, a grim reminder that too large a proportion of black families in North Carolina and every other Southern state "live outside of every legal, medical, and social advance our nation has made in this century."[124]

A Summing Up

An underlying assumption of the preceding pages is that much can be learned about a society — its workings and values — by examining the ways it cares for its sick and diseased. If this is true — i.e., if health history can serve as a sort of social mirror — what image of Southern society does one see?

It is not a particularly complimentary one. In the forefront of the picture are white physicians. In their collective, social role Southern doctors were hardly the kindly, self-sacrificing servants of myth and hagiographic literature. Norman Rockwell's dutiful, grandfatherly figure dispensing care beside his roll-top desk looks as if he might have talked at length about the virtues of doctor-patient relationships and physician collegiality. But when it came to enabling black physicians (and medical students) to become better practitioners or allowing them to minister to their own patients in community hospitals (or even admitting black patients there), the actual members of the Southern white profession for years proved more concerned about enforcing medical segregation than about providing care and healing. Along with physicians everywhere, Southern professionals also chose to ignore mounting problems of occupational health, partly because their schools gave no training in such matters but partly, too, because they feared intruding in the domain of local economic elites. Textile executives, after all, had more favors to bestow than their many thousand employees — no matter the dangers those employees faced at work.

To be sure, in regard to workplace health, it was the South's public, not private, physicians who bore the greater responsibility. And the kindest thing that might be said of public health officers was that they did not see where their duty lay. Most argued that, given the political and economic realities of the day, a cautious, educational approach was their best and only strategy. They did indeed have to be cautious, but surely the educational process could have begun years earlier. The example of forthright action by PHS surgeon Goldberger against pellagra suggested that tougher, more direct challenges could have been mounted by state industrial hygienists without fear of legislative reprisal. North Carolina officials finally made such an effort in the late 1960s; the pity was that it was not done sooner.

Outside the workplace, private physicians played a large part in frustrating the goals of preventive medicine. Instead of getting strongly behind needed projects, such as VD control, home nursing, comprehensive health care, and nutrition improvement, Southern doctors, especially, preferred to fret about encroachments on private medicine and to ring the alarm against socialized medicine and state control. The result, more so in the South than elsewhere because of weaker countervailing forces, was a stifling of public effort and sometimes absolute denial of help to people who could not have afforded a private doctor anyway. Sadly, a chance for helpful public leadership by Southern physicians was for too long sacrificed to the narrow concerns of special interest.

To give Southern white doctors their due, they did yield on the matter of medical segregation without much fuss, when black colleagues finally began pressing for integration in the 1950s and 1960s. The long years of professional contact across racial lines had prepared the white doctor to accept new relationships. Moreover, professionalism, though it had long taken a back seat to medical segregation, was a constant reminder to white physicians (who because of their professional involvements were never as racist as other whites) that they were not doing their best for their black colleagues and their patients. The relatively speedy acceptance of black doctors into professional societies and the eventual integration of white schools and hospitals were not only victories for Southern moderates but a race relations story of which the South could be proud.

As for Southern black physicians, while they did ultimately join the challenge against medical segregation and second-rate patient care, their "Johnny-come-lately" record did them little credit. Certainly it could be dangerous pressing against most racial barriers, but segregated medicine and health care proved to be two areas where much earlier and stronger efforts could have been safely made. With many notable exceptions, the generality of black physicians did not seem eager even to work for improved care within a segregated system. The better record there was registered by black "laymen"— many, if not most of them, women. Far too many, perhaps a majority, of black physicians, according even to their own leaders, had a greater interest in income than social equity. The contention for power among and between black physicians and many black hospital staffs was both deplorable and unfortunate. In Columbia, such divisions cost that city's blacks a much-needed new hospital. Only as the civil rights movement gathered real momentum in the late 1950s would most Southern black physicians enlist in the battle for health and medical equality, and even then they did so as followers, not leaders. Though there were many, many exceptions, an acceptance (even a preference) for the segregationist status quo was long a potent force within the Southern black medical profession.

The story of improvements in the health of Southern mill hands was in some respects a similar one: their self-proclaimed leaders (mill owners, in this case) were far less interested in maintaining a healthy work force than in maintaining high profits, whatever their pronouncements about their deep concern for their help. Health conditions did improve, both in village and mill, but it was hardly a result of owners' conscious design. In the mill villages it was government-mandated wage hikes and heightened post-war prosperity that worked most of the change. In the area of workplace health, improvements were primarily tied to changes in production techniques, such as installation of air conditioning, undertaken for the most part in the interests of greater efficiency and profits. A success for the free-enterprise system, surely—but such successes were a long time coming. Meanwhile workers, not owners, bore the cost of waiting. And for byssinosis victims the cost of delay was high indeed.

Southern state regulatory agencies (in health and labor) had frequently proclaimed their intention to secure the well-being of workers. But the close alliance between government and industry rendered those agency promises meaningless. As one South Carolina labor department chief actually admitted, "our people" were the owners of textile mills, not their employees. Perhaps those state agencies (and the legislatures that empowered them) really did believe in owners' vision of a benevolent industrial society, having no need for the intervening hand of the state but piloted on a true course solely by employers' sense of fair play. If so, the actions of those agencies and those owners suggest that democracy and truly representative government fell far short of the ideal in the twentieth-century South—even for white people.

The social mirror that the foregoing health history provides also reflects something of the Southern mind. At least since the Constitutional period when the South began to contest with the North over the Negro question (among others), the ideas of states' rights and limited government have been worn as talismans below the Mason-Dixon line. Yet by the twentieth century, as the story of black health most clearly reveals, the states' rights, limited-government philosophy was in large part a bankrupt, mean-spirited, and inconsistent, if not dishonest, notion. In the arena of health, at least, the states' rights formula contained little idea of public responsibility. Proclaiming a desire to be left alone to do for themselves, what Southern states really wanted was to be left alone *not* to do for blacks—even when they had TB or malaria or their women and babies were perishing in near-epidemic numbers. And yet if the federal government would pay for the South's health work, Southern legislatures were all too happy to take money from that far-distant big government in Washington — provided of course there were not too many onerous federal controls.

In fact Southern legislatures had no compunction sometimes about taking federal money without paying their agreed-on share and without following agreed-on rules. On occasion it almost seemed that the national health service was in league with the Southern states against the rest of the country. At the very times that Southern states were withholding their full quota of funding (as in the case of the SS grant, VD programs, and industrial hygiene work), PHS officers were bending efforts to see that the South got a special helping because of its greater health needs. And yet, ironically, the image of the federal government as bogeyman, as oppressive foe of freedom, still managed to emerge — and thrive — in the South. Looking at the reflections cast by the health history of the Southern poor — of mill hands and blacks, especially — it was, arguably, the Southern states, not Washington, who more often played the oppressor's role.

Notes

Preface

1.   Quoted in *Biennial Report, North Carolina Board of Health* (1968–70), 55.
2.   Charles E. Rosenberg, *The Cholera Years: The United States in 1832, 1849, and 1866* (Chicago: Univ. of Chicago Press, 1962); Elizabeth Etheridge, *The Butterfly Caste: A Social History of Pellagra in the South* (Westport, Conn.: Greenwood Publishing Co., 1972); Todd L. Savitt, *Medicine and Slavery: The Diseases and Health Care of Blacks in Antebellum Virginia* (Urbana: Univ. of Ill. Press, 1978); James Jones, *Bad Blood: The Tuskegee Syphilis Experiment* (New York: Free Press, 1981); and John Ettling, *The Germ of Laziness: Rockefeller Philanthropy and Public Health in the New South* (Cambridge, Mass.: Harvard Univ. Press, 1981).
3.   Grob's latest volume on the subject is *Mental Illness and American Society, 1875–1940* (Princeton: Princeton Univ. Press, 1983).

Introduction

1.   David L. Carlton, *Mill and Town in South Carolina, 1880–1920* (Baton Rouge: Louisiana State Univ. Press, 1982). In his introduction Carlton elaborates the trauma of the new urban middle class over the millhand invasion.
2.   Quoted in Dewy Grantham, "An American Politics for the South," in Charles G. Sellers Jr., ed., *The Southerner as American* (New York: Dutton, 1966), 153.
3.   Carlton, *Mill and Town*, 11.
4.   Quoted in Cliff Sloan and Bob Hall, "It's Good to Be Home in Greenville," in Marc S. Miller, ed., *Working Lives: The "Southern Exposure" History of Labor in the South* (New York: Pantheon Books, 1980), 237.
5.   George Brown Tindall, *The Emergence of the New South, 1913–1945* (Baton Rouge: Louisiana State Univ. Press and the Littlefield Fund for Southern History of the Univ. of Texas, 1967), 238.
6.   Carlton, *Mill and Town*, 234–44; John Kenneth Morland, *Millways of Kent* (Chapel   315

Hill: Univ. of North Carolina Press, 1958), 183; Lewis's observation is noted in Tindall, *Emergence of New South,* 340.

7. Carlton, *Mill and Town,* 133, 145, 196.

8. Beliefs (and myths) which mill owners held about their hands are examined by Frank Tannenbaum, "The South Buries Its Anglo-Saxons," *Century Magazine* 106 (June 1923), 205–15.

9. Wilbur J. Cash, *The Mind of the South* (New York: Vintage Books, 1941), 206.

10. Quoted in Tindall, *Emergence of New South,* 319; also see Cash, *Mind of South,* 354–55; Daniel Joseph Singal, *The War Within: From Victorian to Modernist Thought in the South 1919–1945* (Chapel Hill: Univ. of North Carolina Press, 1982), 58–82, notes that Mitchell, to preserve his basic, original belief in progress through textile development, had to make it out that second-generation owners had defaulted on original commitments and goals.

11. Tannenbaum, "South Buries Anglo-Saxons," 214.

12. I.A. Newby, *The South: A History* (New York: Holt, Rinehart and Winston, 1978), 411.

13. Sloan and Hall, "Good To Be Home in Greenville," 235; Liston Pope, *Mills Hands and Preachers* (Chapel Hill: Univ. of North Carolina Press, 1942), tells the story of the Gastonia strike.

14. Newby, *The South,* 347–48; the disenfranchisement of significant numbers of Southern whites is detailed in George Stoney, "Who is Fit to Vote in a Democracy?" in *Proceedings of the National Conference of Social Work. Selected Papers* (New York: Columbia Univ. Press, 1941), 173–84.

15. Carlton, *Mill and Town,* 163–64, 225, 228.

16. Lillian Smith, *Killers of the Dream* (Garden City, N.Y.: Doubleday, 1963), 155.

17. Newby, *The South,* 392.

18. Ibid., 370.

19. The sanctuary idea is one of Cash's central points. See, for example, *Mind of the South,* 169–70. Mill owners and their supporters frequently and proudly proclaimed the benevolence inherent in mill-building. See Marjorie Potwin, *Cotton Mill People of the Piedmont* (New York: Columbia Univ. Press, 1927). Potwin was the welfare director for a large South Carolina mill corporation.

20. South Carolina's segregation law is discussed in Carlton, *Mill and Town,* 245, 258. According to Southern historian, Lacy Ford, mill villages "were never devoid of blacks," despite Cash's claims. Blacks lived on the village fringe and performed its menial tasks. Ford, letter to author, Sept. 2, 1985.

21. One study of pellagra incidence in South Carolina about 1912 showed that pellagra struck 104 of every 10,000 mill villagers, which would convert to a mortality rate of about 38–80 percent higher than the black rate.

Chapter 1

1. F.G. Dubose, "The Condition of the Negro in the South," *Southern Medical Journal* 7 (1914):865 (hereafter, *SMJ*).

2. Mortality statistics by race for the early 20th century are in Bureau of the

Census, *Vital Statistics Rates in the United States, 1900–1940* (Washington, D.C., 1943). Hereafter, *Vital Statistics Rates*. On black resistance to malaria and yellow fever see Todd L. Savitt, *Medicine and Slavery* 25–35, 240–41; the growing problem of VD in the late 1800s and its probable effect on fertility is discussed in Reynolds Farley, *Growth of the Black Population: A Study in Demographic Trends* (Chicago: Markham Publishing Co., 1970), 50–58, 225, 226, 235. Also Dr. Francisco Sy (epidemiologist), interview, Sept. 17, 1985.

3. For slaves' working conditions see Savitt, *Medicine and Slavery*, 103–10; data on black urban migration and its medical and economic implications are in Farley, *Growth of Black Population*, 43, 50, 62, and Bureau of the Census, *Negroes in the United States, 1920–32* (Washington, D.C., 1935), 289.

4. White physicians' views on black ill health and their implications are discussed in James Jones, *Bad Blood*, 19–26.

5. Herbert M. Morais, *The History of the Negro in Medicine* (New York: N.Y. Publishers Co., Inc., 1967), 39–58.

6. Ibid., 123. Information on the black hospitals giving free care to indigents was furnished by Savitt, letter to author, Nov. 22, 1985.

7. Farley, *Growth of Black Population*, 58–75, 206–26.

8. *Vital Statistics Rates*, 336–95, *passim*.

9. Savitt, *Medicine and Slavery*, 42–43; also Kenneth Kipple and Virginia King, *Another Dimension to the Black Diaspora: Diet, Disease, and Racism* (Cambridge: Cambridge Univ. Press, 1981), 139.

10. *Palmetto Leader* (Nov. 9, 1935).

11. Bureau of the Census, *Mortality Statistics* (Washington, D.C., 1939), 224; Bureau of the Census, *Manual of the International List of Causes of Death*, 3d ed. (Paris, 1920), 83–84.

12. *Vital Statistics Rates*, 336–95.

13. Robert Wilson, "Some Medical Aspects of the Negro," *SMJ* 7 (1915): 3–6.

14. *Mortality Statistics*, 187; *Manual of Causes of Death*, 126–30, 159c.

15. *Vital Statistics Rates*, 336–95.

16. South Carolina Writers' Project (WPA), Life Histories, file A-3-11, no. 4, South Caroliniana Library, Univ. of South Carolina.

17. Savitt, *Medicine and Slavery*, 36–37.

18. *Vital Statistics Rates*, 336–95.

19. M.O. Bousfield in *Opportunity* 15 (1937):324–25; James Hayne to C.E. Waller, Feb. 3, 1935, State Boards of Health, box 60, South Carolina, file 0245–0425, Public Health Service (PHS) Papers, National Archives.

20. Monroe C. Work, ed. *Negro Yearbook: An Annual Encyclopedia of the Negro, 1925–26* (Tuskegee, Ala.: Negro Yearbook Co., 1925), 409.

21. Rosa Gantt, "Medical Inspection of the Schools in South Carolina," *SMJ* 6 (1913):241.

22. Leon Banov, *A Sanitary Survey of the Rural Portion of Charleston County* (1921), 24, 17–18, 26–28.

23. J.M. Knox and Paul Zentai, "The Health Problem of the Negro Child," *American Journal of Public Health* 16 (1926):808 (hereafter, *AJPH*).

24. Modjeska Simkins, interview, Oct. 10, 1978.

25. Jones, *Bad Blood,* 29.
26. L.E. Burney, "Control of Syphilis in a Southern Rural Area. A Preliminary Report," *AJPH* 29 (1939):1013; see *Negro Yearbook* (1941–46), 329, for percentage of Negro syphilitics in the draft pool; also see J.A. Crabtree and E.L. Bishop, "Syphilis in a Rural Negro Population in Tennessee," *AJPH* 22 (1932):163.
27. Savitt, *Medicine and Slavery,* 26–27.
28. *Vital Statistics Rates,* 336–95; Dr. Francisco Sy, letter to author, Sept. 18, 1985. In North Carolina in 1920 the black malaria mortality rate was 16 and the white, 4.6.
29. *Vital Statistics Rates,* 336–95; Savitt, *Medicine and Slavery,* 19, notes the longevity of malaria: illness from *P. vivax* may last five years and that from *P. malariae* for up to thirty years.
30. James Young, "Malaria in the South," Ph.D. diss. (Univ. of North Carolina, 1972), 155, 143.
31. Ibid., 62.
32. *Palmetto Leader* (Nov. 9, 1935); Paul Cornely, interview, May 14, 1979; *Negro Yearbook* (1941–46), 331, showed TB morbidity among 1941 white draftees to be slightly higher than among blacks.
33. *Negro Yearbook* (1921–22), 367.
34. *AJPH* 31 (1941).
35. *Medical Care for the American People: The Final Report of the Committee on the Cost of Medical Care. Adopted Oct. 31, 1932* (New York: Arno Press and the *New York Times,* 1972), 10. *Negro Yearbook* (1941–46), 331; *Palmetto Leader* (Aug. 30, 1941).
36. C.S. Johnson, "How Much Is the Migration a Flight from Persecution?" *Opportunity* 1 (1923):274.
37. On the Negro migration see, for example, Robert Weaver, *The Negro Ghetto* (New York: Russell and Russell, 1967 [c. 1948]), 14–32.
38. Ibid., also *Negro Yearbook* (1921–22), 387–89.
39. *Negro Yearbook* (1921–22), 387–89.
40. Charles Garvin, "Negro Health," *Opportunity* 2 (1924):341–42.
41. Dorsha B. Hayes, *Chicago* (Chicago: Julian Messner, 1944), 259–60.
42. Bureau of the Census, *Negro Population in the U.S., 1790–1915* (Washington, D.C., 1918), 331, 320.
43. C.E. Terry, "The Negro a Public Health Problem," *SMJ* 7 (1914):460.
44. The relationship between urban migration and awareness of black health problems is illustrated by the history of interest in sickle cell anemia. See Todd Savitt, "The Invisible Malady: Sickle Cell Anemia in America, 1910–70," *Journal of the National Medical Association* 73 (1981):739–46 (hereafter, *JNMA*).
45. "Mortality Among Negroes in Cities," *Atlanta Univ. Publications,* no. 1 (1903), Robert W. Woodruff Library, Atlanta Univ.
46. Ibid., 15.
47. "Is the Negro Dying Out," *Colored American Magazine* 15 (1909):670; Eugene K. Jones, "Urban Health and Sanitation," *Howard Univ. Record* 12 (1918):22–25.
48. "New Trends in Mortality," *Opportunity* 2 (1924):290–91; George Hubbard, "The Prevalence of Contagious and Infectious Disease Among the Negro," *The Hu-*

*man Way (*1913), Neighborhood Union Collection, Robert Woodruff Library, Atlanta Univ.

49. For a discussion of the white profession's historic outlook see James Jones, *Bad Blood,* 19-29; public health physicians, by contrast, were more liberated racially. As an example see the special Negro health issue, *AJPH* 5 (1915); the basis of the race extinction thesis is noted in "Is the Negro Dying Out," 670; also see Algernon Jackson, "The Need of Health Education Among Negroes," *Opportunity* 2 (1924):235.

50. See various articles discussing Negroes' health future in 1914 *SMJ* volume; for example, Terry, "Negro a Public Health Problem," 459.

51. Louis Dublin, "The Effect of Health Education on Negro Mortality," *Opportunity* 2 (1924):234.

52. *Negroes in the U.S., 1920-32,* 320, 370-75.

53. *AJPH* 7 (1917):510-11; *AJPH* 8 (1918):249; Rev. William Holmes Borders, interview, Mar. 1979; on earlier clinical programs for whites see George Rosen, *A History of Public Health* (New York: M.D. Publications, 1958), 357.

54. *Negroes in the U.S., 1920-32,* 293.

55. Ibid., 204-5, 255.

56. Ibid., 282.

57. Ibid., 238, 241, 803.

58. Abbott, "Methods By Which Children's Health May Be Improved," *Opportunity* 2 (1924):6.

59. *Negroes in the U.S., 1920-32,* 606; *Negro Population in the U.S., 1790-1915,* 331; *Negro Yearbook* (1914-15) and (1921-22); Bousfield, "Reaching the Negro Community" *AJPH* 24 (1934):209.

60. *Vital Statistics Rates,* 336-95; *Negroes in the U.S., 1920-32,* 460.

61. *Negroes in the U.S., 1920-32,* 591.

62. Banov, *A Sanitary Survey,* 21, 5-7.

63. S.C. Life Histories, file A-3-7, no. 3.

64. For a discussion of the early studies of pellagra in the South and the dietary basis of the disease see Elizabeth Etheridge, *Butterfly Caste.*

65. Mary Frayser, "Children of Pre-school Age in Selected Areas of South Carolina," *South Carolina Agricultural Experiment Station Bull.,* no. 260 (1929), 29-39, 74-77.

66. Ada Moser, "Farm Family Diets in the Lower Coastal Plains of South Carolina," *South Carolina Agricultural Experiment Station Bull.,* no. 319 (1939), 7-32.

67. William H. Frasier, "Child Health in Tuskegee," *Opportunity* 13 (1935):360-63.

68. D.F. Milam, "A Nutritional Survey of a Small North Carolina Community," *AJPH* 32 (1942):406-12.

69. S.C. Life Histories, file A-3-14, no. 5.

70. Newell D. Easom, "The Negro of North Carolina Forsakes the Land," *Opportunity* 14 (1936):116.

71. *Palmetto Leader* (Aug. 30, 1930).

72. Maude Callan, interview, June 23, 1978.

73. J.E. McTeer, *High Sheriff of the Low Country* (Beaufort, S.C., Beaufort Book Co.,

1970), 19–41; Newell N. Puckett, *Folk Beliefs of the Southern Negro* (Chapel Hill: Univ. of North Carolina Press, 1962), 201–08, 359.

74.   Rev. I. Dequincey Newman, interview, Dec. 17, 1979; also Hylan Lewis, *Blackways of Kent* (Chapel Hill: Univ. of North Carolina Press, 1955), 74–90; South Carolina Writers' Project, H-1-53.

75.   Newman White, *Popular Beliefs and Superstitions from North Carolina,* vol. 4 of *The Frank C. Brown Collection of N.C. Folklore* (Durham: Duke Univ. Press, 1961), 308.

76.   Ibid.

77.   *Opportunity* 4 (1926):271.

78.   Hubbard, in *The Human Way,* 66.

79.   Modjeska Simkins interview.

80.   A discussion of the medical value of the plants noted in the text may be found in Julia F. Morton, *Folk Remedies of the Low Country* (Miami: E.A. Seeman Publishing Co., 1974), 31, 35, 60, 74, 112, 156: also see John Kosa and Irving Zola, eds., *Poverty and Health. A Social Analysis* (Cambridge, Mass.: Harvard Univ. Press, 1975), 239–40.

81.   Hubbard, in *The Human Way,* 68.

82.   Paul Cornely, interview, May 14, 1979.

83.   For discussions of black attitudes toward their health and the stresses they lived under, see I.A. Newby, *Black Carolinians* (Columbia: Univ. of South Carolina Press, 1973), 217–18; Edward Suchman, *Sociology and the Field of Public Health* (N.Y.: Russell Sage Foundation, 1963); Howard Freeman et al., *Handbook of Medical Sociology* (New York: Prentice-Hall, 1963).

84.   S.C. Life Histories, file A-13-15; for a discussion of the lay referral system see Kosa and Zola, *Poverty and Health,* 239–50.

85.   Minutes of the Palmetto Medical, Dental, and Pharmaceutical Association (1920); also, *Negro Population in the U.S.*; *Negroes in the U.S.,* 517–20; also, Theodore Hemmingway, "A History of Black Folks in South Carolina," Ph.D. diss. (Univ. of South Carolina, 1976), 227, 245.

86.   Hubert A. Eaton to the author, June 17, 1985.

87.   S.C. Life Histories, file A-3-7, no. 3.

88.   I.D. Newman, interview, Dec. 17, 1979.

89.   *The Journal of Negro Education: Special Health Issue* 18 (1949):321.

90.   Septima Clark, interview, Dec. 15, 1977.

91.   James Clark before the South Carolina Association of Health Educators conference on "The Black Health Experience in South Carolina," Dec. 1978.

92.   Hemmingway, "A History of Black Folks," 245; *Jour. of Negro Education,* 320; Laura Blackburn and Minier Padgett, *History of the Columbia Hospital* (Columbia, S.C.: R.L. Bryan Co., 1953), 34; "The Good Samaritan Hospital" report, Mar. 26, 1935, N.C. and S.C. Hospital and County Files, box 180, Duke Endowment Archives, William R. Perkins Library, Duke Univ.

93.   L.W. Long, interview, 1978.

94.   Algernon Jackson, "Need of Health Education Among Negroes," 239.

95.   *Negro Yearbook* (1913–38); for activity of the Duke Endowment see Secretary's Reports, 1925–46, Duke Endowment Archives.

96.   Louis Dublin, "The Health of the Negro. The Outlook for the Future," *Opportunity* 6 (1928):199.

97.   Charleston Welfare Council, "Charleston Looks at Its Health Services for Negroes" (unpublished, 1946), B-12.

98.   Lawrence Lee, "The Negro as a Problem in Public Health Charity," *AJPH* 5 (1915):208-9.

99.   Montague Cobb, "Medical Care and the Plight of the Negro," *JNMA* 54 (1947):204.

100.   *Negro Population of the U.S., 1790-1915*, 521-22; "History of Maternal and Child Health Policy in North Carolina" (unpublished report, North Carolina State Board of Health Library, Raleigh, n.d.), 22-24; James Hayne in *Trans. of the 22d Annual Conference of State and Territorial Health Officers* (1924), 97.

101.   "Maternal and Child Health Policy in North Carolina," 22-24.

102.   S.C. Life Histories, file A-3-14, Jan. 27, 1939; Newby, *Black Carolinians* 121; Terry, "The Negro as a Public Health Problem," 461.

103.   "Maternal and Child Health Policy in N.C.," 22-24; *Biennial Report of the State Board of Health of Georgia* (1927-28), 25. For a detailed report on the activity of Southern midwives in the period after regulation, see "Nurse Midwife Maude Callan Eases Pain of Birth, Life, and Death," *Life* (Dec. 3, 1951), 144.

104.   "Negro Families in Need," Atlanta School of Social Work, Neighborhood Union Collection.

Chapter 2

1.   Bureau of the Census, *13th Census, vol. 9: Manufactures* (Washington, D.C., 1910), 230, 912, 1152; also *14th Census, vol. 9: Manufactures* (Washington, D.C.: 1920), 282, 1119, 1395.

2.   *13th Census, vol. 9: Manufactures*, 230, 912, 1152; *14th Census, vol. 9: Manufactures*, 282, 1119, 1395; on the proportion of South Carolinians in the industry see David L. Carlton, *Mill and Town*, 134.

3.   Marjorie Potwin, *Cotton Mill People of the Piedmont*, 13.

4.   W.S. Rankin to S.W. Rankin, June 2, 1913, box 27, Personal Files of W.S. Rankin, 1912-15, North Carolina Div. of Archives and History, Raleigh.

5.   *Family Budgets of Typical Cotton Mill Workers*, vol. 16 of *Condition of Woman and Child Wage Earners in the United States* (Washington, D.C., 1911), Sen. Doc. 645, 61st Cong., 2d Sess.

6.   Ibid., 154, 119, 61, 91, 99, 107.

7.   Ibid., 119, 51.

8.   For a brief history of state, federal, and private efforts in occupational health in the 1900-40 era, see George Rosen, *A History of Public Health*, 426-39; also see Alice Hamilton, *Exploring the Dangerous Trades* (Boston: Little, Brown, 1943).

9.   S.C. Life Histories, file A-3-3, no. 12.

10.   Mrs. John Van Vorst and Marie Van Vorst, *The Woman Who Toils: Being the Ex-*

periences of Two Gentlewomen as Factory Girls (New York: Doubleday, 1903), 226, 248–50.

11. *Family Budgets of Cotton Mill Workers,* 29, 180.

12. *Annual Report, South Carolina Board of Health* (1903), 521, 523 and (1907), 22, 23.

13. Ibid., (1907), 28 and (1908), 3, 52–67.

14. S.C. Life Histories, file A-3-11, no. 2.

15. Belief in a connection between mill work and TB is revealed in *Causes of Death Among Woman and Child Cotton Mill Operatives,* vol. 14 of *Condition of Woman and Child Wage Earners,* 31–33; for the modern-day explanation of mill TB, see James B. Wyngaardan and Lloyd H. Smith, *Textbook of Medicine* (Philadelphia: W.B. Saunders, 1982), 541; also Dr. Donald Robinson (industrial hygienist), interview, May 20, 1983.

16. *Causes of Death Among Woman and Child Operatives,* 49–51, 18–21. It was mill conditions—fatigue, crowding, lack of ventilation—not dust, which explained the higher incidence of female deaths. Sarah Woolbert (head of South Carolina maternal and child health work), interview, Sept. 17, 1985.

17. One of the earliest studies of the region's malarial incidence was done by the Southern Medical Association in 1912. Much of the following account of malaria is taken from Young, "Malaria in the South," especially 26, 31, 35, 37–41.

18. Kenneth Maxcy, "Epidemiological Principles Affecting the Distribution of Malaria in the Southern U.S.," *Public Health Reports* 39, no. 20 (1924):113–27; also see *Family Budgets of Cotton Mill Workers.*

19. Young, "Malaria in the South," 59; Harriett L. Herring, *Welfare Work in Mill Villages: The Story of Extra-Mill Activities in North Carolina* (Chapel Hill: Univ. of North Carolina Press, 1929), 169–72.

20. Quoted in Herring, *Welfare Work in Mill Villages,* 169.

21. Young, "Malaria in the South," 50; quoted in Herring, *Welfare Work,* 170.

22. John Ettling, *Germ of Laziness,* 23–48, 99–100. The "American parasite" was later shown to be native to Africa and likely carried to America by slaves; also see Henry Frank Farmer, "The Hookworm Eradication Program in the South, 1909–25," Ph.D. diss. (Univ. of Georgia, 1966), 9.

23. Charles W. Stiles, *Hookworm Disease Among Cotton Mill Operatives,* vol. 17 of *Condition of Woman and Child Wage Earners* (Washington, D.C., 1910), 36, 10; also see Stiles, "Hookworm Disease in Three Cotton Mills in North Carolina," *Public Health Reports* 25, no. 12 (1910), 354–55.

24. Farmer, "Hookworm Eradication Program" 16–17.

25. Stiles, *Hookworm Disease,* 31.

26. Ibid., 25; also Stiles, "Hookworm in Three Mills," 354–55.

27. Besides the Ettling, Stiles, and Farmer studies, a succinct and lively account of hookworm, as well as other Southern ills, appears in Thomas D. Clark, *The Emerging South* (New York: Oxford Univ. Press, 1968), 24–39.

28. Ettling, *Germ of Laziness,* 47, 44.

29. August Kohn, *Cotton Mills of South Carolina* (Columbia: Dept. of Agriculture, Commerce, and Immigration, 1907), 78.

30.   Farmer, "Hookworm Eradication Program," 1188; Ettling, *Germ of Laziness,* 159–63.

31.   Ettling, *Germ of Laziness,* 159–63; also Farmer "Hookworm Eradication Program," 118.

32.   Ettling, in letter to author, Nov. 16, 1981, recalled the "dearth of correspondence" between Rockefeller Commission officials and mill owners; also "Public Health in North Carolina. A Guidebook for County Commissioners," unpublished report (Raleigh: Board of Health, n.d.) 4; *Annual Report, S.C. Board of Health* (1918), 128.

33.   Stiles, *Hookworm Disease,* 31, 37.

34.   Joseph Goldberger et al., "A Study of the Relation of Factors of a Sanitary Character to Pellagra Incidence in Seven Cotton Mill Villages in S.C. in 1916," *Public Health Reports* 35, no. 29 (July 16, 1920), 1709; also Herring, *Welfare Work in Mill Villages,* 151; *Conference of State and Territorial Health Officers* (1916), 57; also *Report of South Carolina Dept. of Agriculture, Commerce, and Industry* (1918), 18, noted the inability of the two-inspector staff to keep up with its duties.

35.   Much of the story of pellagra which follows was taken from Elizabeth Etheridge, *The Butterfly Caste.*

36.   Ibid., 3–7, 131, 193; the death rate of the Alabama asylum patients was 64 percent.

37.   Etheridge, *Butterfly Caste,* 50.

38.   *Family Budgets of Cotton Mill Workers,* 61, 64, 67.

39.   Goldberger et al., "Relation of Factors of a Sanitary Character to Pellagra Incidence," 1663; on why women were more often afflicted see Etheridge, *Butterfly Caste,* 131; Dr. Sara Woolpert, in interview, Sept. 9, 1985, noted that the repeated pregnancies of early mill women would have kept them in a pellagra state. That view and Goldberger's observation are confirmed by recent studies of malnutrition in the third world, where women and girls are disproportionately affected. See *RF Illustrated* (Sept. 1985), 5.

40.   Goldberger et al., "A Study of the Relation of Family Income and Other Economic Factors to Pellagra Incidence in Seven Cotton Mills in S.C. in 1916," *Public Health Reports* 35, no. 46 (Nov. 12, 1920), 2696–2700.

41.   Etheridge, *Butterfly Caste,* 137; Goldberger et al., "A Study of the Relation of Income to Pellagra," 2690–91.

42.   Etheridge, *Butterfly Caste,* 91–96, 116–17, 182, 189; Hayne revealed his opposition to Goldberger's ideas at national health officers meetings. See *Conference, State and Territorial Health Officers* (1916), 27; also G.A. Wheeler to Surgeon General, July 15, 1930, file 0620–1680, box 61, Record Group 90, State Boards of Health, South Carolina, PHS Papers; Etheridge, *Butterfly Caste,* 116–17, 182, 189.

43.   Etheridge, *Butterfly Caste,* 110–13.

44.   Ibid., 130–35; Goldberger et al., "A Study of the Relation of Family Income to Pellagra," 2073.

45.   *14th U.S. Census, vol. 9: Manufactures,* 1119, 1395; *15th Census. vol. 2: Manufactures* (Washington, D.C., 1930), 248.

46.   Quoted in Etheridge, *Butterfly Caste,* 143.

47.   Ibid., 147, 192–93.

48.   "Lost Time and Labor Turnover in Cotton Mills. A Study of Cause and Extent," *Bull. of the Women's Bureau,* no. 52 (Washington, D.C.: U.S. Dept. of Labor, 1926), 14–16.

49.   "Causes of Absences for Men and for Women in Four Cotton Mills," *Bull. of the Women's Bureau,* no. 69 (1929), 2–3.

50.   One PHS study of the cause of worker absences, reflecting management's view, argued that much short-term illness was due regular hands' practice of staying home so extra hands could work. Rollo Brittain et al., "The Health of Workers in a Textile Plant," *Public Health Bull.,* no. 207 (July, 1932), 14–15.

51.   Evelyn Barnett, "The Story of My Life," box ii. Will Lou Gray Papers, South Caroliniana Library.

52.   Ibid.

Chapter 3

1.   The description of the milling process comes from *Cotton Textile Industry,* vol. I of *Report on the Condition of Woman and Child Wage-Earners in the U.S.* (Washington, D.C., 1910), 339–409.

2.   Ibid., 409; also *Annual Report, S.C. Board of Health* (1908), 54.

3.   *Cotton Textile Industry,* 399–409; Barbara H. Caminita et al., "A Review of the Literature Relating to Affectations of the Respiratory Tract in Individuals Exposed to Cotton Dust," *Public Health Bull.* 297 (1947), 3; "The Methods of Dust Extraction in Cotton-Carding Engines," *Scientific American* 105 (1911):592; "Vacuum Cleaning Applied to Machines in Textile Mills," *Scientific American Supplement* 74 (1912):216.

4.   *Hearings Before the Subcommittee on Labor of the Committee on Labor and Public Welfare* (Sept. 3, 1969–April 28, 1970), 589, U.S. Sen., 91st Cong., 1st and 2d Sess., on S. 2193 and S. 2788; also Carey P. McCord et al., "Noise and Its Effect on Human Beings," *JAMA* 110 (1938): 1555.

5.   *Cotton Textile Industry,* 37.

6.   Kohn, *Cotton Mills of South Carolina,* 84; also *Cotton Textile Industry,* 37.

7.   Kohn, *Cotton Mills of South Carolina,* 84; also *Annual Report, S.C. Board of Health* (1908), 58.

8.   North Carolina Life Histories, no. 2, WPA Papers, Southern Historical Collection; also see *Cotton Textile Industry,* 407; and Arthur Perry, "Preventable Death in Cotton Manufacturing Industries," *Bureau of Labor Statistics Bull.,* no. 251 (Oct. 1919), 95.

9.   *Causes of Death Among Woman and Child Cotton-Mill Operatives,* 32.

10.   George Kober, "Industrial Hygiene," *Bull. of the Bureau of Labor* 16 (Mar. 1908), 486.

11.   "The Vacuum Cleaner in Cotton Mills: Modern Methods Applied to Industrial Sanitation," *Scientific American* 107 (1912):276.

12.   Kober, "Industrial Hygiene," 541–42; *Cotton Textile Industry,* 361, 361; "Mortality Among Cotton Operatives," *AJPH* 5 (1915): 178–79; also H.W. Clark and S.D. Gage, "A Study of the Hygienic Condition of the Air in Certain Textile Mills," *AJPH* 3 (1913):1176, 1182–83, which suggested that it was the frequent move-

ment from warmer (and damper) mill environments to colder outside atmospheres that broke workers' health.

13. The Massachusetts study was reported in Clark and Gage, "Study of the Hygienic Condition of the Air," 1306-09.
14. Kober, "Industrial Hygiene," 541-42.
15. Fred Lee, "The Effects of Temperature and Humidity on Fatigue," *AJPH* 3 (1913):865, 864.
16. "Effect of Fatigue on Industrial Output," *AJPH* 6 (1916): 92; "The Problem of Fatigue Among Munitions Workers," *AJPH* 6 (1916): 185.
17. The Bureau of Mines study is reported in "Heat and Humidity in Factory Conditions," *Scientific Supplement* 88 (1938):12. Present-day understanding of fatigue is summarized in Rutherford Johnston and Seward Miller, *Occupational Diseases and Industrial Medicine* (Philadelphia: W.B. Saunders Co., 1961), 406-10; insight was also gained through the following interviews: Dr. Donald Robinson, May 20, 1983; Dr. John Preston (former public health officer), May 31, 1982; and George Dwiggins (industrial medicine professor at the Univ. of South Carolina), Sept. 16, 1985.
18. McCord, "Noise and Its Effect," 1555-56.
19. N.C. Life Histories, no. 33; for an interpretation of various decibel levels see McCord, "Noise and Its Effect," 1555; North Carolina Life Histories, no. 63A.
21. N.C. Life Histories, no. 42.
22. J.L. Wood, interview, Aug. 16, 1979.
23. Ibid.; Mr. Wood and two friends (who sat in on the interview), all retirees from a Columbia mill, communicated with each other partly by lip reading; also see McCord, "Noise and Its Effect," 1557-59.
24. N.C. Life Histories, no. 38.
25. Wood, interview, Aug. 16, 1979.
26. N.C. Life Histories, no. 24.
27. Ibid.
28. As late as 1947 South Carolina's industrial hygienist lamented that mills in the state were altogether too humid and hot, and he put the blame squarely on mill foremen. See James Hammond, "Hygiene Problems in the Textile Industry," *Safety Engineering* (May 1947): 66-69.
29. Kohn, *Cotton Mills of South Carolina,* 74; also *Cotton Textile Industry,* 374-75.
30. N.C. Life Histories, no. 89.
31. *Textile World* 78 (1929):47. The first indication that opinion in textiles was changing on the rest period issue came in 1931. See *Textile World* 80 (1931):1524.
32. N.C. Life Histories, no. 22.
33. Ibid., no. 52, 53; management's defense is summarized in B.B. Gossett, "Urges More Effective Cooperation Between Mills and Labor," *Textile World* 76 (1929):38.
34. N.C. Life Histories, no. 24.
35. Ibid.
36. Ibid., no. 26.
37. Ibid., no. 52.
38. Ibid., no. 32.

Chapter 4

1. Todd L. Savitt, "The Education of Black Physicians at Shaw University [Leonard Med. School]," in Jeffrey Crow and Flora Hatley, *Black Americans in North Carolina and the South* (Chapel Hill: Univ. of North Carolina Press, 1984), 160–87. The other two schools ceased operation before the 1910 report, casualties of negative influences other than Flexner. Savitt suggests that other black medical schools, especially Leonard and Flint (New Orleans) could have continued to play an important role had adequate funding been available.

2. James Summerville, *Educating Black Doctors: A History of Meharry Medical College,* (University: Univ. of Alabama Press, 1983), 54; Montague Cobb, "Progress and Portents for the Negro in Medicine," *Crisis* 55 (1948): 116, 118; *Jour. of Negro Education,* 346.

3. Foundation support is noted in Summerville, *Meharry Medical College,* 64, 66–67, 96; Cobb, "Progress and Portents," 115; Cobb, "Medical Care and the Plight of the Negro," 201–11.

4. Cobb, "Medical Care and the Plight of the Negro," 202.

5. Peter Marshall Murray to Joseph L. Johnson, Sept. 26, 1928, box 5, Peter Marshall Murray Papers, Moorland-Spingarn Research Center, Howard University.

6. Ibid.

7. Cobb, "Progress and Portents," 112; Summerville, *Meharry Medical College,* 64, 66–67, 96. Financial problems at Howard Medical School are discussed in Kenneth Manning, *Black Apollo of Science: The Life of Ernest E. Just* (New York: Oxford Univ. Press, 1983), 93, 117–20, 140–41.

8. Giles to Peter Marshall Murray, Mar. 1, 1931, "Correspondence, Ge-Gl" file, box 76-5, Murray Papers; "Negro Doctors and Hospitals," *Opportunity* 3 (1925):227.

9. Montague Cobb, interview, May 22, 1979.

10. Suzanne Linder, *Medicine in Marlboro County, 1736–1980,* (Baltimore: Gateway Press, 1980), 62; National Medical Assn.—Miscellaneous Medical and Surgical Assn. file, box 58-2, Joseph L. Johnson Papers, Moorland-Spingarn Research Center.

11. Paul Cornely, "Trends in Public Health Activities among Negroes in 96 Southern Counties During the Period 1930–39," *AJPH* 32 (1942):1123; on hospital exclusion see Cornely, "Race Relations in Community Health Organization," *AJPH* 36 (1946):990; and Cobb, "Medical Care and the Plight of the Negro," 209.

12. In the 1950s, when the North Carolina Medical Society took its first step toward integration, it created a limited membership category for black doctors to avoid this very thing. See *Raleigh News and Observer* (May 10, 1961).

13. Paul Cornely, interview, May 14, 1979.

14. Quoted in Cobb, "Louis T. Wright, 1891–1952," *JNMA* 35 (1953):135–36.

15. *Palmetto Leader* (Mar. 22, 1930).

16. *JNMA* 38 (1946) through 54 (1962).

17. Cobb interview.

18. Dr. Peter Kelly, interview, June 23, 1978.
19. Minutes of the Palmetto Medical Assn., 1920; *JNMA* 1 (1909).
20. Summerville, *Meharry Medical College,* 43–45; Cobb, "Medical History," *JNMA* 46 (1954):79; Cobb, "John A. Kenney, MD, 1874–1950," *JNMA* 42 (1950):175.
21. Cobb, "Medical History," *JNMA* 51 (1959):407–9.
22. Cobb, "Medical History," *JNMA* 52 (1960):382; Walter Weare, *Black Business in the New South: A Social History of the North Carolina Mutual Life Insurance Company* (Urbana: Univ. of Illinois Press, 1973), 110–11, 128; on Moton, see Cobb, "Medical History," *JNMA* 53 (1961):34.
23. *Palmetto Leader* (Mar. 22, 1930); Jesse T. Hill and John Evans, interview, June 22, 1977; George Bunch to "To Whom It May Concern," Dec. 28, 1906, letter in possession of Mrs. Hill; Mariana Davis, *South Carolina's Blacks and Native Americans, 1776–1976* (Columbia: Bicentennial Commission, 1976), 157–58.
24. *The Negro Health Journal* 1 (1916):1, 4–5. A set is available at the Waring Medical History Library, Charleston.
25. *Palmetto Leader* (June 21, 1930), (Sept. 20, 1930), (Sept. 27, 1930), (Jan. 30, 1932); "A Brief History of the Evans Clinic" (1932), pamphlet in possession of author.
26. L.W. Long, interview, July 6, 1977.
27. Ibid.; *Union Daily Times* (Apr. 23, 1979).
28. Long, "Presidential Address," Minutes, Palmetto Assn., 1941, 3.
29. Program of Community Hospital Annual Clinic (1932); Long, interview, July 6, 1977; *Union Daily Times* (Apr. 23, 1979).
30. Long "Presidential Address," 3; Long interview.
31. Long, "Presidential Address," 6.
32. Ibid., 2.
33. Ibid., 2–4.
34. Joseph Robinson to Long, Mar. 17, 1941, in Long, "Presidential Address," 3–4.
35. "A Prominent Colored Surgeon," *Colored American Magazine* 14 (1908):481.
36. Ibid.
37. On Bousfield see *Who Was Who,* vol. 2 (Chicago: Marquis-Who's Who, Inc., 1950), 72; biographical data on Murray is available in the catalogue of the Murray Papers; information on Cornely and Poindexter was obtained from an interview with Cornely, May 14, 1979.
38. The Howard ethic of service and Johnson's role in advancing it is discussed in Henry and Katherine Pringle, "America's Leading Negro Univ.," *Saturday Evening Post* 201 (1949): 36–37, 96–98. Johnson's authoritarian manner is discussed in Manning, *Black Apollo of Science,* 208–37.
39. The author is indebted to Prof. Martin Pernick for suggesting this perspective on the Northern medical reformers.
40. *Palmetto Leader* (May 7, 1932); Bousfield to Murray, n.d., but c. June 1932, box 4, Murray Papers.
41. Murray to Bousfield, November 17, 1932, box 4, Murray Papers.
42. The Atlanta session and Murray's concerns are discussed in Murray, "President's Address," *JNMA* 24 (1932): 1.
43. Quoted in *Palmetto Leader* (May 7, 1932).
44. Murray to Bousfield, Nov. 17, 1932; also see Murray, "President's Address," 1.

45.   Bousfield to Murray, c. June 1932; Bousfield's connection with Rosenwald is noted in *Who Was Who,* 72.
46.   The founding, purposes, and operation of the Duke Endowment are covered in "Proposed Plan of Work" (c. 1925), Hospital Section file, box 28-D, Watson Smith Rankin Papers, Duke Endowment Archives. Also Marshall Pickens, interview, Dec. 15, 1982.
47.   On the early history and medical operations of the Rosenwald Fund see Edwin Embree, *Investment in People: The Story of the Julius Rosenwald Fund* (New York: Harper, 1949), chs. 4, 5.
48.   On Davis's work see Embree, *Rosenwald Fund,* 122–31.
49.   Davis's general interest in black health is recounted in Jones, *Bad Blood,* 52–60. The syphilis experiments involved a denial of treatment to a large group of black syphilitics, who were made to serve as an experimental control group. The Rosenwald Fund was not involved in that project.
50.   Murray to Bousfield, Nov. 17, 1932; in citing Davis's "Virginia upbringing" Bousfield was apparently confusing him with Dr. Taliaferro Clark, a PHS officer—and a Virginian—who was assigned to the Rosenwald Fund as a consultant in Negro Health. See *Who Was Who* 2 (for Clark) and 5, 173 (for Davis); also W.S. Rankin to Taliaferro Clark, Dec. 20, 1930, N.C. and S.C. Hospital Files, box 180, Duke Endowment Archives.
51.   Murray to Bousfield, Nov. 17, 1932.
52.   Murray, "President's Address," 8.
53.   Cobb, "Integration in Medicine: A National Need," *JNMA* 49 (1957): 4; also Murray to Oscar DePriest, Mar. 12, 1932, box 4, Murray Papers.
54.   Murray to DePriest.
55.   Cobb, "Integregation in Medicine," 4.
56.   Murray to Bousfield, Nov. 17, 1932.
57.   Ibid.
58.   On efforts to get blacks on health department staffs, see Murray, "President's Address," 1–10 and (for Bousfield's efforts) Embree, *Rosenwald Fund,* 111–12, 116–17; also see *Who Was Who* 2, 72; Bousfield, "Reaching the Negro Community," *AJPH* 24 (1934): 209–15.
59.   Bousfield, "Reaching the Negro Community," 210.
60.   Ibid., 214.
61.   Ibid., 210–11.
62.   Hildrus Poindexter, "Handicaps in the Normal Growth and Development of Rural Negro Children," *AJPH* 28 (1938): 1049. Information on Poindexter is in *Who's Who Among Black Americans, 1977–78,* 2d ed., vol. 1 (Northbrook, Illinois: 1978), 720.
63.   Cornely interview.
64.   For the Atlanta Univ. publications see, for example, "Mortality Among Negroes in Cities," *Atlanta Univ. Publication,* no. 1 (1903), 23. The two Census Bureau reports are *The Negro Population in the U.S., 1790–1915* and *Negroes in the U.S., 1920–32.*
65.   Cornely, "Observations on the Health Progress of Negroes in the U.S. During the Past Two Decades," *SMJ* 34 (1941):1286.

66. Cornely, "Trends in Public Health Activities," 1117–23; also see Cornely, "Segregation and Discrimination in Medical Care in the U.S.," *AJPH* 46 (1956):1074–81.

67. See for example Cornely, "Morbidity and Mortality from Scarlet Fever in the Negro," *AJPH* 29 (1939):999–1005.

68. The work which did most to create the image of an uncaring black middle class was E. Franklin Frazier, *Black Bourgeoisie: The Rise of a New Middle Class* (New York: The Free Press, 1957), esp., 112, 228, 235–38. The poetry of LeRoi Jones echoes Frazier's analysis: see "Black Bourgeosis" in Lettie J. Austin, *The Black Man and the Promise of America* (Glenwood, Ill.: Scott, Foresman and Co., 1970), 331. Also see Weaver, *The Negro Ghetto,* which reveals sharp class divisions among blacks who migrated north.

69. *JNMA* 3 (1911):327–30; *Negro Yearbook* (1913), 241.

70. *JNMA* 3 (1911):63.

71. "The NMA c. 1932, Murray's Presidential Address" file, box 10, Murray Papers; M.O. Bousfield to [hospital] Superintendents, Nov. 11, 1935, box 4, Murray Papers.

72. "The Case Against the AMA," *Opportunity* 17 (1939): 194.

73. Cobb interview.

74. Minutes, Palmetto Assn., 1914; W.H. Young, "Presidential Address," 7, Minutes, Palmetto Assn., 1942.

75. Report of Howard Payne, Apr. 1939, Private Papers of Modjeska M. Simkins.

76. B.M. Rhetta et al., "Report of the Committee on the VD Situation," Mar. 1932, box 4, Murray Papers.

77. Young, "Presidential Address," 7.

78. Bousfield to Murray, c. June, 1932.

79. Murray to Bousfield, Nov. 17, 1932.

80. Dublin, "The Health of the Negro," 200.

81. Rhetta, "Report on the VD Situation."

82. *Palmetto Leader* (May 7, 1932).

83. Septima Clark, interview, Dec. 15, 1977.

84. Graham Davis to Michael Davis, June 23, 1930, box 7, Graham Davis Correspondence, Duke Endowment Archives.

85. W.S. Rankin to Lillian Rhodes, June 10, 1927, box 180, N.C. and S.C. Hospital and County files, Duke Endowment Archives; Memo, Good Samaritan Hospital, March 19, 1929, ibid.; R. Beverly Herbert to Rankin, June 18, 1939, ibid.; G.P.H. "Good Samaritan Hospital, Columbia," Oct. 14, 1931, ibid.; Graham Davis Memo, Waverly Fraternal Hospital, n.d., ibid.

86. G.F.H. Memo for Rankin, July 2, 1938, ibid.

87. Davis Memo, Waverly Fraternal Hospital.

88. Cornely interview.

89. Ibid.; on the teaching at Negro medical schools, see Peyton Anderson, MD, "The Neglected One-Tenth," *Opportunity* 13 (1935): 210.

90. Cornely interview.

Chapter 5

1. For background on the Virginia group see "Clean-up Week in Virginia," *Southern Workman* 43 (1914):272. Jones, *Bad Blood,* 34–35, notes the tie between the Virginia organization and National Negro Health Week. APHA attention is shown in "The Negro and Public Health," *AJPH* 4 (1914):624–25. For a discussion of the Health Movement, itself, see Herbert Morais, *The History of the Negro in Medicine,* 86–87; also *Hygeia* 9 (1931):336, and 10 (Apr. 1932):349. The 1930s volumes (April issues) of the *Palmetto Leader,* a South Carolina black paper, reveal the local activities of Health Week. A health venture similar to Negro Health Week was the health commission launched in 1927 by the black Elks organization. Focusing on education but also sponsoring nursing and clinic programs, the Elks served a large number of mostly Northern blacks. See Dennis Dickerson, "Medicine for the Masses: The Health Commission of the IBPOE 1927–42," paper delivered at the 1985 meeting of the American Association for the History of Medicine.

2. Septima Clark, *Echo in My Soul* (New York: Dutton, 1962), 41–42, 50, 73, 74, 110–11, 138; also Septima Clark, interview, Dec. 15, 1977. Cornely, interview, May 14, 1979.

3. Carl Degler, *At Odds: Women and the Family in America from the Revolution to the Present* (New York: Oxford Univ. Press, 1981), 298–327.

4. 1912–13 file, box 1, Neighborhood Union Papers (hereafter, NU).

5. Ibid.; also see Gerda Lerner, "Early Community Work of Black Club Women," *Jour. of Negro History* 59 (1974):163. *Atlanta Constitution* (June 21, 1914); also see Report of the Emergency Committee of the NU, 1934, 1914–16 file, box 1, NU Papers.

6. 1912–13 file, box 1, NU Papers; To Mayor, State Board of Education, Superintendent of City Schools, Sept. 29, 1923, 1923–25 file, box 1, NU Papers. Also see Lerner, "Black Club Women," 163–64.

7. *Atlanta Constitution* (June 21, 1914). Report of the Emergency Committee of the NU, NU Papers.

8. "Outline of Anti-TB work," in Hope to Edith Thompson, Mar. 6, 1922, 1920–22 file, box 2, NU Papers.

9. Hope, "The Program for 1926–27: Health and Recreation," 1926–27 file, box 2, NU Papers.

10. 1923–25 file, box 2, NU Papers.

11. Report of NU Activities, by Helen Foster, 1927–30 file, box 2, NU Papers.

12. Ibid.; Report of Colored Dept. for the Year 1919, 1917–19 file, box 1; office report for June, 1923, 1923–25 file, box 2, NU Papers.

13. Report of Colored Dept. (1919), 1917–19 file, box 1, NU Papers.

14. 1917–18 file, box 1. Report of the Emergency Committee of NU, 1934, NU Papers.

15. Hope to Thomas Jesse Jones, 1926, 1926–30 file, box 2; also Report of the Emergency Committee; also L.D. Shivery Note, 1933, 1926–30 file, box 2, NU Papers.

16. L.D. Shivery Note, 1933, NU Papers; Report of the Emergency Committee, NU Papers.

17. Report of the Emergency Committee, NU Papers.

18. Mary Antin to Hope, Apr. 19, 1922, 1921–22 file, box 2, NU Papers.

19. "Modjeska," *Columbia Record* (Dec. 12, 1974).

20. Simkins, interview, Dec. 14, 1976.

21. Simkins, interview, Oct. 10, 1978.

22. Simkins, interview, Dec. 14, 1976.

23. Ibid.; *Palmetto Leader* (Feb. 27, 1932).

24. *Palmetto Leader* (June 7, 1941).

25. Simkins, interview, Oct. 10, 1978.

26. *Palmetto Leader* (Oct. 15, 1932).

27. "Planning the Health Education Institute for Ministers at Dillard Univ., New Orleans, Louisiana, June 7–17, 1943," private files of Modjeska Simkins.

28. W.A.C. Hughes to D. McL. MacDonald, n.d., private files of Modjeska Simkins.

29. See *Palmetto Leader* (Feb. 16, 1935), (Oct. 22, 1938); undated memo, private files of Modjeska Simkins.

30. Simkins, interview, Oct. 10, 1978.

31. *Palmetto Leader* (Dec. 7, 1936); Simkins, interview, Oct. 10, 1978.

32. MacDonald to C. St. C. Guild, Apr. 9, 1936, private files of Modjeska Simkins.

33. "Modjeska," *Columbia Record*. "Planning the Health Institute for Ministers."

34. Simkins, interview, Dec. 14, 1976.

35. "The Good Samaritan-Waverly Hospital Building Fund Campaign," 1945, private files of Modjeska Simkins.

36. Maude Callan, interview, June 23, 1978. *Negro Yearbook* (1925–26), 24, 25.

37. See Embree, *Rosenwald Fund* for a survey of that group's work; for a synopsis of the Endowment program see "Proposed Plan of Work" (c. 1925), Duke Endowment, Rankin Papers.

38. S.L. Smith, "Some Early Activities of the Julius Rosenwald Fund in Health Among Negroes in the South," pp. 1–3: speech delivered at the annual meeting of the Southern Tuberculosis Conference, Houston, Texas, Sept. 16, 17, 18, 1935, private files of Modjeska Simkins.

39. Ibid., 1–4.

40. Ibid.; Embree, *Rosenwald Fund,* 109.

41. Cobb, "Progress and Portents," 115; also Embree, *Rosenwald Fund,* 111, 112; Smith, "Some Early Accounts of Julius Rosenwald Fund," 3–4.

42. H.A. Taylor to Talliaferro Clark, Sept. 16, 1930, box 25 (1930), North Carolina Board of Health Papers, North Carolina Div. of Archives and History. Also see Summary of Health Problems, May 30, 1932, box 4, Murray Papers.

43. In responding to North Carolina's suggestion Rosenwald's Embree referred to North Carolina's "statesmanlike concern for her total population. . . . " Embree to C.V. Reynolds, Oct. 29, 1935, box 33, 1926–35, North Carolina Board of Health Papers; also Embree, *Rosenwald Fund,* 111, 112.

44. C. O'H. Laughinghouse to Dr. D.A. Dees, Mar. 8, 1930, box 25, North Carolina Board of Health Papers; also *Biennial Report, N.C. Board of Health* (1934–36), 37, 41.

45. Cornely, "Health Assets and Liabilities of the Negro," *Opportunity* 23 (1945):198. Embree, *Rosenwald Fund,* 113–15; the history of the Tuskegee experiment is found

in Jones, *Bad Blood,* especially 78-91; federal involvement with VD in the late
1930s is detailed in Thomas Parran and R.A. Vonderlehr, *Plain Words about
VD* (New York: Raynal and Hitchcock, 1941).

46. Cornely, "Health Assets and Liabilities," 200; Embree, *Rosenwald Fund,* 115; Dr.
James Fouche, in interview, Nov. 27, 1984, recounted his experience with lung
collapse therapy.

47. Bousfield to Murray, June 4, 1932, box 4, Murray Papers; also Laughinghouse
to Michael Davis, June 10, 1930, box 25, North Carolina Board of
Health Papers; also H.A. Taylor to Taliaferro Clark, ibid.

48. Cobb, "Louis T. Wright," *JNMA,* 130-45.

49. Quoted in Murray to Bousfield, Nov. 17, 1932, box 4, Murray Papers.

50. Ibid.

51. Ibid.

52. Smith, "Some Early Accounts of the Rosenwald Fund," 3-4.

53. Cornely, "Health Assets and Liabilities of the Negro," 200.

54. Secretary's Reports, 1925-46, Duke Endowment, Hospital Section, box 28-D,
Rankin Papers.

55. On Davis see Hospital Section file, box 28-D, Rankin Papers.

56. "Proposed Plan of Work."

57. Ibid.; also Secretary's Reports, 1925-46, box 1, Duke Endowment Archives.

58. Secretary's Reports, 1925-26, box 1, Duke Endowment Archives; also Duke
Endowment, *Annual Report of Hospital Section,* (1930), 34-37.

59. *Annual Report of Hospital Section* (1930), 34-37; also "Hospital Section," *Duke Endowment Yearbook* (1940), 21-27.

60. *Duke Endowment Yearbook* (1940), 21-27; Hospital Section file, box 28-D, Rankin
Papers. G.L. Davis to Lawrence A. Oxley, May 21, 1939, Davis Correspondence,
box 7, Duke Endowment Archives; also *Annual Report of Hospital Section* (1930),
34-37.

61. *Annual Report of Hospital Section* (1930), 34-37; also *Duke Endowment Yearbook,* 21-27.

62. Marshall Pickens to the author, July 12, 1985.

63. Memo, Good Samaritan, Apr. 20, 1927; Memo, Good Samaritan Hospital,
Mar. 19, 1929; J.W. Crews to Rankin, Feb. 24, 1928; G.P.H. Memo: Good Samaritan Hospital, Nov. 21, 1940 — all in N.C. and S.C. Hospital and County
files, box 180, Duke Endowment Archives.

64. R.A. Meares to Embree, Dec. 26, 1929, ibid.

65. Rankin to Taliaferro Clark, Jan. 20, 1930, ibid.

66. See Graham Davis to Michael Davis, Feb. 10, 1930, ibid.; Graham Davis to
S.R. Green, July 22, 1930, ibid.

67. Graham Davis to S.R. Green, July 20, 1930, ibid.; Graham Davis to Michael
Davis, Jan. 28, 1931, Davis Correspondence, box 7, Duke Endowment Archives.

68. *The [South Carolina] State* (Dec. 28, 1931).

69. Ibid.

70. Ibid. (Dec. 27, 1931). On white opposition to giving Negroes the old hospital
see editorial, *The State* (Dec. 23, 1931).

71. *Palmetto Leader* (Dec. 19, 1931).

72. Ibid.

73. Ibid.
74. Ibid. (Feb. 25, 1939). By the end of World War II the hospital was entirely inadequate for its volume of patients. Led by Modjeska Simkins, trustees sought to raise funds for a new facility, with assurance of matching funds from Duke if they could gather $100,000. The effort succeeded in the early 1950s, and the Waverly-Good Samaritan was finally able to take up Duke's twenty-year-old offer; see "The Good Samaritan-Waverly Hospital Building Fund Campaign," private files of Modjeska Simkins.
75. Blackburn and Padgette, *History of Columbia Hospital*, 34. "The Good Samaritan Hospital, Columbia," N.C. and S.C. Hospital and County files.
76. The Duke Endowment, Hospital Section file, Rankin Papers; also Secretary's Reports, 1925-46, Duke Endowment Archives.
77. Robert Toomey, interview, Nov. 19, 1977.

Chapter 6

1. Permanent health officers were named in Georgia in 1903, North Carolina in 1910, and South Carolina in 1910. See T.F. Abercrombie, *A History of Public Health in Georgia, 1733-1950* (Atlanta: Dept. of Public Health, n.d.), 54, and B.E. Washburn, *A History of the North Carolina Board of Health, 1877-1925* (Raleigh: Board of Health, 1966), 35; for South Carolina see *Annual Report, S.C. Board of Health* (1910), 23; on vital statistics collection see ibid. (1903), 515, which argued that such work was needed to refute Yankee claims that the state was an unhealthy place.
2. See *SMJ* 1 (1908), to 10 (1917) and *AJPH* 1 (1911) to 7 (1917). Jones, *Bad Blood*, 19-26, illustrates the narrower thinking of private physicians.
3. F.L. Hoffman, *Race Traits and Tendencies of the American Negro,* (New York: Macmillan, 1896), 148, 328; also see Josiah Morse, in James E. McCulloch, *The Human Way* (Nashville: The Southern Sociological Congress, 1913), 59.
4. Terry, "The Negro a Public Health Problem," 459.
5. Quoted in Louis Dublin, "The Health of the Negro, 198.
6. Lee, "The Negro as a Problem in Public Health," 209-11.
7. Ibid., 211.
8. Terry, "The Negro a Public Health Problem," 466.
9. Martin L. Graves, "The Negro a Menace to the Health of the White Race," *SMJ* 9 (1916):413.
10. Quoted in Terry, "The Negro a Public Health Problem," 466.
11. William Brunner, "The Negro Health Problem in Southern Cities," *AJPH* 5 (1915):187, 188-89.
12. Martin Sloan, "The Urgent Need of Hospital Facilities for Tuberculous Negroes," *SMJ* 10 (1917):662.
13. Terry, "The Negro and His Relation to Public Health in the South," *AJPH* 3 (1913):303, 305.
14. Terry, "The Negro a Public Health Problem," 463.
15. Sloan, "Urgent Need of Hospital Facilities for Tuberculous Negroes," 663.

16. "Health Departments of States and Provinces of the U.S. and Canada," *Public Health Bull.* no. 184 (1932), 355, 477, 533. The first county health departments were created in Kentucky (1908) and North Carolina (1911), but growth of the movement was slow, as states offered little aid; see Francis Allen, "Public Health Work in the Southeast, 1872–1941: The Study of a Social Movement," Ph.D. diss. (Univ. of North Carolina, 1945), 360.

17. See *Annual Report, S.C. Board of Health* (1915), 3–15.

18. Washburn, *North Carolina Board of Health,* 55; also see "North Carolina," *AJPH* 11 (1921): 583; *Biennial Report, Georgia Board of Health* (1929–30), 116; *Annual Report, S.C. Board of Health* (1915), 8–9.

19. Sloan, "Urgent Need of Hospital Facilities for Tuberculous Negroes," 654, 656.

20. Ibid., 654–62.

21. *Annual Report, S.C. Board of Health* (1918), 3, and (1919), 50–51; also see *The State* (Jan. 2, 1918) and (Jan. 19, 1918).

22. *Annual Report, S.C. Board of Health* (1917), 12–13, 44, 46, and (1918), 11. *The State* (April 8, 1918) and (Jan. 19, 1919).

23. *Annual Report, S.C. Board of Health* (1918), 11.

24. E.H. Beardsley, "Allied Against Sin: American and British Responses to VD in WWI," *Medical History* 20 (1976):193–94; also *The State* (Feb. 27, 1919).

25. *Acts and Joint Resolutions of the General Assembly of South Carolina* (1918), 890; *The State* (Apr. 18, 1918) and (Feb. 27, 1919); and *Annual Report, S.C. Board of Health* (1918), 46, 48–56, 111–12.

26. *Annual Report, S.C. Board of Health* (1919), 50–51; *The State* (Feb. 27, 1919).

27. J. Stanley Lemons, "The Sheppard-Towner Act," *Jour. of American History* 55 (1969):776–77.

28. *Annual Report, S.C. Board of Health* (1918), 3; also *The State* (Jan. 19, 1918).

29. *Annual Report, S.C. Board of Health* (1917), 44–45, 53–55; (1918), 43–44; and (1919), 9, 32, 62; also *The State* (Feb. 25, 1918), (Jan. 19, 1919), (Feb. 20, 1918), and over the course of April 1918.

30. *Annual Report, S.C. Board of Health* (1919), 60, and (1921), 9.

31. Ibid., 8; also *The State* (Jan. 19, 1919) and (Apr. 19, 1918). An illustration of state and federal concern to meet the needs of returning veterans were the land-settlement programs inaugurated after World War I. One project of that sort, in Wisconsin's cut-over district, is discussed in E.H. Beardsley, *Harry L. Russell and Agricultural Science in Wisconsin* (Madison: Univ. of Wisconsin Press, 1969), 121–37.

32. Quoted in *Conference of State and Territorial Health Officers* (1923), 60; also *Public Health Bull.,* no. 184 (1932), 552.

33. *Annual Report, S.C. Board of Health* (1919), 73; also *The State* (Jan. 16, 1919) and (Jan. 22, 1919); on South Carolina's black sanatorium wing see *Report of the Comptroller General* (1919), and *The State* (Jan. 16, 1919).

34. Washburn, *North Carolina Board of Health,* 66, 51; "North Carolina," *AJPH* 11 (1921):583; *Biennial Report, Georgia Board of Health* (1927–29), 116.

35. The history of Sheppard-Towner is covered in Lemons, "The Sheppard-Towner Act," 776–86. Boll Weevil infestation is treated in Francis Butler Simkins and Charles P. Rolland, *A History of the South* (New York: Knopf, 1972), 31–33, and

in Lewis P. Jones, *South Carolina: A Synoptic History for Laymen* (Columbia: R.L. Bryan, 1971), 235-36. Gilbert Fite and Jim E. Reese, *An Economic History of the United States* (Boston: Houghton-Mifflin, 1959), 551-55, surveys Southern economic conditions in the early 1920s.

36.   Solomon Blatt, interview, June 25, 1979. Blatt was the most powerful figure in state politics after World War II.

37.   Quoted in *Opportunity* 2 (1924):132.

38.   Jackson, "The Need of Health Education Among Negroes," 239.

39.   *Public Health Bull.,* no. 184 (1932), 240-47; on the attitude of Georgia doctors toward public health see Abercrombie, *Public Health in Georgia,* 57, and *Biennial Report, Georgia Board of Health* (1927-29), 29, and (1929-31), 46, 55; also Allen, "Public Health Work in the Southeast, 1872-1941."

40.   *Annual Report, S.C. Board of Health* (1921), 37, and (1925), 93-103; on the cooperative agreement see ibid. (1930), 25, 29; malaria work in the 1920s is noted in Andrew Peeples, "Historical Aspects of Health Administration," 54-55, unpublished manuscript in office of director of South Carolina DHEC; also see *Report of the Comptroller General* for 1925-29; also Dr. G.E. McDaniel, interview, Mar. 9, 1977.

41.   *Annual Report, S.C. Board of Health* (1921), 3, (1923), 107, and (1925), 14. The decline in funding for child hygiene work is also noted in *Report of the Comptroller General* for 1916-32. Also see Peeples, "Historical Aspects of Health Administration," 38.

42.   See discussions of TB in *Annual Report, S.C. Board of Health* (1920-1930), especially (1929), 10.

43.   Ibid. (1919), 10; opposition to VD work is noted in ibid. (1920), 62; for evidence of the open discussion of this once secret subject see *The State* (Jan. 26, 1919), (Feb. 13, 1919), and (Mar. 7, 1919), as well as *Annual Report, S.C. Board of Health* (1919), 52; funding is noted in ibid. (1920), 61, and (1921), 85. The brief protest against VD funding termination is documented in ibid. (1924), 3, 11 and (1925), 1-30 *passim.*

44.   See *Public Health Bull.,* no. 184. Federal aid came in the form of the LaFollette-Bullwinkle Act of 1938 (chapter 7).

45.   *Biennial Report, Georgia Board of Health* (1927-29), 29, 116 and (1929-31) 46, 55; Abercrombie, *Public Health in Georgia,* 108-9, notes the loss of significant amounts of Sheppard-Towner money because of legislative refusal to match available federal dollars.

46.   Washburn, *North Carolina Board of Health,* 72; also *Public Health Bulletin,* no. 184: 477, and "Public Health in North Carolina: A Guidebook for County Commissioners," 4.

47.   "North Carolina, " *AJPH* 11 (1921): 94; also see Washburn, *North Carolina Board of Health,* 71; also *Public Health Bull.,* no. 184: 118-19, 476-77.

48.   George Cooper, "Progress in Health Work for Negroes," address before the North Carolina Commission on Interracial Cooperation, May 14, 1931, George Cooper file, box 28, North Carolina Division of Archives and History. Also see *Public Health Bull.,* no. 184: 476-77. Not until 1926 did total monies available for school inspection exceed those for operation of the maternal-infant bu-

reau. See also "A Synopsis of the Child Hygiene Laws of the Several States," *Public Health Bull.*, no. 110 (May 1925), 49.

50.   Black population figures are in Bureau of the Census, *Historical Statistics of the United States*, part 1 (Washington, D.C.: 1975), 26, 32, 34.

51.   *Public Health Bull.*, no. 184.

52.   G.E. McDaniel, M.D., "James Adams Hayne, M.D., Dr. Public Health," unpublished paper, copy in possession of the author.

53.   Hayne before *Conference of State and Territorial Health Officers* (1918), 64.

54.   See *Annual Report, S.C. Board of Health* (1936–37), 24; (1940–41), 28; and (1942–43), 7–8; also Hayne before *Conference of State and Territorial Health Officers* (1918), 40.

55.   Hayne before *Conference of State and Territorial Health Officers* (1924), 97.

56.   Ibid. (1925).

57.   *Annual Report, S.C. Board of Health* (1921), 28; also *Negroes in the U.S. 1920–32*, 803–5.

58.   Hayne before *Conference of State and Territorial Health Officers* (1921), 64–65.

59.   McDaniel, "James A. Hayne"; also Hardy Wickwar, interview, July 11, 1978; for Hayne's limited interest in VD, see director's summary in *Annual Report, S.C. Board of Health* (1920–30). In ibid. (1921), 10, Hayne attacked the legislature for its shortsightedness in failing to fund VD work adquately, but this concern was not typical and later (p. 84) he stressed economic aspects of syphilis (the chance to save public money) to the exclusion of any other factor.

60.   Arthur Miller memo for Dr. Draper, Jan. 14, 1926, box 60, Record Group 90, State Boards of Health, South Carolina, PHS Papers; also Wickwar, interview, July 11, 1978.

61.   L.M. Fisher of Dr. Draper, Jan. 3, 1925, box 60, Record Group 90, State Boards of Health, South Carolina, PHS Papers; also see Miller, Memo for Draper, ibid.

62.   Fisher to Draper, Jan. 3, 1925, ibid., and L.L. Williams to L.L. Lumsden, Mar. 8, 1924, file 0620–1680, box 61, ibid.

63.   H.S. Cumming to Hayne, Feb. 26, 1929, file 0620–1680, box 61, ibid.

64.   Hayne to Cumming, July 5, 1930, box 60, ibid.

65.   G.A. Wheeler to Surgeon General, July 15, 1930, ibid.; also Cumming to Hayne, Aug. 6, 1930, ibid.

66.   James F. Gifford, letter to the author, June 5, 1985. Gifford is presently writing a biography of Rankin. Also *Who Was Who* 6:336, and *National Cyclopaedia of Amer. Biog.* 56 (Clifton, N.J.: James T. White and Co., 1975), 264.

67.   "North Carolina," *AJPH* 10 (1920):384.

68.   Rankin, "The Medical Profession and the Laity from the Standpoint of the Health Officer," *AJPH* 13 (1923):361, 362.

69.   The national Life Extension Institute is discussed in Paul Starr, *The Social Transformation of American Medicine* (New York: Basic Books, 1982), 192–93; also Washburn, "The North Carolina Plan of County Health Work," *SMJ* 11 (1918):428; also Washburn, *North Carolina Board of Health*, 64, 63; also *Public Health Bull.*, no. 184:476–77, and no. 110.

70.   Rankin, "The Medical Profession and the Laity," 500–1.

71.   Ibid., 501, 502.

72. Quoted in R.B. Wilson to Rankin, Oct. 30, 1919, Personal File of W.S. Rankin, 1912–25, North Carolina Archives.

73. "North Carolina," *AJPH* 11 (1921):94–95.

74. Washburn, *North Carolina Board of Health*, 93; also *Public Health Bull.*, no. 184: 477, 533, 247.

75. John A. Ferrell, "Health Problems Peculiar to the Southern States," *AJPH* 23 (1933):449.

76. Cooper, "Progress in Health Work for Negroes"; on Bousfield's activism see "Reaching the Negro Community," 209–15.

77. Sloan, "Urgent Need of Hospital Facilities for Tuberculous Negroes," 658.

78. Smith, "Some Early Accounts of the Rosenwald Fund," 1–3; Cooper, "Progress in Health Work for Negroes"; also Charles O'H. Laughinghouse to Michael Davis, June 10, 1930, box 25, North Carolina State Board of Health Papers; on the Negro doctor, see *Biennial Report, N.C. Board of Health* (1935–36), 37, 41.

79. T.F. Abercrombie to H.S. Cumming, Dec. 29, 1930, box 20, State Boards of Health, Georgia, Record Group 90, PHS Papers. The national experience is reflected in *AJPH* 22 (1932):395–96, and Sept. 1932 editorial.

80. Abercrombie to Cumming, Dec. 29, 1930, PHS Papers.

81. Ibid.

82. Hayne and Ben Wyman statement on Dillon Co., Feb. 24, 1931, box 60, State Boards of Health, South Carolina, ibid.; also Hayne to Cumming, Feb. 16, 1931, ibid.

83. Hayne to H.S. Cumming, July 26, 1932, ibid.

84. Cumming to Laughinghouse, July 31, 1920, box 25, North Carolina Board of Health Papers.

85. M.V. Ziegler to C.E. Waller, Mar. 30, 1933, box 51, State Boards of Health, North Carolina, Record Group 90, PHS Papers.

86. Ibid.; also Ziegler to Waller, May 25, 1933, ibid.

87. Waller to Abercrombie, Dec. 6, 1932, file 0115–0135, box 19, State Boards of Health, Georgia, ibid.; also Hayne to Cumming, Feb. 16, 1931, South Carolina, ibid.

88. Laughinghouse to Michael Davis, June 10, 1930, box 25, North Carolina Board of Health Papers; also H.A. Taylor to Talliaferro Clark, Sept. 16, 1930, ibid.

89. John Hamilton to James Parrott, Dec. 5, 1931, file 1850–2223, box 25, State Boards of Health, North Carolina, Record Group 90, PHS Papers; also "Public Health in North Carolina: A Guidebook for County Commissioners," 4.

90. Waller to Abercrombie, Dec. 6, 1932, file 0115–0135, box 19, State Boards of Health, Georgia, Record Group 90, PHS Papers; also *Annual Report, S.C. Board of Health* (1931–32), 65–66, and (1932–33), 65.

91. On the mortality rise see *Annual Report, S.C. Board of Health* (1932–33), 4.

92. "Emergency Employment in Mississippi," *Opportunity* 10 (1932): 3

93. *Atlanta World* (April 29, 1931).

94. F.B. Long to George Power, Oct. 12, 1933, "Medical Care-Hospitalization," FERA Old Subject file, FERA Papers, National Archives.

Chapter 7

1. Roy Lubove, "The New Deal and National Health," *Current History* 72 (1977):200, 225, discusses the centralizing of both program planning and funding which took place in American public health work in the New Deal era. Although such federal relief agencies as the FERA, CWA, and CCC had significant influence on health activities in the states, it was the Social Security Act, chiefly, which made Washington (mainly the PHS and the Children's Bureau) the center of a new national public health program.

2. Quoted in Hopkins to Governors and State Relief Administrators, Aug. 25, 1933, "Medical Care General, A-H" file, FERA old subject files, FERA Papers.

3. W.K. Fishburne to Hopkins, June 21, 1933, "Medical Care-Hospitalization" file, FERA old subject files.

4. Ibid.; Bruce McClure to James F. Byrnes, July 12, 1933, ibid.; also C.M. Bookman to Kendall Emerson, July 17, 1933, "Medical Care-Nursing Service" file, ibid.

5. Waller to Parrott, July 1, 1933, 0115–0135 file, box 51, State Boards of Health, North Carolina, Record Group 90, PHS Papers. The Waller letter sums up state health officers' concerns. Also see Parrott to Edward Pou, July, 1933, ibid.

6. On FERA's relation to black doctors see M.O. Bousfield to C.E. Waller, Jan. 3, 1945, "Medical Care General" file, FERA subject files, FERA Papers; Bousfield et al., Statement, n.d. but c. Sept. 1933, ibid.; Peter M. Murray to Hopkins, Oct. 27, 1935, ibid.; on black doctors' claims of discrimination see J.B. Walker (Spartanburg black dentist) to Hopkins, May 3, 1935, South Carolina "Medical Care" file, state files, 1933–36, FERA Papers; also George Zerbst to J.B. Walker, May 11, 1935, ibid.

7. On the work relief aspect of FERA health grants see Abercrombie, *Public Health in Georgia*, 137; on the impact in South Carolina see *Annual Report, S.C. Board of Health* (1933–34), 48; for Georgia see Abercrombie, 135 and *Biennial Report, Georgia Board of Health* (1933–35), 137.

8. C.L. White to James Silver, Jan. 23, 1940, box 39, correspondence and reports, State Board of Health Papers, 1937–46, North Carolina Archives; on South Carolina see *Annual Report, S.C. Board of Health* (1935–36), 10; *Vital Statistics Rates in the U.S., 1900–40*, 358–59, 394–95.

9. Abercrombie, *Public Health in Georgia*, 135; "Appropriations" file 0135, box 34, North Carolina, WPA, Record Group 90, PHS Papers; also Summary of Proposals, "Appropriations" file, South Carolina, ibid.; also *Biennial Report, N.C. Board of Health* (1934–36), 72.

10. Gastonia ERA Canning Project Report, Nov. 1934, box 26, Correspondence by Counties, 1934, State Administrative Offices, State Administrative Records, North Carolina ERA Papers, North Carolina Div. of Archives and History.

11. *Palmetto Leader* (Apr. 11, 1936). Roger Sargent (Univ. of S.C. nutritionist), in interview, Sept. 16, 1985, rated the nutritional quality of that commodities allotment as excellent.

12. Quoted in Cambell, *Brother to a Dragonfly* (New York: Continuum Publishing Co., 1980), 34.

13. "U.S. Community Improvement Appraisal," Mar. 1938, file 6551.363, State of South Carolina, WPA Records, National Archives.

14. On the CCC see Richard Morris, *Encyclopedia of American History* (New York: Harper and Row, 1961), 342; the Indian story was related by a former CCC recruit, interview, May 11, 1982; on physical growth see Kenneth Holland and Frank E. Hill, *Youth in the CCC* (New York: Arno Press, 1974), 191.

15. Carl Rice, "CCC Medical Program," Health Officer, Miscellaneous Reports, 1940–42, NYA Papers, National Archives.

16. On Williams see *Who's Who in America* 21 (1940), 2770; *Palmetto Leader* (Oct. 5, 1940); also see NYA Resident Centers, State Correspondence, 1940–42, box 7, South Carolina, NYA Papers.

17. "NYA Resident Work Centers," Health Officer, Misc. Reports, NYA Papers.

18. *Palmetto Leader* (Oct. 5, 1940); Rosa Clark to R.L. Coe, Apr. 4, 1941, State Correspondence, 1940–42, box 7, South Carolina, NYA Papers.

19. Dr. George Waters to Carol Rice, Dec. 3, 1941, Health Office, State Health Program Reports, box 7, North Carolina, NYA Papers.

20. See Roderick McIver to Helen Harris, Mar. 30, 1942, State Correspondence, box 7, South Carolina, NYA Papers.

21. See Paul Cornely, "Report to Rosenwald Fund" (unpublished, 1940); on Alexander, see Wilma Dykeman and James Stokely, *Seeds of Southern Change: The Life of Will Alexander* (New York: Norton, 1962).

22. Ibid., 235–38; letter to Health Officers of 35 North Carolina Counties, n.d. but c. 1940, FSA file, North Carolina Board of Health, Administrative Services, Central Files, Miscellaneous Correspondence, box 2, 1939–40, North Carolina Archives.

23. Dykeman and Stokely, *Will Alexander*, 235–38; Cornely "Report to Rosenwald Fund."

24. Roy Lubove, "The New Deal and National Health," 199–200.

25. Ibid.

26. Ibid., 200; Lemons, "The Shepphard-Towner Act," 781.

27. Waller to Dr. E.L. Bishop, Aug. 28, 1935, file 0135–58, box 51, State Boards of Health, North Carolina, PHS Papers.

28. Lubove, 225, 226; in 1930 only 35 Georgia counties (with 46 percent of the population) had full-time departments; by 1940, if one added to the full-time counties those with public health nursing services (also paid for by SS), some 74.5 percent of Georgia's people got regular services (Abercrombie, *Public Health in Georgia,* 156).

29. Williams to Parran, Sept. 21, 1942, General Classified Records, Group 3, States, 1936–44, PHS Papers.

30. North Carolina School of Public Health, "News" (Winter 1951–52): 1–13.

31. Parran to Hayne, Jan. 21, 1939, file 0505, box 97, General Classified Records, South Carolina, PHS Papers; also Hayne to Parran, Feb. 10, 1939, ibid.

32. Note, 1937 "MCH" file, box 6, Director's General Administrative Records,

Record Group 26-2-3, Board of Health Papers, Georgia Dept. of Archives and History; the Children's Bureau aided post-graduate education of black doctors as well as white; see Cornely, "Health Assets and Liabilities of the Negro," 199.

33. *Annual Report, S.C. Board of Health* (1936–37), 56, 62.

34. J.C. Knox to Dr. James Watson, Sept. 28, 1940, "Charities and State Board of Public Welfare" file, Miscellaneous Correspondence, 1939–40, box 2, Administrative Services, Central Files, North Carolina Archives.

35. Report in T.F. Abercrombie to Governor Talmadge, Sept. 22, 1941, "Governor" file, box 18, Record Group 26-2-3, Director's General Administrative Records, Georgia Board of Health Papers.

36. Ibid.

37. J.H.M. Knox, "Reduction of Maternal and Infant Mortality in Rural Areas," *AJPH* 25 (1935):73; also *Annual Report, S.C. Board of Health* (1937–38), 25–27.

38. Betty Ficquette, interview, Aug. 1, 1979; also *Annual Report, S.C. Board of Health* (1942–43), 153–61. The board wanted midwives to turn away patients who had not reported to a clinic before the 6th month, but that struck most of them as unrealistic, and they were generally unwilling to follow it.

39. *Annual Report, S.C. Board of Health* (1936–36), 105; (1940–41), 145, 149; and (1939–40), 175, 179; for North Carolina see *Biennial Report, North Carolina Board of Health* (1936–38), 68; and for Georgia see Maternal and Child Health file, Director's General Administrative Records, 1944, Georgia Board of Health Papers.

40. *Annual Report, S.C. Board of Health* (1939–40), 179; *Biennial Report, N.C. Board of Health* (1936–38), 68; *Biennial Report, Georgia Board of Health* (1948), 107.

41. Amealie Brown to Mrs. Roosevelt, Apr. 12, 1943, South Carolina file 651.329, WPA Papers.

42. Maude Fleming to Abbie Weaver, Sept. 24, 1938, Director's General Administrative Records, Georgia Board of Health Papers.

43. Arnall to Abercrombie, Dec. 5, 1944, and Abercrombie to Arnall, Dec. 7, 1944, "Governor" file, box 27, ibid.

44. Abercrombie, *Public Health in Georgia*, 56; also see, for example, *Annual Report, S.C. Board of Health* (1940–41), 92, 131. In 1940–41 the federal grant of $36,000 called for $68,300 from South Carolina; the state actually gave $3000.

45. Cornely, "Race Relations in Community Health Organization," 987.

46. Cornely, "Report to the Rosenwald Fund"; Cornely, "The Nature and Extent of Health Education Among Negroes," *Jour. of Negro Education*, 374; Cornely, "Health Assets and Liabilities of the Negro," 198, 288.

47. Cornely, "Race Relations in Community Health Organization," 991.

48. Septima Clark, interview, Dec. 15, 1977.

49. Cornely, "Race Relations in Community Health Organization," 988.

50. Simkins, interview, Dec. 14, 1976.

51. Parran and Vonderlehr, *Plain Words About VD*, 169–70. The Southern states simply were not able to mount a VD program until money came from Washington in the late 1930s. In 1945 the South Carolina health officer admitted that improvement in the quality of local health work (including chiefly VD

control) was dependent on increases in federal sponsorship. See *Annual Report, S.C. Board of Health* (1944-45), 17.

52. Parran and Vonderlehr, *Plain Words About VD*, 10.

53. Ibid., 32; *Annual Report, S.C. Board of Health* (1935-36), 116-17; (1936-37), 56; and (1937-38), 47-51.

54. L.E. Burney, "Control of Syphilis in a Southern Rural Area," *AJPH* 29 (Sept. 1939): 1007, 1009, 1014; also Walter Davenport, "Bad-Blood Wagon," *Collier's* 103 (May 27, 1939): 28.

55. Burney, "Control of Syphilis in a Southern Rural Area," 1008.

56. Ibid., 1006-14; Parran and Vonderlehr, *Plain Words About VD*, 174.

57. *Biennial Report, N.C. Board of Health* (1936-38), 39; Parran and Vonderlehr, *Plain Words About VD*, 173.

58. See for instance *Biennial Report, N.C. Board of Health* (1936-38), 39. North Carolina got an $80,000 federal grant, plus an annual sum of over $100,000 from the Reynolds Foundation, to give it an exceptionally large fund.

59. J.R. Heller, "Progress in Syphilis Control in the Southern States," *SMJ* 33 (July 1940): 681.

60. *Annual Report, S.C. Board of Health* (1938-39), 48, 47; (1939-40), 63, 73, 78; and (1941-42), 123-24; also Heller, "Progress in Syphilis Control, " 681.

61. *Annual Report, S.C. Board of Health* (1943-44), 25.

62. Parran and Vonderlehr, *Plain Words About VD*, 17-18.

63. Clarence Smith to Surgeon General, Oct. 4, 1941, file 0425, box 97, States, South Carolina, PHS General Classified Records, Group III.

64. Ibid.; also *Annual Report, S.C. Board of Health* (1942-43), 9, 86, 141.

65. *Annual Report, S.C. Board of Health* (1940-41), 91, 92, 131; (1941-42), 94; and (1942-43), 86, 141.

66. Ibid., (1944-45), 142; Abercrombie *Public Health in Georgia,* 171-2; *Biennial Report, N.C. Board of Health* (1944-46), 160.

67. *Annual Report, S.C. Board of Health* (1944-45), 142, 10-11; (1945-46), 146-47; and (1946-47), 23, 59; *Biennial Report, N.C. Board of Health* (1944-46), 60, 160; on syphilis decline, see Minutes of North Carolina State Board of Health, Jan. 30, 1947, VD—State Aid, State Health Director, Administrative Division, Papers North Carolina Board of Health.

68. Parran, "Public Health-the Base of Progress," *Opportunity* 6 (July 1928): 198-200.

69. James H. Conrad, "Health Services of the U.S. Children's Bureau, 1935-53," Ph.D. diss. (Ohio State Univ. 1974), 99-114; *Biennial Report, N.C. Board of Health* (1942-44), 59, for the growing pressures there; on the problem of follow-up care see "MCH" box 26, 1944, Director's General Administrative Records, Georgia Board of Health Papers.

70. Conrad, "Health Services U.S. Children's Bureau," 119-20; Georgia Division of Maternal and Child Health, box 26 and 27, 1944, Director's General Administrative Records. *Annual Report, S.C. Board of Health* (1942-43), 19, 39; and (1943-44), 17, 21, 153; "Children's Bureau" box 33, 1947, Director's General Administrative Records.

71.   *Biennial Report, N.C. Board of Health* (1942–44), 59.

72.   Conrad, "Health Services U.S. Children's Bureau," 118, 129; also Georgia Division of Maternal and Child Health, box 27, 1944, Director's General Administrative Records.

73.   Conrad, "Health Services U.S. Children's Bureau," 125; Georgia Division Maternal and Child Health, box 27, 1944, Director's General Administrative Records.

74.   Georgia Division Maternal and Child Health, box 27, 1944, Director's General Administrative Records.

75.   Ibid.; "Children's Bureau" box 33, 1947, Director's General Administrative Records.

76.   *Annual Report, S.C. Board of Health* (1944–45), 207; Cornely, interview, May 21, 1979.

77.   Conrad, "Health Services U.S. Children's Bureau," 111; *AJPH* 39 (1949):1579–80.

78.   "Hospital Boom," *Time* 48 (Aug. 26, 1946):70; also "More than 16,000,000 Entered Hospitals in 1944," *Science Newsletter* 47 (Aug. 7, 1945):217.

79.   "Hospital Boom," 70; also James Burrow, *AMA: Voice of American Medicine* (Baltimore: Johns Hopkins Univ. Press 1963), 237–51; on blacks' hospital insurance see Hospital Advisory Council minutes, 5, Nov. 14, 1951, box 16460, Executive Committee minutes, South Carolina Board of Health Papers, State Archives.

80.   "Our Health and Our Hospitals," *Collier's* 117 (May 11, 1946): 90.

81.   Lister Hill, "Health in America: A Personal Perspective," in *Health in America, 1776–1976* (Washington, D.C.: HEW 1976), 12–13; Marshall Pickens, in interview, Dec. 15, 1982, noted the Duke Endowment Influence.

82.   "The Hospital Survey and Construction Program," *AJPH* 39 (Nov. 1949):1468–69; "A Decade of Hill-Burton," *AJPH* 47 (Nov. 1957):1446–47; "Our Health and Our Hospitals," 90.

83.   "How to Get a Hospital," *U.S. News and World Report* 21 (Aug. 30, 1946):38–39, 46; "Health Centers and the Hill-Burton Act," *AJPH* 38 (Dec. 1948):1653–1655; "Progress Report," *AJPH* 39 (July 1949): 889; "Hospital Survey and Construction Program," *AJPH* 39 (Nov. 1949):1468.

84.   "Our Health and Our Hospitals," 90; Hill, "Health in America," 12–13.

85.   For a discussion of bed-to-population ratios see folder 1, Southern Regional Council study, "Progress in Southern States, 1946–48" box 18, SRC Papers, Trevor Arnett Collection; also "Hospital Survey and Construction Program," *AJPH* 39 (Nov. 1949):1468; Cornely commented on the state of Southern black hospitals in "Race Relations in Community Health Organization," *AJPH* 36 (Sept. 1946): 990.

86.   Cobb, "Progress and Portents for the Negro in Medicine," *Crisis* 55 (Apr. 1948): 117.

87.   "More Than 16,000,000 Entered Hospitals in 1944," 217.

88.   A few Southern states, such as Arkansas and Oklahoma, did give priority attention to blacks, and all gave first attention to their poorest rural areas. See SRC Hospital Study, folder 1. Nationwide, 53 percent of projects were in communities of less than 5000. See "A Decade of Hill-Burton," *AJPH* 47 (Nov. 1957):1146–47.

89. Jack Parker to Ben Wyman, Apr. 26, 1946, Apr. 1946 file, box 16459, container 21, Executive Committee minutes, South Carolina Board of Health Papers; also minutes, Palmetto Association, 1947.

90. "Relative Need Report," Apr. 27, 1948, June 1948 file, Executive Committee minutes, South Carolina Board of Health Papers; folder 1, SRC Hospital Study.

91. Minutes, Palmetto Assn., 1947.

92. Mar. 17, 1948, file, box 16451, Executive Committee minutes, South Carolina Board of Health Papers.

93. Lynch to Wyman, Feb. 16, 1948, Feb. 1948 file, Executive Committee minutes, ibid.; Lynch to Wyman, Mar. 17, ibid.

94. Minutes of Public Meeting, ibid.; also *Annual Report, S.C. Board of Health* (1948–49), 10.

95. J.D. Guess to Executive Committee, Sept. 7, 1948, Sept. 1948 file, box 16451, Executive Committee minutes, South Carolina Board of Health Papers.

96. "Relative Need Report, Revised, Apr. 27, 1948," June 1948 file, ibid.

97. Hospital Advisory Council Minutes, Dec. 7, 1949, file, ibid.; Advisory Council minutes, Mar. 14, 1950, pp. 7, 9, March 29, 1950, file, box 16460, ibid.

98. Ibid., 7.

99. Ibid. The decline in the already scarce number of black doctors was a regional problem. Hubert Eaton in his autobiography, *Every Man Should Try* (Wilmington, N.C.: Bonaparte Press, 1984), 197, reports the same situation in Wilmington.

100. Advisory Council minutes, Mar. 14, 1950, p. 7, Mar. 29, 1950, file, box 16460, Executive Committee minutes, South Carolina Board of Health Papers; also Project Report, Sept. 5, 1954, file, ibid.

101. "Relative Need Report, Revised, Apr. 27, 1948," June 1948 file, box 16451, ibid. Memo of Nov. 21, 1951, Nov. 21, 1951, file, box 16460, ibid.

102. Hospital Advisory Council minutes, Nov. 14, 1951, p. 5, ibid.

103. H.M. Fairley, memo, Nov. 21, 1951, ibid.; Wyman to Fairley, Nov. 24, 1951, ibid.

104. Executive Committee minutes, Jan. 23, 1952 and Aug. 13, 1952, ibid.

105. Hospital Advisory Council minutes, Nov. 14, 1951, p. 7, ibid.

106. Ibid., p. 16; Hospital Advisory Council minutes, p. 4, Jan. 23 and Aug. 13, 1952, ibid.

107. Hill-Burton projects, 1948–55, Sept. 15, 1954, file, ibid.

108. Advisory Council minutes, Oct. 15, 1952, and Nov. 19, 1952, ibid.; also Norman to Governor Byrnes, Sept. 24, 1952, ibid.

109. Hill-Burton projects, 1948–55, ibid.

110. R.C. Williams, "One Year of Operating Experiences of 17 Hospitals Built Under Hill-Burton," *Jour. of the Medical Assn. of Georgia* (Dec. 1952).

111. C.C. Spaulding to Gov. R.G. Cherry, Apr. 24, 1945, and W.S. Rankin to Spaulding, Apr. 25, 1945, Lincoln Hospital Records, North Carolina 32A, Duke Endowment Archives, Charlotte.

112. Marshall Pickens, interview, Dec. 15, 1982.

113. *The Jour. of Negro Education. Special Health Issue*, 331; also *JNMA* 42 (Mar. 1950):115.

114. "How to Get a Hospital," 38–39; also "Deny Hospital Fund Increase," *Architectural Record* 107 (May 1950):76.

115.   "A Decade of Hill-Burton," *AJPH* (Nov. 1957):1146–47.
116.   Freeman et al., *Handbook of Medical Sociology,* 354.
117.   W.H. Young, "Presidential Address," Apr. 22, 1941, minutes, Palmetto Association.
118.   "Public Services," *Negro Yearbook* (1952), 317–18.
119.   "President's Inaugural Address," *JNMA* 1 (Sept. 1958): 373.

Chapter 8

1.   A penetrating analysis of the Southern mill village and the cultural and civic sterility that characterized it is found in Tannenbaum, "The South Buries Its Anglo-Saxons."
2.   Morland, *Millways of Kent,* 176.
3.   Kohn, *Cotton Mills of South Carolina,* 23.
4.   Ibid.
5.   Stiles, *Hookworm Disease,* 26. Stiles was an enthusiast for mill development and sometimes overstated owner contributions to employee health. He did concede (p.31) that sanitary conditions in "so many mills" were terrible, but argued they were not as bad as on farms that mill hands left.
6.   Potwin, *Cotton Mill People,* 50–51; Stiles, *Hookworm Disease,* 25.
7.   Kohn, *Cotton Mills of South Carolina,* 77–78.
8.   Herring, *Welfare Work in Mill Villages,* 149, 161–63; also Kohn, *Cotton Mills of South Carolina,* 84. Kohn reports that physicians' clubs operated in about half the mills of South Carolina. On the use of clubs in other industries, see Burrows, *AMA: Voice of American Medicine,* 174.
9.   SMJ 9 (1916):32.
10.   Report of South Carolina Dept. of Agriculture, Commerce, and Industry (1917), 10.
11.   *The Cotton Textile Industry,* 597, 598.
12.   *Report of South Carolina Department of Agriculture, Commerce, and Industries* (1915), 1118 (hereafter *Report ACI*).
13.   Carlton, *Mill and Town,* 154–60.
14.   Herring, *Welfare Work in Mill Villages,* 19, 151, 155, 170; also Carleton, *Mill and Town,* 154–60.
15.   On the matter of resident nurses, see *The Cotton Textile Industry,* 596; *Annual Report, S.C. Board of Health* (1908), 3, 67; Herring, *Welfare Work in Mill Villages,* 20; Carleton, *Mill and Town,* 154–60.
16.   Tannenbaum, "The South Buries Its Anglo-Saxons," 211.
17.   Herring, *Welfare Work in Mill Villages,* 155–60.
18.   Ralph Barbare, "Community Welfare Work in the Mill Villages of Greenville, South Carolina," 75, M.A. thesis (Univ. of S.C., 1930).
19.   Herring, *Welfare Work in Mill Villages,* 177–81; Potwin, *Cotton Mill People,* 151–52.
20.   Herring, *Welfare Work in Mill Villages,* 177–81.
21.   Broadus and G.S. Mitchell, *The Industrial Revolution in the South* (Baltimore: Johns Hopkins Univ. Press, 1930), 236, 54, 56, 59; Broadus Mitchell's ambivalence

toward the South's textile leadership is discussed in Singal, *The War Within: From Victorian to Modernist Thought in the South, 1919–45*, 58–82.

22. Edward Sydenstricker et al., "Disabling Sickness Among the Population of Seven Cotton Mill Villages of South Carolina in Relation to Family Income," *Public Health Reports* 33 (Nov. 22, 1918), 2044, 2051.

23. Herring, *Welfare Work in Mill Villages*, 173, 160.

24. Ibid., 156.

25. Many mills never started nursing work. A 1927 North Carolina study found that more than 40 percent sponsored no health activity. A South Carolina examination of twelve Greenville mills in 1929 found about 50 percent declining to offer any health services. Herring, *Welfare Work in Mill Villages*, 174; Barbare, "Community Welfare Work," 71.

26. Etheridge, *Butterfly Caste*, 149, 146–48.

27. Ibid., 146–69.

28. Potwin, *Cotton Mill People*, 54; Herring, *Welfare Work in Mill Villages*, 165; Etheridge, *Butterfly Caste*, 184–85.

29. Herring, *Welfare Work in Mill Villages*, 196.

30. For North Carolina see "Public Health in North Carolina," 4; *Annual Report, S.C. Board of Health* (1918), 6, and (1930), 5–8; Potwin, *Cotton Mill People*, frontispiece (map of mill distribution in the Carolinas).

31. Herring, *Welfare Work in Mill Villages*, 154–55.

32. *Annual Report, S.C. Board of Health* (1923), 76–78, and (1929), 12; Etheridge, *Butterfly Caste*, 183–84.

33. Etheridge, *Butterfly Caste*, 196–203. In North Carolina the decline in pellagra deaths was even sharper, falling 85 percent between 1930 and 1940. See *Vital Statistics Rates in the U.S., 1900–40*, 353. Final conquest of the disease, however, awaited discovery of the specific anti-pellagra factor (nicotinic acid, or niacin, in 1937), plus an improvement in the South's economy, which got underway in WW II. See Etheridge, *Butterfly Caste*, 206–17.

34. Hugh William Close, interview, Dec. 7, 1979.

35. South Carolina Life Histories, A-3-13, no. 6.

36. W.G. Gaston to Mrs. Thomas O'Berry, Nov. 20, 1934, Correspondence by Counties, box 26, State Administrative Offices, State Administrative Records, ERA Papers.

37. Harry G. Wilson and Robert M. Brown, *An Evaluation of the Industrial Hygiene Problem in South Carolina* (Industrial Hygiene Div., 1938), 18, 19.

38. J.L. Wood, interview, Aug. 16, 1979. South Carolina Life Histories, A-3-13, no. 6; Lacy Wright, interview, Oct. 13, 1981.

39. Hughes, interview, Dec. 21, 1978.

40. See, for example, *Annual Report, S.C. Board of Health* (1934–35), 90–91.

41. "Societal Engineering," *Textile World* 73 (1928):3286.

42. Wilson and Brown, *Industrial Hygiene Problem in South Carolina*, 17.

43. S.C. Life Histories, file A-3-9, no. 11.

44. Ibid., file A-3-10, no. 2.

45. Ibid., files A-3-4, no. 2; A-3-19, no. 5; A-3-13, no. 6; A-3-14, no. 3; A-3-19, no. 11, A-3-16, no. 1.

46. Ibid., file A-3-19, no. 10.
47. Ibid., files A-3-4, no. 2, and A-3-16, no. 1.
48. Milam, "A Nutritional Survey of a Small N.C. Community," 406-7.
49. Ibid., 411.
50. Ibid.
51. Ibid., 410.
52. "Labor in the South," *Bureau of Labor Statistics Bull.*, no. 898 (1947), 99.
53. Ibid., 72-73, 110-111.
54. Ibid., 79, 72.
55. Morland, *Millways of Kent,* 83, 88, 145-46; also Francis Bell (retired v.p. of The Springs Corp.), interview, June 1983.

Chapter 9

1. Beverage in *Congressional Records — Senate,* 41, pt. 2 (Jan. 28, 1907), 1821, 59th Cong., 2d Sess.
2. See Kohn, "Health of the Help," *Cotton Mills of South Carolina,* 75; for background see Lewis Parker, "Condition of Labor in Southern Cotton Mills," *Annals of the American Academy of Political and Social Science* 32 (Mar. 1909): 354-62.
3. Kohn, *Cotton Mills of South Carolina,* 78, 75.
4. William P. Few, "The Constructive Philanthrophy of a Southern Cotton Mill," *Atlantic Monthly* 8 (Jan. 1909):87.
5. *Cotton Textile Industry,* 365-66; Southern industrial historian Tom E. Terrill, in interview, Oct. 2, 1984, estimated that the shift to fine goods manufacture was well underway by WW I.
6. Arthur Perry, "Preventable Death in Cotton Manufacturing Industries," *Bureau of Labor Statistics Bull.*, no. 251 (Oct. 1919), 95.
7. *Textile World* 55 (1919):40.
8. Economic statistics for the cotton textile industry for the post-war decade are found in *Fifteenth Census of the U.S.: Manufactures: 1929* ii (1933), 248.
9. "In the Cotton Mills," *The Survey* 43 (1920):493-94.
10. Gompers's address was reported in the *New York Times* (Sept. 13, 1921), 10:3; also see "No 'Murder,'" *Literary Digest* 21 (1921): 32.
11. Adelaid Smith, M.D., "Health Hazards in Textiles," *The Survey* 57 (1926):225-26.
12. For a sketch of the bishop see *Christian Century* 46 (1929): 1239-41; the churchmen's response is described in "The Southern Cotton Mills Reply," *New Republic* 55 (June 6, 1928):59-60.
13. *Textile World* 73 (1928):3281; also see *Literary Digest* 82 (1927):30.
14. *Textile World* 73 (1928):3281.
15. Ibid.
16. The shift of Northern mills continued steadily, except during World War II; by 1947 the South had 80 percent of all *cotton* textile workers and about 50 percent of employees in cotton and synthetics industries, combined ("Labor in the South," 72).

17. "Modern Trends in Mill Construction," *Textile World* 55 (1919):421.
18. *Textile World* 65 (1923):76; also "Why We Moved South," *America's Textile Reporter* 83 (1969):37.
19. Massachusetts's early start is discussed in Clark and Gage, "Hygienic Condition of the Air in Certain Mills," 1176; for a summary of Massachusetts's factory law see *Labor Laws and Factory Conditions* (1912), 446–50, vol. 19 of *Women and Child Wage Earners in the U.S.;* also see Rosen, *History of Public Health,* 426–27; for an example of the *AJPH* as a forum see Edward Clapper, "Child Labor and Public Health," *AJPH* 1 (1911):322–23.
20. *Conference of State and Territorial Health Officers* (1914), 74.
21. Ibid. (1914), 18, and (1916), 57; Robert Brown, interview, Jan. 23, 1979; difficulty with physician reporting is also noted in *Annual Report, S.C. Board of Health* (1935–36), 107; (1939–40), 210; and (1940–41), 174.
22. Ibid. (1935–36), 107; Brown, interview, Jan. 23, 1979.
23. Rankin to Messrs. Fuller and Reade, Mar. 22, 1913, box 27, personal file of Watson Smith Rankin, 1912–25.
24. Story (told by Alice Hamilton) is quoted in Ludwig Teleky, *History of Factory and Mine Hygiene* (New York: Columbia Univ. Press, 1948), x.
25. *Labor Laws and Factory Conditions,* 880–81, 1016–17, 1072–73; North Carolina had a factory inspection law, but as of 1915 the legislature had failed to provide funds for a factory inspector; see "Child Workers in North Carolina Cotton Mills," *The Survey* 33 (1915): 573.
26. *Labor Laws and Factory Conditions,* 880–81, 1016–16, 1072–73; for South Carolina see *Report ACI* (1915–35).
27. *Report ACI* (1917), 10; (1922), 14; and (1923), 11.
28. Ibid., (1925), 11.
29. Wilson and Brown, *Industrial Hygiene Problem in South Carolina,* 43–44.
30. Hazelhurst, "The Role of the State in Industrial Hygiene," *AJPH* 15 (1925):685.
31: *The State* (Mar. 23, 1932); also *Annual Report, S.C. Board of Health* (1932–33), 13; also see David G. Adams, "Report of Board of Health," *Jour. of the [S.C.] Senate* (Jan. 18, 1933), 56–72.
32. *Jour. of the [S.C.] Senate,* 57.
33. *Biennial Report, N.C. Board of Health* (1934–36), 33; *Annual Report, S.C. Board of Health* (1935–36), 11, 12, 107.
34. *Annual Report, S.C. Board of Health* (1934–35), 12, 13.
35. Asbestosis was first clearly identified by English physician W.E. Cooke in 1924, though South Carolina pathologist Kenneth Lynch followed closely behind in suggesting a connection between asbestosis-textile work and lung cancer. See Paul Brodeur, "The Magic Mineral," *The New Yorker* 44 (Oct. 12, 1968): 126; and James Hammond, interview, January 1979. Knowledge of silicosis goes back further. The disease was identified by 1870, and interest in it grew in the early 20th century. By 1930 its etiology had been worked out and experimental work begun on animals. Donald Hunter, *The Diseases of Occupations* (Boston: Little, Brown, 1962), 902–7, and *AJPH* 31 (1941): 190–91 S; for North Carolina initiatives see *Biennial Report, N.C. Board of Health* (1934–36), 32–33,

and (1938–40), 43; also "Program of Industrial Hygiene," June 15, 1935, Plan
and Policy File, Box 64, Subject File Inactive, 1910–65, Central Files, N.C.
Board of Health Papers; also Memo from H. Robert Coler to Dr. J.W.R. Norton, May 1955, ibid.

36.   R.R. Sayers, Memo for L.R. Thompson, July 31, 1935, file 0525–0875, box
51, State Board of Health, North Carolina, PHS Papers; also W.R. Draper
to James Hayne, Mar. 30, 1936, file 0875, box 98, General Classified Records,
Group III, States, 1936–44, South Carolina, ibid.; *Biennial Report, N.C. Board
of Health* (1934–36), 110. Also see Wilson and Brown, *Industrial Hygiene Problem
in South Carolina.*

37.   Ibid., 49, 3, 43–44.

38.   Ibid., 15–16, 17.

39.   J.J. Bloomfield et al., "A Preliminary Survey of the Industrial Hygiene Problem in the U.S.," *Public Health Bull.,* no. 259 (1940), 42–43.

40.   Wilson and Brown, *Industrial Hygiene Problem in South Carolina,* 46.

41.   *Biennial Report, N.C. Board of Health* (1934–36), 108.

42.   Wilson and Brown, *Industrial Hygiene Problem in South Carolina,* 49, 46.

43.   Louis Newman, "What Industry Expects of Industrial Hygiene Agencies,"
AJPH 43 (1933):330–33.

44.   *Annual Report, S.C. Board of Health* (1935–36), 107.

45.   Hammond, interview, Jan. 1979.

46.   *Biennial Report, N.C. Board of Health* (1934–36), 114.

47.   Fran Lynn, "The Dust in Willie's Lungs," *The Nation* 222 (1976): 209–12.

48.   Brown, interview, Jan. 23, 1979.

49.   Joseph A. Page and Mary-Winn O'Brien, *Bitter Wages: Ralph Nader's Study Group
Report on Disease and Injury on the Job* (New York: Grossman Publishers, 1973),
85; a West Virginia doctor charged that the truth about the cotton dust hazard had been withheld from Southern workers by public health officials, doctors, and industry (*Hearings Committee on Labor and Public Welfare,* 583).

50.   J.L. Wood and Mr. Smith, interview, Aug. 16, 1979.

51.   *Biennial Report, N.C. Board of Health* (1938–40), 127, and (1964–66), 63; only during WW II did North Carolina's board give attention to health conditions
in textiles, but at that time no notice was given to problems associated with
the milling process. See Textile Mills, Miscellaneous file, Occupational Health,
box 65, Subject files, Central files, N.C. Board of Health Papers.

52.   Brown, interview, Jan. 23, 1979.

53.   For a discussion of the connection between economic considerations and work-
place reforms in another industry, see William Graebner, "The Regulatory
State: Safety in the Coal Mines," in Graebner and Richards, eds., *The American
Record* 2 (New York: Knopf, 1982), 157.

54.   *Textile World* 100 (1950): 109; also James Townsend, "Medical Phases of Industrial Hygiene," *SMJ* 35 (1942):939.

55.   Ibid.; "Dermatitis Scare," *Textile World* 91 (1941):114; also see ibid. 94 (1944):107,
and "The Industrial Health Nurse Sells Health and Safety," ibid. 95 (1945):102–3.

56.   "The Workers Speak for Themselves," Textile Workers Union of America Re-

search Report, c. 1970, in Papers of the South Carolina Council for Human Rights, South Caroliniana Library.

57. William Gafafer, ed., *Manual of Industrial Hygiene* (Philadelphia: W.B. Saunders Co., 1943), 479.

58. Raymond Arsenault, "The End of the Long Hot Summer: The Air Conditioner and Southern Culture," *Jour. of Southern Hist.* 1 (1984): 602–5.

59. *Textile World* 91 (1941):74.

60. Ibid. 94 (1944):151; also ibid. 95 (1945): 131, 204; and "Pete and Bill," ibid., 177.

61. "In-plant Feeding Fortifies the Worker," ibid. 94 (1944): 60–62.

62. Ibid. 94 (1944): 140; also *Annual Report, S.C. Board of Health* (1943–44), 120–23.

63. *Textile World* 97 (1947): 4.

64. Division of Labor Standards, "Atmospheric Conditions in Cotton Textile Plants," *Special Bull.*, no. 18 (June 1945), iii, 5.

65. James Hammond, "Health Hazards in Cotton Textile Manufacture," (n.d. but c. 1947), 2, 3, speech before the Southern Safety Conference (copy in author's possession); also "Air Conditioning of Mills Requires Engineering Skill," *Textile World* 97 (1947):164.

66. *Annual Report, S.C. Board of Health* (1943–44), 120–23; also James Hughes, interview, Dec. 21, 1978.

67. J.L. Wood, interview, Aug. 16, 1979.

68. *Textile World* 97 (1947):120–21.

69. "Pacolet's New Air Conditioned Weave Room," ibid., 104 (1954):106–7.

70. See, for example, ibid. 94 (1944):151, and 100 (1952):118.

71. Ibid. 95 (1945):118.

72. Ibid. 97 (1947):129; also ibid. 98 (1948):112.

73. For labor problems in textiles see ibid. 95 (1945): 131, and 95 (1945):156.

74. "Atmospheric Conditions in Cotton Textile Plants," 17.

75. *Textile World* 98 (1948):4; also "Personnel Relations," ibid. 97 (1947): 116, and 98 (1948):4; also "The Union Again," ibid. 106 (1956):79; and "Cotton Textile Industry Launches Public Relations Program," ibid. 97 (1947): 149.

76. "Individual Employee is Center of Attention in 1950," ibid. 100 (1950):116; also ibid. 98 (1948):4; also "The Union Again," ibid. 106 (1956):79; and ibid. 47 (1947):115.

77. *Annual Report, S.C. Board of Health* (1957–58), 18; for the industry's view that AC was essential see *Textile World* 47 (1947):115; ibid. 105 (1955) to 108 (1960) contained no mention of AC. By 1960 mills without AC were described as backward. See ibid. 106 (1960):43.

78. *JAMA* 160 (1956):421; also *Hearings, Committee on Labor and Public Welfare,* 589.

79. Dr. Lee Heaphy, in interview, Nov. 12, 1979; Allen Sloan, in interview, June 22, 1978; and Logan Robertson in interview, June 19, 1979, alluded to the traditional disdain of private physicians for public health work; Alice Hamilton recalled the disdain of European occupational health specialists for American work. See Hamilton "Exploring the Dangerous Trades," *Atlantic Monthly* 171 (Feb. 1943): 119. Also see Suchman, *Sociology and the Field of Public Health,* 114.

80. Logan Robertson, interview, June 19, 1979.

81.   George Perkel, letter to author, June 8, 1983; also Bernard Coleman, "The Union Contract and Industrial Hygiene," *AJPH* 37 (1947): 1449–53; also "Air Conditioning in Textile Mills," TWUA paper (mimeographed, 1948).

82.   Page and O'Brien, *Bitter Wages,* xv, xi, xiv.

83.   Perkel, letter to author, June 8, 1983; also Emil Rieve (TWUA president), letter, Aug. 20, 1948, in "Air Conditioning in Textile Mills," 5, 6.

84.   No mention of such a bill appeared in *Jour. of the Sen. of the State of North Carolina* (1947, 1949) or in *Jour. of the House of the State of North Carolina* (1947, 1949).

85.   *The State* (Feb. 9, 1949); also ibid. (Apr. 15, 1949).

86.   *Biennial Report, N.C. Board of Health* (1948–50), 190; between 1948 and 1950, hygienists visited 215 plants and examined over 6000 endangered workers. By 1960 silicosis was reduced to one case in 400 according to the *Biennial Report* for 1960–62 (79); also Memo from Dr. Coler to Dr. J.W.R. Norton (May 1955), 2.

87.   *Biennial Report, N.C. Board of Health* (1950–52), 156.

88.   Memo from Dr. Coler to Dr. J.W.R. Norton (May (1955), 2; also Textile Mills, Miscellaneous file, box 65, Subject File Inactive, 1910–65, Central Files, N.C. Board of Health Papers; *Biennial Report, N.C. Board of Health* (1948–50), 190.

89.   Memo from Dr. Coler to Dr. J.W.R. Norton (May 1955), 1, 3.

90.   *Biennial Report, N.C. Board of Health* (1956–58), 101; also W.L. Wilson to J.W.R. Norton, Feb. 19, 1964, Plan and Policy file, box 64, Subject File Inactive, N.C. Board of Health Papers. Textiles was not one of the areas identified as needing attention.

91.   Hammond, "Hygiene Problems," 67–68.

92.   Reid, interview, Oct. 29, 1979.

93.   For explanations of the abolition of the industrial hygiene division, see Sinway Young, interview, July 12, 1979 (Labor's view); Dr. G.E. McDaniel, interview July 16, 1979 (rivalry with Wyman and budget problems); also see *Annual Report, S.C. Board of Health* (1950–51), 17, 96.

94.   *Annual Report, S.C. Dept. of Labor* (1957–58), 17.

95.   Ibid. (1954–55), 10.

96.   Francis Bell, interview, June 20, 1983.

97.   Johnson and Miller, *Occupational Diseases,* 392–93; "How Noise Control Affects You," *Textile World* 119 (1969):46.

98.   *Hearings, Committee on Labor and Public Welfare,* 982–83; Coley Lynch, interview, Sept. 10, 1979; "How Noise Control Affects You," 46.

99.   Ibid., 45.

100.   *Hearings, Committee on Labor and Public Welfare,* 589; Nixon's national-unity phase is discussed in Jonathan Schell, *The Time of Illusion* (New York: Vintage Books, 1976), 17–27.

101.   George Perkel, letter to the author, June 8, 1983; Francis Bell, interview, June 20, 1983.

Chapter 10

1. Several later American studies recount the British work of the 1920s. See H. Leonard Bolen, "Byssinosis — Report of Two Cases and Review of the Literature," *Journal of Industrial Hygiene and Toxicology* 25 (1943):215 (hereafter, *Jour. Ind. Hyg.*); Rollo Brittain et al., "The Health of Workers in a Textile Plant," *Public Health Bull.*, no. 207 (1932), 19; and B.H. Caminita et al., "Affections of the Respiratory Tract in Individuals Exposed to Cotton Dust," 19, 43–44; an early warning of "so-called byssinosis" was sounded by George M. Kober, M.D., "Industrial Hygiene," 484–85.
2. Caminita, "Affections of the Respiratory Tract," 43–44; Brittain, "Health of Workers," 19; Bolen, "Byssinosis," 222.
3. Caminita, "Affections of the Respiratory Tract."
4. Ibid.
5. Brittain "Health of Workers"; also J.J. Bloomfield and W.C. Dreessen, "Exposure to Dust in a Textile Plant," *Public Health Bull.*, no. 208 (1933); "Health of Workers in Dusty Trades," *Monthly Labor Review* 27 (1928):712–15.
6. Brittain, "Health of Workers," 20.
7. Bloomfield and Dreessen, "Exposure to Dust," 22–23.
8. Brittain, "Health of Workers," 14–15.
9. Ibid.
10. Ibid., 1; on comparative dust measurements see C.B. McKerrow and R.F.S. Schilling, "A Pilot Inquiry into Byssinosis in Two Cotton Mills in the U.S.," *Journal of the American Medical Association* 177 (1961): 108 (hereafter *JAMA*).
11. Both North Carolina and South Carolina created divisions of industrial hygiene within their respective boards of health in 1936, and in South Carolina, at least, cotton dust did gain some recognition as a "hazardous substance"; see Wilson and Brown, *Industrial Hygiene Problem in South Carolina*, 43–44.
12. Robert Brown, interview, Jan. 23, 1979.
13. Wilson and Brown, *Industrial Hygiene Problem in South Carolina*, 51–52.
14. James Hughes, interview, Dec. 21, 1978.
15. M.F. Trice, "Card-Room Fever," *Textile World* 90 (1940):68.
16. Ibid.
17. *Monthly Labor Review*, 52 (1941):629–30.
18. Caminita, "Affections of the Respiratory Tract," 42.
19. *Monthly Labor Review*, 629–30; also see *JAMA*, 116 (1941): 156; Caminita "Affections of the Respiratory Tract," 19.
20. *Monthly Labor Review*, 630, provided the first report of the British law.
21. Bolen, "Byssinosis," 220.
22. Ibid., 215.
23. Wayne Ritter and Morris Nussbaum, "Occupational Illness in Cotton Industries, II: Chronic Respiratory Problems," *Jour. Ind. Hyg.* 27 (1945): 49, 50–51.
24. Ibid., 47, 50–51.
25. *Textile Research Journal* 15 (1945):167–68.
26. "Atmospheric Conditions in Cotton Textile Mills, " *Jour. Ind. Hyg.* 28 (1946):19.

27. Ibid.
28. Caminita, "Affections of the Respiratory Tract, " 23.
29. Ibid.
30. Ibid.
31. Ibid.
32. Attention is properly put on Southern mills because by 1947 80 percent of all cotton textile workers labored in the South. See "Labor in the South," *Bureau of Labor Statistics Bull.*, no. 898 (1947), 70.
33. Trice, "Card-Room Fever," 68; also see "Byssinosis," *Textile Research Journal* 17 (1947):654.
34. In 1947 James Hammond spoke on "Health Hazards in Cotton Textile Manufacture," before textile groups and before the Southern Safety Conference.
35. Hugh William Close, interview, Dec. 7, 1979.
36. Hammond, "Health Hazards," 2.
37. Liston Pope, *Millhands and Preachers* (Chapel Hill: Univ. of North Carolina Press, 1942), 148; also see Tannenbaum, "The South Buries Its Anglo-Saxons," 205–15.
38. Hugh Close interview.
39. James Hammond, interview, Jan., 1979; Allen Sloan, in interview, June 22, 1978, noted that as late as the middle 1950s the Medical College of South Carolina curriculum offered no instruction on occupational medicine. Also Logan Robertson, interview, June 19, 1979; Leo Heaphy, interview, Nov. 12, 1979.
40. "Queries and Minor Notes," *JAMA* 146 (1951):607–8.
41. R.S.F. Schilling, "The Epidemiology of Byssinosis—Adventure and Misadventure," *Jour. of Occupational Medicine* 1 (1959): 33–38.
42. Ibid., 34.
43. Ibid., 35–36.
44. Ibid., 33; on the rising number of awards see "Parliament," *The Lancet* (1953):1042. Between 1942 and 1947 only 30 cotton workers were judged totally disabled and therefore eligible for compensation. By 1953 byssinosis awards had risen to 106. Also see R.S.F. Schilling, "Byssinosis in Cotton and Other Textile Workers," *The Lancet* (1956): 261–65; *JAMA* 160 (1956): 1167.
45. Schilling, "Epidemiology of Byssinosis," *Jour. of Occup. Med.* 1 (1959):36–37.
46. C.B. McKerrow and R.F.S. Schilling, "A Pilot Inquiry into Byssinosis," *JAMA* 177 (1961):850–53.
47. R.S.F. Schilling, "Worldwide Problems of Byssinosis," *Chest* 79S (1981 Supplement):4S.
48. Leo Heaphy, interview, Nov. 12, 1979; Schilling, letter to author, Oct. 10, 1981.
49. McKerrow and Schilling, "A Pilot Inquiry into Byssinosis," 110, 111. The two researchers used a different breathing test than they had employed earlier. Now, they measured the volume of air that a worker could expel in 0.75 seconds. A standard test today, it is referred to as the F.E.V. (forced expiratory volume).
50. McKerrow and Schilling, "A Pilot Inquiry into Byssinosis."
51. Schilling, "Worldwide Problems of Byssinosis," 4S-5S.
52. *Hearings, Committee on Labor and Public Welfare*, 586.

53.   T.F. Forbes (Georgia Textile Manufacturers Assn.) to Gentlemen, June 4, 1964, copy in possession of author.

54.   Arend Bouhuys et al., "Byssinosis in Cotton Textile Workers: Respiratory Survey of a Mill with Rapid Labor Turnover," *Annals of Internal Medicine* 71 (1969):257-69.

55.   Leo Heaphy, interview, Nov. 12, 1979.

56.   *Biennial Report, N.C. Board of Health* (1962-64), 80, 81, and (1964-66), 63.

57.   John Lumsden, interview, Jan. 10, 1982; Bouhuys, "Byssinosis in Carding and Spinning Workers. Prevalence in the Cotton Textile Industry," *Arch. of Environ. Health* 19 (1969): 670; *Hearings, Committee on Labor and Public Welfare,* 973; *Biennial Report, N.C. Board of Health* (1966-68), 69.

58.   Bouhuys, "Byssinosis in Carding and Spinning Workers," 670-71. Lumsden, interview, Jan. 10, 1982.

59.   Bouhuys, "Byssinosis in Carding and Spinning Workers," 670; *Biennial Report, N.C. Board of Health* (1966-68), 69. By the late 1970s Bouhuys had hiked his estimate of the number with severe lung impairment to 35,000, a figure which included both active and retired mill workers. See Bouhuys et al., "Epidemiology of Chronic Lung Disease in a Cotton Mill Community," *Lung* 154 (1977):167-86.

60.   "Research Seeks to Define Causes of Industrial Respiratory Ills," *Textile World* 119 (1969):47.

61.   "It All Depends," *America's Textile Reporter* 83 (1969); front cover, 27.

62.   Ibid., 27. John Lumsden, interview, Jan. 10, 1982. The Burlington Survey involved over 10,000 workers in about a score of mills. See Harold Imbus and Moon Seek, "Byssinosis: A Study of 10,133 Textile Workers," *Arch. of Environ. Health* 26 (1973):183-91.

63.   "Research Seeks to Define Causes," *Textile World* 119 (1969): 47. Charles McLendon, interview, Oct. 13, 1981.

64.   "Here Come the Image-busters," *Textile World* 118 (1968): 57; also "Is the Textile Industry Losing Its Cool?" ibid., 118 (1968):47.

65.   "Is the Textile Industry Losing Its Cool?" 47.

66.   *Textile World* 116 (1966): 53-54.

67.   Ronald C. Davis, "Diagnosis, Brown Lung; Prognosis, Misery," *Textile World* 122 (1972):49-50; ibid., 119 (1969): 34; ibid., 121 (1971):31.

68.   Ibid., 121 (1971):31.

69.   The continued uncertainty about byssinosis among medical scientists is reflected in the James Merchant article in Robert W. Crandell and Lester B. Lane, eds., *The Scientific Basis of Health and Safety Regulation* (Washington, D.C., 1981), 71-91, and in the National Research Council study, *Byssinosis: Clinical and Research Issues* (Washington, D.C., 1982). The federal standards issue and the matter of preventive measures in industry are taken from Rachel Scott, *Muscle and Blood* (New York: Dutton, 1974), 200-03; Kaye H. Kilburn et al., "Byssinosis: Matter from Lint to Lungs," *Amer. Jour. of Nursing* 73 (1973); and Jerry Reeves (South Carolina Dept. of Labor), interview, Dec. 10, 1984.

70.   Davis, "Diagnosis, Brown Lung," 39.

Chapter 11

1. Black activist doctors like Montague Cobb held their colleagues in low
    esteem when it came to medical-rights issues. For example, see Cobb,
    "Special Problems in the Provision of Health Services for Negroes," *Jour.
    of Negro Education,* 341–45; on the earnings of black doctors see *JNMA* 43
    (Mar. 1951).
2. W.E.B. DuBois et al., "Statement on the Denial of Human Rights to Minori-
    ties" (n.d., but c. 1948), Countee Cullen-Harold Jarman Collection, Atlanta
    University.
3. Paul Cornely, "Report of the Health Consultant for Charleston, South Caro-
    lina," Community Relations Project of the National Urban League (unpub-
    lished, n.d., but c. 1947), copy at the Waring Medical History Library, Medi-
    cal Univ. of South Carolina.
4. Arnall to Abercrombie, Dec. 5, 1944, "Governor" file, box 27, Director's General
    Administrative Records, Record Group 26-2-3, Georgia Board of Health
    Papers; also Abercrombie to Arnall, Dec. 7, 1944, ibid.
5. "Integration Battlefront," *JNMA* 49 (1957):353.
6. Montague Cobb, "The Crushing Irony of Deluxe Jim Crow," *JNMA* 44
    (1952):387; also Cobb, "Medical Care and the Plight of the Negro," 201–11.
7. Awareness of racism's international implications is discussed in Lillian Smith,
    Killers of the Dream, 4–7, and John P. Roche, *The Quest for the Dream* (Chicago:
    Quadrangle Books, 1969), 236. Parran's outlook is shown in "Public Health—
    The Base of Progress," *Opportunity* 23 (1945):196; for earlier studies of race rela-
    tions and medical discrimination see Cobb, "Progress and Portents for the
    Negro in Medicine" and Cornely, "Race Relations in Community Health
    Organization."
8. Cobb, "Progress and Portents," 118.
9. *Modern Hospital* 76 (1951): 49.
10. Cobb, interview, May 22, 1979; also Cobb, "Removing Our Health Burden"
    Crisis 53 (1946):268.
11. *Jour. of Negro Education,* 341; also Cobb, "Progress and Portents," 107.
12. *Jour. of Negro Education,* 341.
13. Ibid., 340; also "The 17th of May," *JNMA* 46 (1954):270.
14. Cobb, "Progress and Portents," 116.
15. Cobb, "No Room for Money-Changers in the Temple of Aesculapius," *JNMA*
    42 (1950):112–13.
16. Cobb, "The Los Angeles Convention," *JNMA* 47 (1955):408; Cobb, "Medical
    Care and Plight of Negro," 201–11.
17. Cobb, "Medical Care and Plight of Negro," 201–11.
18. Cobb recalled those divisions in *JNMA* 47 (1955):408.
19. Ibid., 48 (1956):272.
20. *JNMA* 45 (1953):333–39 outlines the national health program of the NAACP;
    also see "Support the Fighting Fund for Freedom," *JNMA* 46 (May 1954):192–3.
    Also *JNMA* 47 (1955):198 on success of the membership drive.

21. *JNMA* 48 (1956):272; for an example of an "Integration Battlefront" column see *JNMA* 49 (1957):198–201.

22. Dwight Anderson to Dr. Morris Weintraub, May 18, 1949, Peter Marshall Murray Papers.

23. Ibid.

24. "The AMA Resolutions," *JNMA* 42 (1950):324.

25. Ibid.

26. *JNMA* 53 (1961):524.

27. Minutes, Palmetto Assn., 1951.

28. "Charleston County Medical Assn. Admits Negro Physicians," *JNMA* 45 (1953):153–4; also minutes, Palmetto Assn., 1952.

29. "Presidential Address," minutes, Palmetto Assn., 1955.

30. "Charleston Co. Medical Society Admits Negro Physician," 153–54; also see *JNMA* 45 (1953):75, and 46 (1954):284–5; Cornely, "Segregation and Discrimination in Medical Care in the U.S.," *AJPH* 46 (1956):1077–78.

31. *JNMA* 49 (1957):115, and 50 (1958):223.

32. *Raleigh News and Observer* (May 10, 1961).

33. James L. Curtis, *Blacks, Medical Schools, and Society* (Ann Arbor: Univ. of Michigan Press, 1971), 17–18, discusses the decrease in black doctors; also see *Jour. of Negro Education,* 205.

34. Minutes (undated, but c. 1946), box 4, Medical Training for Negroes, Medical Care Commission Papers, North Carolina Div. of Archives and History.

35. Minutes (Sept. 18, 1946), box 1, ibid.

36. Ibid., 2; on the 70 percent figure see minutes (undated), ibid.; on Meharry's origination of the plan see minutes (Apr. 9, 1946), ibid.

37. Cobb, "Progress and Portents," 116; also Cobb, "Open Medical Schools," *JNMA* 41 (1949):129.

38. *JNMA* 45 (1953):337.

39. "Open Medical Schools," 129.

40. "Slow Grinding Mills," *JNMA* 47 (1955): 49–50; also see "Medical Deans and Discrimination," *JNMA* 42 (1950): 42–3.

41. McFall in *Negro Yearbook* (1952), 317–18.

42. *Jour. of Negro Education,* 344.

43. Minutes, Palmetto Assn., 1952; also see ibid., 1951; Emory Univ. was one of the few hold-outs that desegregated before 1967: Rebecca C. Dillard, letter to author, Sept. 24, 1984. The 1967 acceptances are confirmed in Ann Donato, letter to author, July 24, 1984 (South Carolina); Charles B. Johnson, letter to author, Aug. 15, 1984 (Duke); Velna G. Watts, letter to author, Aug. 16, 1984 (Bowman Gray); and James E. Carter III, letter to author, Aug. 28, 1984 (Georgia).

44. Cornely, "Race Relations in Community Health Organization," 990.

45. Cornely, "Trend in Racial Integration in Hospitals in the U.S.," 10.

46. Advisory Council, minutes, Nov. 14, 1951, box 16460, South Carolina Executive Committee, minutes; also *JNMA* 45 (1953): 284–85.

47. "A Decade of Hill-Burton," 1145–47.

48.   Robert Toomey, interview, Nov. 19, 1979; also "Self-Study Report," SRC Papers.
49.   Henry Collier, interview, May 20, 1982.
50.   B.D. Mayberry to William F. Andrews, Oct. 29, 1962, Memorial Hospital of Wake Co., North Carolina, file 92C, Duke Endowment Papers.
51.   Andrews to Pickens, Dec. 29, 1961, ibid.
52.   *Raleigh News and Observer* (July 14, 1961).
53.   Ranzy Weston, interview, May 20, 1982.
54.   Toomey interview.
55.   Weston interview.
56.   Mayberry to Andrews, Oct. 29, 1962.
57.   Cornely, "Trend in Racial Integration in the U.S.," 9.
58.   Cornely, "Segregation and Discrimination in Medical Care in the U.S.," 1079.
59.   "Imhotep Conference Proceedings: Local Area Reports," *JNMA* 49 (1957):198, 198–201; also ibid., 212–13, 351–42; also Simkins, interview, Dec. 14, 1979.
60.   Kirshner, in interview, Sept. 20, 1985, said that Gen. Omar Bradley, Veterans' Affairs Administrator until 1948, was the catalyst of the directive. Determined to make needed changes in the VA system, he also believed that if blacks were good enough to fight for their country they were also deserving of equal medical care. The only facility exempt from the order was Tuskegee's all-black hospital. Ferguson in interview, Aug. 12, 1985, recalled that the VA dispatched human relations specialists to local hospitals to prepare staff for upcoming integration.
61.   *Jour. of Negro Education,* 342.
62.   Cobb, "The Crushing Irony of Deluxe 'Jim Crow,'" 387.
63.   "Memphis NAACP Branch Rescinded Endorsement of Negro Hospital," *JNMA* 44 (1952):314; on Columbia see "Negro Voters Defeat Hospital Bond Issue," ibid. 45 (1953):438; on St. Petersburg see ibid 52 (1960):216. The involvement of the NAACP is shown in Cobb, "The National Health Program of the NAACP," 337; "Support the Fighting Fund for Freedom," 192–93, and *JNMA* 46 (1954): 274; also Thurgood Marshall to Cobb, Sept. 7, 1954, in ibid. 46 (1954):439, 441.
64.   "Proceedings, Imhotep National Conference on Hospital Integration," *JNMA* 49 (1957):199.
65.   Ibid., 198.
66.   Ibid., 213.
67.   Ibid., 199, 200.
68.   Cornely, "Segregation and Discrimination in Medical Care in the U.S.," 1081.
69.   Cornely, "Segregation and Discrimination in Medical Care in the U.S.," 1086; see also "Rann Holds Imhotep Planning Meetings," *JNMA* 53 (1961): 646; also "New Weapons," *JNMA* 47 (1955):342.
70.   "Jairtts Bill to End Hospital Discrimination under Hill-Burton Act," *JNMA* 54 (1962): 120–23.
71.   "Rann Holds Imhotep Planning Meetings," *JNMA* 53 (1961):645.
72.   Ibid.; also see "An Appraisal of the Imhotep Conference," *JNMA* 49 (1957):181; "Imhotep Conference Proceedings," ibid., 50 (1958):225.
73.   Davis is quoted in "Proc., Imhotep National Conference," 198; for Cobb's re-

marks, see "An Appraisal of the Imhotep Conference," 181; Cornely's views are in "Imhotep Conference Proc.," *JNMA* 49 (1957): 233.

74. "Second Imhotep Conference on Hospital Integration," *JNMA* 50 (1958): 381, 383; see also, "NAACP Resolutions on Health, 1959," *JNMA* 51 (1959):399, 401.

75. "Fourth Imhotep National Conference," *JNMA* 52 (1960):283–86; see also, "Call for Nationwide Formation of Local Imhotep Committees," ibid. 53 (1961):83; the recollection of black and white physicians and hospital administrators was that the NAACP played little or no role in hospital integration in the late 1950s and 1960s; see interviews with Toomey, Nov. 19, 1979; I.D. Newman, Dec. 17, 1979; and Marshall Pickens, Dec. 15, 1982.

76. Cornely and Emory Rann, "The Imhotep Conference—Why a Conference?" *Crisis* 70 (1963):275.

77. Cornely, interview, May 14, 1979.

78. Cobb interview.

79. Paul H. Douglas, *In the Fullness of Time: The Memoirs of Paul H. Douglas* (New York: Harcourt, Brace, Jovanovich, 1971), 298.

80. Cobb interview.

81. Collier interview.

82. Toomey interview.

83. Glenn, interview, Jan. 26, 1983.

84. The account that follows of the *Cone* case is taken from *Federal Reporter* 2d series, 323 (St. Paul: West Publishing Co., 1964), 959–77.

85. Ibid., 970.

86. *Orangeburg Democrat* (Jan. 19, 1965).

87. Ibid.; Timmerman had resigned by the time of the re-trial.

88. *Charleston News and Courier* (Feb. 21, 1965).

89. Ibid. (April 21, 1965); when Columbia's Richland Memorial opened on a totally integrated basis in 1972 there was a large flight of white patients, causing financial instability; see Diane Berry, interview, Feb. 8, 1983. White abandonment of Southern public hospitals has continued, posing the problem of gathering sufficient revenues from paying patients to offset the load of no-pay and part-pay patients, many of whom are black and whose government insurance covers only a part of costs (Blease Graham, interview, Mar. 31, 1983). Also see Charlotte LeGrand, letter to editor, *The State* (Apr. 3, 1983).

90. *Orangeburg Democrat* (Jan. 15, 1965).

91. Ibid.

92. *The State* (July 7, 1965); for the state mental hospital investigation, see *Orangeburg Democrat* (Feb. 7, 1965).

93. Dr. Frank Owens, interview, Feb. 2, 1978; on the pace of Columbia Hospital integration, see Graham, interview, Mar. 31, 1983.

94. Owens interview.

95. Toomey interview.

96. Pickens, interview, Dec. 15, 1982.

97. Ibid.

98. Owens interview.

99. *Columbia Record* (June 13, 1969); as late as 1969 the NAACP complained strongly
     that HEW was certifying hospitals which continued to discriminate against
     both black patients and physicians. See *JNMA* 61 (1969):357.
100. "NAACP Health Resolutions," *JNMA* 61 (1969):357.
101. *Raleigh Times* (July 12, 1966).
102. *Raleigh News and Observer* (Aug. 1, 1970).
103. *Charlotte Evening Post* (July 30, 1968); the story of the integration of "New Roper"
     is taken from *United States v. Medical Society of South Carolina,* 298 F Supplement
     145 (1969).
104. The Roper Hospital case proved influential, not only in pushing segregated
     private hospitals to integrate but also in adding strength both to the 1964 law
     and to the federal courts' ability to implement it. See, for example, *Gray v.
     Greyhound Lines, East* in *Federal Reporter,* 2d series, 545 (1976), 176; and *United States
     v. Medical Society of South Carolina* in *American Law Reports, Federal* (1972), 734. The
     publication of the Roper case in *American Law Reports* was one sign of the im-
     portance which lawyers and judges assigned to it.
105. Collier interview. Ranzy Weston, in 1982 interview, noted that black doctors
     were not pushing very strongly for desegregation.
106. Collier interview. Weston reported the same sort of sudden reversal.
107. Weston interview.
108. Ibid.; Pickens interview.
109. Pickens interview.
110. Anne Bishop (Duke Endowment), in letter to the author, Feb. 28, 1983, re-
     ported that in 1964 the Endowment was aiding 15 black hospitals in the Caro-
     linas; but that by 1976 only 1 of them (L. Richardson Memorial in Greens-
     boro) was still operating; also see "Hospital Survives Alone," *Greenville [North
     Carolina] Daily News* (Aug. 29, 1982). Not all change was loss: Lincoln Hospital
     (Durham) survives in spirit, today, as a modern $5 million health center, thanks
     largely to the efforts of long-time Lincoln surgeon Charles Watts (Watts, in-
     terview, May 17, 1984).
111. On the Columbia Hospital see *The State* (Aug. 30, 1967) and *Columbia Record*
     (Mar. 4, 1972). Waverly remains (1986) a derelict, unused structure, still for sale.
112. Collier interview.

Chapter 12

1. *Annual Report, S.C. Board of Health* (1945–46), 52.
2. "Sick for Justice," Special Issue of *Southern Exposure* 6 (Summer 1978): 106. The
   Special reprinted portions of the magazine's first issue of 1947.
3. Godfrey Hodgson, *America in Our Time* (New York: Vintage Books, 1976), 446–62,
   discusses the emergence of a permanent, two-tiered, two-class black society
   in America. Hodgson believes the lower tier may contain nearer 50 percent
   of American blacks.
4. *Jour. of Negro Education,* 3; also see Parran, "Public Health—The Base of Progress," 196.

5.   Cornely, "Race Relations in Community Health Organizations," 984-85.

6.   Ibid., 986-87.

7.   Ibid., 991, 986.

8.   Charleston Welfare Council, "Charleston Looks at Its Services for Negroes" (1947) C-2.

9.   *Jour. of Negro Education*, 340.

10.   Ibid.

11.   Minutes of the Executive Secretary, July 12, 1952, box 1, North Carolina Medical Care Commission Papers.

12.   C.V. Reynolds, Annual Report to North Carolina Medical Society, in *Biennial Report, N.C. Board of Health* (1942-44), 89.

13.   *Annual Report, S.C. Board of Health* (1945-46), 156, and (1951-52), 312; also *Biennial Report, Georgia Board of Health* (1947-49), 106; also *Biennial Report, N.C. Board of Health* (1946-48), 105. North Carolina stopped tabulating by race in 1948.

14.   Miriam Cadwallader, interview, Mar. 28, 1979.

15.   Ibid.

16.   *Annual Report, S.C. Board of Health* (1969-70), 140, 144.

17.   For example, *Annual Report, S.C. Board of Health* (1949-50), 159, reported 27,950 new and old Negro maternity patients, while the total number of live and still-born babies in calendar year 1949 was 27,840, according to *Vital Statistics of the U.S.* (1949).

18.   "Nurse Midwife Maude Callan Eases Pain of Birth, Life and Death," 144.

19.   Dugdale Baird, "Social and Economic Factors Affecting the Mother and Child," *AJPH* 42 (1952):516-20.

20.   Statements based on data from *Vital Statistics of the United States, 1945*, part 1 (1947), and *Vital Statistics of the United States, 1957*, 1 (1959).

21.   Statements based on data from *Vital Statistics, 1945*, part 1, and *Vital Statistics, 1957*, 1. Also see Robert D. Grove and Alice M. Hetzel, *Vital Statistics Rates in the United States, 1940-1960* (Washington, D.C.: HEW, 1968) for fetal death statistics for 1957.

22.   Statements based on data from *Vital Statistics, 1945*, part 1, and *Vital Statistics, 1957*, 1. Also see Charles Williams, Jr., et al., "Community Health Services for Children in 8 Selected States," *AJPH* 38 (1948):81.

23.   Bureau of the Census, Current Population Reports, *The Social and Economic Status of the Black Population in the U.S.: An Historical View* (Washington, D.C., n.d. but c. 1980), x.

24.   Ibid., 28; Bureau of the Census, "Characteristics of the Population of South Carolina," *1970 Census of Population*, vol. 1, part 42 (1970), 126, 135.

25.   Statements based on data from *Vital Statistics, 1957*, 1, and *Vital Statistics, 1969*, 2: *Mortality*, part B (Rockville, Md.: National Center for Health Statistics, 1973). Also Grove and Hetzel, *Vital Statistics Rates, 1940-60*.

26.   *Jour. of Negro Education*, 425.

27.   George Peabody College, *Spartanburg County Schools: A Survey Report* (1949), 60, 93-94; *Annual Report, S.C. Board of Health* (1955-56), 73; Gov. James F. Byrnes of South Carolina initiated a program of Negro school construction in the

early 1950s in hopes of avoiding desegregation. See Byrnes, *All in One Lifetime* (New York: Harpers, 1958), 407–09.

28. A new attitude of the part of Georgia state officials toward Negro TB is revealed in Herman Talmadge to "Dear Friend," Dec. 23, 1949, Governor file, box 49, Director's General Administrative Records, Georgia Board of Health Papers. For the increasing attention in South Carolina see reports of TB control division and of TB sanatorium in *Annual Report, S.C. Board of Health* (1960–61) through (1969–70), but esp. (1963–64), 187. National vital statistics show that Negro TB mortality declined 41 percent from 1910–20, but that it dropped 47 percent in the 1940s and 80 percent in the 1950s. See *Social and Economic Status of the Black Population,* and Grove and Hetzel, *Vital Statistics Rates, 1940–60.*

29. *Annual Report, S.C. Board of Health* (1963–64), 187, and (1965–66), 170–74; also Grove and Hetzel, *Vital Statistics Rates, 1940–60* (1945) and *Statistical Abstracts of the U.S.* (1940 and 1950) for data to estimate 1945 rates and their subsequent decline.

30. *Annual Report, S.C. Board of Health* (1948–49), 155–57.

31. *Vital Statistics of the U.S.* (1945) and 1 (1970) for decline in syphilis deaths; though seldom a cause of death, gonorrhea, which caused sterility in females, was also on the rise; in 1968 South Carolina reported 9285 cases among blacks and 2025 among whites. Those totals were up from 1783 and 304 cases in 1962. See *Annual Report, S.C. Board of Health* (1967–68), 221, and (1962–63), 227.

32. Statements based on data from *Vital Statistics, 1949*, part 1, and *Vital Statistics, 1969*, 2; also *Vital Statistics, 1970*, 1.

33. For a comparison of 1940 and 1970 mortality roles, see *Social and Economic Status of the Black Population,* 124–25; for Southern states see *Vital Statistics, 1945*, part 1, and *Vital Statistics, 1970*, 1; on byssinosis, see ch. 10.

34. Statements based on data from Grove and Hetzel, *Vital Statistics Rates, 1940–60.*

35. Ibid.

36. Ibid.; also see, Federal Security Administration, *State Life Tables: 1949–51* 1, 2 (Washington, D.C., 1957), HEW, *State Life Tables: 1959–61* 1, 2 (Washington, D.C., 1966), and HEW, *State Life Tables: 1969–71* 1, 2 (Washington, D.C., 1975).

37. *Annual Report, S.C. Board of Health* (1967–68), 8, and (1969–70), 27.

38. "South Carolina," *Hearings before the Select Committee on Nutrition and Human Needs of the U.S. Senate,* part 4 (Feb. 18–20, 1969), 1220, 90th Cong., 2d Sess. and 91st Cong., 1st Sess.

39. Raymond Wheeler, *The Problem of Hunger and Poverty in North Carolina* (Univ. of North Carolina School of Social Work, 1968), 1; the best book on the hunger crusade, by journalist Nick Kotz, is *Let Them Eat Promises* (Englewood Cliffs, N.J.: Prentice Hall, 1969).

40. James Donnelly, "Who Knows, Who Cares," *America* 120 (1969): 250–52.

41. *Hearings, Select Committee on Nutrition,* part 4, 1214.

42. Ibid.

43. Wheeler, *The Problem of Hunger,* 1.

44. Elizabeth B. Drew, "Going Hungry in America: Government's Failure," *Atlantic* 122 (Dec. 1968):55.

45. Robert Coles and Harry Huge, "FBI on the Trail of the Hunger Mongers," *New Republic* 159 (Dec. 21, 1968):11–13.

46. *U.S. News and World Report* 64 (May 27, 1968):45.

47. Robert Coles and Harry Huge, "Strom Thurmond Country," *The New Republic* 159 (Nov. 30, 1968):19.

48. Recollection of the author who attended the meeting (and was vice president of the organization), which took place in fall, 1969.

49. Nick Kotz, "The Politics of Hunger," *The New Republic* 101 (Apr. 30, 1984): 22; *Readers Guide to Periodical Literature* for 1968 and 1969 listed 45 articles under the heading "Nutrition Problems, U.S."; also see Coles and Huge, "FBI on the Trail," 11–13; and Alan Mermann, "When Did We See Thee Hungry," *Christian Century* 86 (1969):473, 374.

50. For a critique of existing food supplement programs see Drew, "Going Hungry in America," 54–55, and Paul Matthias's testimony in *Hearings, Select Committee on Nutrition,* part 4, 1261; also ibid., part 1 (Dec. 17–19, 1968), 161; also Kotz, "Politics of Hunger," 22.

51. Drew, "Going Hungry in America," 58; Donnelly, "Who Knows, Who Cares," 251, notes the hold-up of Schaefer's study and his eventual report to the McGovern Committee.

52. Quoted in F. Glen Lloyd, "Finally Facts on Malnutrition in the U.S., " *Today's Health* 47 (1969):33, 31.

53. "The Face of Hunger," *Newsweek* 73 (Feb. 3, 1969):66. Schaefer's final report confirmed his earlier one. See Schaefer, *Ten State Nutrition Survey, 1968–70* (Washington, D.C.: HEW, 1972).

54. *Hearings, Select Committee on Nutrition,* part 4, 1165.

55. Ibid.

56. *Hearings, Select Committee on Nutrition,* part 1, 154.

57. Ibid., 155.

58. Ibid., part 4, 1218.

59. Ibid., 1232.

60. Milam, "A Nutritional Survey of a Small North Carolina Community."

61. *Hearings, Select Committee on Nutrition,* part 4, 1215, 1216.

62. Poindexter, "Handicaps in the Normal Growth and Development of Rural Negro Children," 1049. Also *Annual Report, S.C. Board of Health* (1951–52), 312.

63. Margaret Hickey, "Rural Community Works for Better Health. West Edgecombe, North Carolina," *Ladies' Home Journal* 71 (Mar. 1954):29; also see "Down with Parasites," *The Rotarian* 82–83 (June 1953):40–41, and "Florida Schools Tackle Vitamin Deficiency," *Practical Home Economics* 34 (Oct. 1955): 48–49.

64. Ernest E. Neal, "Health Is What You Think It Is," *Nursing Outlook* 2 (1954):478–80.

65. "Racially Rationed Health," *Time* 95 (Apr. 6, 1970):90–91; one close study of blacks' economic status in the 1970s put 42 percent of that population in the poor and near-poor category. See Robert Engs, "A Bold, Necessarily Ambiguous Appraisal of the Condition of Blacks," *The Chronicle of Higher Education* (Oct. 14, 1975): 17.

66. Edward A. McSweeney and Paul W. Matthias, *Sick Unto Death* (Columbia: South Carolina Council for Human Rights, 1972), 19.

67. John Ransom to Dr. John Stillwell, Nov. 5, 1949, Hospital Services — Last Half of 1949 file, box 41, Director's General Administrative Records, Georgia Board of Health Papers; *Hearings, Select Committee on Nutrition,* part 4, 1170.

68. Hearings, Select Committee on Nutrition, part 4, 1179.

69. Ibid., 1224.

70. Quoted in *South Today* 2 (May 1971):6; also see Drew, "Going Hungry in America," 55.

71. Drew, "Going Hungry in America," 55; also Carl Rowan and David Mazie, "Hunger. It's Here, Too," Reader's Digest 93 (Nov. 1968):127-34.

72. *Hearings, Select Committee on Nutrition,* part 4, 1224.

73. Mermann, 476.

74. *U.S. News and World Report* 64 (June 3, 1968):24; for confirmation of the nutritional inadequacy of commodity surplus and school lunch programs, see Kotz, *Let Them Eat Promises,* 49-50, 58.

75. Mermann, "When Did We See Thee Hungry?" 476.

76. See for example, "When You Turn on the Tap," *New Republic* 171 (Nov. 30, 1974):8, which notes that health officials move effectively against known water contaminants (eg., bacteria) but are ineffective in the case of carcinogenic pollutants.

77. Shaeffer's study noted all these as common defects. See "One-sixth of a Nation," *Time* 93 (Jan. 31, 1969): 74.

78. *Hearings, Select Committee on Nutrition,* part 4, 1224.

79. Paul Starr, *Social Transformation of American Medicine,* charts the historic dominance of public medicine by organized private medicine and traces the relationship to the early 20th century. See esp. pp. 21-22, 27, 28, 181-89.

80. South Carolina health officer Wyman not only took private physicians' side against national health insurance but felt that private medicine should be in control of public health work. See *Annual Report, S.C. Board of Health* (1944-45), 12; on the reorganization of S.C. and N.C. boards see (for S.C.) I.D. Newman, interview Dec. 17, 1979, and *Annual Report, Dept. of Health and Environmental Control of South Carolina* (1973-74), 6, 8; for N.C. (which also reorganized in 1973), see *Session Laws of North Carolina,* General Assembly, 1st sess. (1973), 621, and Mrs. Elnora Turner, letter to author, June 28, 1984. In Georgia, new governor Jimmy Carter reorganized his state's board in 1972 against strong opposition from the state medical society. See Betty Glad, *Jimmy Carter: In Search of the White House* (New York: Norton, 1980), 169.

81. Margaret Setin to George Mitchell, Sept. 18, 1947, folder 1, Southern Regional Council Papers.

82. *Biennial Report, N.C. Board of Health* (1950-52), 103, 104.

83. *Biennial Report, N.C. Board of Health* (1958-60), 48.

84. In North Carolina, for example, cancer detection clinics were open without regard to income, whereas in South Carolina indigency was the primary test; see *Biennial Report, N.C. Board of Health* (1950-52), 180, 182.

85. *Annual Report, S.C. Board of Health* (1953-54), 8, 43.

86. *Annual Report, S.C. Board of Health* (1950-51), 204-5 and (1945-46), 190.

87. *Vital Statistics of the U.S.,* 1 (1970); also see *Annual Report, S.C. Board of Health* (1969-

70), 58; compared to the large proportion of public patients who were black, only 7 percent of private cancer patients were; for the racial break-down for public and private physicians see ibid. (1965–66), 152. Also Cancer Control Division report, ibid. (1946–70).

88. *Annual Report, S.C. Board of Health* (1967–68), 47, 64.

89. Ibid. (1965–66), 252 and (1967–68), 47, 64.

90. Gatch appeared at a 1969 public meeting in Columbia, along with Richland Co. health officer John Preston. Gatch's introductory remark was that had he known who else would be on the program he would not have accepted. Recollection of the author, who set up the meeting.

91. Coles and Huge, "Strom Thurmond Country," 19; Bynum Shaw, "Let Us Now Praise Dr. Gatch," *Esquire* 69 (June 1968):111.

92. Shaw, "Let Us Now Praise Dr. Gatch," 108.

93. *Biennial Report, N.C. Board of Health* (1968–70), 42; *Hearings, Select Committee on Nutrition,* part 1, 182–95.

94. Phillip Lee to the Honorable Charles Percy, Dec. 24, 1968, in *Hearings, Select Committee on Nutrition,* part 4, 1174.

95. *Annual Report, S.C. Board of Health* (1968–69), 294. North Carolina's board of health began to respond to the hunger question a year earlier. See *Biennial Report, N.C. Board of Health* (1968–70), 42.

96. *Annual Report, S.C. Board of Health* (1968–69), 299.

97. On negotiations for a reduction in food stamp costs, see Joseph Clark in *Hearings, Select Committee on Nutrition,* part 1, 10; *New Republic* 57 (July 15, 1969):4; Drew, "Going Hungry in America," 56, 57. "In 1968 Freeman lowered the cash payment requirement to $.50 per person per month for the totally indigent. See *U.S. News and World Report* 66 (June 3, 1968): 22.

98. *U.S. News and World Report,* 22.

99. Ibid., 24.

100. "Hunger and Malnutrition: HEW Says Nation Must Know More and Do More," *Science* 160 (1968):1433; also *U.S. News and World Report,* 22.

101. "Making Hunger a Has-been," *Todays Health* 40 (Nov. 1969): 38–40.

102. See relevant entries in *Readers' Guide to Periodical Literature* (1970–73).

103. "TRB," *New Republic* 167 (May 16, 1970): 6; also Ernest F. Hollings, "The Reality of American Hunger," *The Nation* 212 (1971):521, 518–20.

104. Ibid., 521.

105. Quoted in "Frontline: Bread, Butter, and Politics," (ETV Program, June 4, 1984); also Kotz, "Politics of Hunger," 22. Kotz sees a resurgence of hunger in the 1980s, but this time among the "blue-collar" middle class.

106. *Biennial Report, N.C. Dept. of Social Services* (1970–72), 42; Charles Dunn before *Hearings, Select Committee on Nutrition,* part 1, 187, and I.D. Newman before ibid., part 4, 1236; also *Annual Report, S.C. Board of Health* (1969–70), 106.

107. *South Today* 3 (July-Aug., 1971): 8.

108. Ibid.

109. *Sick Unto Death,* 47. Dr. Charles Watts, in interview, May 22, 1984, noted that the low welfare cut-off level was a problem in North Carolina, as well.

110. *Sick Unto Death,* 47, 27. At the very time South Carolina was rejecting supple-

mental Medicaid programs, state leaders were proudly touting their multi-million dollar reserve fund and the grade-A credit rating that it brought them from N.Y.C. banks.

111. *Annual Report, S.C. Board of Health* (1968–69), 249; *Sick Unto Death,* 13, 24.

112. *Sick Unto Death,* 1–2.

113. Ibid., 2, 13; also *Annual Report, S.C. Board of Health* (1968–69), 249.

114. Eaton, *Every Man Should Try,* 231–32.

115. Ibid., 249; the Dept. of Human Resources was a new state agency subsuming the old boards of health and public welfare. It was the welfare division which was largely responsible for Medicaid administration (as it was in South Carolina).

116. Ibid., 232, 238. The refusal of physicians to participate in Medicaid was a nationwide problem, though Southern doctors opted out at a greater rate apparently. One study noted that by 1974, 40 percent of California doctors had reduced or were about to reduce their involvement, while in Michigan, active physician participation had declined from 83.5 to 68.3 percent between 1974 and 1977. Dewey D. Gardner et al., "Factors Affecting Physician Participation in a State Medicaid Program [Mississippi's]," *Medical Care* 17 (Jan. 1979): 43–58.

117. Eaton, *Every Man Should Try,* 240.

118. Ibid., 248.

119. Ibid., 236, 244, 249.

120. *Sick Unto Death,* 26.

121. "Sick for Justice," 105.

122. "Foreword," *Sick Unto Death.*

123. Ibid.

124. Ibid.; the statistical summary was in North Carolina Dept. of Human Resources, letter to author, Dec. 14, 1983. Both black men and women had a lower rate for chronic obstructive pulmonary disease, while only Negro women died less frequently from auto accidents.

Bibliographic Essay

I. The Health of Southern Blacks

The search for sources relating to twentieth century Southern health history, especially the history of the region's poor, is burdened by a number of handicaps, some a function of Southern history itself. Except for its response to hookworm (a project generously funded by outsiders), the South was generally not known for any significant public concern for the well-being of its lower orders. Such exclusion applied particularly to blacks, but it also carried over to the region's textile hands, who were left in the care (and keeping) of virtually autonomous mill owners. As a result, until federal funding beefed up Southern health programs in the 1930s, there was little official record of what their health histories had actually been. Nor were there any rich collections of private material (published or unpublished) relating to health history, as there were in the fields of political, diplomatic, ethnic, and women's history. Not only does health lack the drama needed to attract chroniclers, but both physicians and their poor patients have, for quite differing reasons, left scant record of their service or their suffering. Moreover, the record that has survived is mostly the drab, fleshless prose of bureaucrats—with their preference for statistical arrays over the human story.

But historians, after all, should not expect easy access to their subject, and if they but cast their nets broadly enough and keep alert for the unlikely source, materials on Southern health history can be found in some abundance. The health and medical history of Southern blacks (patients and physicians) is more easily documented than that of mill hands. Among published, primary materials, black periodicals offer an obvious and useful record. *Opportunity*, the organ of the National Urban League, which dates from 1922, took a continuing interest in health conditions of blacks. Al-   365 though started earlier (1909), the NAACP's *Crisis* was less attuned to health issues. However, Montague Cobb's "Progress and Portents of the Negro in Medicine" (1948) is valuable for its look at historic barriers confronting black doctors. *The Negro Yearbook,* begun in 1910 by sociologist Monroe C. Work of Tuskegee Institute, contains demographic and professional data not available elsewhere, though Work's statistics are, understandably, not always accurate. Also useful are the reports of the Atlanta University Conferences on the Negro, a set of which is on file at the University's Robert Woodruff Library. Of particular importance, especially for the post-World War II era, when Cobb held its editorship, is the *Journal of the National Medical Association.* Its "Medical History" and "Integration Battlefront" sections reflected the impact of racism and of the civil rights movement on black health history. It also published the proceedings of the "Imhotep Conferences" (1958–63), which provided a record of the movement and showed the need to desegregate Southern hospitals.

Probably the single most important periodical source, however, is the 1949 "Special Health Issue" of the *Journal of Negro Education.* Written by leading black and white professionals, the articles deal with virtually every health problem facing the black patient and physician in the 1930s and 1940s. "White" periodicals are occasionally a good source for information about black health conditions. White physicians and health officers were no less intrigued by the "Negro question" than any other group of Southerners, and their interest is particularly evident in the *American Journal of Public Health* (established 1910) and only slightly less so in the *Southern Medical Journal* (1907). In the pre–World War I era, parent organizations of both periodicals gave large attention to the health crisis among Southern urban Negroes. The March 1915 issue of the *AJPH* provides a veritable treasure of information on black health conditions, as well as a look at how white health officers defined their duty to the submerged race. The *AJPH* also from time to time opened its pages to black physicians. M.O. Bousfield's 1934 challenge to the APHA, Hildrus Poindexter's 1938 piece on malnourished black children, and several key articles by Howard's Paul Cornely in the 1940s and 1950s appeared in the *AJPH.*

General periodicals are also helpful, particularly in pursuing topics in the area of social medicine. The developing hospital crisis of World War II, which culminated in passage of the Hill-Burton Act, was mirrored in the pages of *Time, Newsweek, Collier's,* and *U.S. News and World Report.* When hunger exploded as an issue in the late 1960s, the periodical press—notably liberal journals like *Atlantic Monthly, The New Republic,* and *Christian Century*—again provided all the ugly details, as well as a running account of Congress's response. But the most thorough description of American hunger is found in the *Hearings Before the Select Committee on Nutrition and Human*

Needs of the U.S. Senate (1968–69) or, as popularly known, the McGovern Committee.

There are, in fact, a number of government publications, which give useful insights and information about the state of health of black Southerners. Of primary value are two volumes of historical statistics on the Negro prepared by the Census Bureau, *Negro Population in the United States, 1790–1915* (Washington, D.C., 1918) and *Negroes in the United States, 1920–32* (Washington, D.C., 1932). Besides vital statistics each volume contains a wealth of related social data, such as housing costs, occupation, size of families, and literacy rates. Also helpful, particularly in comparing black and white mortality rates, are two volumes of general historical statistics, *Vital Statistics Rates in the United States, 1900–40* (Washington, D.C.: U.S. Census Bureau, 1943) and the companion volume, *Vital Statistics Rates in the United States, 1940–1960* (Washington, D.C.: HEW, 1968).

Newspapers help fill in other parts of the story. Black papers are useful in revealing community concern about health issues. Besides national papers such as the Chicago *Defender* and Baltimore's *Afro-American,* each Southern state also had its black weeklies. Many were short-lived, but one which remained in print from the 1920s to the 1940s and gave large coverage to health matters such as TB, VD, and maternal and infant health was South Carolina's *Palmetto Leader*. White papers, too, like *The [South Carolina] State,* reported on black health and medical matters. But their coverage was so occasional that unless a scholar knows exactly what to look for, investment of time is hardly warranted. North Carolina's State Archives (Raleigh) have a useful index file for several state papers, including the *Raleigh News and Observer,* and while the file is nowhere near complete, it does span most of the twentieth century, and a fair amount of relevant information can be garnered quickly there.

Unpublished papers and manuscript collections bearing on black health history are few and far between. But because of that, those few are all the more valuable. The "Life Stories" collected by interviewers with the Federal Writers Project (WPA) contain occasional goldmines of information. The South Carolina narratives, in the South Caroliniana Library of the University of South Carolina, hold testimonies of a black midwife, a public health nurse, and several black tenants who talked about their many ills. The General Administrative Records of the director of the Georgia Board of Health contains files of correspondence with various Georgia governors (beginning in the 1930s), which proved unexpectedly rich. In those files are scores of letters from plain folk, white and black, appealing for help in handling one or another kind of health crisis. The letters provide a measure of changing health conditions, as well as an index of the effectiveness of government agency responses.

In the collections of the National Archives are papers of similar use-fulness. The papers of the United States Public Health Service and the health-related materials in the FERA Subject Files, the WPA Records, and the NYA Papers allow a glimpse at black (and white) health conditions on a region-wide basis in the midst of the Depression. One of the voluminous holdings of black materials in the Robert Woodruff Library of Atlanta University is the Neighborhood Union Collection. Spanning the 1905 to 1935 era, these papers document Negro ill-health in a major Southern city. Another holding, the Southern Regional Council Archives, was still being processed when the present study was underway, but even so it was useful in documenting health matters in the post–World War II South. Finally, mention should be made of the collections at the Waring Medical History Library at the Medical University of South Carolina (Charleston). Particularly useful are the *Sanitary Survey of the Rural Portion of Charleston County* (unpublished 1921) and the report prepared by the National Urban League and the Charleston Welfare Council, "Charleston Looks at Its Services for Negroes" (unpublished, 1964). Together, the two studies permit a glimpse at Negroes' changing health status over a quarter century.

There are few published memoirs of health professionals, but four deserve mention for insights they gave. Leon Banov's *As I Recall: The Story of the Charleston County Health Department* (Columbia: R.L. Bryan Co., 1970) recounts the work of a highly regarded local health officer in the pre–1940s era. Hubert A. Eaton's, *Every Man Should Try* (Wilmington, N.C.: Bonaparte Press, 1984) recounts the life of a N.C. medical rights activist of the post-war period and provides an especially helpful critique of Medicaid. Septima Clark's *Echo in My Soul* (New York: Dutton, 1962) contains sections dealing with health problems among Sea Island blacks. And while only an extended article, the *Life Magazine* feature, "Nurse Midwife Maude Callan Eases Pain of Birth, Life and Death" (Dec. 3, 1951), provides an intimate look at maternal and child health, sanitation, and housing problems.

With so few surviving written recollections, taped interviews with participants in Southern health reform efforts took on added value. Collected from the body of black health professionals and lay leaders, these oral histories dealt not only with physician and health agency responses to illness and death but with problems from the point of view of the victim as well. Among the most useful interviews (all to be deposited in the South Caroliniana Library archives) were those conducted with Septima Clark, Maude Callan, Modjeska Simkins, Dr. L.W. Long, and I. Dequincey Newman of South Carolina; Dr. Paul Cornely of Howard; Dr. Charles Watts of North Carolina; and Miriam Cadwallader, Dr. Ranzy Weston, and Dr. Henry Collier of Georgia.

Finally, among sources for black health history are a number of secondary works. James Young, "Malaria in the South" (Ph.D. diss., University of North Carolina, 1972), and Henry Frank Farmer, "The Hookworm Eradication Program in the South, 1909–225" (Ph.D. diss., University of Georgia, 1966), focus on the whole Southern population but contain relevant information on blacks as well. James Summerville, *Educating Black Doctors: A History of Meharry Medical College* (University: Univ. of Alabama Press, 1983), tells the story of one of the two major institutions for training black physicians for the South. James Jones's *Bad Blood: The Tuskegee Syphilis Experiment* (New York: Free Press, 1981) provides basic information on VD and recounts the infamous Tuskegee trials. James Stokely and Wilma Dykeman's biography of FSA administrator Will Alexander, *Seeds of Southern Change* (New York: Norton, 1962) highlights the economic malaise which underlay such health problems and also portrays the efforts of one New Deal agency to correct them. Finally, several monographs are helpful in gaining an understanding of how the poor respond to illness. Among them are Edward Suchman, *Sociology and the Field of Public Health* (N.Y.: The Russell Sage Foundation, 1963), and John Kosa and Irving Zola, eds., *Poverty and Health: A Social Analysis* (Cambridge, Mass.: Harvard Univ. Press, 1975). The list of key secondary works is admittedly short, but that is merely a sign of how much remains to be done in the area of black health history.

II. The Health of Southern Textile Workers

When one turns to sources bearing on the health of Southern mill workers one finds far less primary material. For the pre–1930s era, at least, it is almost as if a conspiracy of silence has been plotted to stifle discussion of the issue. What sources do turn up are mostly research publications of federal bureaus, plus a handful of studies undertaken by Northern state agencies. Health professionals themselves were not much attuned to industrial hygiene in that early era. When Alice Hamilton attended an international industrial health conference on the eve of World War I, she saw how far behind Americans were—the European view of American work, in fact, was that it did not exist.

But that was a distortion, and the most useful study for the present investigation was the multi-volumed *Report on the Condition of Women and Child Wage-Earners in the U.S.* (Washington 1911). A project of the U.S. Labor Bureau (and published as a Senate Document), several volumes speak to the issue of health among textile hands. Three of the most valuable are *Family Budgets of Typical Cotton Mill Workers* (v. 16), *Causes of Death Among Women and Child Cotton Mill Operatives* (v. 14), and Charles Wardell Stiles's *Hookworm Disease Among Cotton Mill Operatives* (v. 17).

The *American Journal of Public Health* (established 1910) is also an indispensable source, containing a large number of reports by individual professionals, plus some key investigations by Northern state boards of health, such as Massachusetts's "A Study of the Hygienic Condition of the Air in Certain Textile Mills," *AJPH* 3 (Nov. 1913). Beginning in the post–World War I period, *Public Health Reports* and *Public Health Bulletins* are often a mine of information, especially in regard to pellagra among mill hands and the relation between income and health. From the 1920s, the *Bulletins of the Woman's Bureau* (U.S. Dept. of Labor) contain a number of useful studies of morbidity among textile workers, in particular "Lost Time and Labor Turnover in Cotton Mills" (no. 52, 1926).

Then in the 1930s, as Southern states created public agencies (with Social Security money) to investigate hygiene problems, information began to appear on a regular basis. The South Carolina study of Robert Brown and George Zerbst, *An Evaluation of the Industrial Hygiene Problem in South Carolina* (Industrial Hygiene Div., 1938), provides the statistics needed to measure the past performance of mill owners in guarding employee health. In North Carolina, M.F. Trice's investigation, "Card Room Fever" in *Textile World* 90 (Mar. 1940), is an early warning of byssinosis. Trice's piece should be examined alongside "A Nutritional Survey of a Small North Carolina Community," *AJPH* 32 (Apr. 1942), which suggested that health problems of equal magnitude were found in mill villages, as well.

Not all sources emphasized problems. Textile management and their spokesmen stressed improvements in health, often picturing mill villages and mills as settings where good health was enhanced, not destroyed. August Kohn's *Cotton Mills of South Carolina* (Columbia: Dept. of Agriculture, Commerce and Industry, 1907) was a classic defense of mill paternalism. *Textile World,* the industry's leading trade journal, also made its appearance in the pre–World War I era, and while emphasizing management's position, it was not unwilling to concede the existence of health problems. In the pre–World War II period most of its attention was directed at improvements in mill villages. After the war the central focus was on problems (and solutions) within the mill itself. Though *Textile World* is a good source for management's outlook on health, its usefulness is severely limited by the absence of a yearly index to its bulky volumes. Further, any use of *Textile World* for the pre-1940s should be balanced by a reading of Harriett L. Herring, *Welfare Work in Mill Villages* (Chapel Hill: Univ. of North Carolina Press, 1929), which offers a more objective look at how well owners were doing by their hands.

One problem which management shied clear of, until quite recently, was byssinosis. The primary sources for the history of that problem began their appearance in the 1930s and were found either in government publications or in various industrial hygiene journals. Among the former the earliest important source is Bloomfield and Dreessen, "Exposure to Dust in a Textile Plant," *Public Health Bulletin,* no. 208 (July 1933), which was published in response to earlier British findings of an alarming amount of byssinosis in their mills. By far the most useful source, however, is B.H. Caminita et al., "A Review of the Literature Relating to Affections of the Respiratory Tract in Individuals Exposed to Cotton Dust," *Publish Health Bulletin,* no. 297 (1947).

The major occupational health journals to give attention to the disease were *The Journal of Industrial Hygiene and Toxicology* and *Archives of Environmental Health.* The *Journal of the AMA,* too, ran occasional pieces, most notably McKerrow and Shilling's study "A Pilot Inquiry into Byssinosis" 177 (Sept. 1961). State boards of health, especially North Carolina's, began investigations of "brown lung" in the late 1960s. Particularly useful is the 1966–68 *Biennial Report of the North Carolina Board of Health.* Congress, too, was awakened by the rising public clamor over byssinosis, and in the *Hearings before the Senate Subcommittee on Labor of the Committee on Labor and Public Welfare* (1969–70), Sen., 91st Cong., 1st and 2d Sess., the historian finds much useful testimony by all parties to the dispute. Finally, in the 1970s, industry was forced to take note of the problem, too, and the record of its action is best charted in *Textile World,* especially in its special byssinosis issue, 119 (Dec. 1969).

As with the black health issue there are few collections of unpublished papers bearing on textile health problems. The Will Lou Gray papers at the South Caroliniana Library contain a box of "life stories" by students in Miss Gray's "Opportunity School" (a literacy project), which occasionally offer an intimate look at ill health and economic hardships among Carolina mill families. Much more useful along that line are the narratives collected by interviewers for the WPA Federal Writers Project. The North Carolina FWP collection in Chapel Hill contains a large number of textile sketches, detailing health problems inside the mills, while the South Carolina collection (South Caroliniana Library) has accounts of ill health in village and family settings. Finally, the papers of the South Carolina Council for Human Rights has a slim file of material generated by the Textile Workers Union of America, in which actual byssinosis victims relate their experiences.

Just as they did for the subject of black health history, personal interviews generated a rich store of material relating to the history of occupational health. Every important textile city (Columbia, for example) has a union headquarters and often a "Brown Lung Association" chapter, which can provide contacts with retired mill hands. Among the more valuable tapes produced by the present project (and deposited at the South Caroliniana Library with other tapes) were those of interviews with Coley Lynch and J.L. Wood of South Carolina and Lacy Wright of North Carolina. On the other side of the issue, the author also found corporate executives willing to discuss industrial health. Two of the most valuable interviews were with executives at Springs Mills Corporation (Lancaster, South Carolina) and Burlington Industries (Winston Salem). Those on the medical side were helpful, too. Occupational health consultants Leo Heaphy and Logan Robertson provided an interesting (and mostly critical) perspective on the profession's attitude toward occupational health. John Lumsden took part in several byssinosis studies of the North Carolina Board of Health, and his comments revealed the relationships between the regulators and the regulated—as did an interview with former South Carolina occupational health physician James Hughes. Two especially important interviews were those conducted with Robert Brown and James Hammond, hygienists with the South Carolina Board of Health in the 1930s and 1940s. They dealt with a range of topics, including the accommodation which regulatory agencies had to make with an economically (and politically) powerful industry.

In contrast to most other kinds of material, secondary sources are more abundant for the textile health story than for black history, perhaps because of the recent vogue of occupational health. A useful background to the story (which leaned strongly to the workers' side) is Rachel Scott's *Muscle and Blood* (New York: Dutton, 1974). Also helpful, but stridently anti-business, is Joseph Page and Mary Winn O'Brien's *Bitter Wages: Ralph Nader's Study Group Report on Disease and Injury on the Job* (New York: Grossman Publishers, 1973). The human toll associated with a long-ignored problem like byssinosis is graphically presented in Mimi Conway, *Rise Gonna' Rise: A Portrait of Southern Textile Workers*. Two older views of the world of Southern mill hands, which see employer arrogance at the base of most problems, are Frank Tannenbaum, "The South Buries Its Anglo-Saxons," *Century Magazine* 116 (June 1923), and Broadus Mitchell, *The Industrial Revolution in the South* (Baltimore: Johns Hopkins Univ. Press, 1930). The latter piece needs to be balanced by a reading of the Mitchell chapter in Daniel Singal, *The War Within: From Victorian to Modernist Thought in the South, 1919 to 1945* (Chapel Hill: Univ. of North Carolina Press, 1982).

Several of the illnesses that took a large toll in mill villages have also had their chroniclers. Elizabeth Etheridge's *The Butterfly Caste* (Westport, Ct.: Greenwood, 1972) examines pellagra, and John Ettling's *Germ of Laziness* (Cambridge: Harvard Univ. Pres, 1981) focuses on hookworm. Also useful are Young's dissertation, "Malaria in the South" and Farmer's dissertation, "The Hookworm Eradication Program." A recent study of Southern urban, middle-class attitudes toward the mill worker, which includes a chapter on village health, is David Carlton, *Mill and Town in South Carolina, 1880–1920* (Baton Rouge: Louisiana State Univ. Press, 1982). Finally, Liston Pope's

Mill Hands and Preachers (Chapel Hill: Univ. of North Carolina Press, 1942) treats the alliance between mill owners and the Southern church, revealing another aspect of the mill worker's subjection.

III. The Response of the Health and Medical Establishments

As might be imagined, the surviving records of health care *providers* is far more voluminous than that generated by the victims of ill health. Published reports of state departments of health and labor were a major foundation for the present study, for they, alone, covered its entire chronological span. For South Carolina, the *Annual Reports of the South Carolina State Board of Health* contained a synopsis of yearly events as well as a record of each administrative division (such as the VD and Local Health divisions). But equally valuable are the occasional unguarded comments, which allow the scholar to look behind the official position to discover motives and attitudes more closely shaped by race and class. The *Reports of the South Carolina Dept. of Agriculture, Commerce, and Industry* and (after 1935) the *Reports of the South Carolina Dept. of Labor,* while documenting concern and programs for the health of the work force, are more useful in showing those agencies as defenders of the interests of the state's textile industry.

In North Carolina the basic source for public health programs for blacks and (after 1935) mill hands is the *Biennial Reports of the North Carolina State Board of Health.* Besides services, the North Carolina *Reports* also reveal a state agency less inhibited by concerns of race and class and more willing to challenge the power of organized doctors in the state. The *Biennial Reports of the Georgia State Board of Health* reflect a state health agency whose historic performance (except for local health work and industrial hygiene, which were organized very late) fell somewhere between those of the two neighboring states.

Useful supplements to the official reports are two memoir/histories by high-ranking health officials in Georgia and North Carolina, T.F. Abercrombie's *A History of Public Health in Georgia, 1733–1950* (Atlanta: Georgia State Board of Health, n.d. but c. 1960) and B.E. Washburn's *A History of the North Carolina Board of Health* (Raleigh: North Carolina State Board of Health, 1966). Both accounts contain information not available elsewhere, though their claims about the impact of public health programs need to be discounted a bit. A memoir which examines those public programs more critically and provides an inside look at a major private foundation active in the South is Edwin Embree, *Investment in People: The Story of the Julius Rosenwald Fund* (New York: Harper and Row, 1949). Finally, a source that permits an evaluation of Southern state programs against others in the region and nation is the *Transactions of the Conference of State and Territorial Health Officers* (first issued in 1902). These reports, published by the PHS, also permit a view of federal health activity in the pre-New Deal era and give an idea of the rôle of the national service in shaping state programs.

In addition to published reports there is also a large volume of unpublished material bearing on the role of state and national health agencies. The National Archives collections (papers of the PHS, NYA, CCC, WPA, FERA, and FSA) have already been noted as a source of information on black health problems. As a yardstick of changing federal-state relations after 1932, they are even more valuable. For example, a number of letters in the state boards of health files of the PHS papers deal very candidly with the perceived role of the federal service and with the quality of state health officers.

At the state level the papers of the North Carolina Board of Health and of its director Watson Smith Rankin, both at the state archives in Raleigh, are equally candid and informative concerning health work in a single state. Rankin's papers as a Duke Endowment executive, as well as the voluminous correspondence and reports of that organization, are also extremely helpful. They are housed at the William R. Perkins Library of Duke University and at the Endowment headquarters in Charlotte. Lastly, the North Carolina ERA papers (in the state archives) allowed a measurement of the effectiveness of New Deal health programs at the grass roots.

In South Carolina the papers of the Executive Committee of the State Board of Health fleshed out the bare-bones accounts offered in the *Annual Reports*. The richest sources in that collection were the files of South Carolina's Hospital Advisory Council, which revealed the politics of Hill-Burton adminstration at the state level. The main drawback of the Executive Committee material was the absence of any files for the pre-1940s period. The largest state collection, though, was the papers of the Georgia State Board of Health, in the state archives in Atlanta. The Director's General Administrative Files, in particular, had primary material on virtually every subject imaginable (cancer, migrant health, malaria, industrial hygiene), from the early twentieth century, and revealed the near impossible task of protecting the public health in states where problems were legion but resources and will in short supply.

As for the health work of black doctors, two collections informed the present study. One was the Peter Marshall Murray Papers in the Moorland-Spingarn Research Center at Howard University. Murray's correspondence for the 1930–50 era reveals the Southern ties of Northern black physicians. The second set of papers were those of South Carolina's Palmetto Medical, Dental, and Pharmaceutical Association (in possession of the Association treasurer). No such collections were located for North Carolina or Georgia, but the South Carolina material was useful in showing the dissatisfaction of leading practitioners with the passivity of most of their colleagues. After World War II that passivity diminished, and the Palmetto Association Papers became an equally good source for black doctors' involvement with desegregation.

Once again, oral histories were a crucial source — this time in shedding light on the activity of health providers. The interview with Paul Cornely was perhaps the best of the lot, but there were a number of others which also aided the present study. They included interviews with Montague Cobb of the *JNMA;* G.E. McDaniel, formerly of the South Carolina Board of Health; Sinway Young of the AFL-CIO in South Carolina; Dr. John Preston, former director of the Richland County Health Department; James Hammond and Robert Brown of South Carolina's Division of Industrial Hygiene; John Lumsden, their counterpart in North Carolina; and Marshall Pickens, emeritus director of the Hospital and Orphans Section of the Duke Endowment.

Finally, a word about secondary works touching on public health administration in the South. George Rosen, *The History of Public Health* (New York: M.D. Publications, Inc., 1958) provides the story of an emerging public health movement in the United States. A number of texts are available to guide understanding of the clinical aspects of industrial illness in textiles, but one which the author found useful for its section on heat-humidity diseases was Rutherford Johnston and Seward Miller, *Occupational Diseases and Industrial Medicine* (Philadelphia: W.B. Saunders Co., 1961). The nagging, seemingly insoluble problem of VD and the federal government's response to it are explored by Thomas Parran and Ron Vonderlehr in *Plain Words about VD* (New York: Raynal and Hitchcock, 1941). Both authors were involved in the federal response of the 1930s. The growth of the overall federal health role since 1933 was the subject of a special issue of *Current History* (May–June 1977). Roy Lubove's piece on the Social Security Act and its health impact was particularly useful.

Not all accounts praise Washington's health role. Among the most critical evaluations are Elizabeth Drew's "Going Hungry in America. Government's Failure," *Atlantic* 22 (Dec. 1968). Also worth noting are reports of two Southern civil rights organizations. One was *Sick Unto Death* (Columbia, 1972), an examination of the operation of Medicaid in South Carolina, published by the South Carolina Council for Human Rights. The other was a special issue of *Southern Exposure* (Summer 1979), the organ of the Southern Regional Council. A survey of the health status of blacks in the period since World War II, the report found that most of the benefits of America's health delivery system went to health providers not to those low-income, white and black Americans who most needed help.

Index

A History of Neglect was designed by Dariel Mayer;
composed by Lithocraft Company, Grundy Center, Iowa;
printed by Thomson-Shore, Inc., Dexter, Michigan; and
bound by John Dekker & Sons, Grand Rapids, Michigan.
The book was set in 10/12 Baskerville and printed
on 60-lb Glatfelter natural.